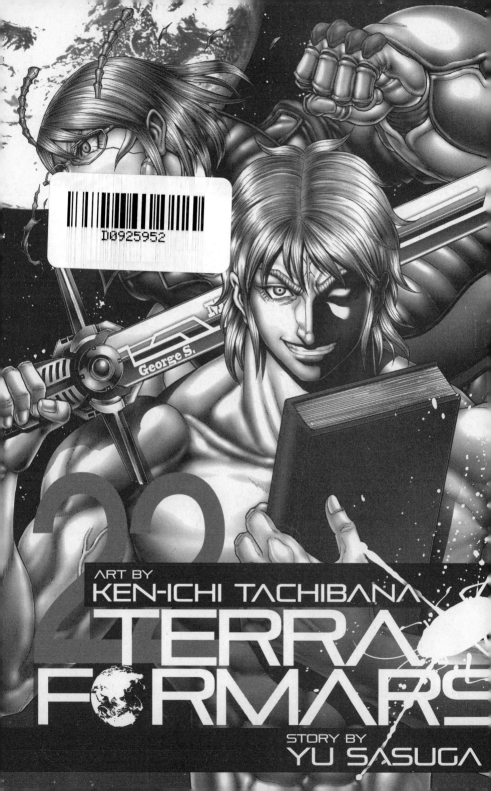

ART BY
KEN-ICHI TACHIBANA

TERRA FORMARS

STORY BY
YU SASUGA

George S.

TERRA FORMARS 22

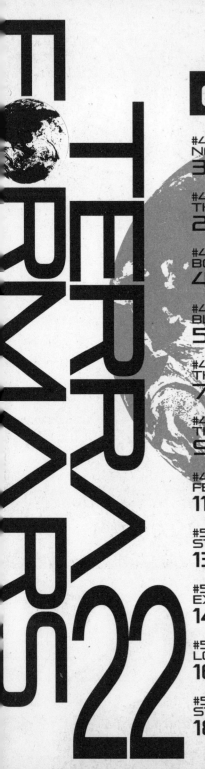

# CONTENTS

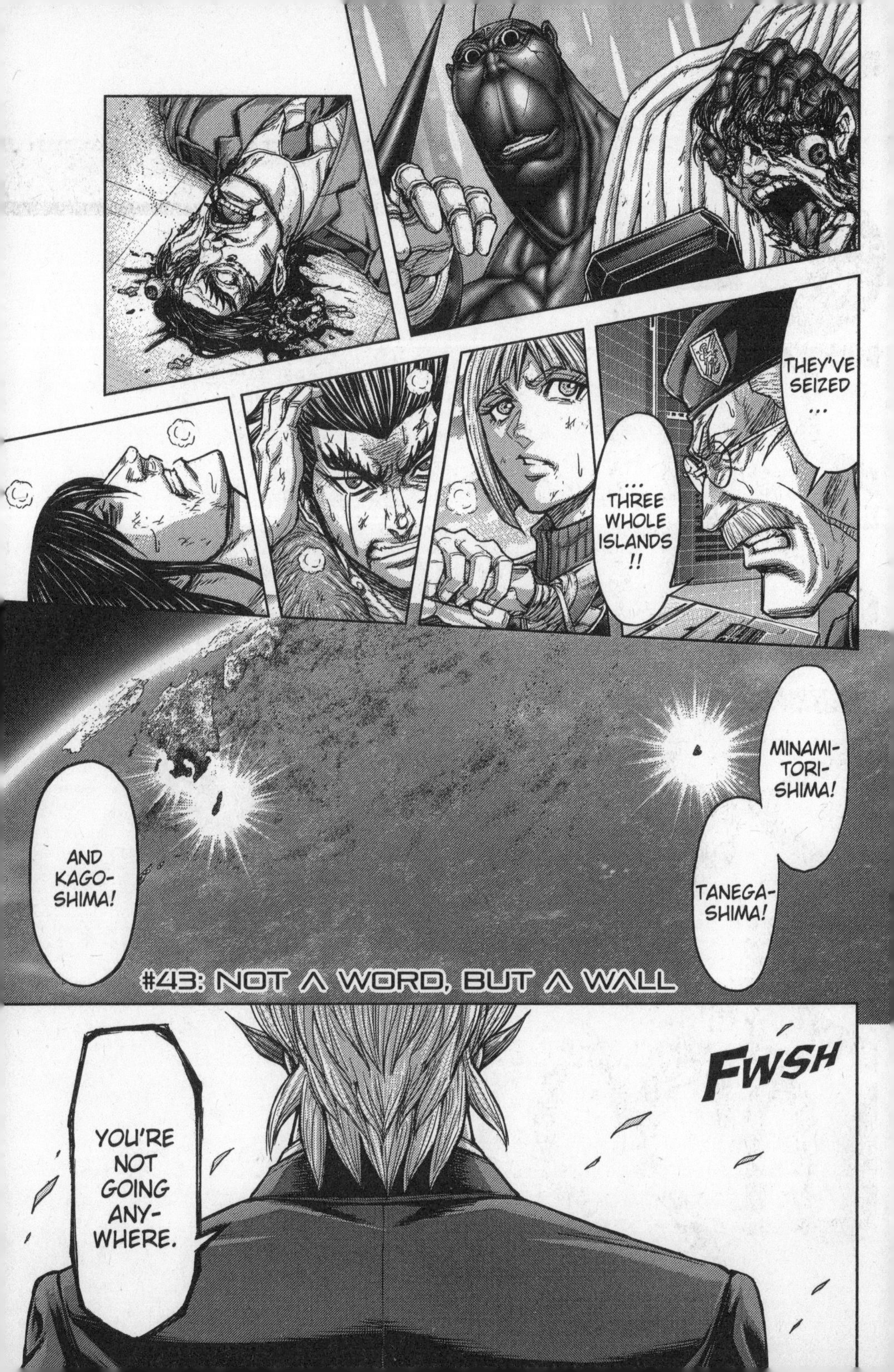
THEY'VE SEIZED ...
... THREE WHOLE ISLANDS !!
MINAMI-TORI-SHIMA!
TANEGA-SHIMA!
AND KAGO-SHIMA!
#43: NOT A WORD, BUT A WALL
FWSH
YOU'RE NOT GOING ANY-WHERE.

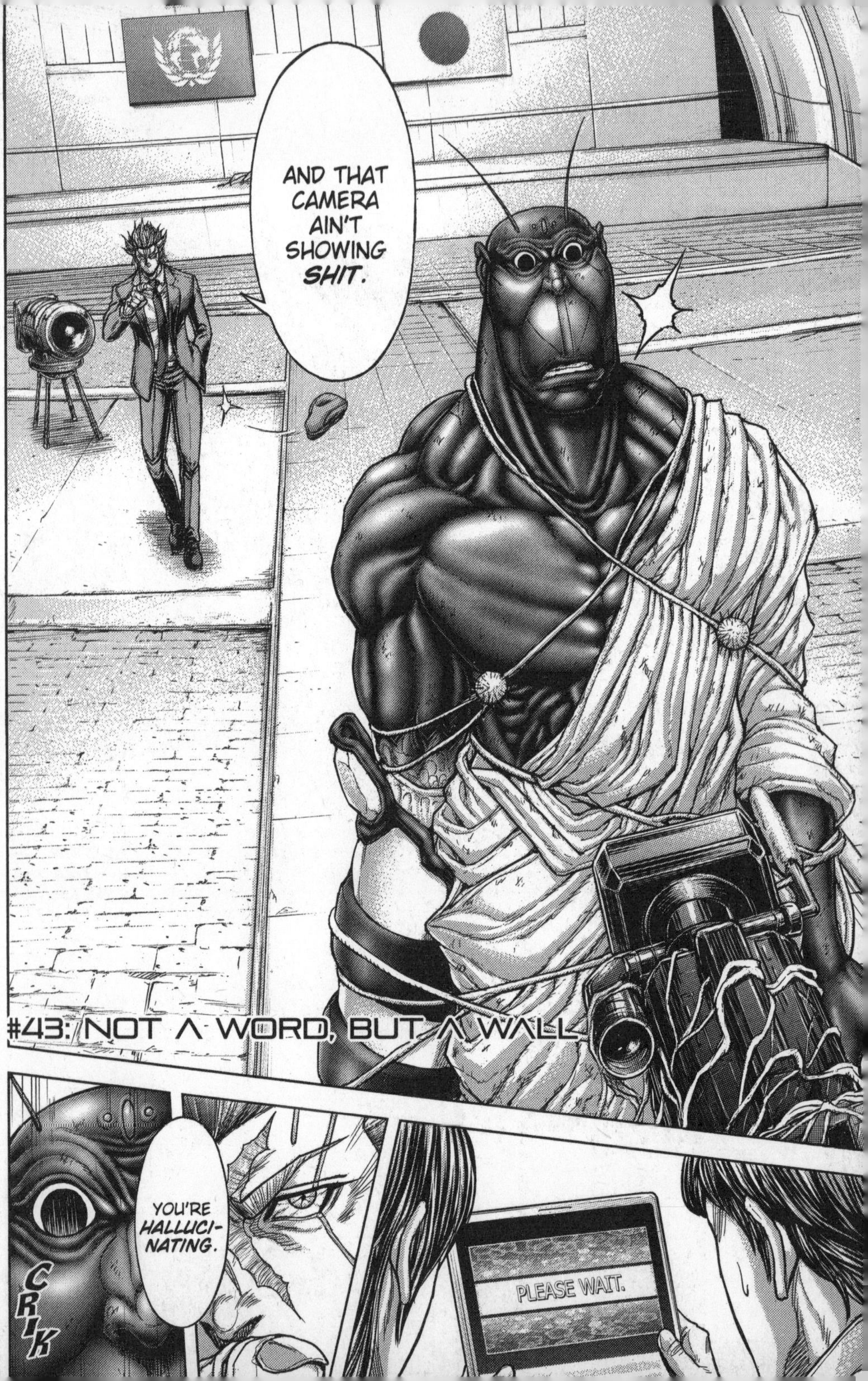
AND THAT CAMERA AIN'T SHOWING SHIT.
#43: NOT A WORD, BUT A WALL
PLEASE WAIT.
YOU'RE HALLUCI-NATING.
CRIK

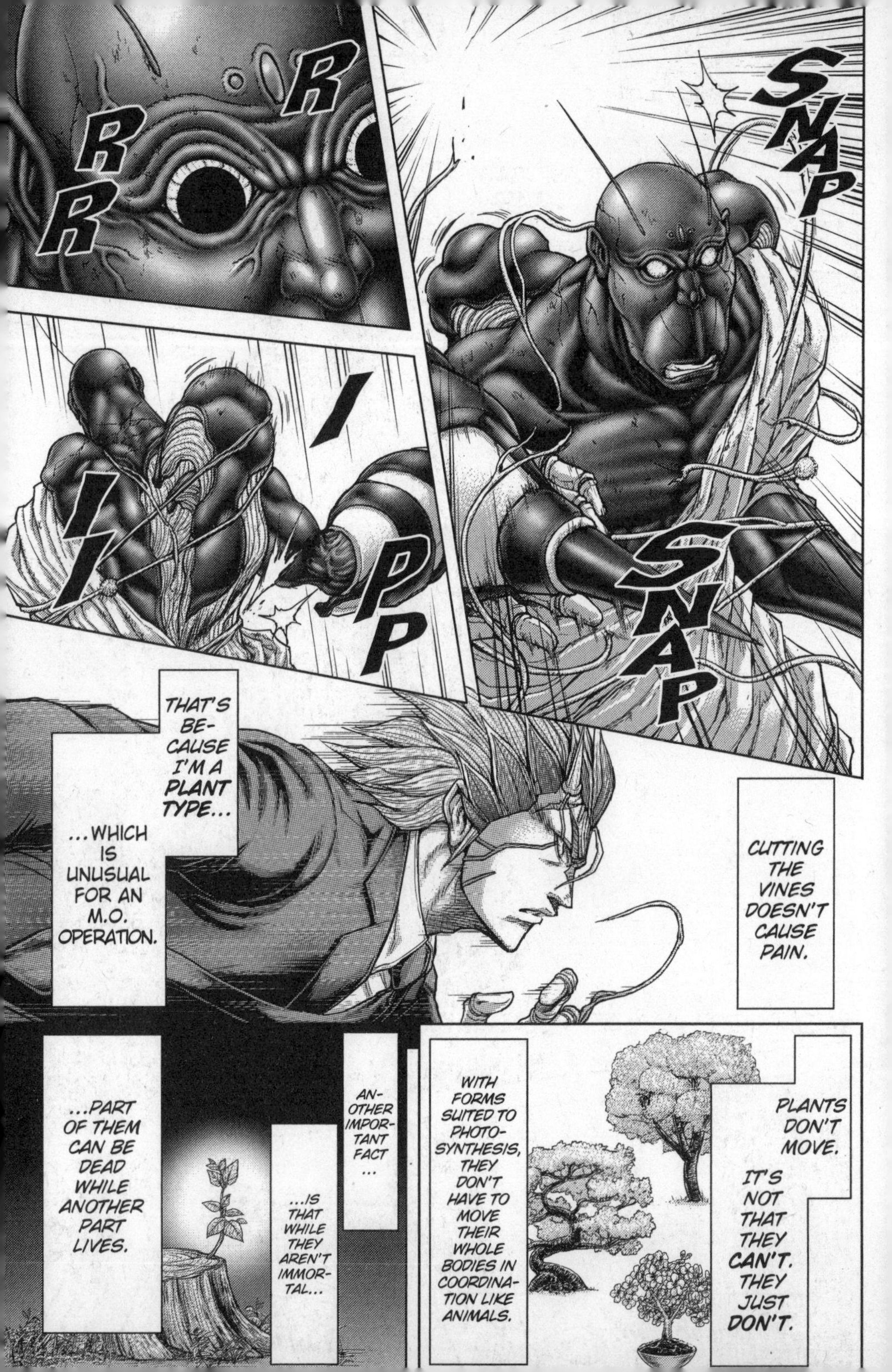
SNAP
SNAP
RRR
IIIPP
CUTTING THE VINES DOESN'T CAUSE PAIN.
THAT'S BECAUSE I'M A **PLANT TYPE**...
...WHICH IS UNUSUAL FOR AN M.O. OPERATION.
PLANTS DON'T MOVE.
IT'S NOT THAT THEY **CAN'T**. THEY JUST **DON'T**.
WITH FORMS SUITED TO PHOTOSYNTHESIS, THEY DON'T HAVE TO MOVE THEIR WHOLE BODIES IN COORDINATION LIKE ANIMALS.
ANOTHER IMPORTANT FACT...
...IS THAT WHILE THEY AREN'T IMMORTAL...
...PART OF THEM CAN BE DEAD WHILE ANOTHER PART LIVES.

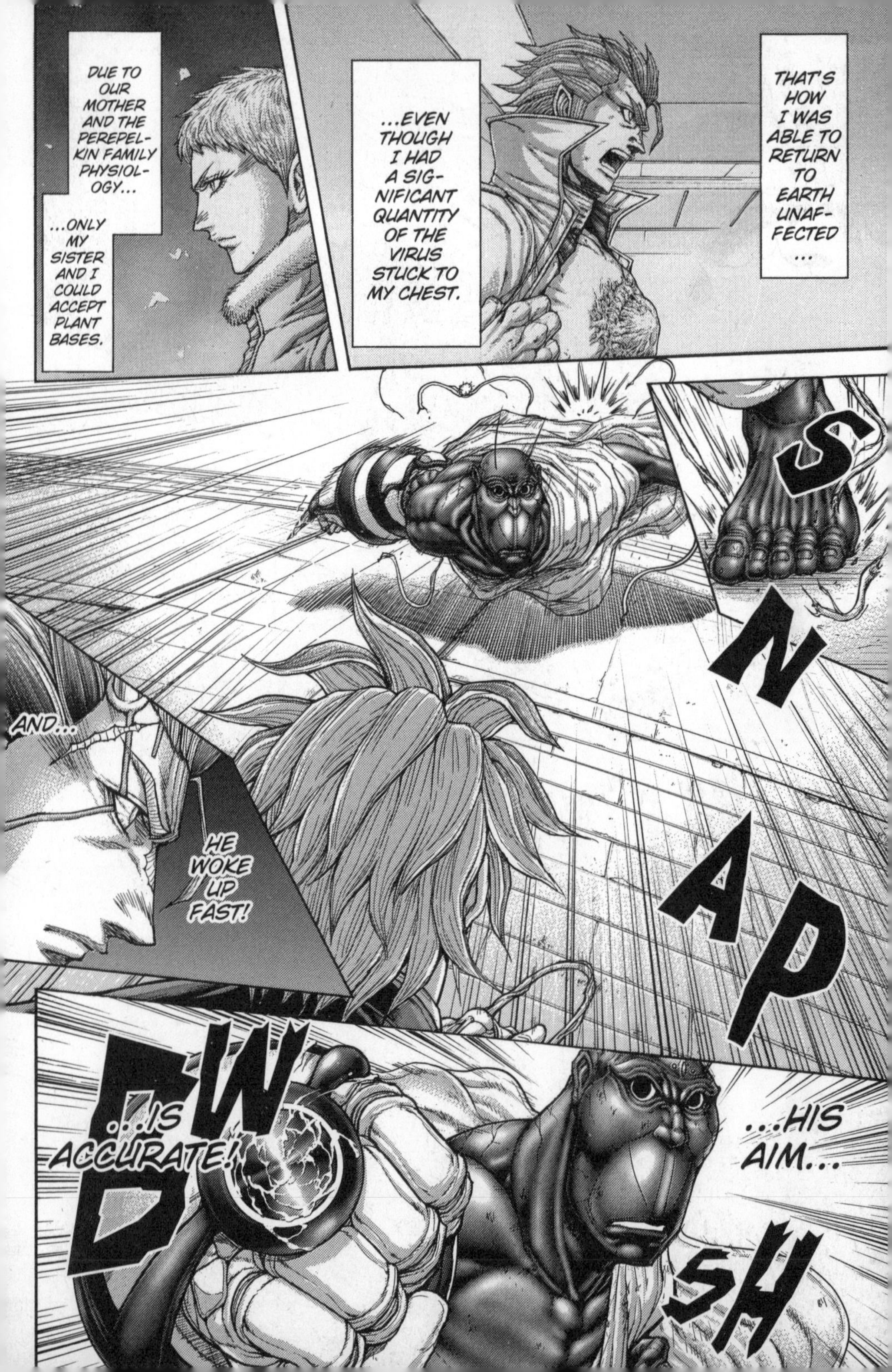
THAT'S HOW I WAS ABLE TO RETURN TO EARTH UNAFFECTED...
...EVEN THOUGH I HAD A SIGNIFICANT QUANTITY OF THE VIRUS STUCK TO MY CHEST.
DUE TO OUR MOTHER AND THE PEREPELKIN FAMILY PHYSIOLOGY...
...ONLY MY SISTER AND I COULD ACCEPT PLANT BASES.
SNAP
AND...
HE WOKE UP FAST!
...HIS AIM...
...IS ACCURATE!
FWSH

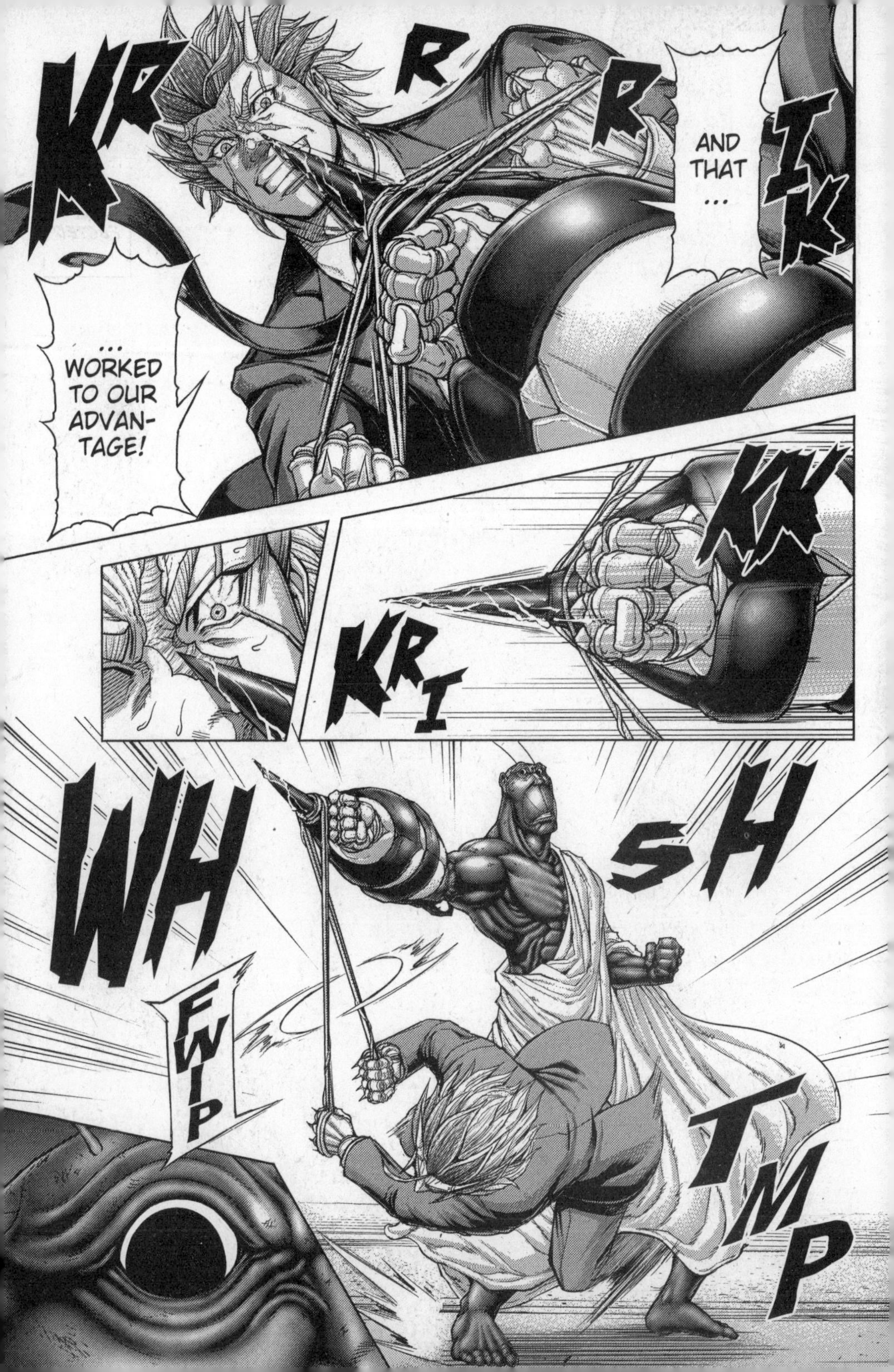

KRRRTIK
AND THAT ...
... WORKED TO OUR ADVANTAGE!
KK
KRI
WHSH
FWIP
TMP

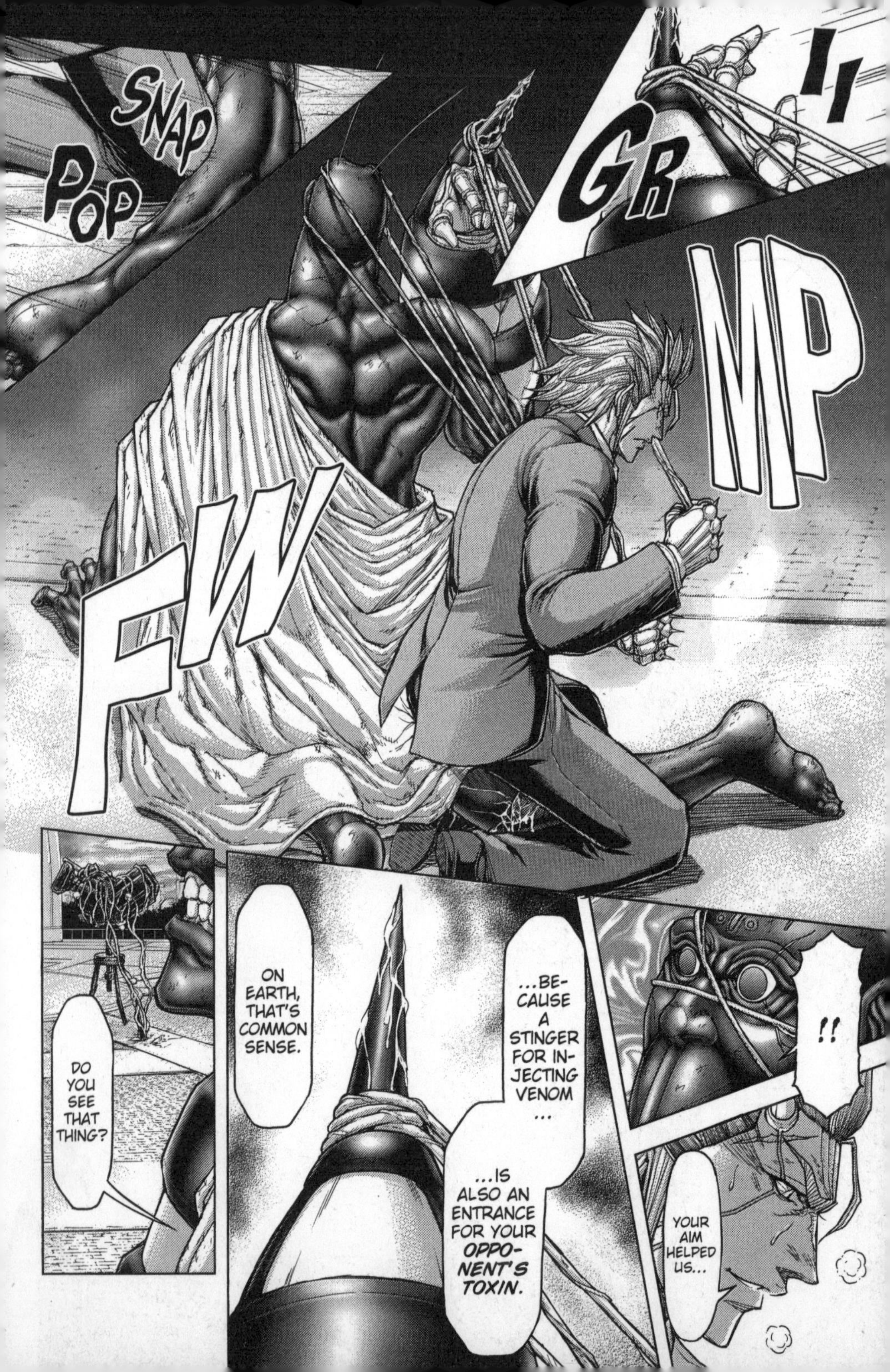
GR
!!
SNAP
POP
MP
FW
!!
YOUR AIM HELPED US...
...BE-CAUSE A STINGER FOR IN-JECTING VENOM...
...IS ALSO AN ENTRANCE FOR YOUR *OPPO-NENT'S TOXIN.*
ON EARTH, THAT'S COMMON SENSE.
DO YOU SEE THAT THING?

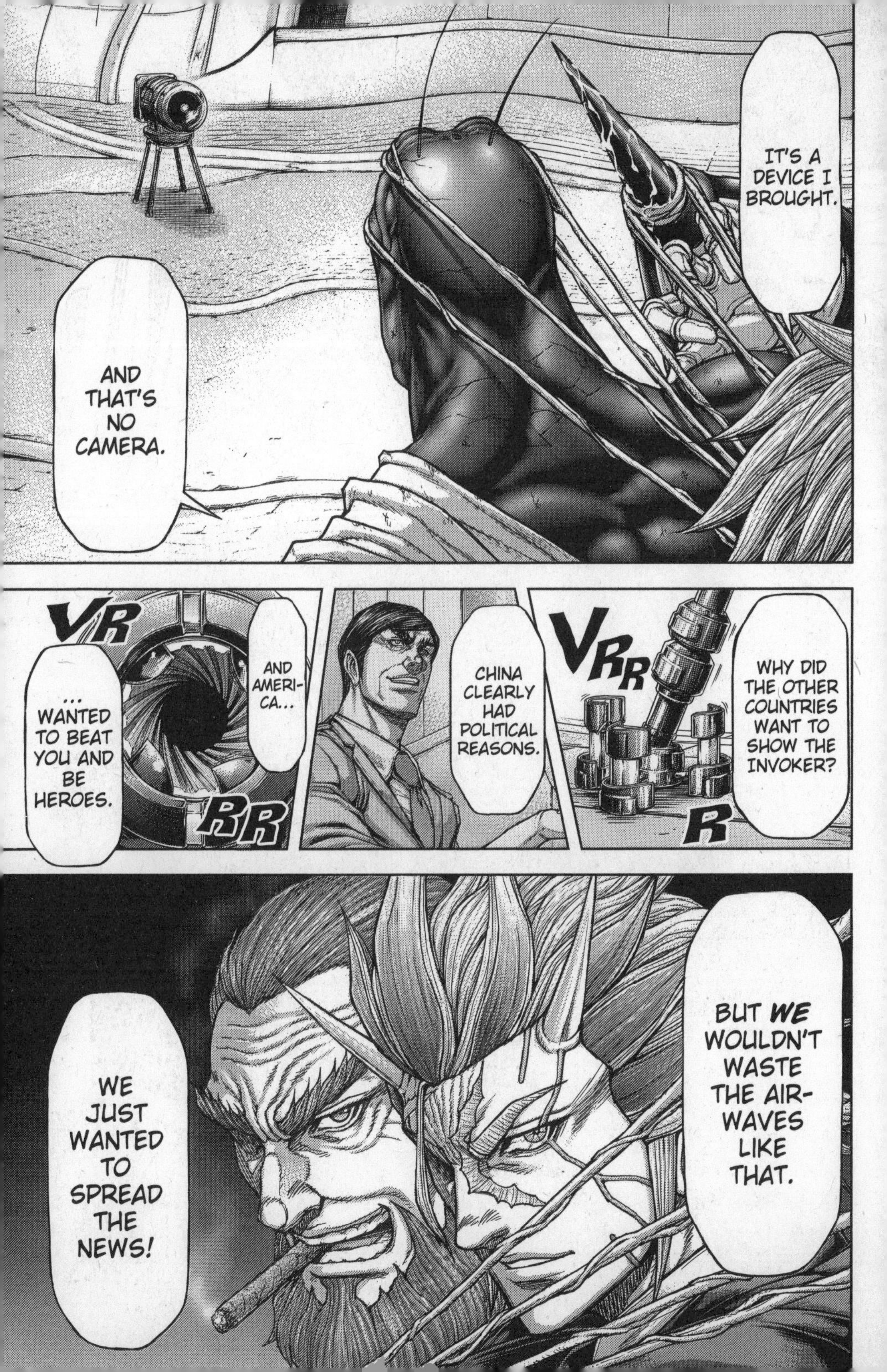
IT'S A DEVICE I BROUGHT.
AND THAT'S NO CAMERA.
VRR
R
WHY DID THE OTHER COUNTRIES WANT TO SHOW THE INVOKER?
CHINA CLEARLY HAD POLITICAL REASONS.
AND AMERI-CA...
VR
RR
...WANTED TO BEAT YOU AND BE HEROES.
BUT *WE* WOULDN'T WASTE THE AIR-WAVES LIKE THAT.
WE JUST WANTED TO SPREAD THE NEWS!

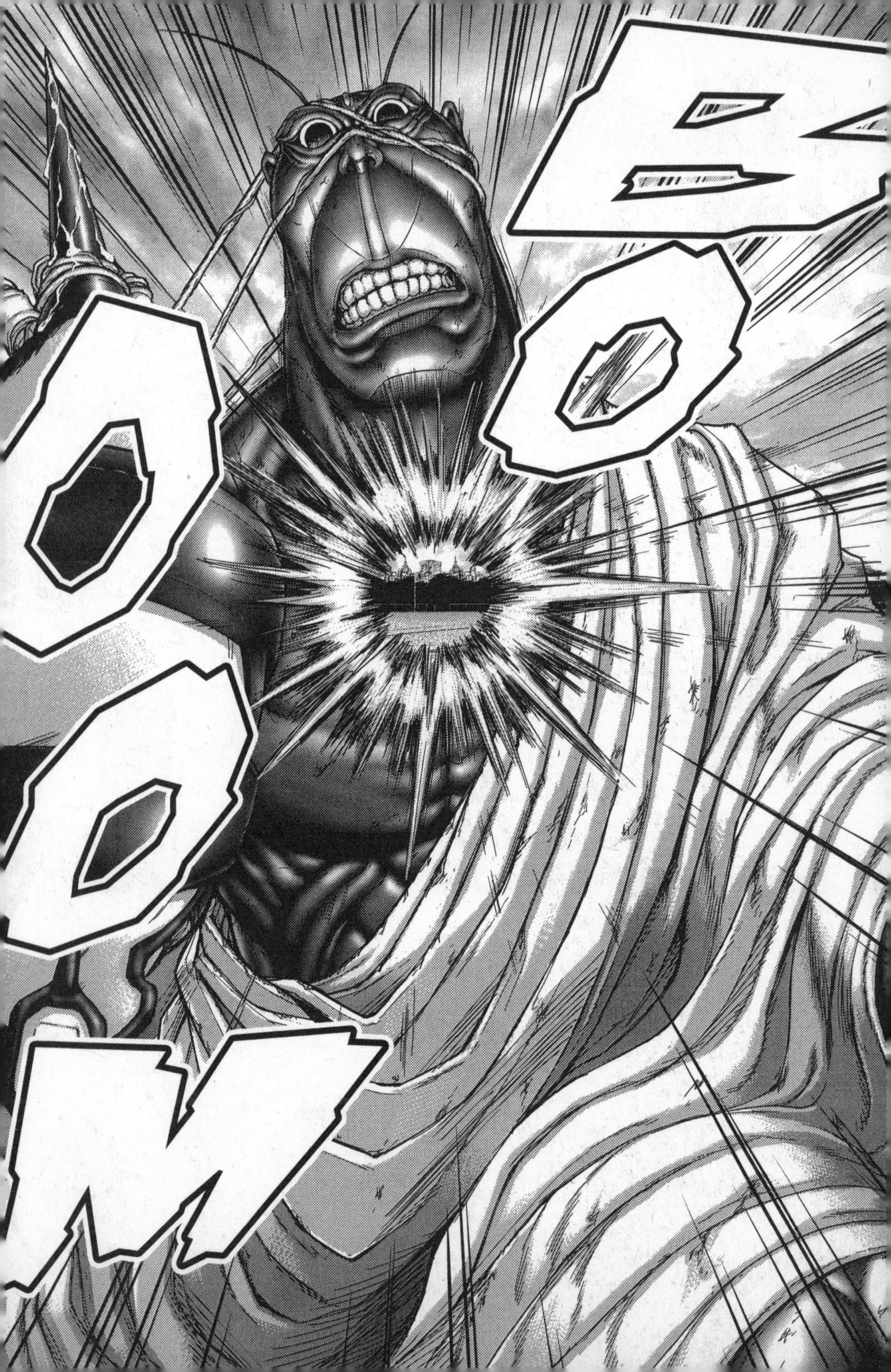
BOOOM

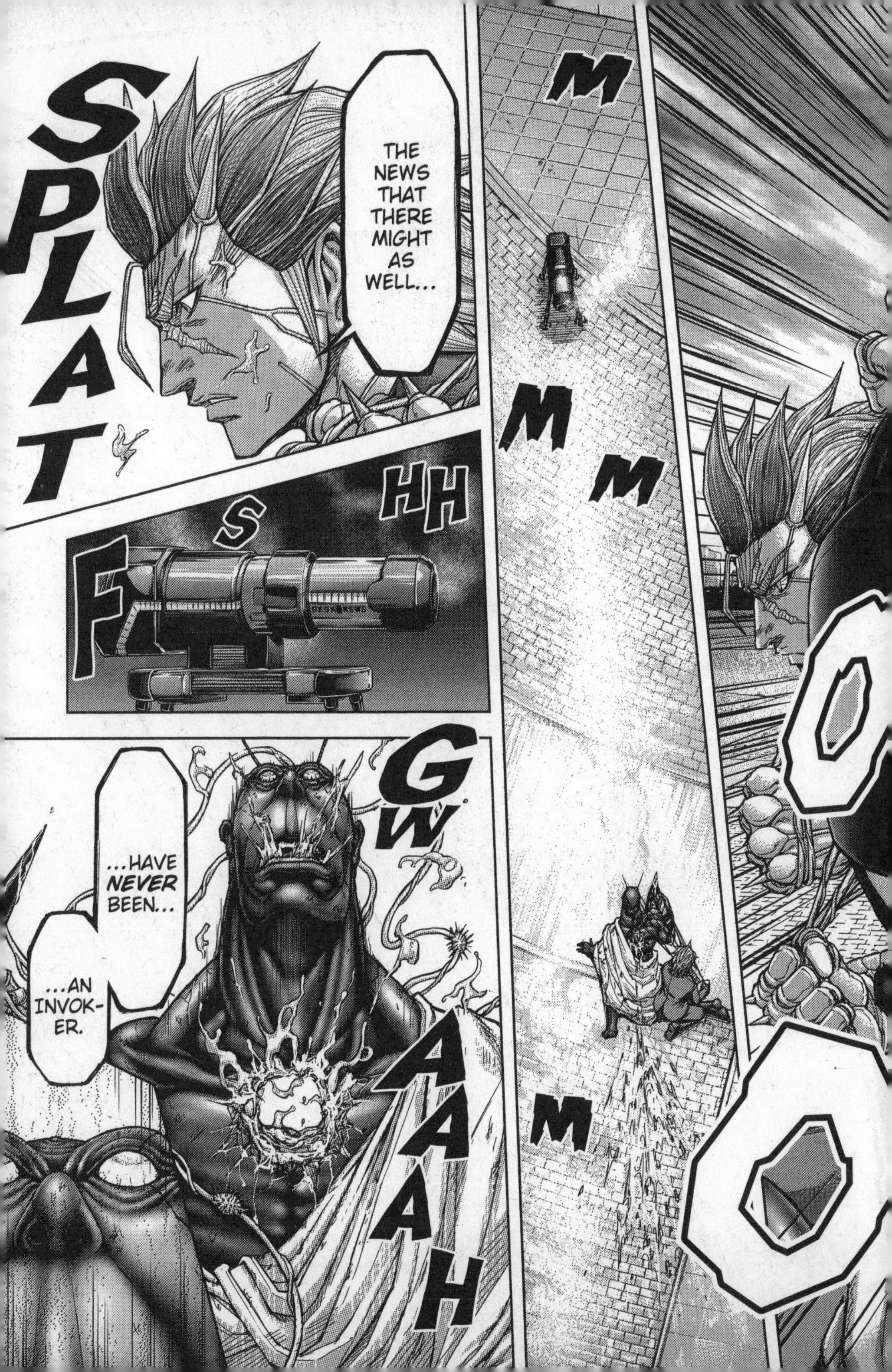
O
O
M
M
M
M
THE NEWS THAT THERE MIGHT AS WELL...
SPLAT
HH
S
F
...HAVE *NEVER* BEEN...
...AN INVOK-ER.
GWAAAAH

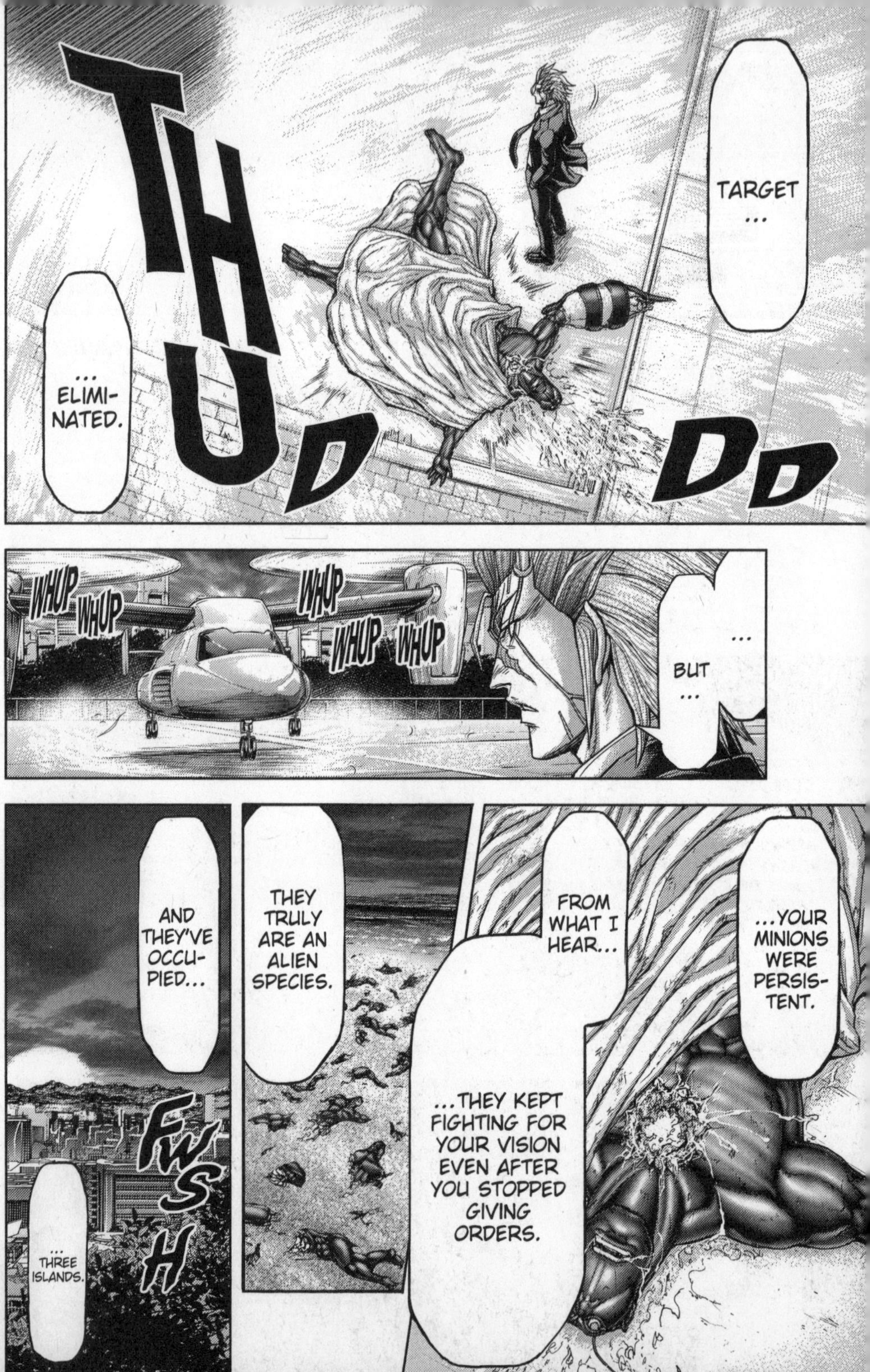
TARGET ...
... ELIMI-NATED.
THUDD
DD
WHUP WHUP
WHUP
WHUP WHUP
... BUT ...
...YOUR MINIONS WERE PERSIS-TENT.
FROM WHAT I HEAR...
...THEY KEPT FIGHTING FOR YOUR VISION EVEN AFTER YOU STOPPED GIVING ORDERS.
THEY TRULY ARE AN ALIEN SPECIES.
AND THEY'VE OCCU-PIED...
FWSH
... THREE ISLANDS.

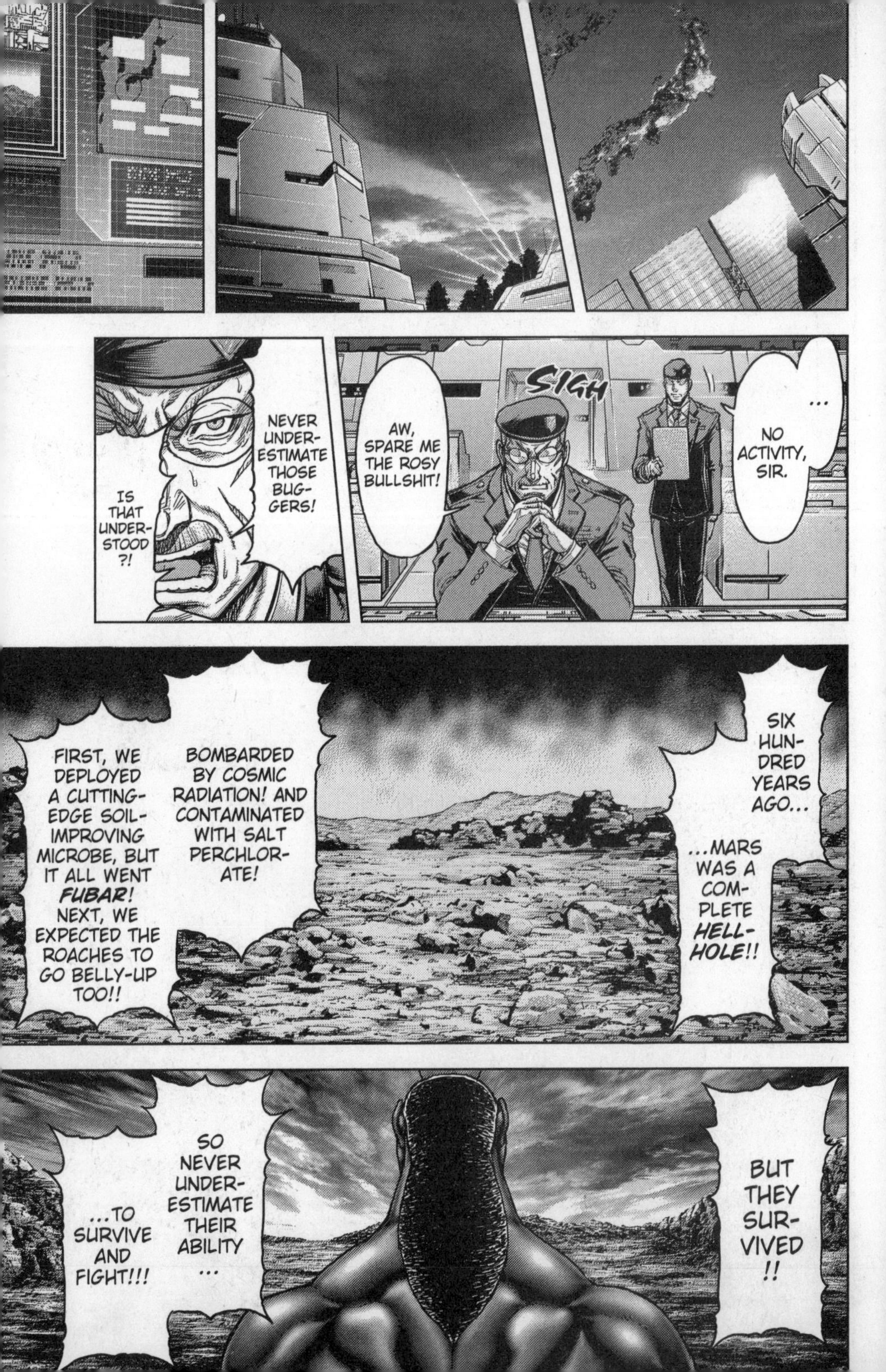
...
NO ACTIVITY, SIR.
SIGH
AW, SPARE ME THE ROSY BULLSHIT!
NEVER UNDERESTIMATE THOSE BUGGERS!
IS THAT UNDERSTOOD?!
SIX HUNDRED YEARS AGO...
...MARS WAS A COMPLETE HELLHOLE!!
BOMBARDED BY COSMIC RADIATION! AND CONTAMINATED WITH SALT PERCHLORATE!
FIRST, WE DEPLOYED A CUTTING-EDGE SOIL-IMPROVING MICROBE, BUT IT ALL WENT FUBAR! NEXT, WE EXPECTED THE ROACHES TO GO BELLY-UP TOO!!
BUT THEY SURVIVED!!
SO NEVER UNDERESTIMATE THEIR ABILITY...
...TO SURVIVE AND FIGHT!!!

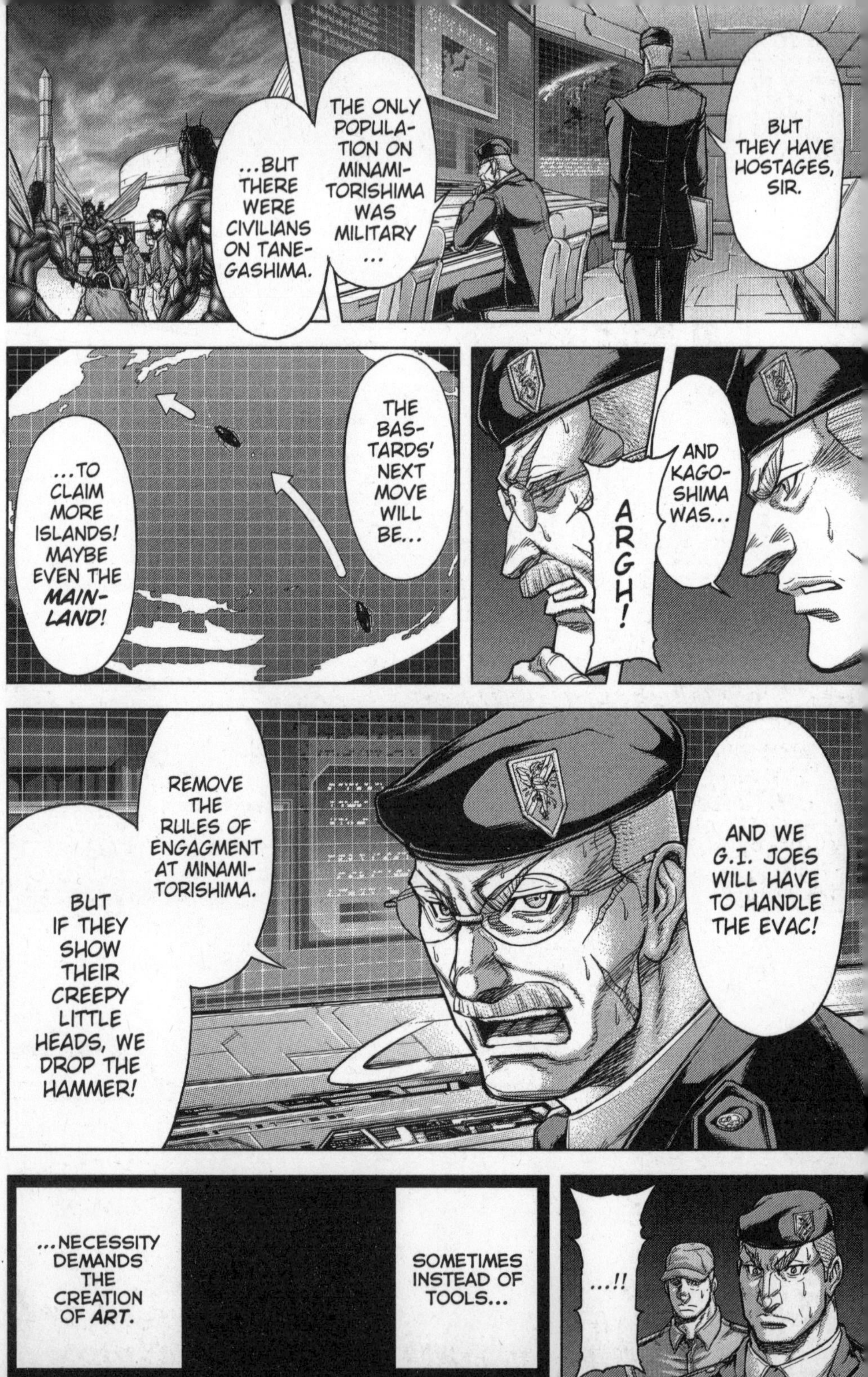
BUT THEY HAVE HOSTAGES, SIR.
THE ONLY POPULATION ON MINAMI-TORISHIMA WAS MILITARY...
...BUT THERE WERE CIVILIANS ON TANEGASHIMA.
AND KAGOSHIMA WAS...
ARGH!
THE BASTARDS' NEXT MOVE WILL BE...
...TO CLAIM MORE ISLANDS! MAYBE EVEN THE *MAINLAND*!
AND WE G.I. JOES WILL HAVE TO HANDLE THE EVAC!
REMOVE THE RULES OF ENGAGMENT AT MINAMI-TORISHIMA.
BUT IF THEY SHOW THEIR CREEPY LITTLE HEADS, WE DROP THE HAMMER!
...!!
SOMETIMES INSTEAD OF TOOLS...
...NECESSITY DEMANDS THE CREATION OF *ART*.

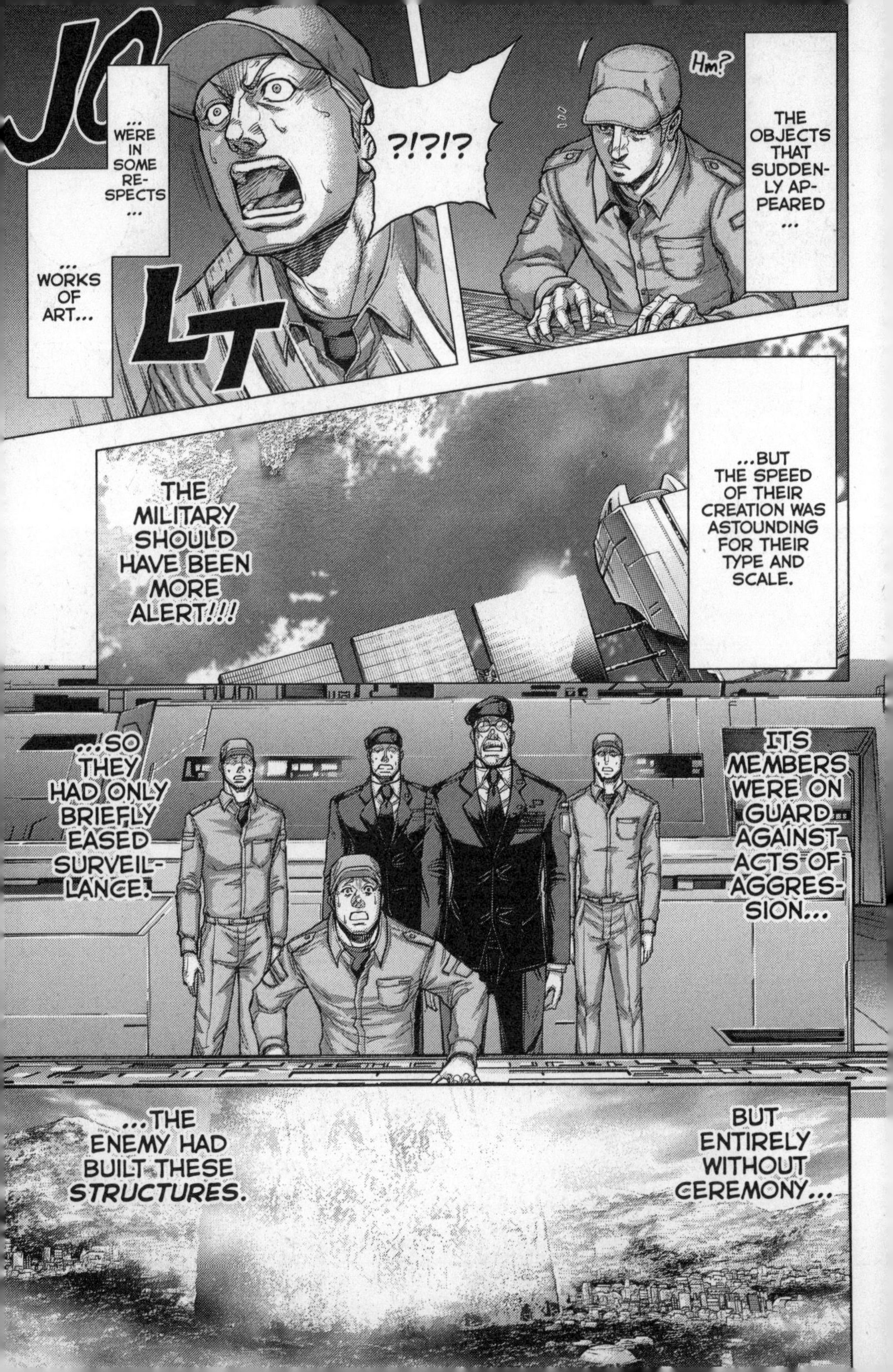

Hm?
THE OBJECTS THAT SUDDEN-LY AP-PEARED ...
JOLT
?!?!?
... WERE IN SOME RE-SPECTS ...
... WORKS OF ART...
...BUT THE SPEED OF THEIR CREATION WAS ASTOUNDING FOR THEIR TYPE AND SCALE.
THE MILITARY SHOULD HAVE BEEN MORE ALERT!!!
ITS MEMBERS WERE ON GUARD AGAINST ACTS OF AGGRES-SION...
...SO THEY HAD ONLY BRIEFLY EASED SURVEIL-LANCE.
BUT ENTIRELY WITHOUT CEREMONY...
...THE ENEMY HAD BUILT THESE *STRUCTURES*.

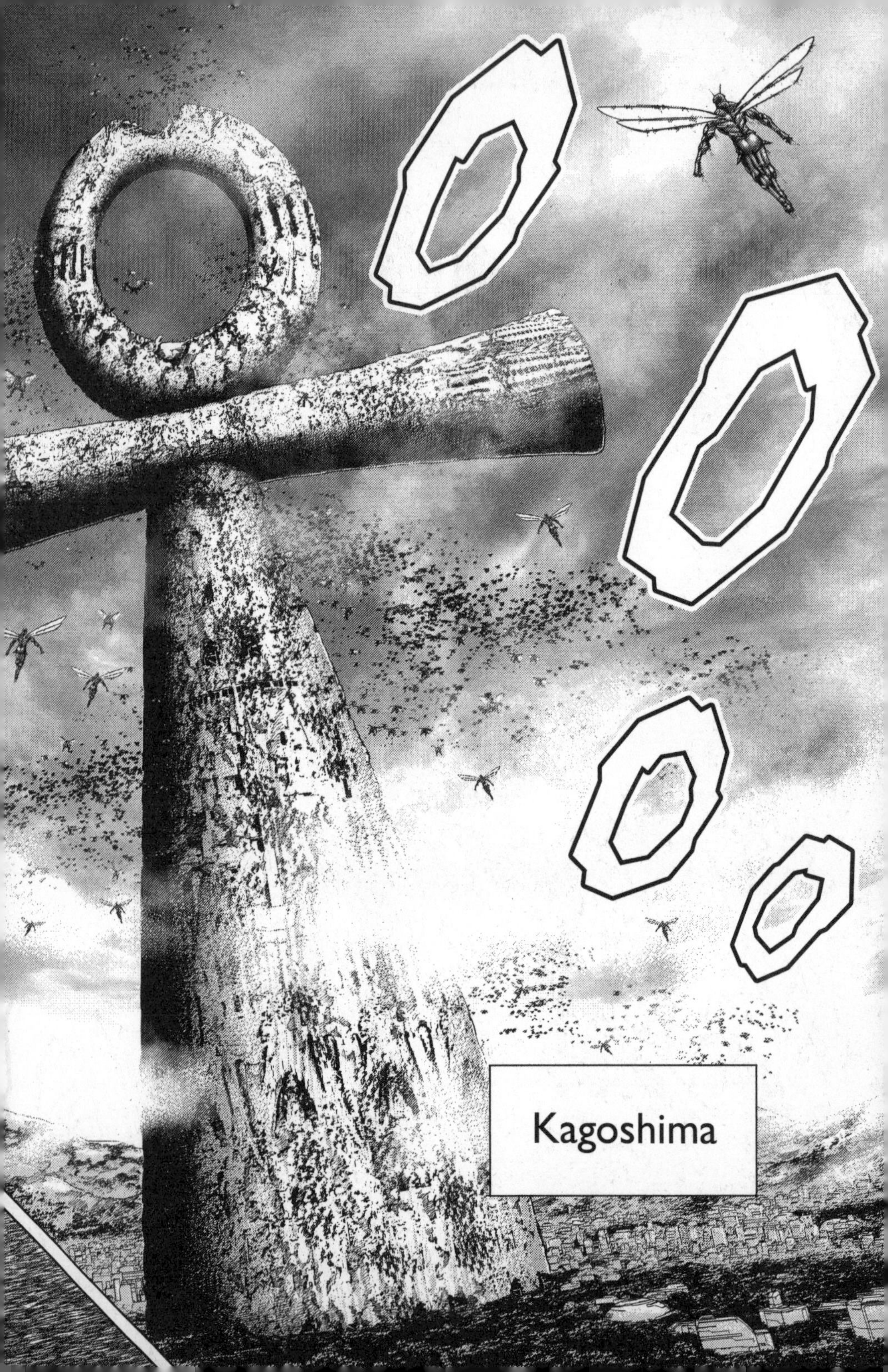
Kagoshima

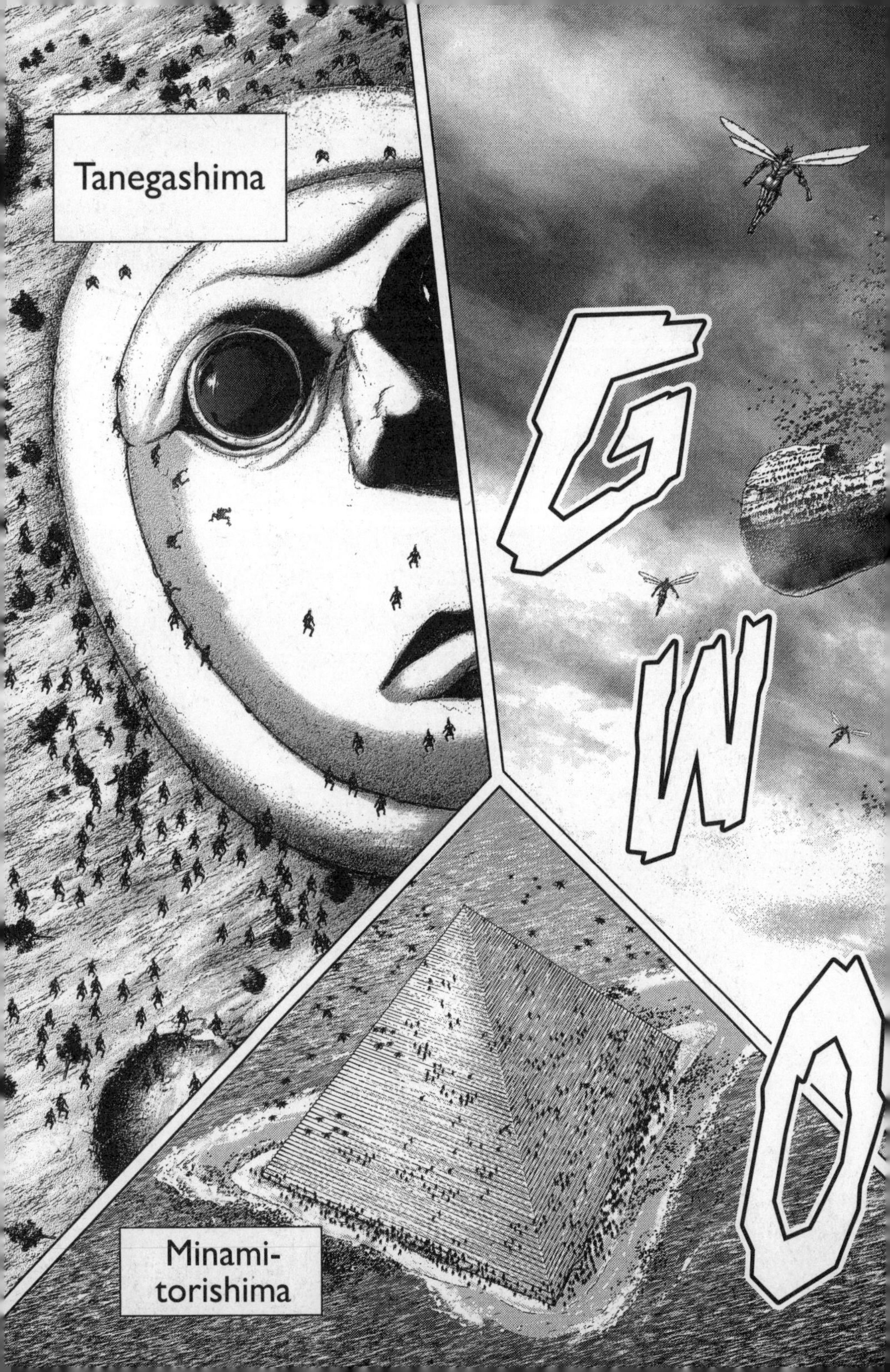
GWO
Tanegashima
Minami-
torishima

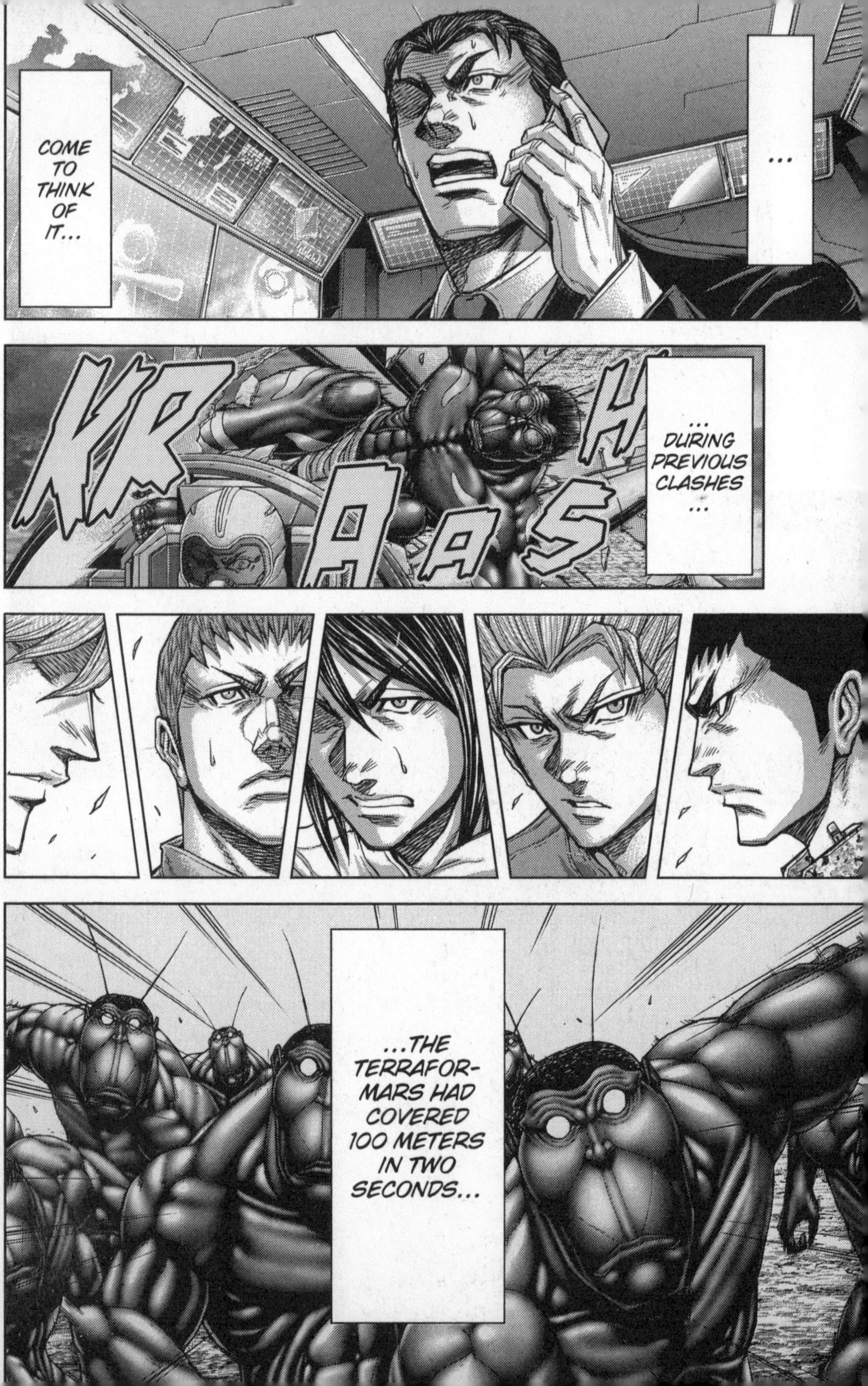
...
COME TO THINK OF IT...
... DURING PREVIOUS CLASHES ...
KRAASH
...THE TERRAFOR-MARS HAD COVERED 100 METERS IN TWO SECONDS...

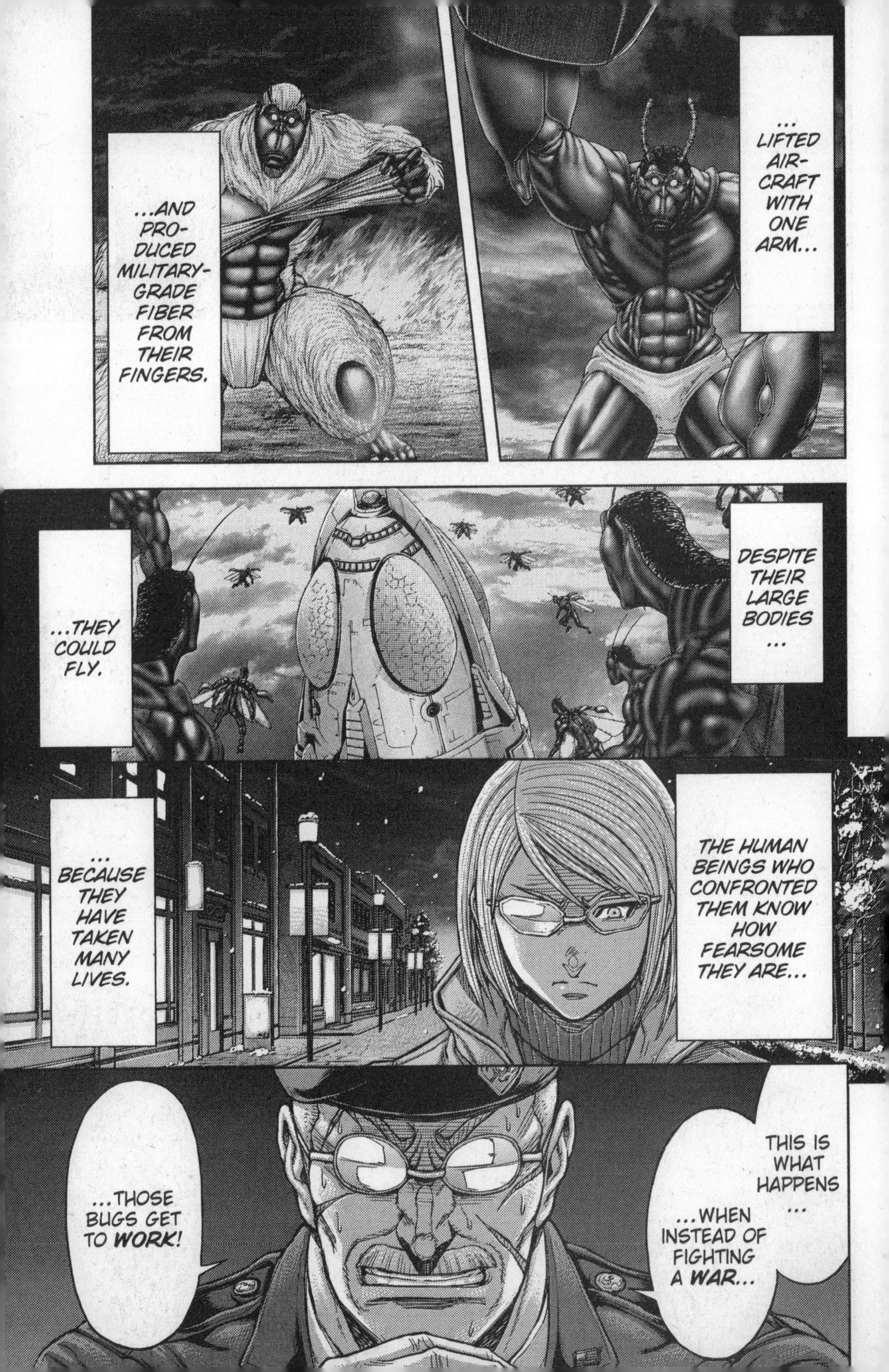
...LIFTED AIRCRAFT WITH ONE ARM...
...AND PRODUCED MILITARY-GRADE FIBER FROM THEIR FINGERS.
DESPITE THEIR LARGE BODIES...
...THEY COULD FLY.
THE HUMAN BEINGS WHO CONFRONTED THEM KNOW HOW FEARSOME THEY ARE...
...BECAUSE THEY HAVE TAKEN MANY LIVES.
THIS IS WHAT HAPPENS...
...WHEN INSTEAD OF FIGHTING A *WAR*...
...THOSE BUGS GET TO *WORK*!

...AS MERE **ROACHES** JACKED UP BY MARTIAN EVOLUTION!

WE DIS- MISSED THEM...

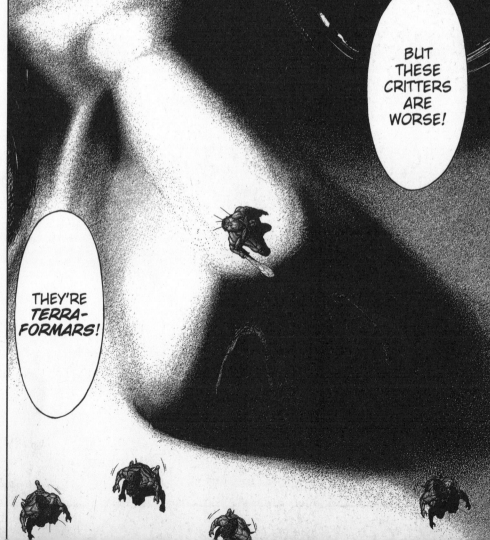

BUT THESE CRITTERS ARE WORSE!

THEY'RE **TERRA- FORMARS!**

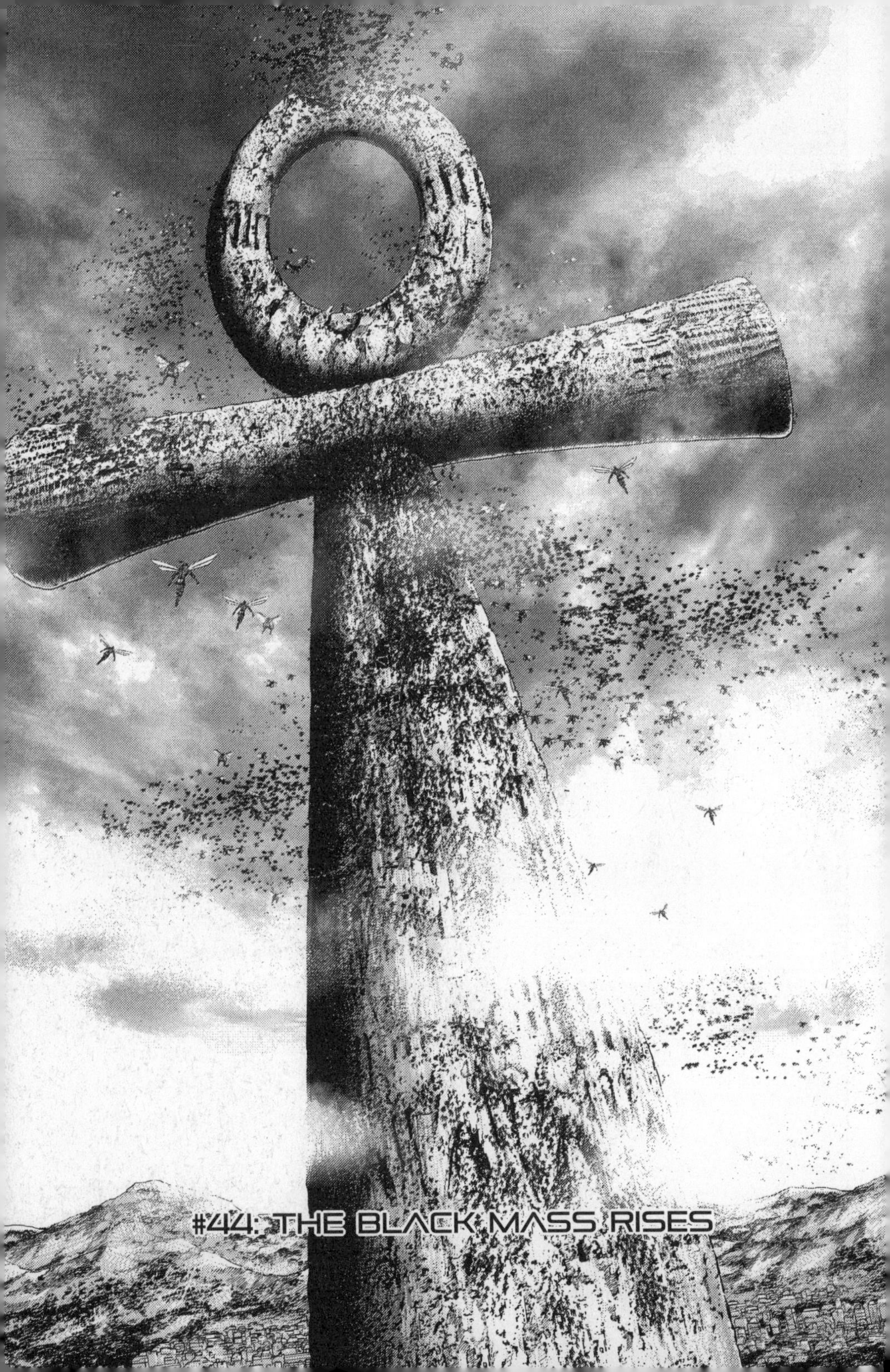
#44: THE BLACK MASS RISES

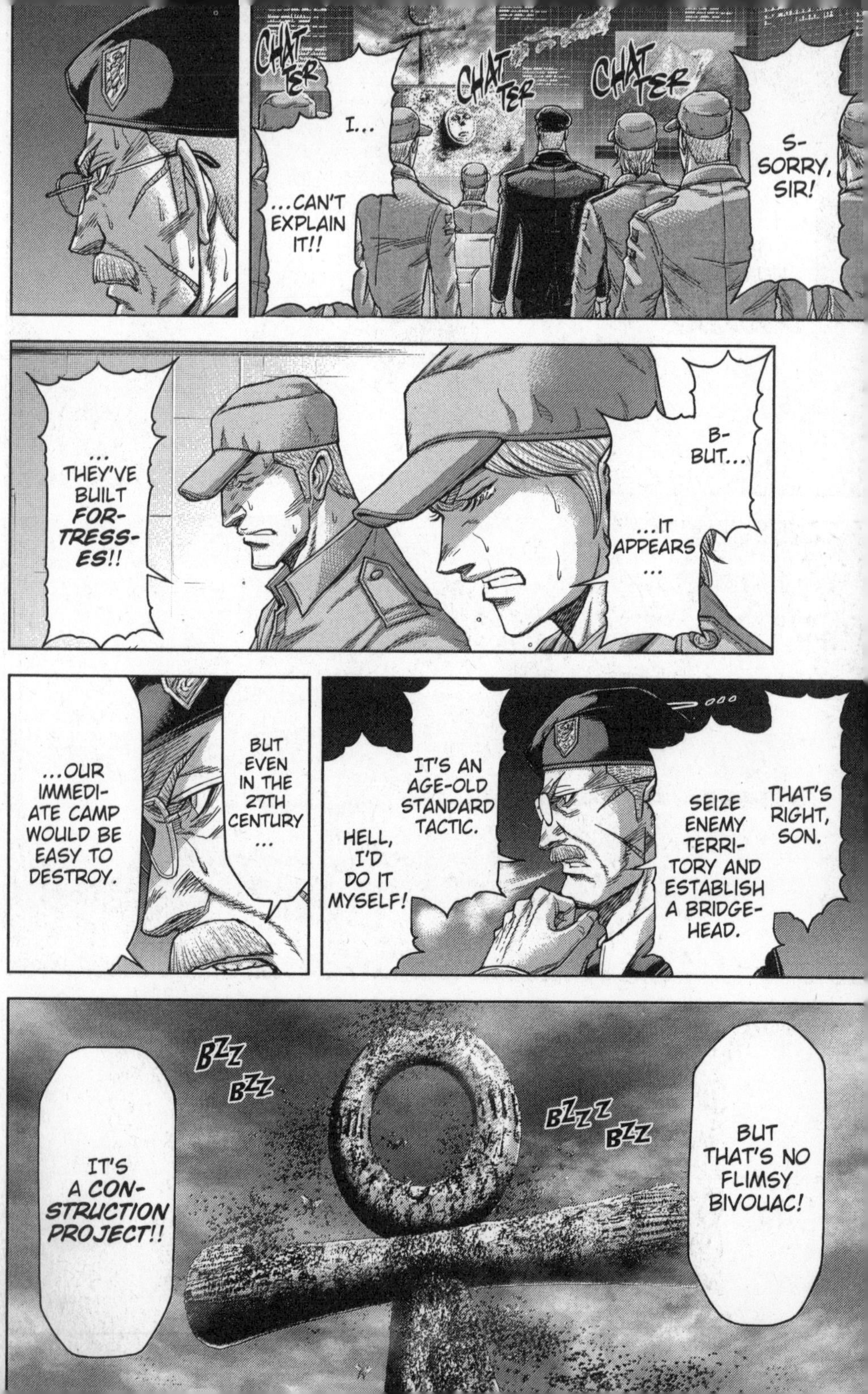
S-SORRY, SIR!
CHATTER
CHATTER
CHATTER
I...
...CAN'T EXPLAIN IT!!
B-BUT...
...IT APPEARS ...
...THEY'VE BUILT *FORTRESSES*!!
THAT'S RIGHT, SON.
SEIZE ENEMY TERRITORY AND ESTABLISH A BRIDGEHEAD.
IT'S AN AGE-OLD STANDARD TACTIC.
HELL, I'D DO IT MYSELF!
BUT EVEN IN THE 27TH CENTURY ...
...OUR IMMEDIATE CAMP WOULD BE EASY TO DESTROY.
BUT THAT'S NO FLIMSY BIVOUAC!
BZZZ
BZZ
BZZ
BZZ
IT'S A *CONSTRUCTION PROJECT*!!

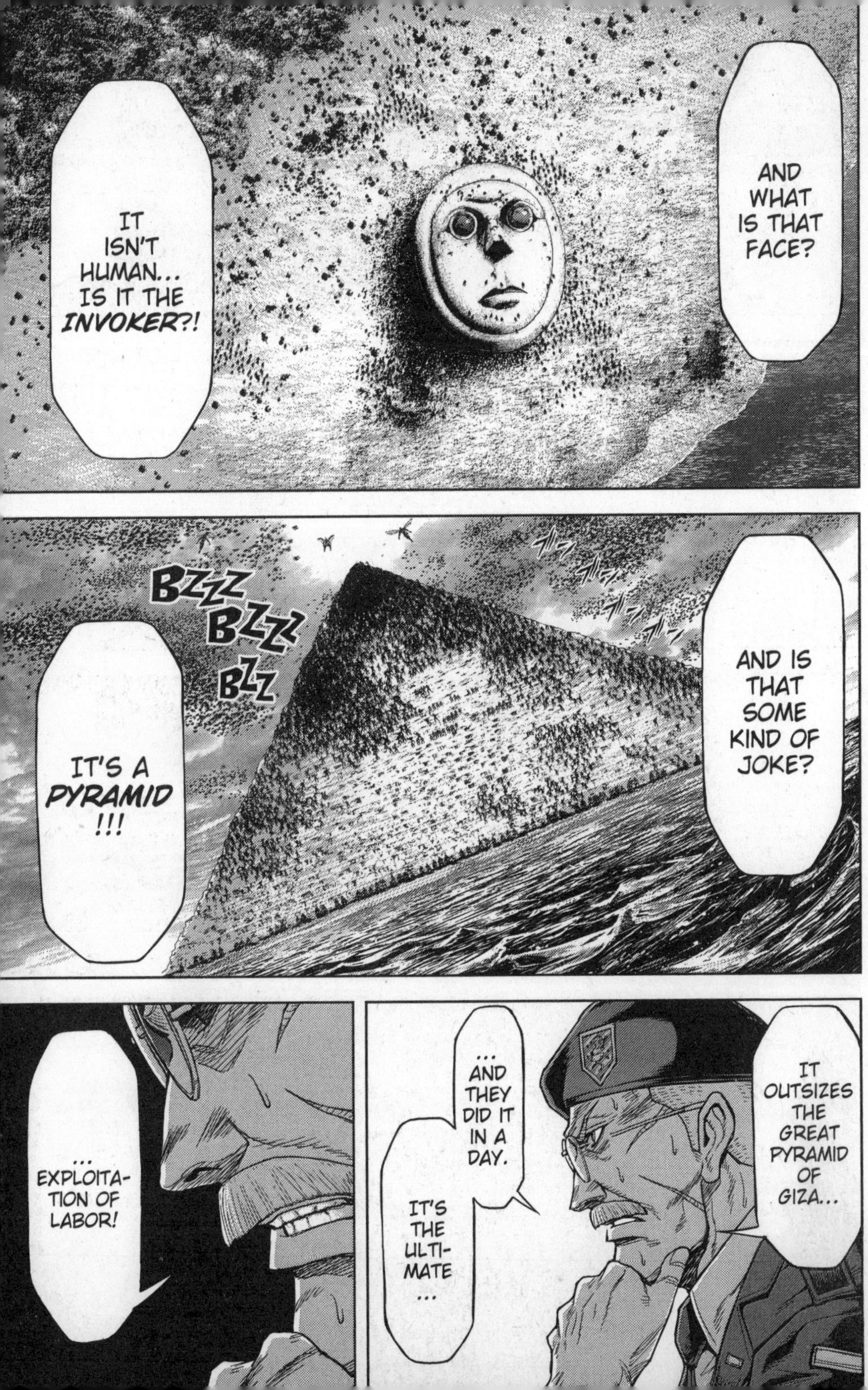
AND WHAT IS THAT FACE?
IT ISN'T HUMAN... IS IT THE *INVOKER*?!
AND IS THAT SOME KIND OF JOKE?
BZZZ BZZZ BZZ
IT'S A *PYRAMID* !!!
IT OUTSIZES THE GREAT PYRAMID OF GIZA...
...AND THEY DID IT IN A DAY.
IT'S THE ULTI-MATE...
...EXPLOITA-TION OF LABOR!

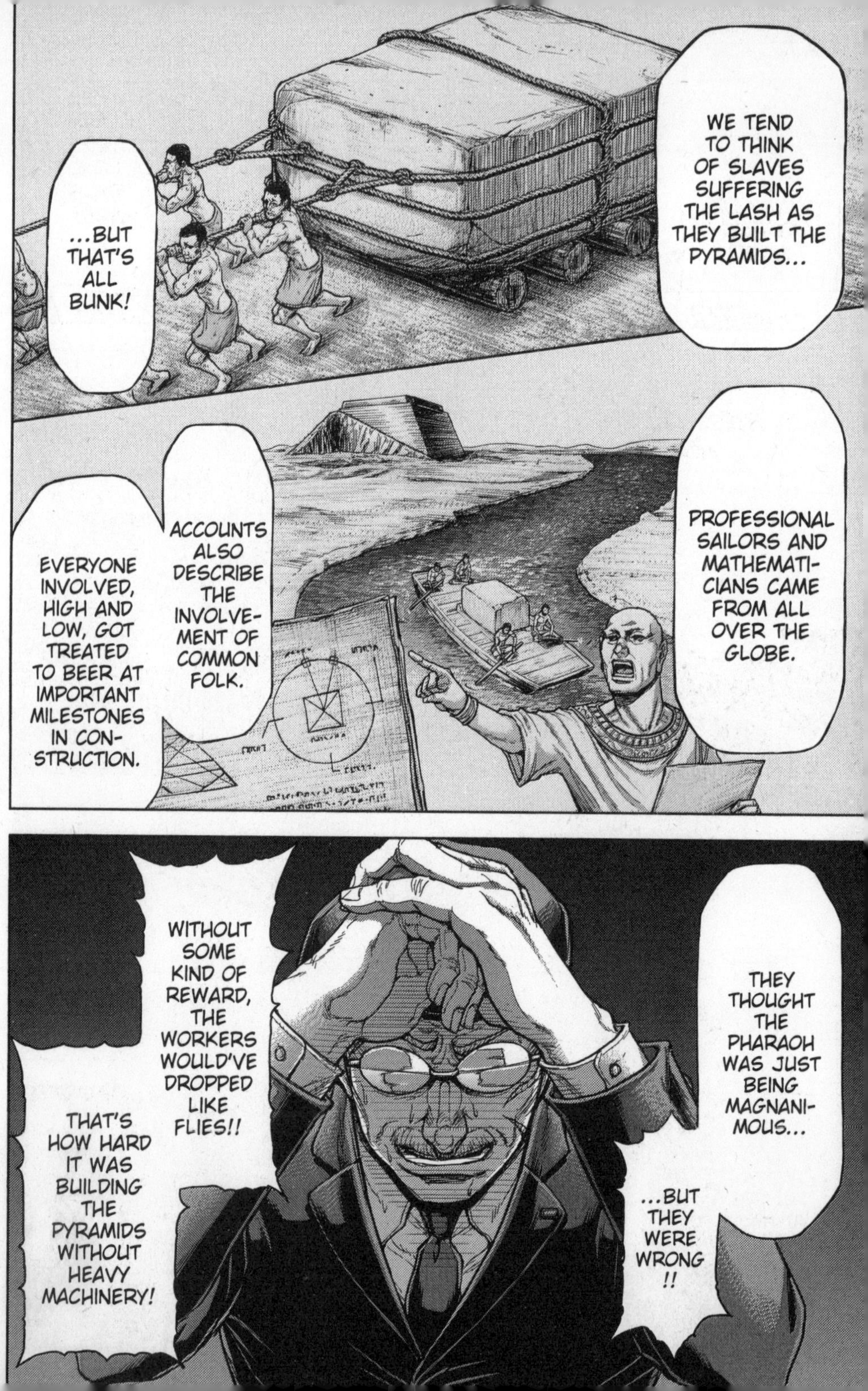
WE TEND TO THINK OF SLAVES SUFFERING THE LASH AS THEY BUILT THE PYRAMIDS...
...BUT THAT'S ALL BUNK!
PROFESSIONAL SAILORS AND MATHEMATICIANS CAME FROM ALL OVER THE GLOBE.
ACCOUNTS ALSO DESCRIBE THE INVOLVEMENT OF COMMON FOLK.
EVERYONE INVOLVED, HIGH AND LOW, GOT TREATED TO BEER AT IMPORTANT MILESTONES IN CONSTRUCTION.
THEY THOUGHT THE PHARAOH WAS JUST BEING MAGNANIMOUS...
...BUT THEY WERE WRONG!!
WITHOUT SOME KIND OF REWARD, THE WORKERS WOULD'VE DROPPED LIKE FLIES!!
THAT'S HOW HARD IT WAS BUILDING THE PYRAMIDS WITHOUT HEAVY MACHINERY!

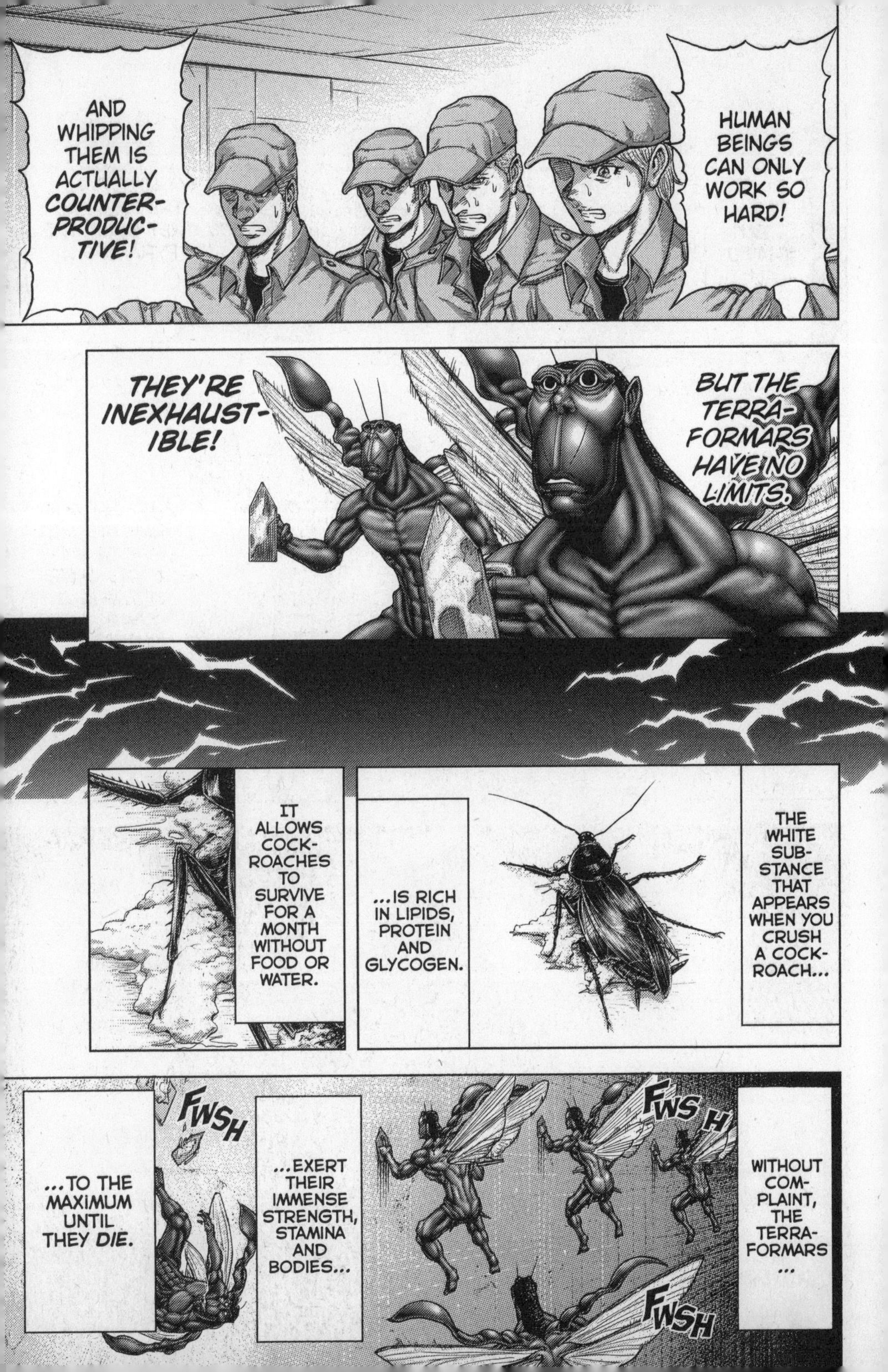
HUMAN BEINGS CAN ONLY WORK SO HARD!
AND WHIPPING THEM IS ACTUALLY COUNTER-PRODUCTIVE!
BUT THE TERRAFORMARS HAVE NO LIMITS.
THEY'RE INEXHAUSTIBLE!
THE WHITE SUBSTANCE THAT APPEARS WHEN YOU CRUSH A COCKROACH...
...IS RICH IN LIPIDS, PROTEIN AND GLYCOGEN.
IT ALLOWS COCKROACHES TO SURVIVE FOR A MONTH WITHOUT FOOD OR WATER.
WITHOUT COMPLAINT, THE TERRAFORMARS...
FWSH
FWSH
...EXERT THEIR IMMENSE STRENGTH, STAMINA AND BODIES...
FWSH
...TO THE MAXIMUM UNTIL THEY DIE.

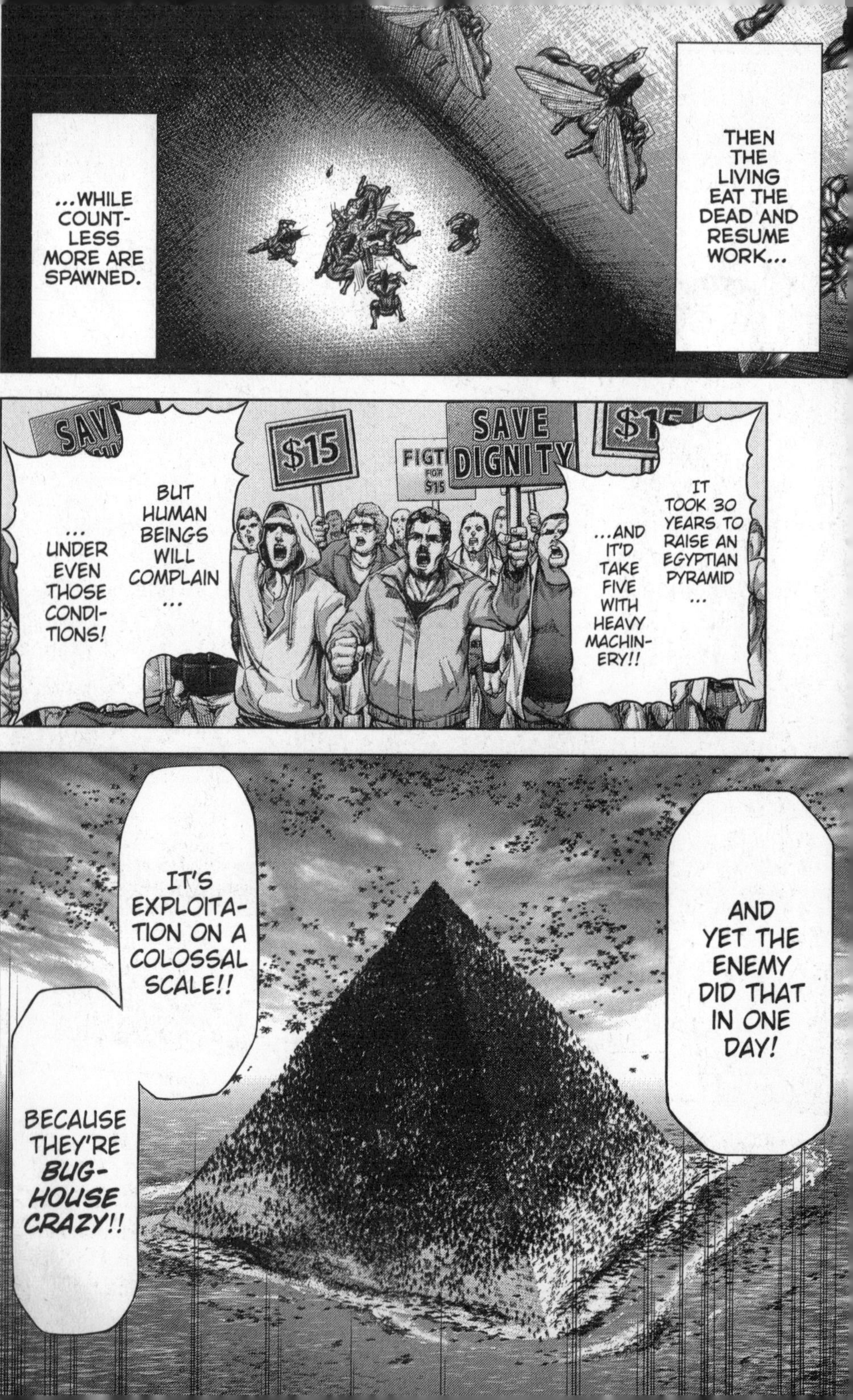
THEN THE LIVING EAT THE DEAD AND RESUME WORK...
...WHILE COUNTLESS MORE ARE SPAWNED.
$15
SAVE DIGNITY
$15
IT TOOK 30 YEARS TO RAISE AN EGYPTIAN PYRAMID...
...AND IT'D TAKE FIVE WITH HEAVY MACHINERY!!
BUT HUMAN BEINGS WILL COMPLAIN...
...UNDER EVEN THOSE CONDITIONS!
AND YET THE ENEMY DID THAT IN ONE DAY!
IT'S EXPLOITATION ON A COLOSSAL SCALE!!
BECAUSE THEY'RE *BUG-HOUSE CRAZY*!!

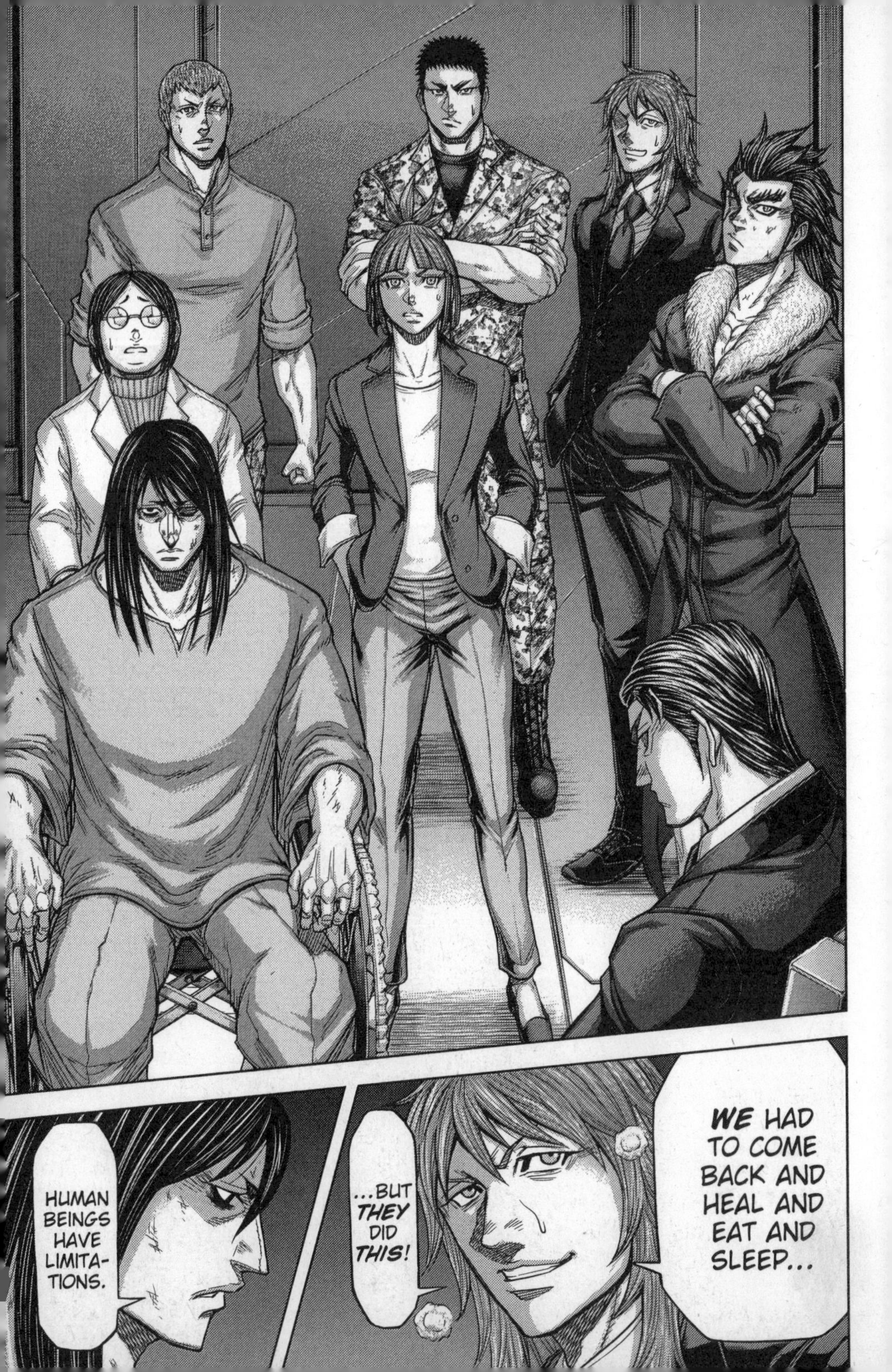
WE HAD TO COME BACK AND HEAL AND EAT AND SLEEP...
...BUT THEY DID THIS!
HUMAN BEINGS HAVE LIMITA-TIONS.

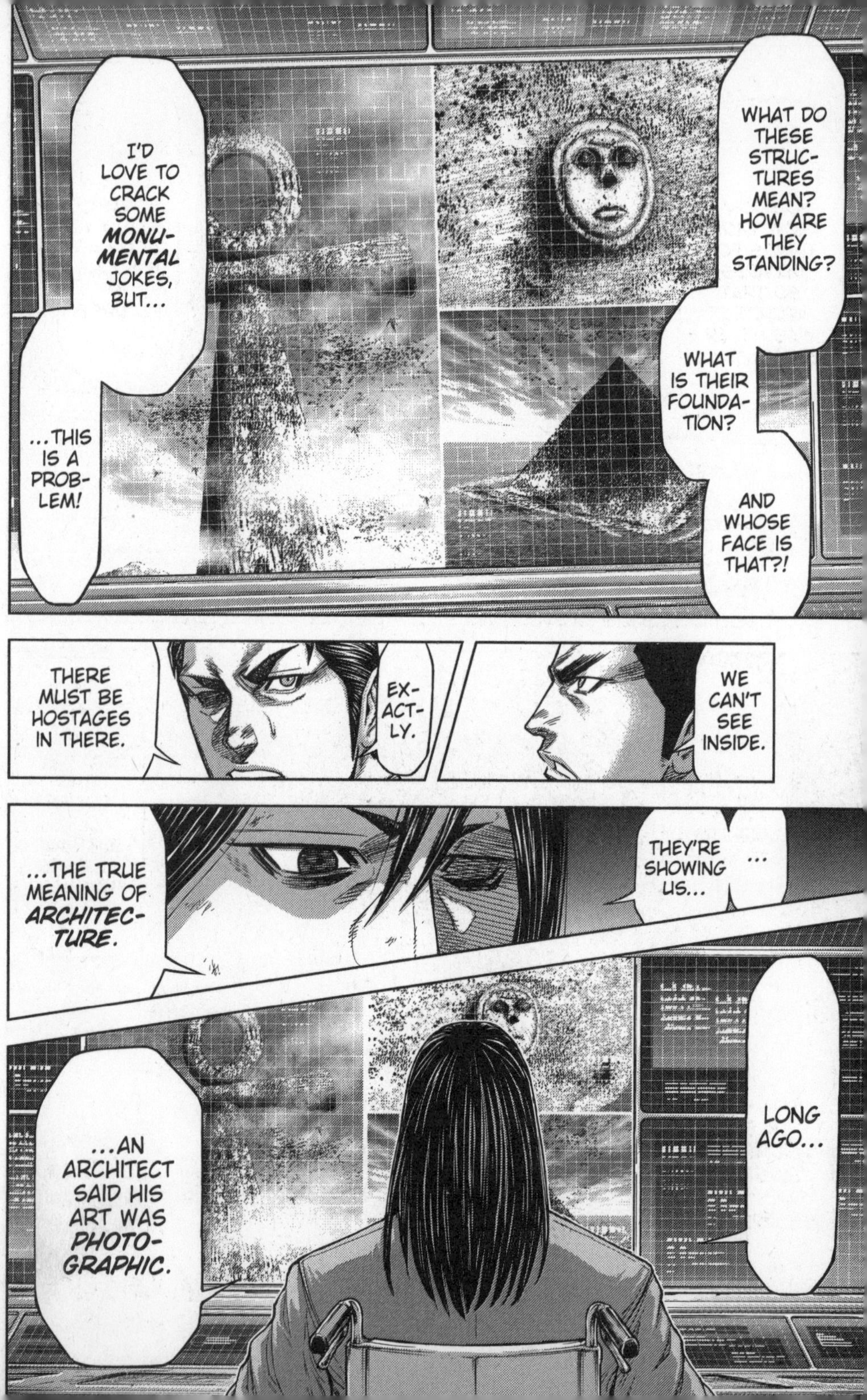
WHAT DO THESE STRUCTURES MEAN? HOW ARE THEY STANDING?
WHAT IS THEIR FOUNDATION?
AND WHOSE FACE IS THAT?!
I'D LOVE TO CRACK SOME MONUMENTAL JOKES, BUT...
...THIS IS A PROBLEM!
WE CAN'T SEE INSIDE.
EXACTLY.
THERE MUST BE HOSTAGES IN THERE.
...
THEY'RE SHOWING US...
...THE TRUE MEANING OF ARCHITECTURE.
LONG AGO...
...AN ARCHITECT SAID HIS ART WAS PHOTOGRAPHIC.

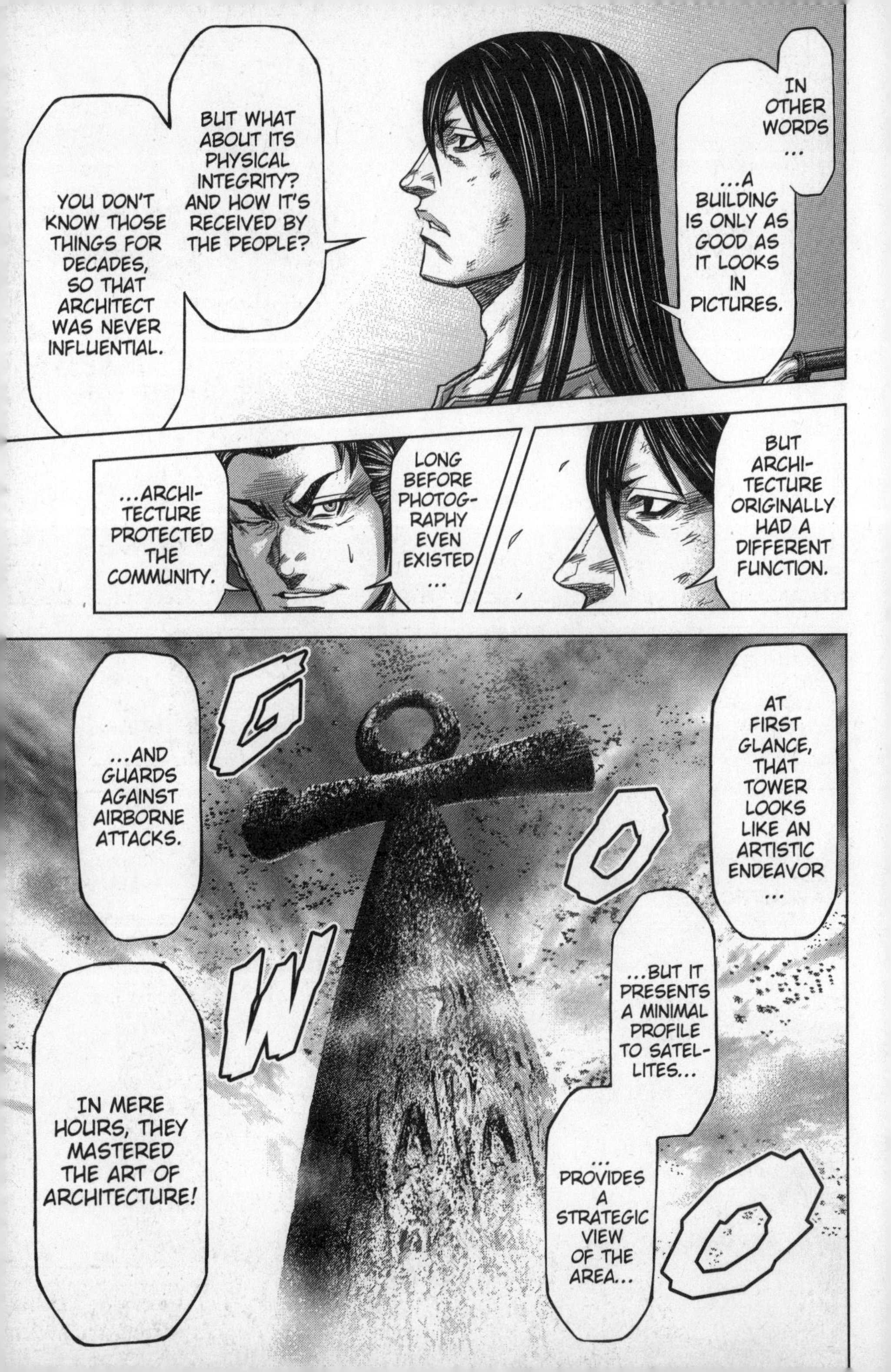
IN OTHER WORDS... ...A BUILDING IS ONLY AS GOOD AS IT LOOKS IN PICTURES.
BUT WHAT ABOUT ITS PHYSICAL INTEGRITY? AND HOW IT'S RECEIVED BY THE PEOPLE?
YOU DON'T KNOW THOSE THINGS FOR DECADES, SO THAT ARCHITECT WAS NEVER INFLUENTIAL.
BUT ARCHI-TECTURE ORIGINALLY HAD A DIFFERENT FUNCTION.
LONG BEFORE PHOTOG-RAPHY EVEN EXISTED...
...ARCHI-TECTURE PROTECTED THE COMMUNITY.
AT FIRST GLANCE, THAT TOWER LOOKS LIKE AN ARTISTIC ENDEAVOR...
...BUT IT PRESENTS A MINIMAL PROFILE TO SATEL-LITES...
...PROVIDES A STRATEGIC VIEW OF THE AREA...
...AND GUARDS AGAINST AIRBORNE ATTACKS.
GOWO
IN MERE HOURS, THEY MASTERED THE ART OF ARCHITECTURE!

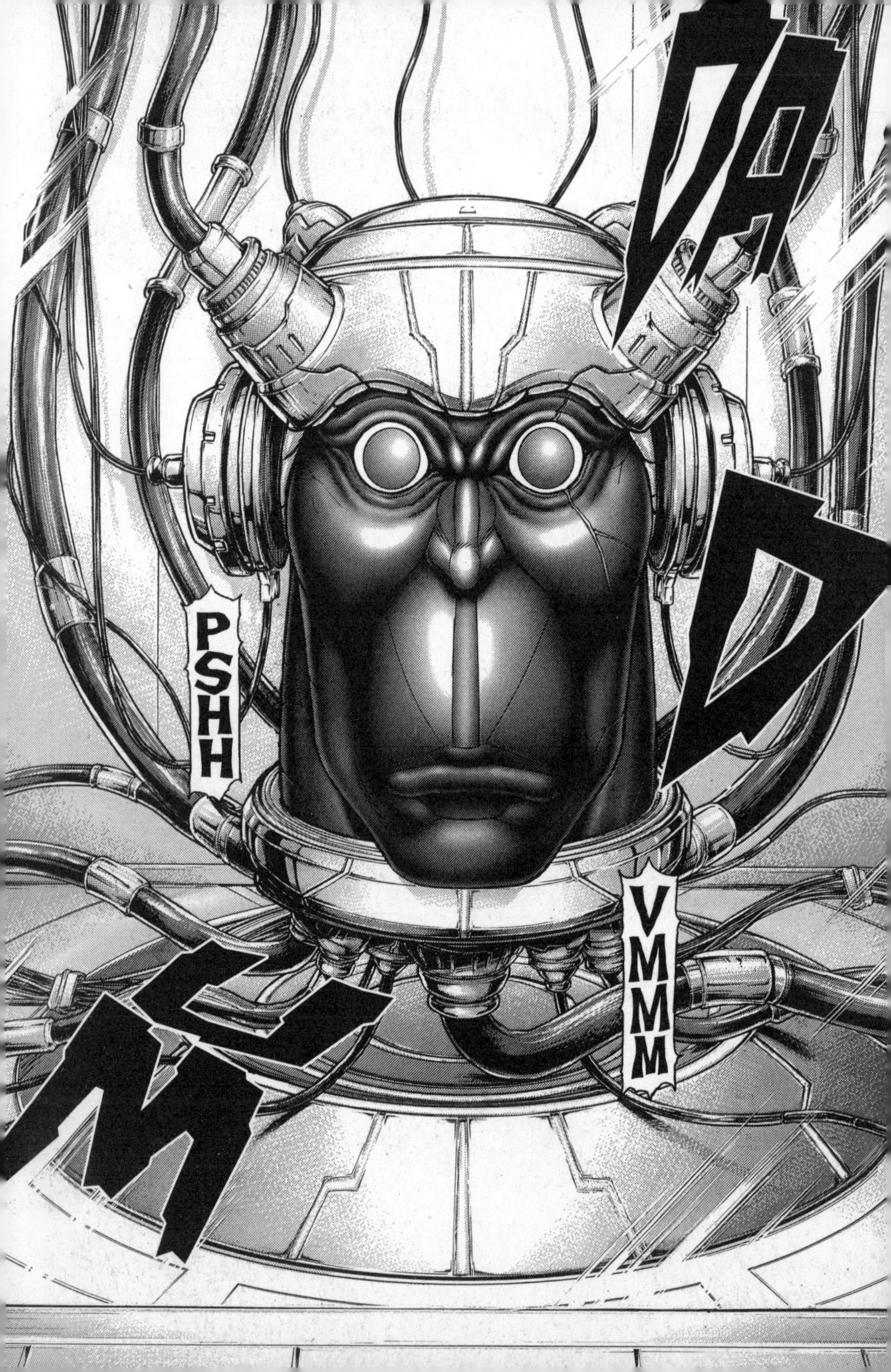
PSHH
VMMM

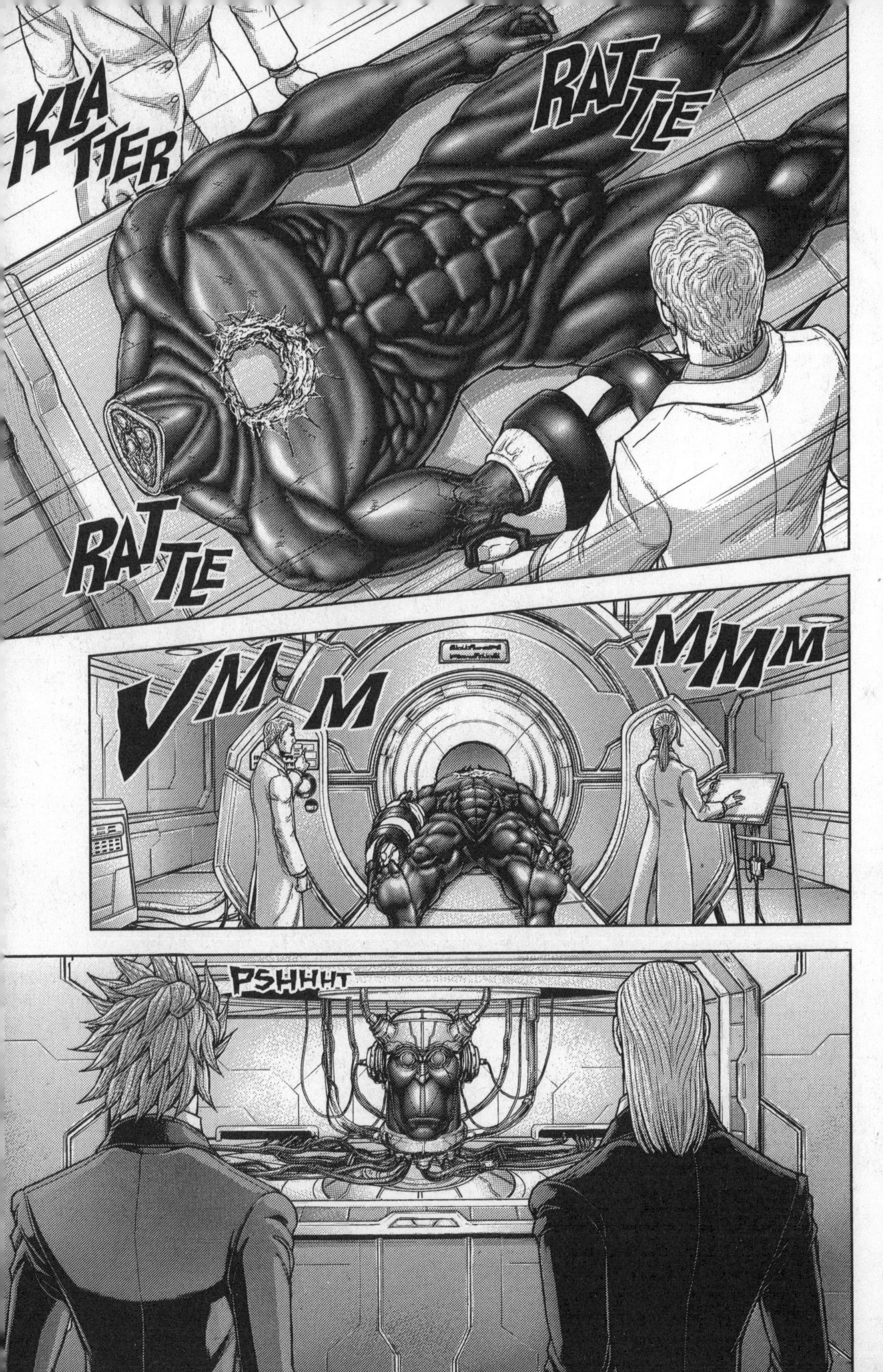
RATTLE
KLATTER
RATTLE
MMMM
VM M
PSHHHT

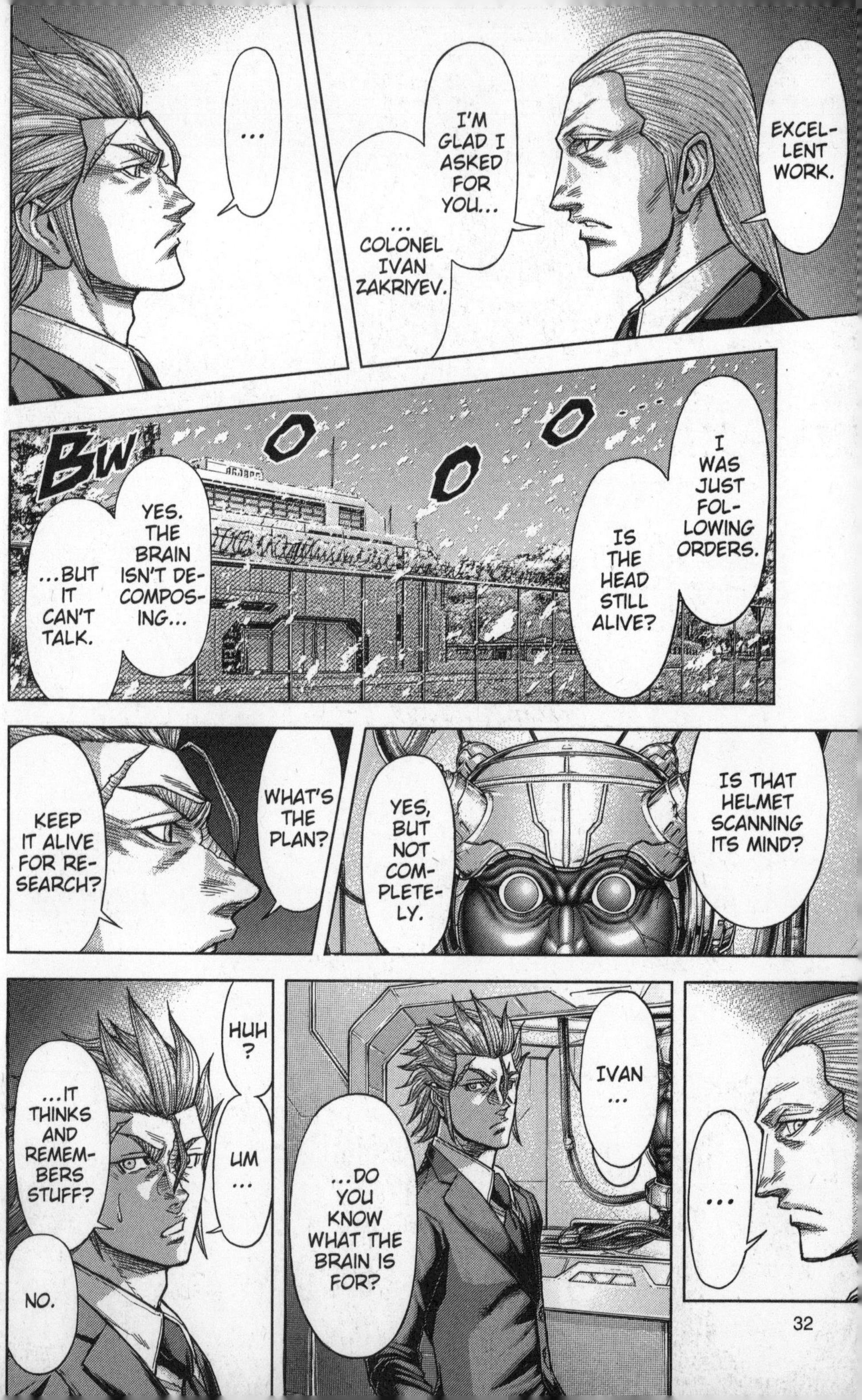
EXCELLENT WORK.
I'M GLAD I ASKED FOR YOU... ...COLONEL IVAN ZAKRIYEV.
...
I WAS JUST FOLLOWING ORDERS.
IS THE HEAD STILL ALIVE?
BWOOO
YES. THE BRAIN ISN'T DECOMPOSING...
...BUT IT CAN'T TALK.
IS THAT HELMET SCANNING ITS MIND?
YES, BUT NOT COMPLETELY.
WHAT'S THE PLAN?
KEEP IT ALIVE FOR RESEARCH?
...
IVAN...
...DO YOU KNOW WHAT THE BRAIN IS FOR?
HUH?
UM...
...IT THINKS AND REMEMBERS STUFF?
NO.

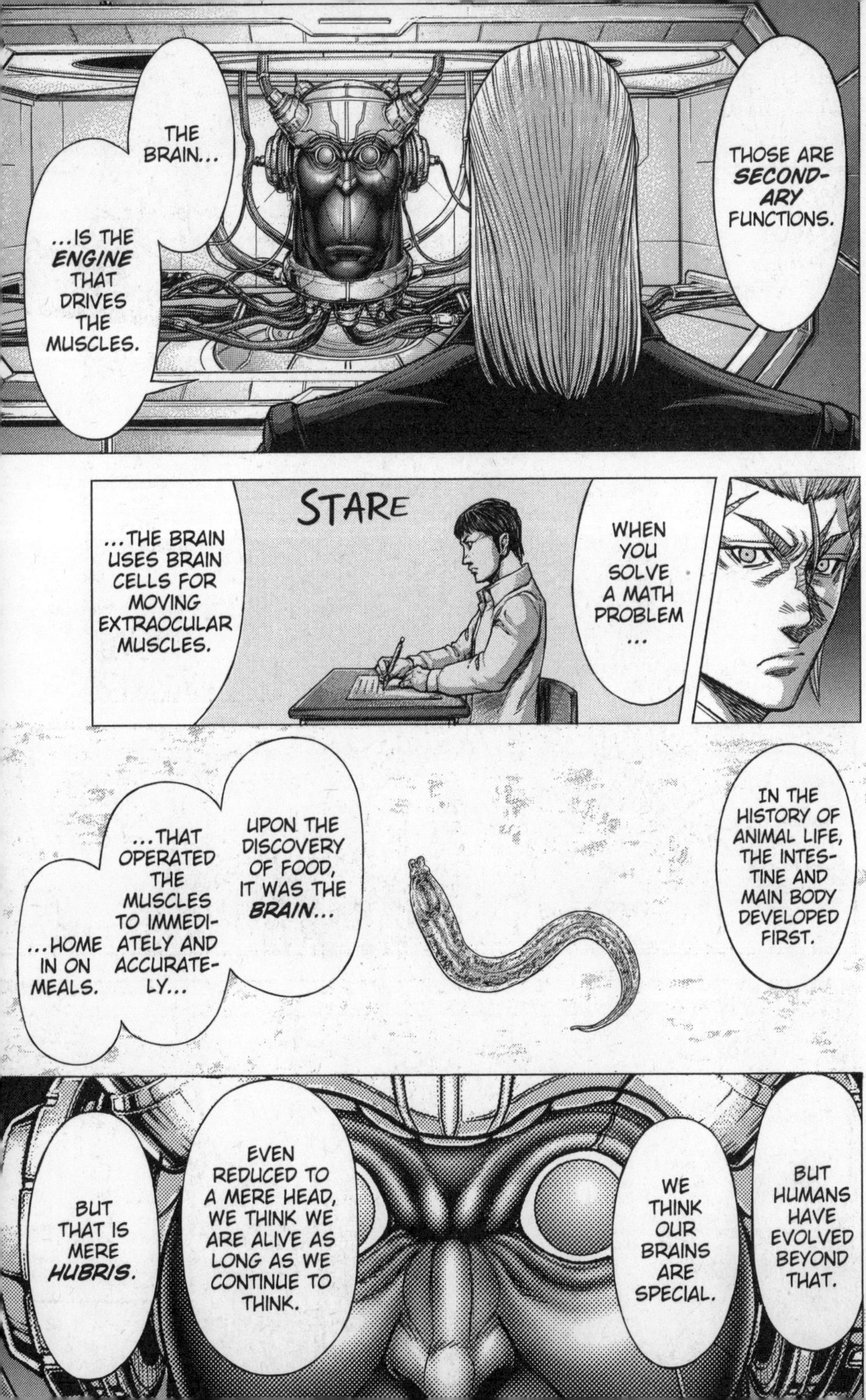
THOSE ARE SECONDARY FUNCTIONS.
THE BRAIN...
...IS THE ENGINE THAT DRIVES THE MUSCLES.
WHEN YOU SOLVE A MATH PROBLEM...
STARE
...THE BRAIN USES BRAIN CELLS FOR MOVING EXTRAOCULAR MUSCLES.
IN THE HISTORY OF ANIMAL LIFE, THE INTESTINE AND MAIN BODY DEVELOPED FIRST.
UPON THE DISCOVERY OF FOOD, IT WAS THE BRAIN...
...THAT OPERATED THE MUSCLES TO IMMEDIATELY AND ACCURATELY...
...HOME IN ON MEALS.
BUT HUMANS HAVE EVOLVED BEYOND THAT.
WE THINK OUR BRAINS ARE SPECIAL.
EVEN REDUCED TO A MERE HEAD, WE THINK WE ARE ALIVE AS LONG AS WE CONTINUE TO THINK.
BUT THAT IS MERE HUBRIS.

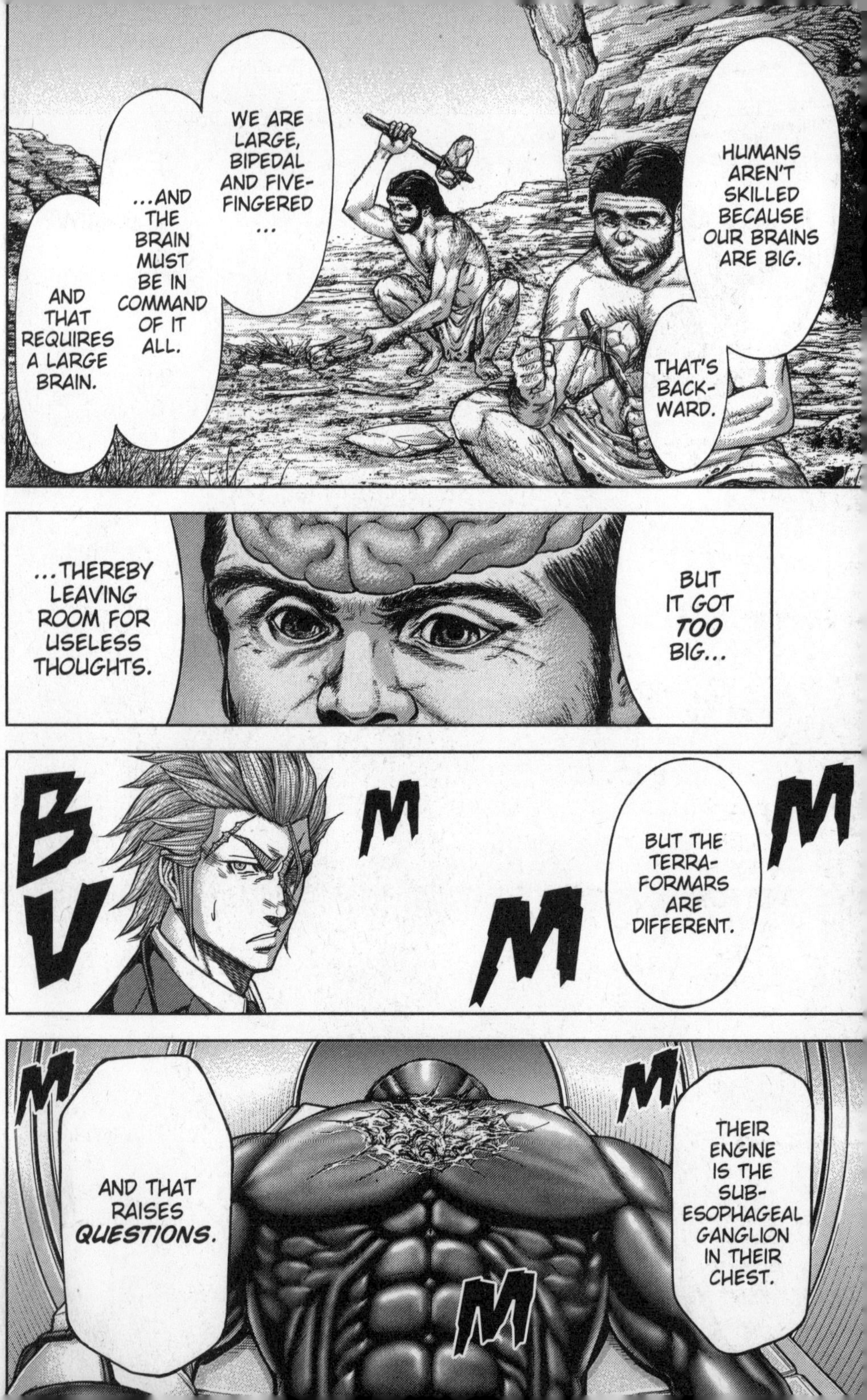
HUMANS AREN'T SKILLED BECAUSE OUR BRAINS ARE BIG.
THAT'S BACKWARD.
WE ARE LARGE, BIPEDAL AND FIVE-FINGERED...
...AND THE BRAIN MUST BE IN COMMAND OF IT ALL.
AND THAT REQUIRES A LARGE BRAIN.
BUT IT GOT *TOO* BIG...
...THEREBY LEAVING ROOM FOR USELESS THOUGHTS.
BVMMM
BUT THE TERRAFORMARS ARE DIFFERENT.
MMMM
THEIR ENGINE IS THE SUB-ESOPHAGEAL GANGLION IN THEIR CHEST.
AND THAT RAISES *QUESTIONS*.

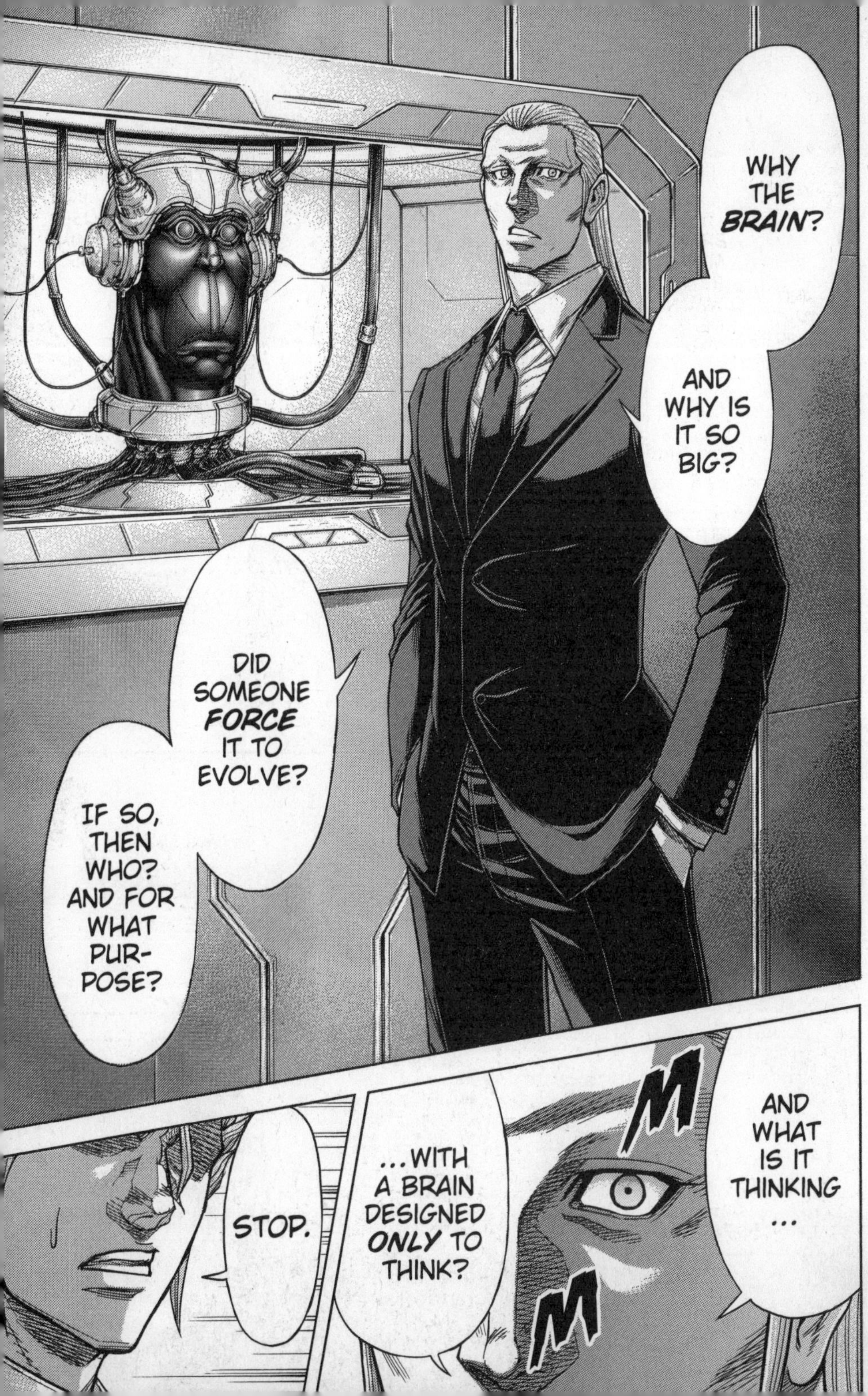
WHY THE BRAIN?
AND WHY IS IT SO BIG?
DID SOMEONE FORCE IT TO EVOLVE?
IF SO, THEN WHO? AND FOR WHAT PUR-POSE?
AND WHAT IS IT THINKING...
M
M
...WITH A BRAIN DESIGNED ONLY TO THINK?
STOP.

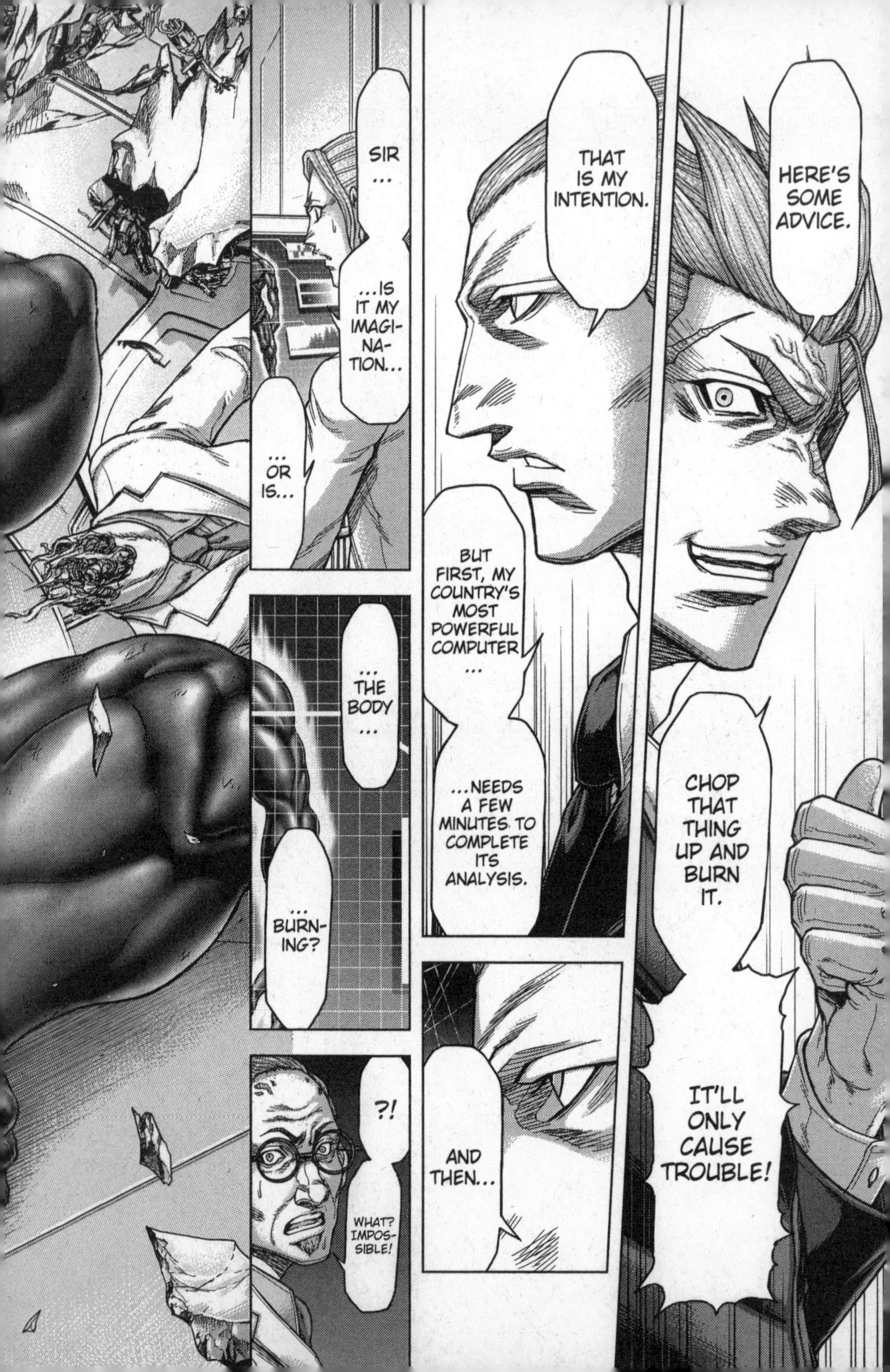
HERE'S SOME ADVICE.
CHOP THAT THING UP AND BURN IT.
IT'LL ONLY CAUSE TROUBLE!
THAT IS MY INTENTION.
BUT FIRST, MY COUNTRY'S MOST POWERFUL COMPUTER...
...NEEDS A FEW MINUTES TO COMPLETE ITS ANALYSIS.
AND THEN...
SIR...
...IS IT MY IMAGINATION...
...OR IS...
...THE BODY...
...BURNING?
?!
WHAT? IMPOSSIBLE!

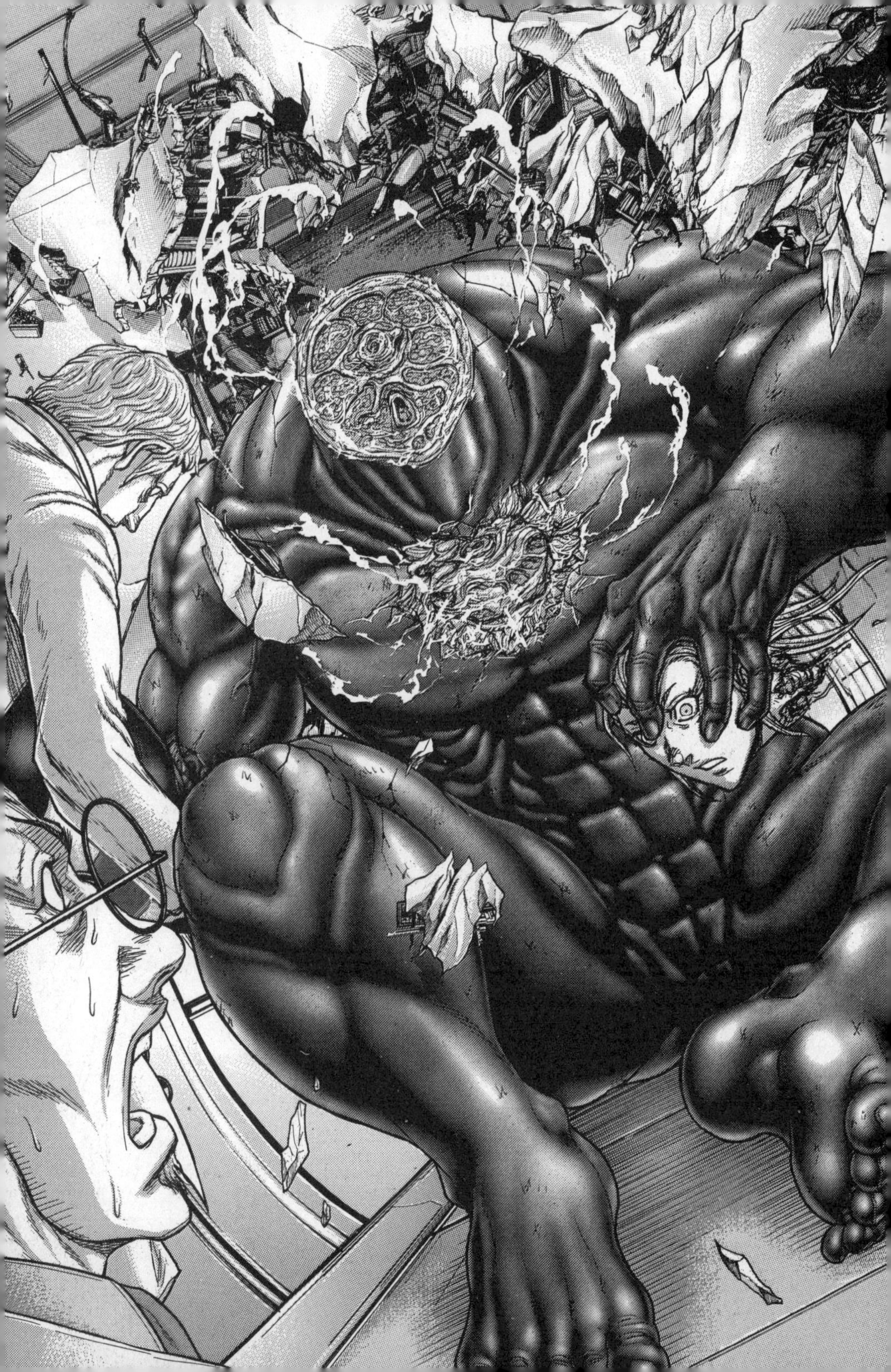

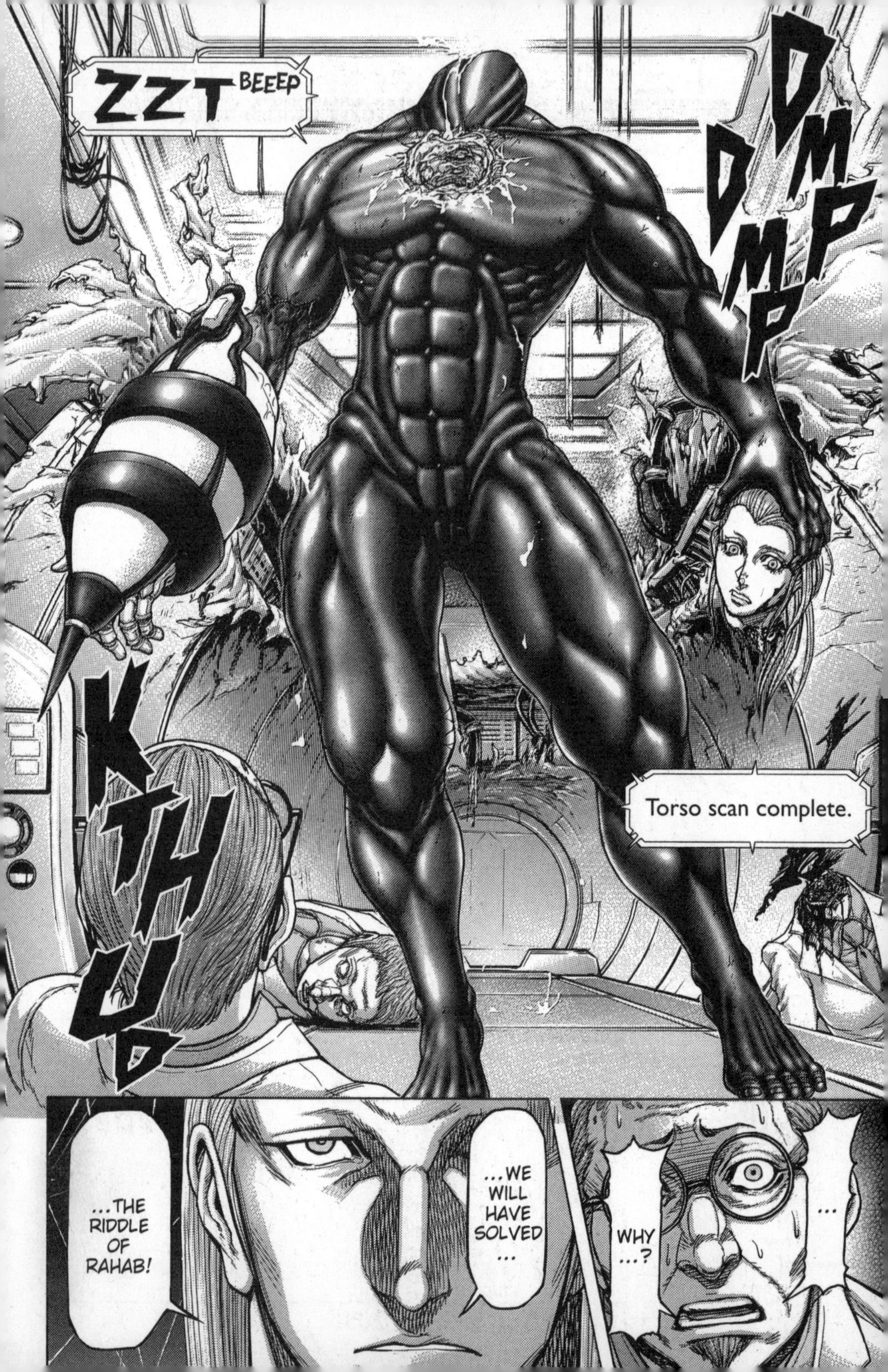
DMP DMP
ZZT BEEEP
Torso scan complete.
KTHUD
...
WHY ...?
...WE WILL HAVE SOLVED ...
...THE RIDDLE OF RAHAB!

# TERRA FORMARS

## Instructor Kazemura's Habits After Becoming Mobile Again, Part 4

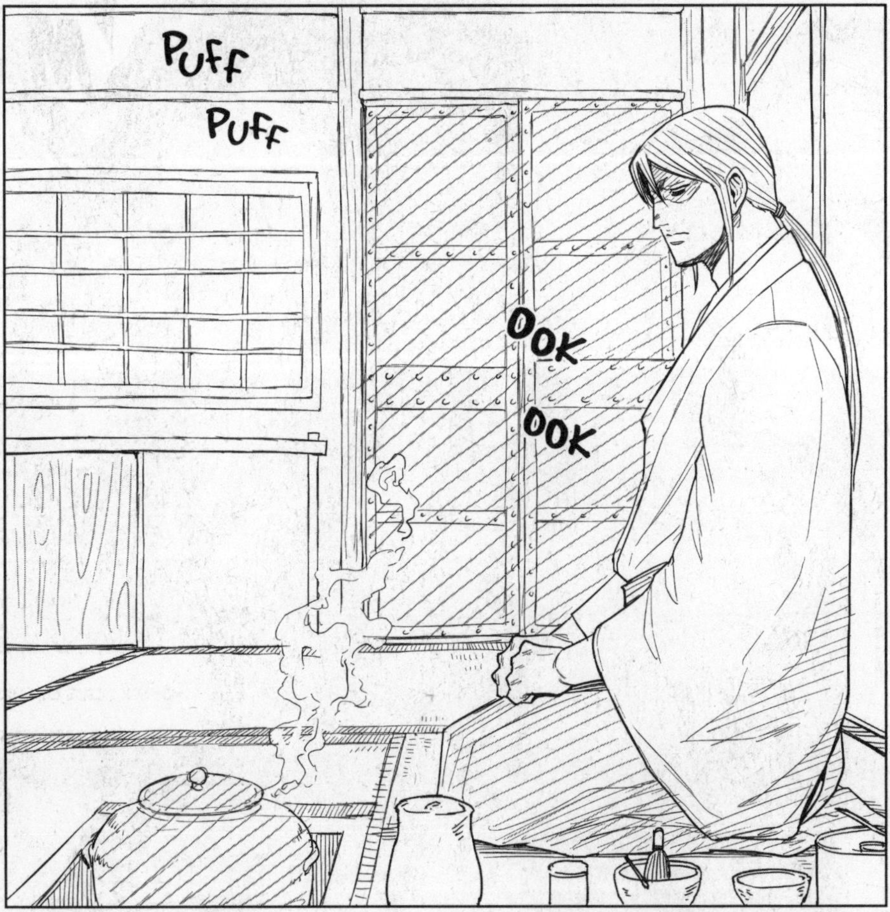

PUFF
PUFF
OOK
OOK


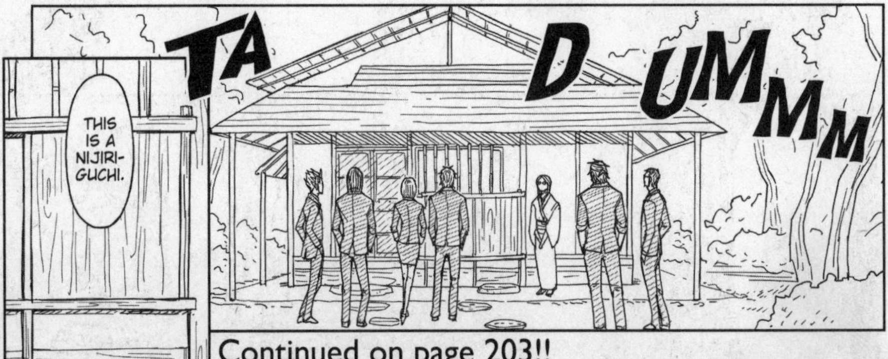

TA DUMMM
THIS IS A NIJIRI-GUCHI.


[A small door for entering a tea ceremony]

Continued on page 203!!

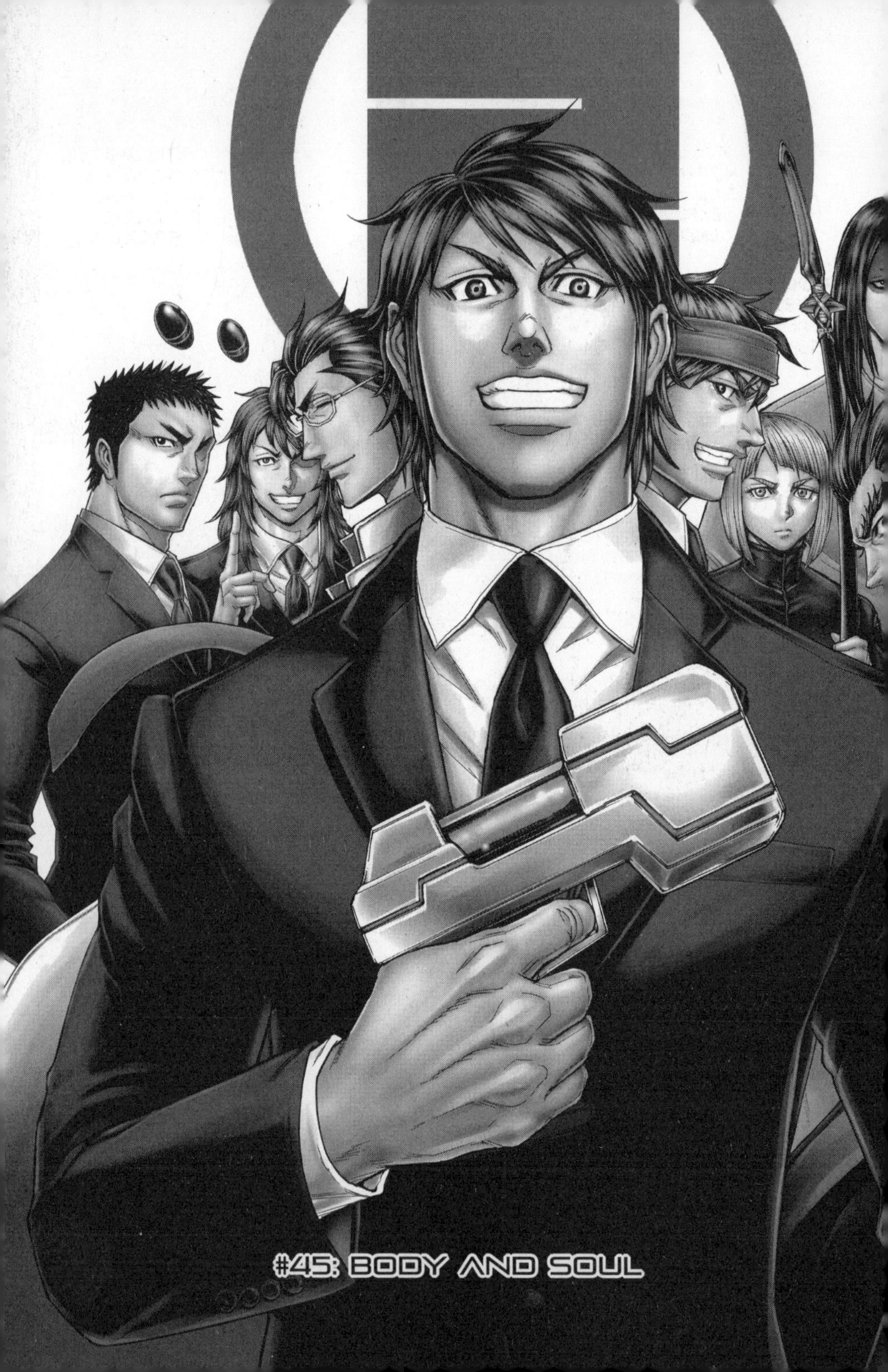
#45: BODY AND SOUL

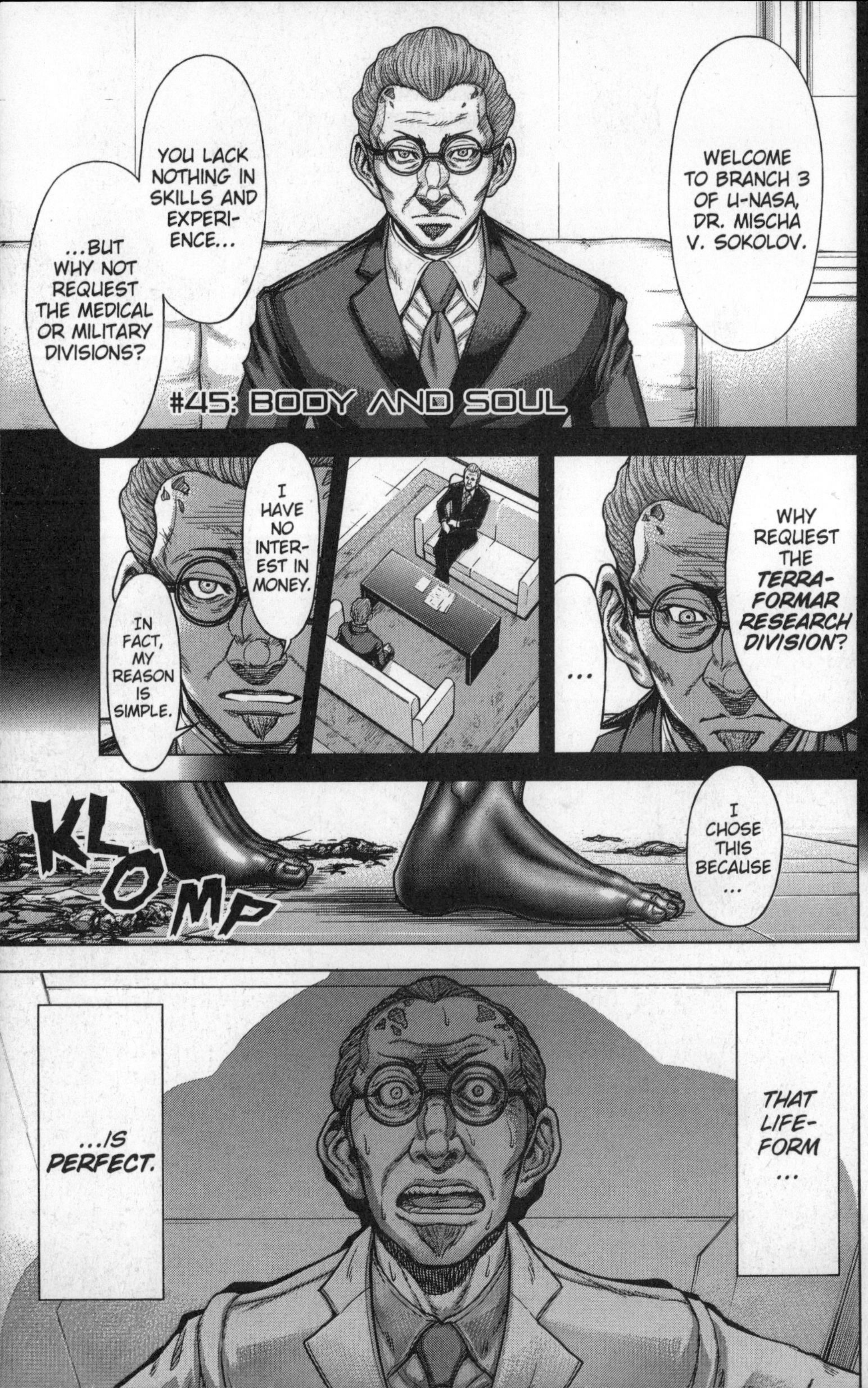
WELCOME TO BRANCH 3 OF U-NASA, DR. MISCHA V. SOKOLOV.
YOU LACK NOTHING IN SKILLS AND EXPERIENCE...
...BUT WHY NOT REQUEST THE MEDICAL OR MILITARY DIVISIONS?
#45: BODY AND SOUL
WHY REQUEST THE *TERRAFORMAR RESEARCH DIVISION*?
...
I HAVE NO INTEREST IN MONEY.
IN FACT, MY REASON IS SIMPLE.
I CHOSE THIS BECAUSE...
KLOMP
*THAT LIFE-FORM...*
*...IS PERFECT.*

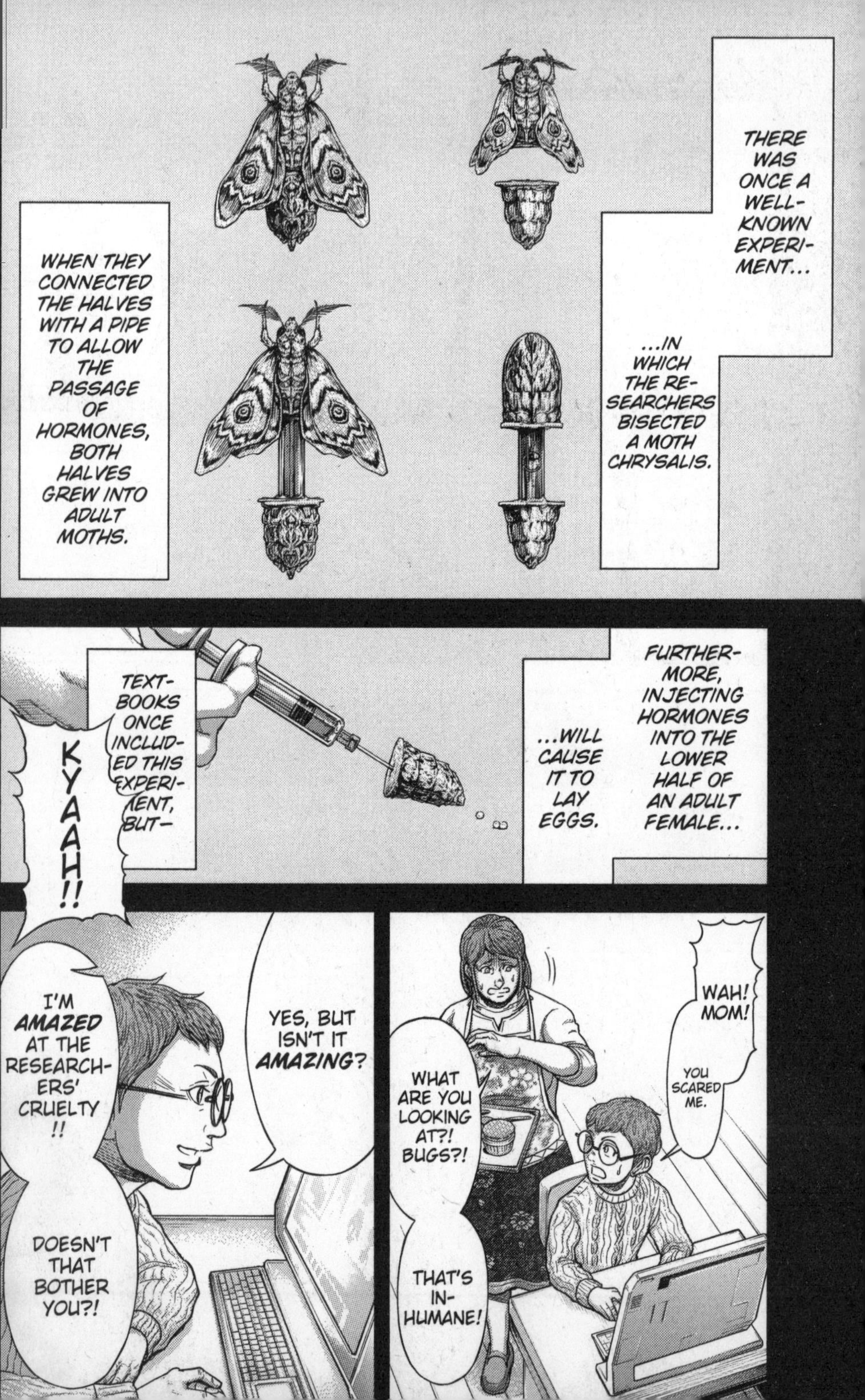
THERE WAS ONCE A WELL-KNOWN EXPERIMENT...
...IN WHICH THE RESEARCHERS BISECTED A MOTH CHRYSALIS.
WHEN THEY CONNECTED THE HALVES WITH A PIPE TO ALLOW THE PASSAGE OF HORMONES, BOTH HALVES GREW INTO ADULT MOTHS.
FURTHERMORE, INJECTING HORMONES INTO THE LOWER HALF OF AN ADULT FEMALE...
...WILL CAUSE IT TO LAY EGGS.
TEXTBOOKS ONCE INCLUDED THIS EXPERIMENT, BUT-
KYAAH!!
WAH! MOM!
YOU SCARED ME.
WHAT ARE YOU LOOKING AT?! BUGS?!
THAT'S INHUMANE!
YES, BUT ISN'T IT AMAZING?
I'M AMAZED AT THE RESEARCHERS' CRUELTY!!
DOESN'T THAT BOTHER YOU?!

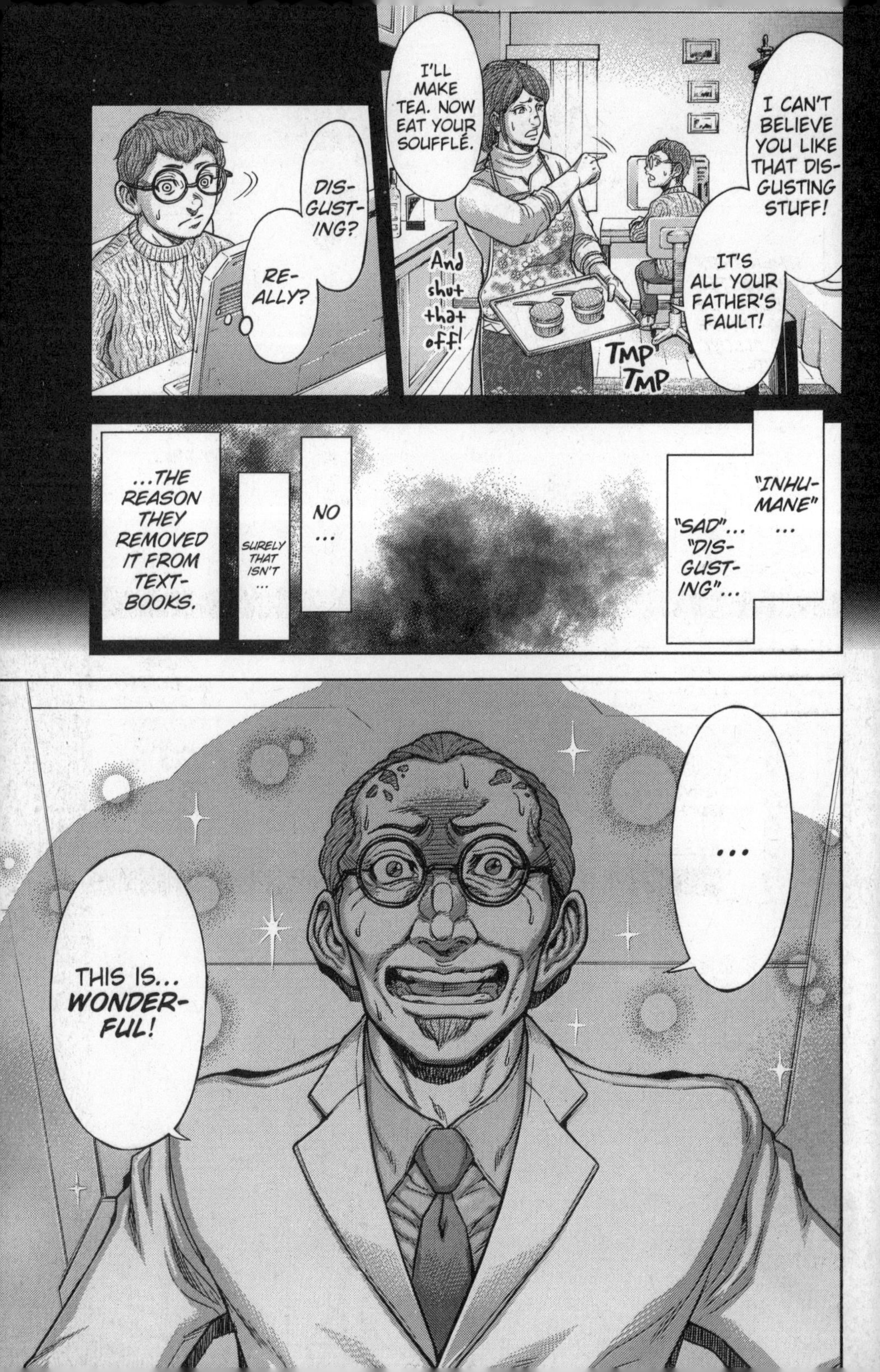
I CAN'T BELIEVE YOU LIKE THAT DIS-GUSTING STUFF!
IT'S ALL YOUR FATHER'S FAULT!
I'LL MAKE TEA. NOW EAT YOUR SOUFFLÉ.
And shut that off!
TMP TMP
DIS-GUST-ING?
RE-ALLY?
"INHU-MANE"...
"SAD"... "DIS-GUST-ING"...
NO...
SURELY THAT ISN'T...
...THE REASON THEY REMOVED IT FROM TEXT-BOOKS.
...
THIS IS... **WONDER-FUL!**

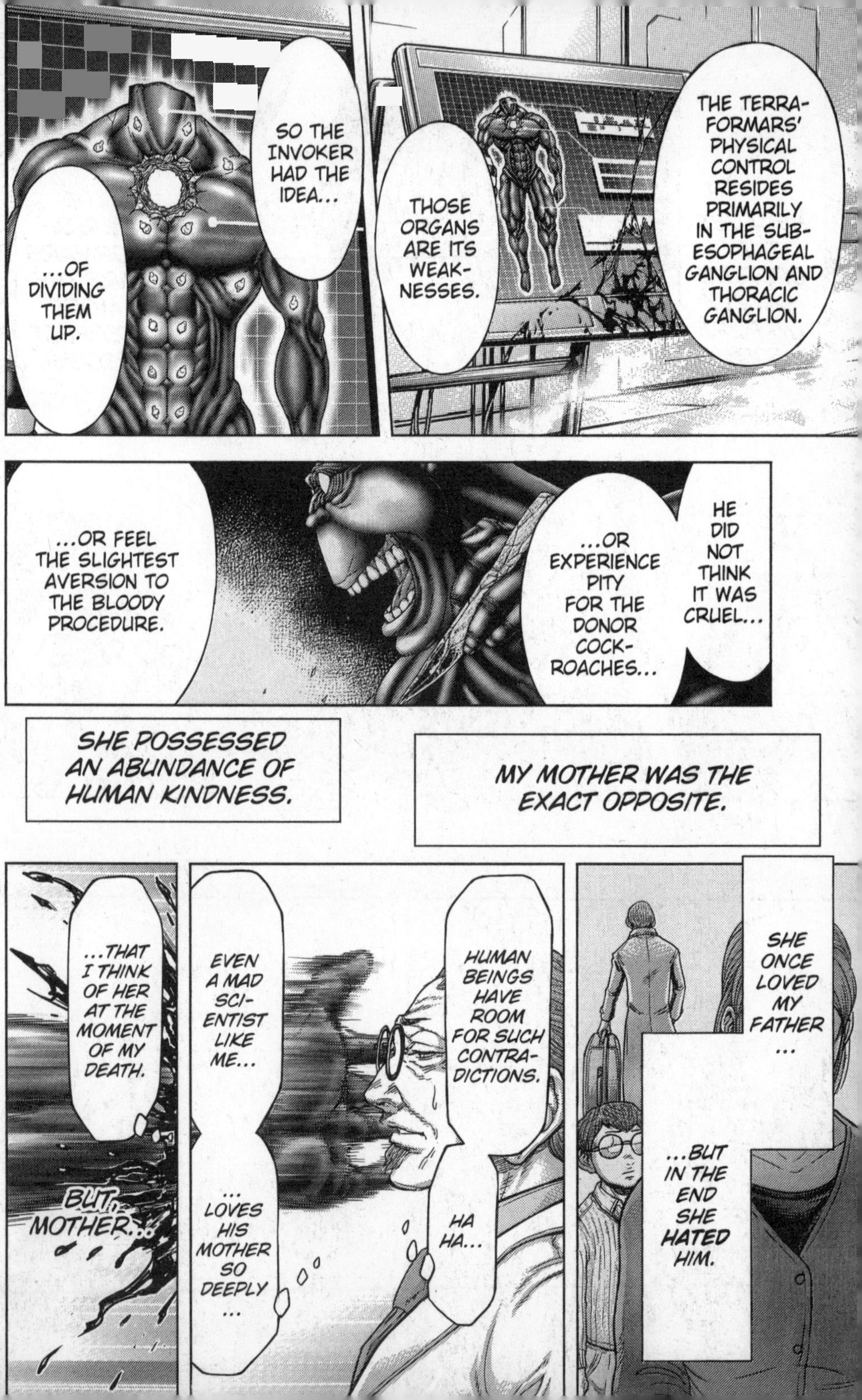
THE TERRA-FORMARS' PHYSICAL CONTROL RESIDES PRIMARILY IN THE SUB-ESOPHAGEAL GANGLION AND THORACIC GANGLION.
THOSE ORGANS ARE ITS WEAK-NESSES.
SO THE INVOKER HAD THE IDEA...
...OF DIVIDING THEM UP.
HE DID NOT THINK IT WAS CRUEL...
...OR EXPERIENCE PITY FOR THE DONOR COCK-ROACHES...
...OR FEEL THE SLIGHTEST AVERSION TO THE BLOODY PROCEDURE.
MY MOTHER WAS THE EXACT OPPOSITE.
SHE POSSESSED AN ABUNDANCE OF HUMAN KINDNESS.
SHE ONCE LOVED MY FATHER...
...BUT IN THE END SHE HATED HIM.
HUMAN BEINGS HAVE ROOM FOR SUCH CONTRA-DICTIONS.
HA HA...
EVEN A MAD SCI-ENTIST LIKE ME...
...LOVES HIS MOTHER SO DEEPLY...
BUT, MOTHER...
...THAT I THINK OF HER AT THE MOMENT OF MY DEATH.

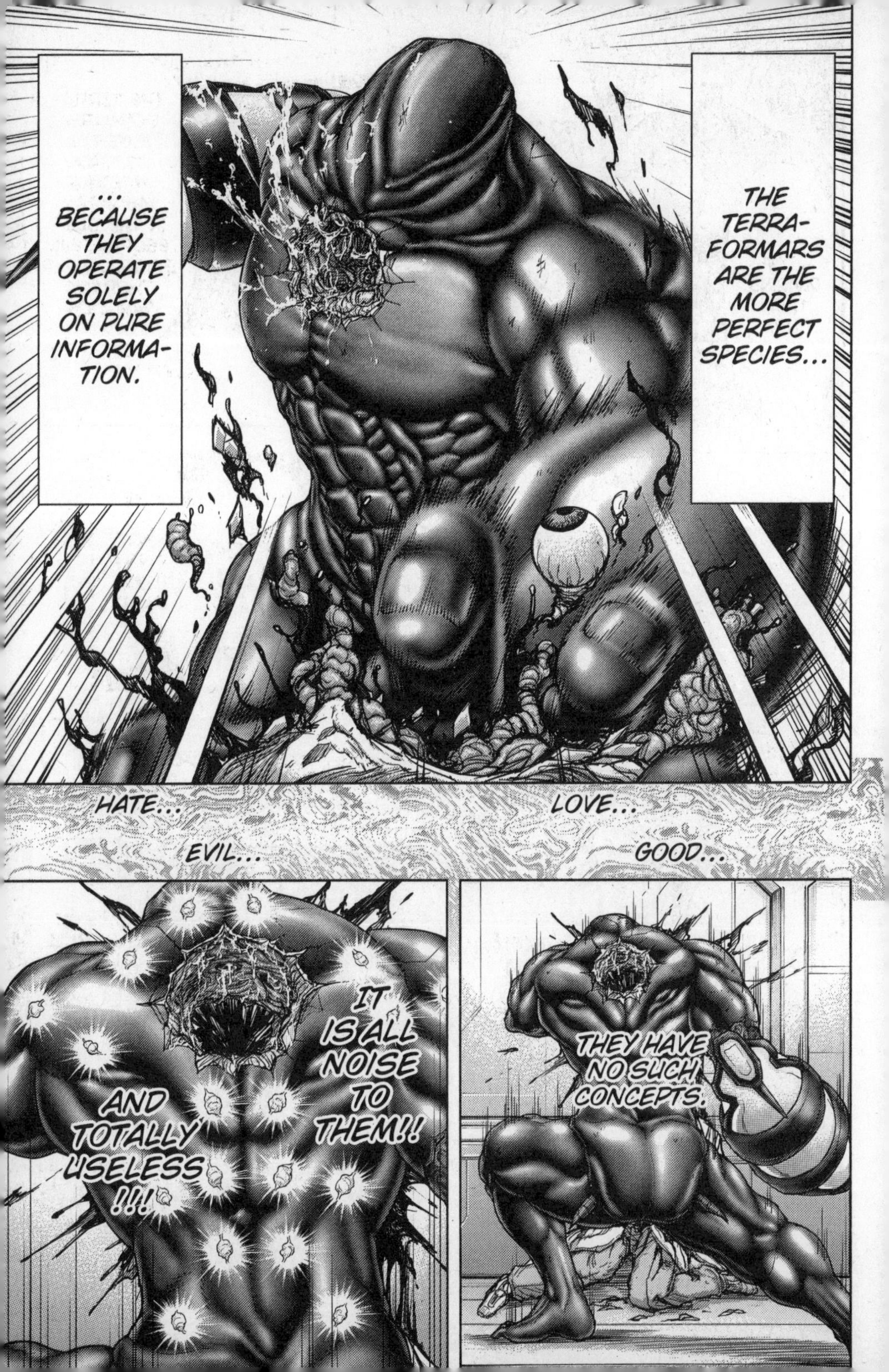
THE TERRA-FORMARS ARE THE MORE PERFECT SPECIES...
...BECAUSE THEY OPERATE SOLELY ON PURE INFORMATION.
LOVE...
HATE...
GOOD...
EVIL...
THEY HAVE NO SUCH CONCEPTS.
IT IS ALL NOISE TO THEM!!
AND TOTALLY USELESS!!!

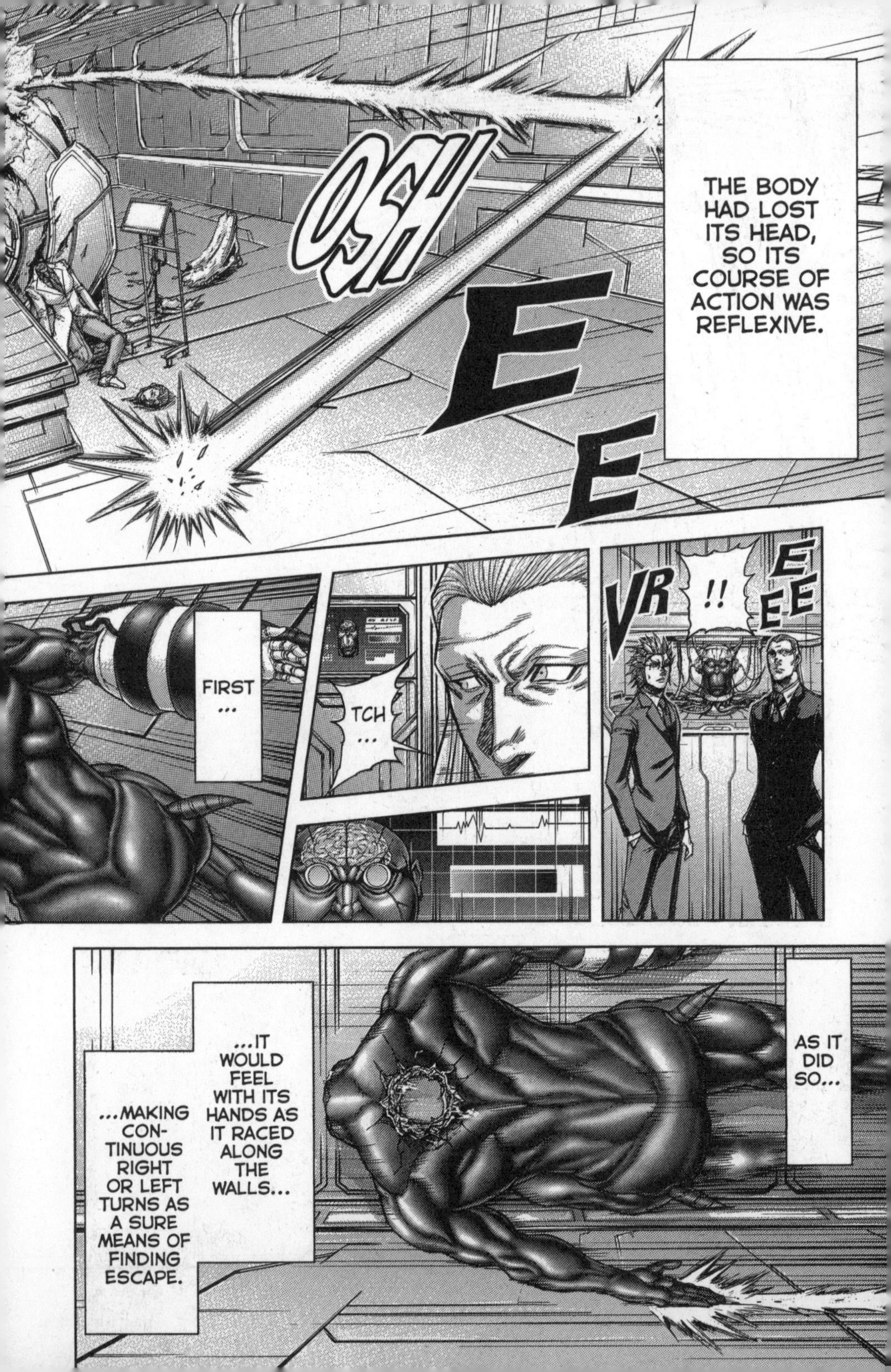
THE BODY HAD LOST ITS HEAD, SO ITS COURSE OF ACTION WAS REFLEXIVE.
OSH
E
E
VR
!!
E
EE
TCH...
FIRST...
AS IT DID SO...
...IT WOULD FEEL WITH ITS HANDS AS IT RACED ALONG THE WALLS...
...MAKING CON-TINUOUS RIGHT OR LEFT TURNS AS A SURE MEANS OF FINDING ESCAPE.

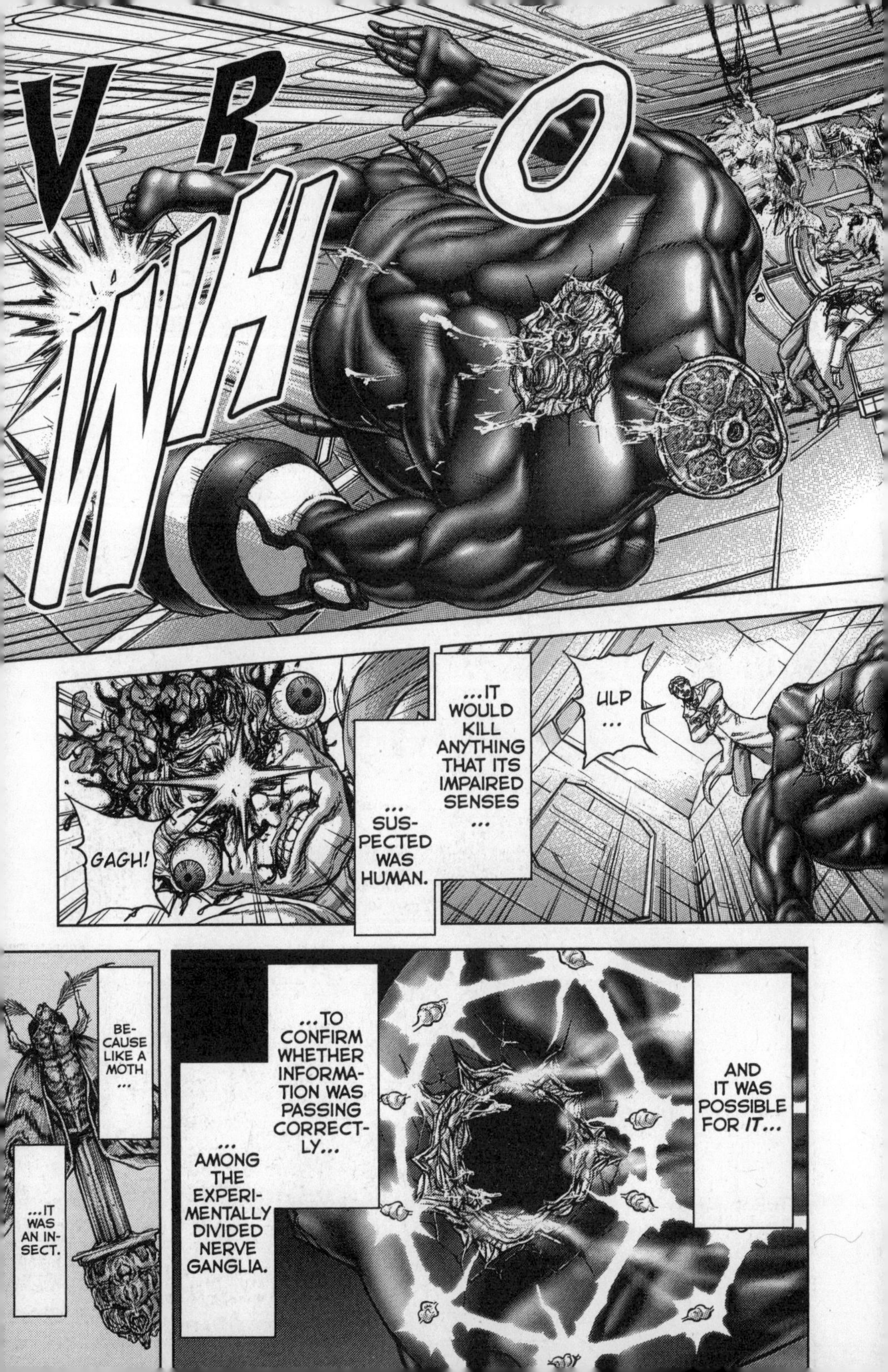
VRO
WH
ULP ...
...IT WOULD KILL ANYTHING THAT ITS IMPAIRED SENSES ...
... SUSPECTED WAS HUMAN.
GAGH!
AND IT WAS POSSIBLE FOR *IT*...
...TO CONFIRM WHETHER INFORMATION WAS PASSING CORRECTLY...
... AMONG THE EXPERIMENTALLY DIVIDED NERVE GANGLIA.
BECAUSE LIKE A MOTH ...
...IT WAS AN INSECT.

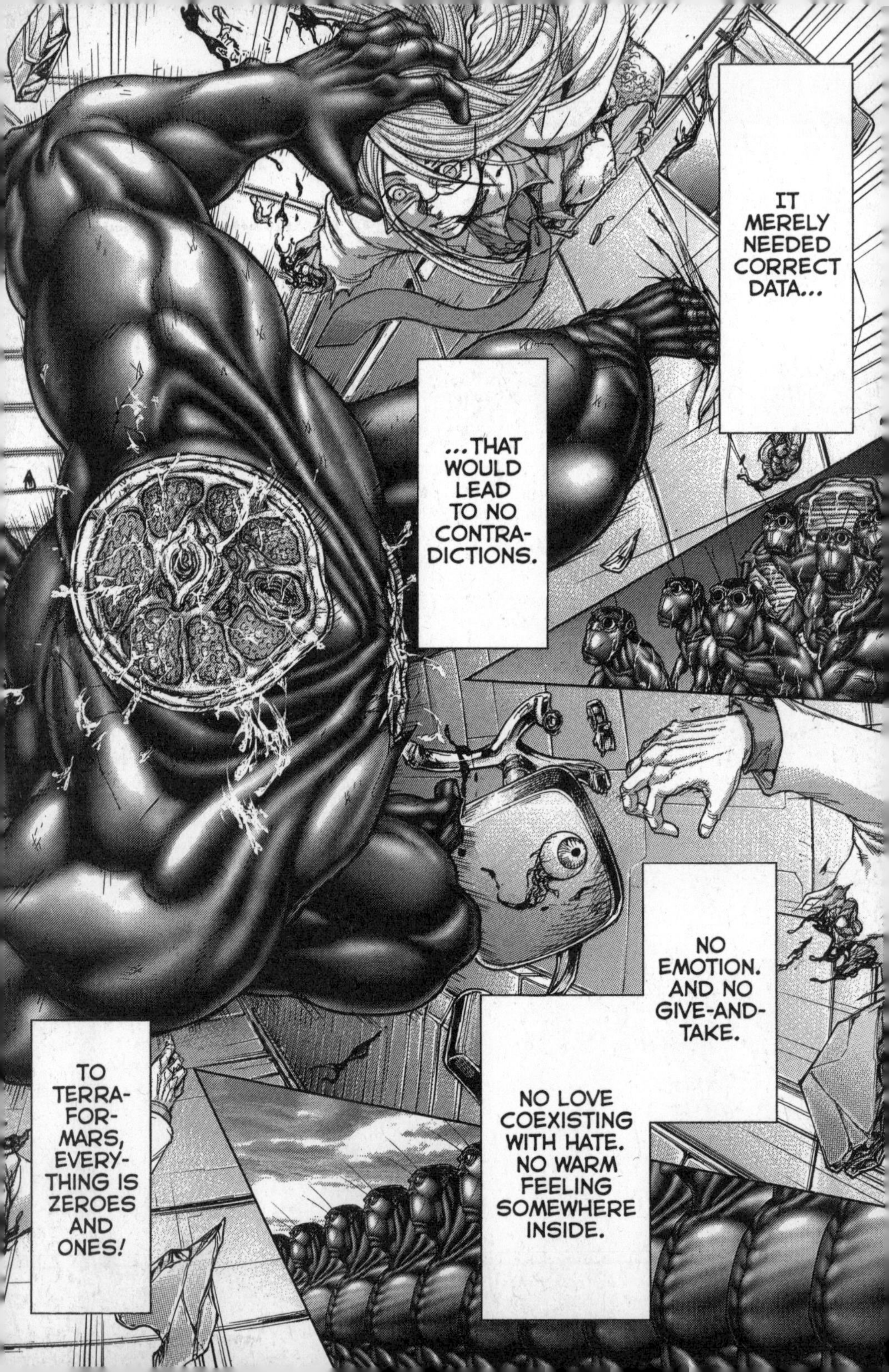
IT MERELY NEEDED CORRECT DATA...
...THAT WOULD LEAD TO NO CONTRA-DICTIONS.
NO EMOTION. AND NO GIVE-AND-TAKE.
NO LOVE COEXISTING WITH HATE. NO WARM FEELING SOMEWHERE INSIDE.
TO TERRA-FOR-MARS, EVERY-THING IS ZEROES AND ONES!

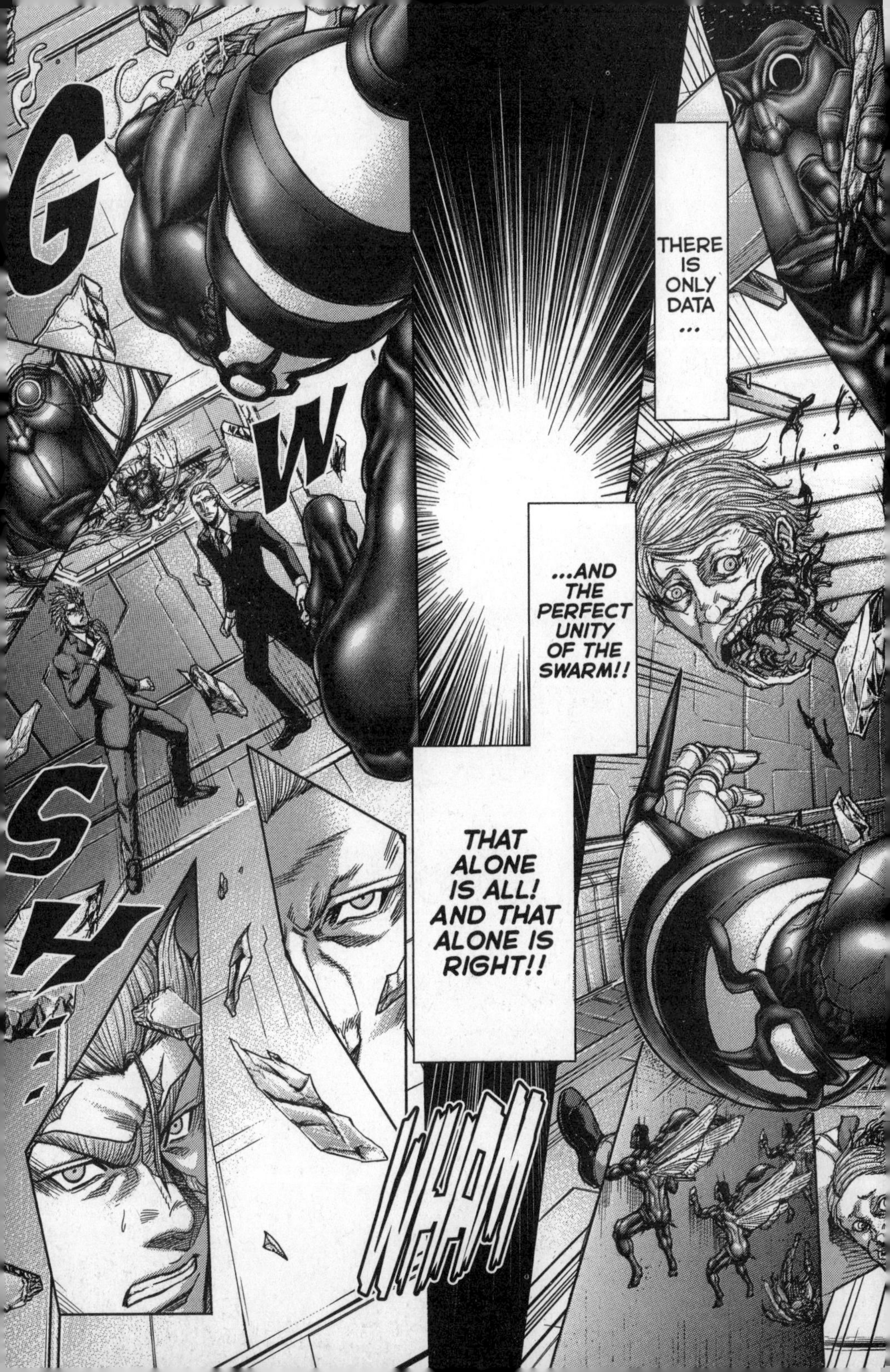
THERE IS ONLY DATA ...
...AND THE PERFECT UNITY OF THE SWARM!!
THAT ALONE IS ALL! AND THAT ALONE IS RIGHT!!

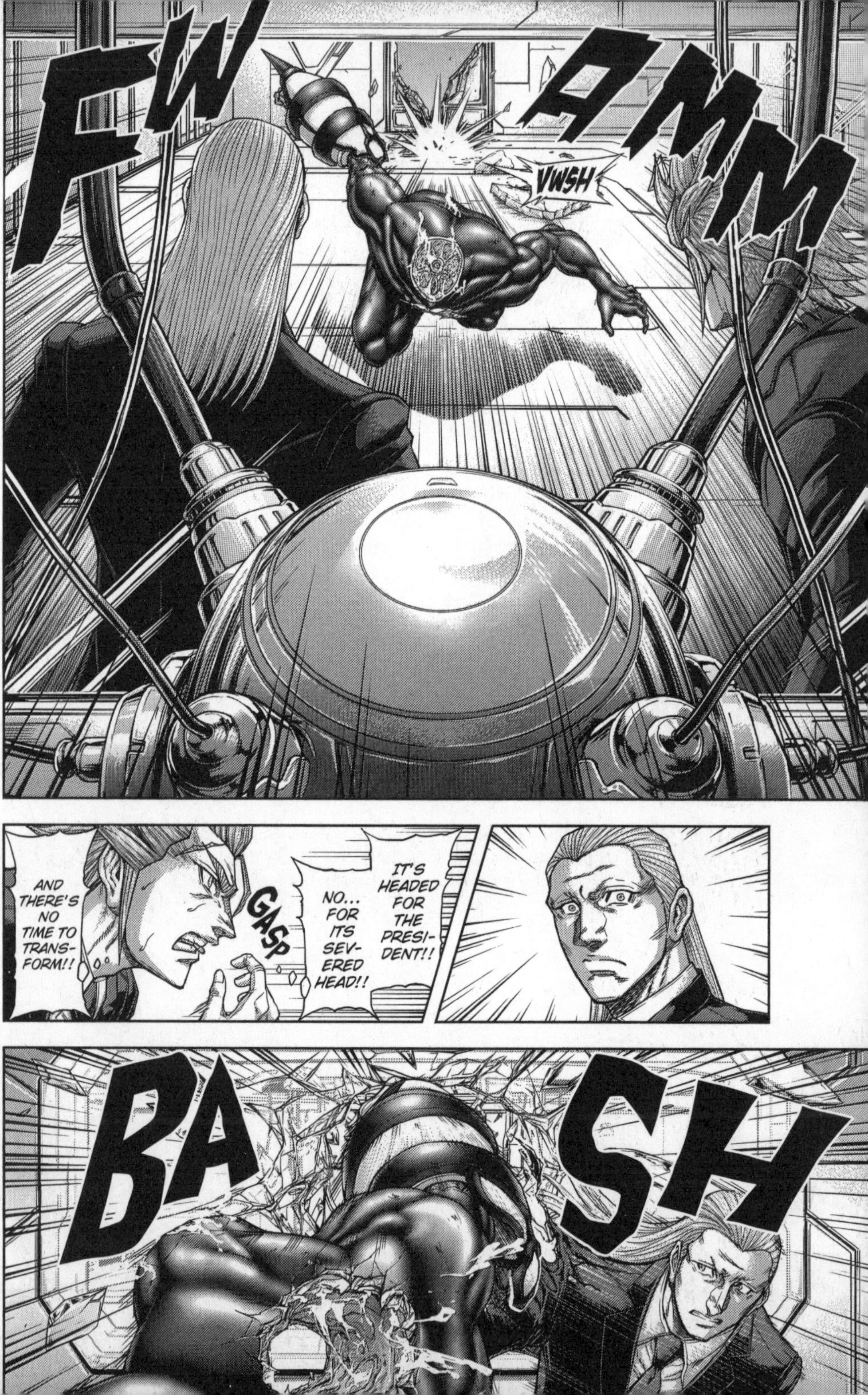
FWAMM
VWSH
IT'S HEADED FOR THE PRESIDENT!!
NO... FOR ITS SEVERED HEAD!!
GASP
AND THERE'S NO TIME TO TRANSFORM!!
BASH

KRUMBL
KRUMBL
KRUMBL
KLOMP
SWIP
Scanning
Time remaining: 1 min
SNAP

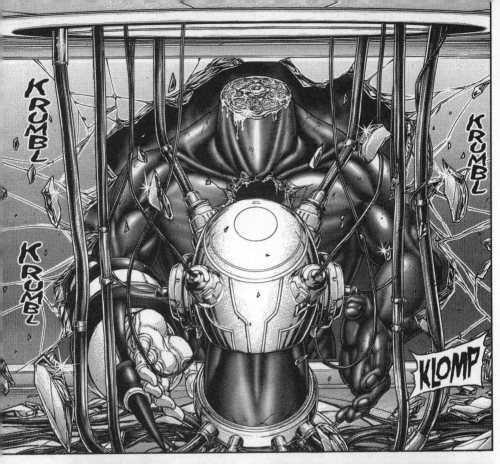

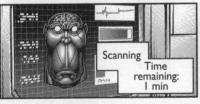

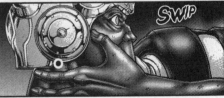

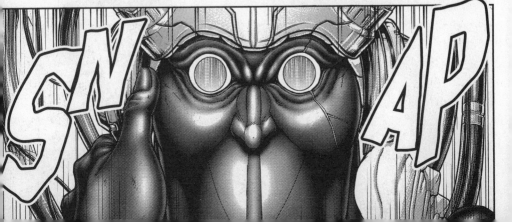

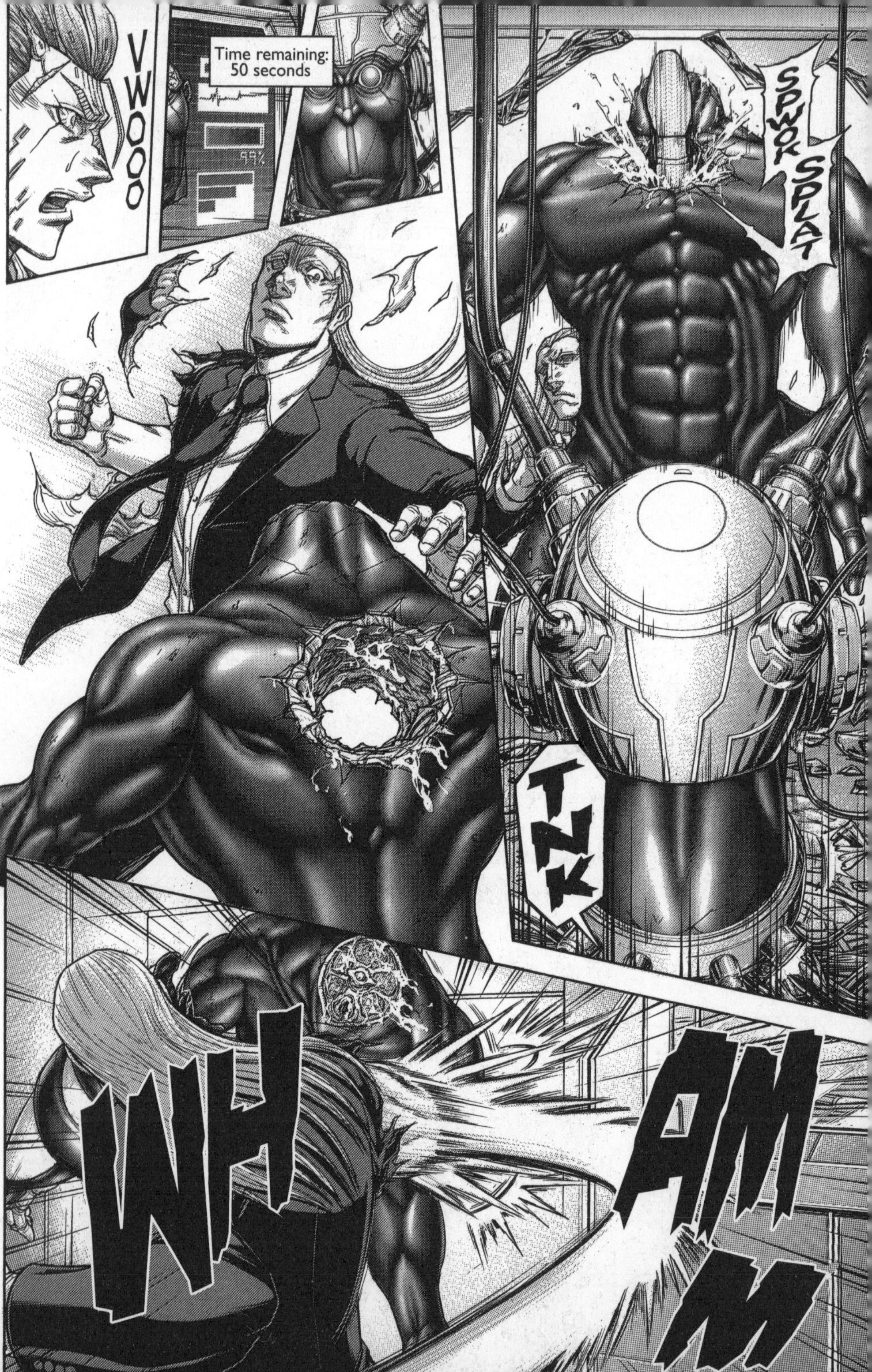
SPWOK SPLAT
TNK
Time remaining: 50 seconds
VWOOO
WHAMM

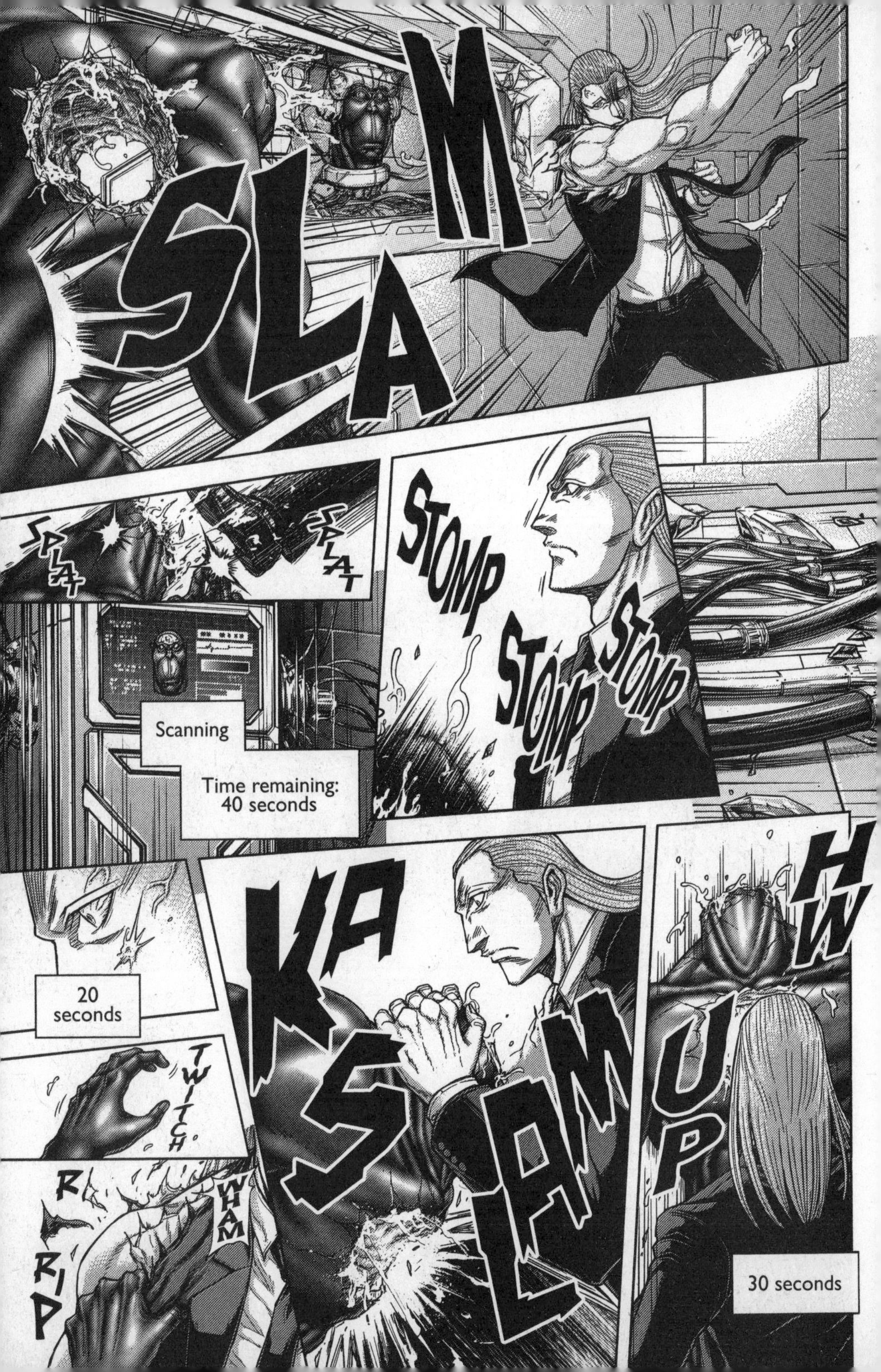
SLAM
STOMP
STOMP
STOMP
SPLAT
SPLAT
Scanning
Time remaining: 40 seconds
WHUMP
30 seconds
KASLAM
20 seconds
TWITCH
WHAM
RIP

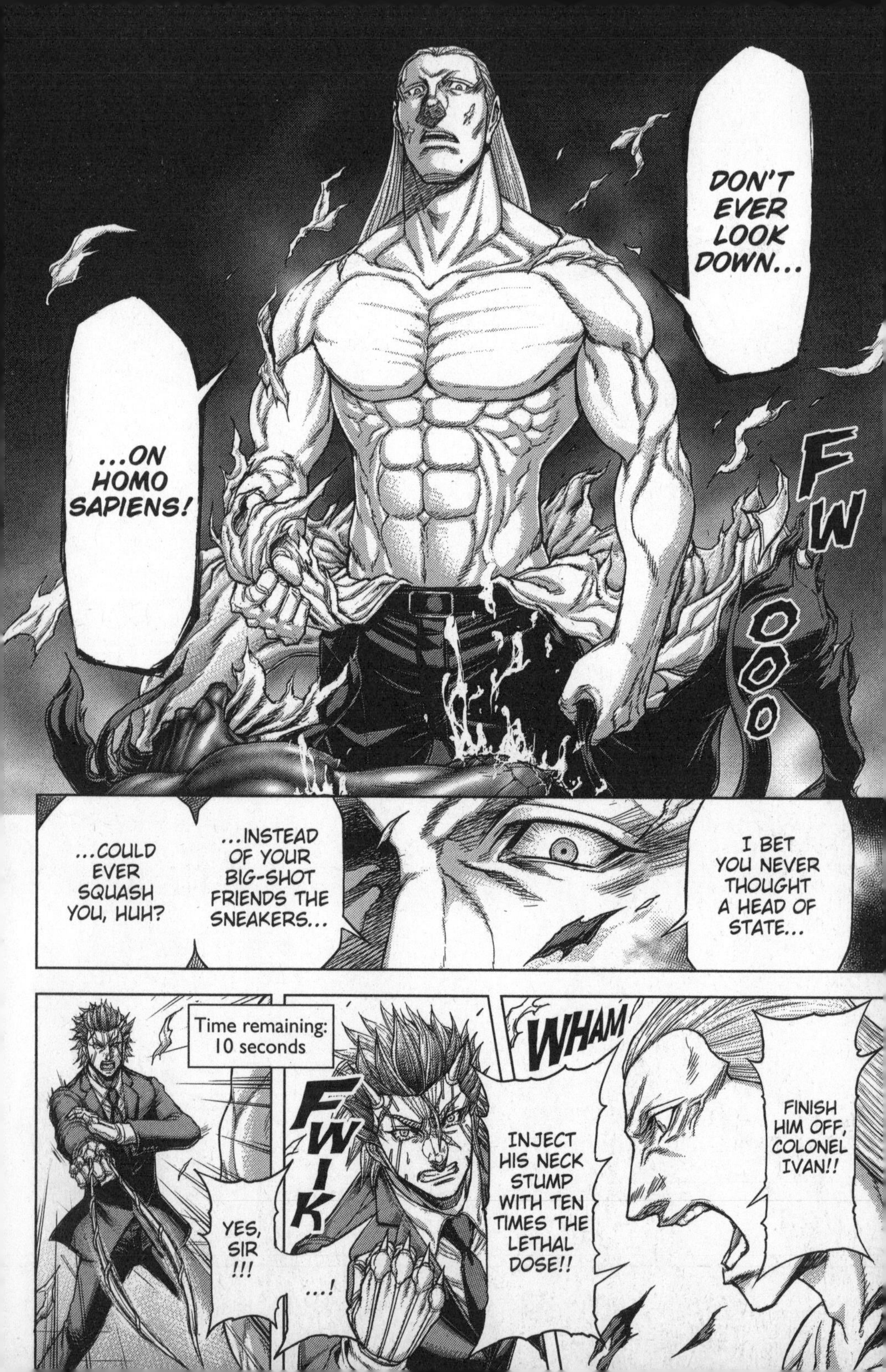
DON'T EVER LOOK DOWN...
...ON HOMO SAPIENS!
FWOOOO
I BET YOU NEVER THOUGHT A HEAD OF STATE...
...INSTEAD OF YOUR BIG-SHOT FRIENDS THE SNEAKERS...
...COULD EVER SQUASH YOU, HUH?
WHAM
FINISH HIM OFF, COLONEL IVAN!!
INJECT HIS NECK STUMP WITH TEN TIMES THE LETHAL DOSE!!
FWIK
...!
Time remaining: 10 seconds
YES, SIR!!!

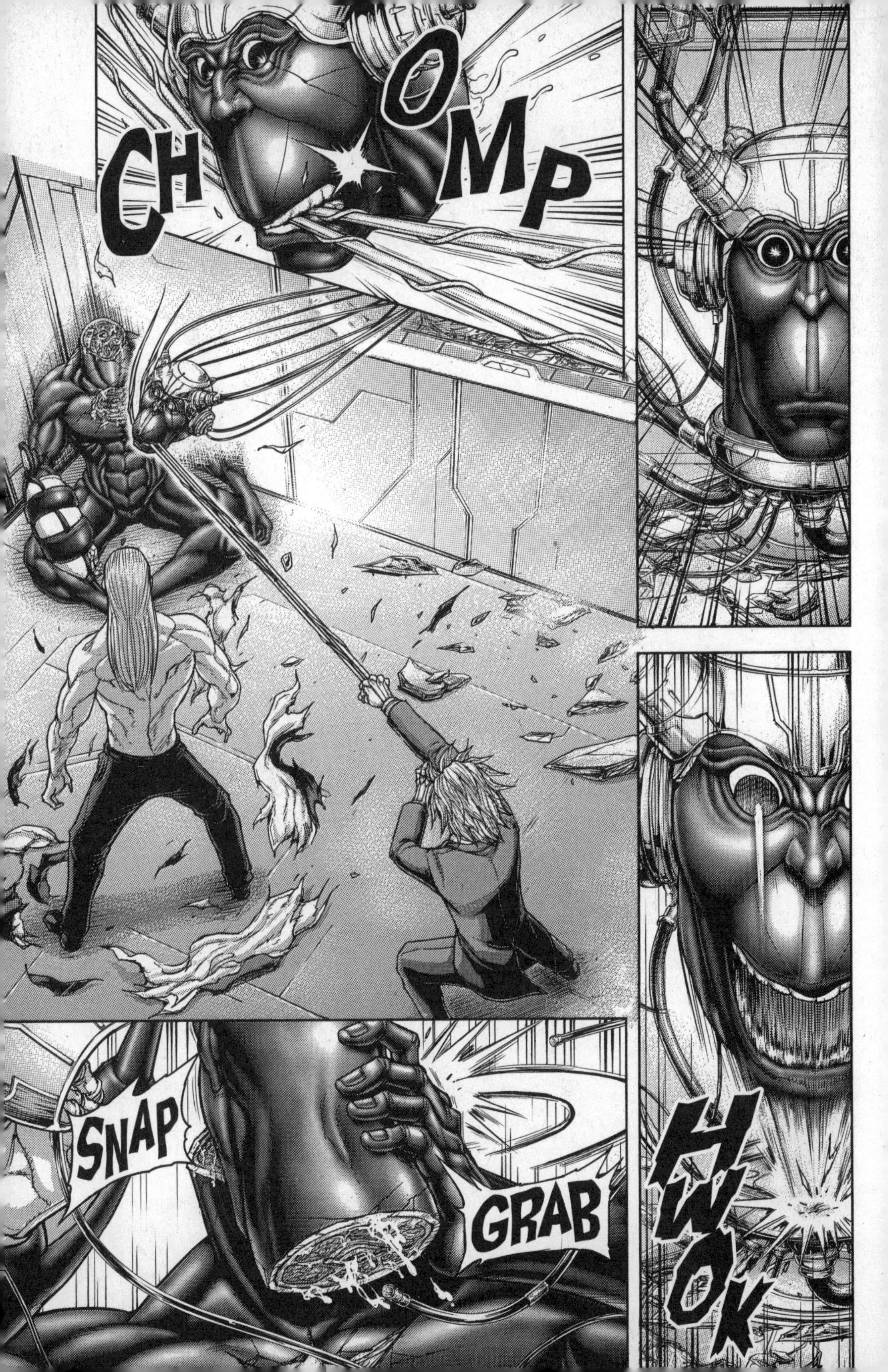
CHOMP
HWOK
SNAP
GRAB

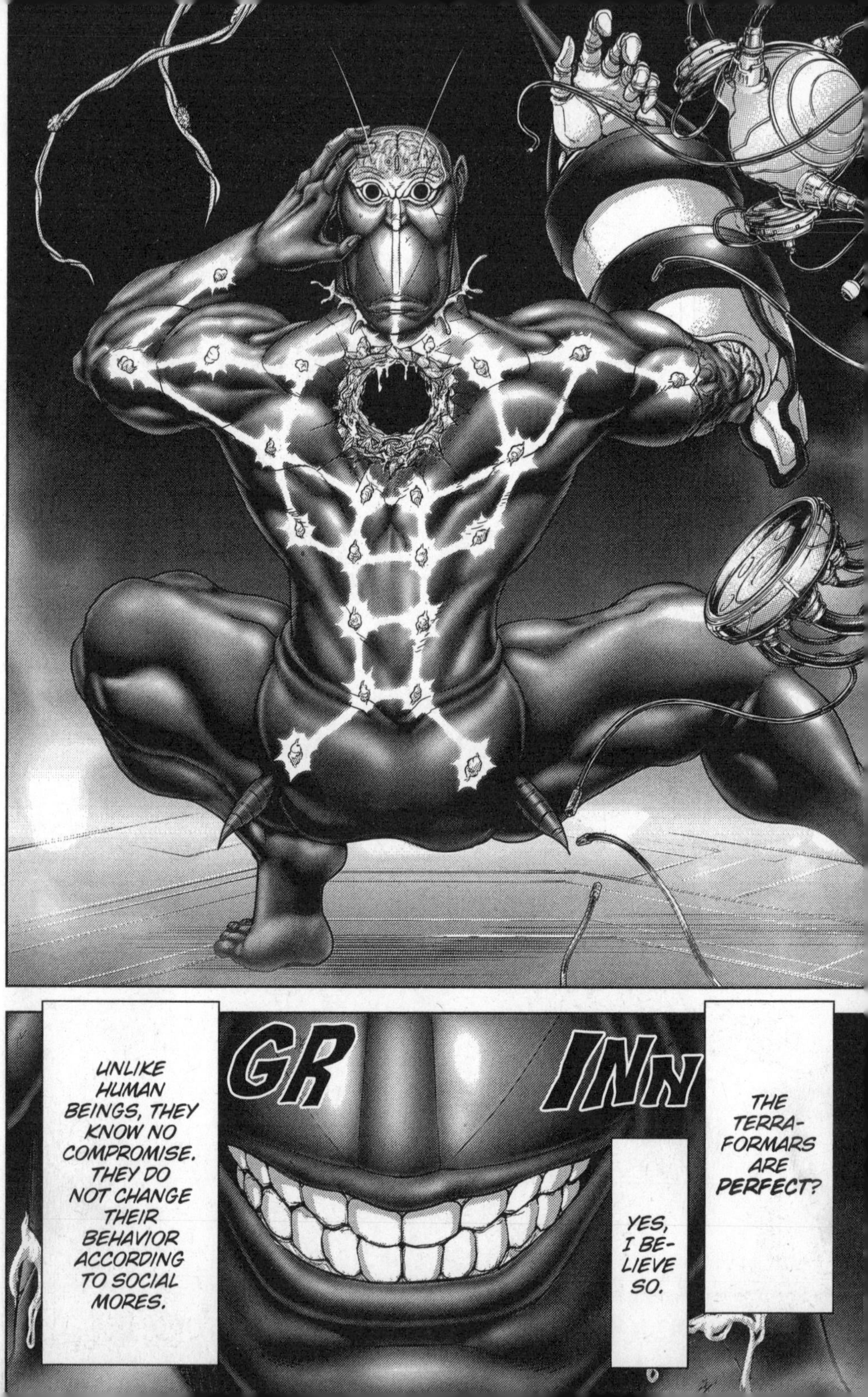
THE TERRA-FORMARS ARE PERFECT?
GR INN
YES, I BE-LIEVE SO.
UNLIKE HUMAN BEINGS, THEY KNOW NO COMPROMISE. THEY DO NOT CHANGE THEIR BEHAVIOR ACCORDING TO SOCIAL MORES.

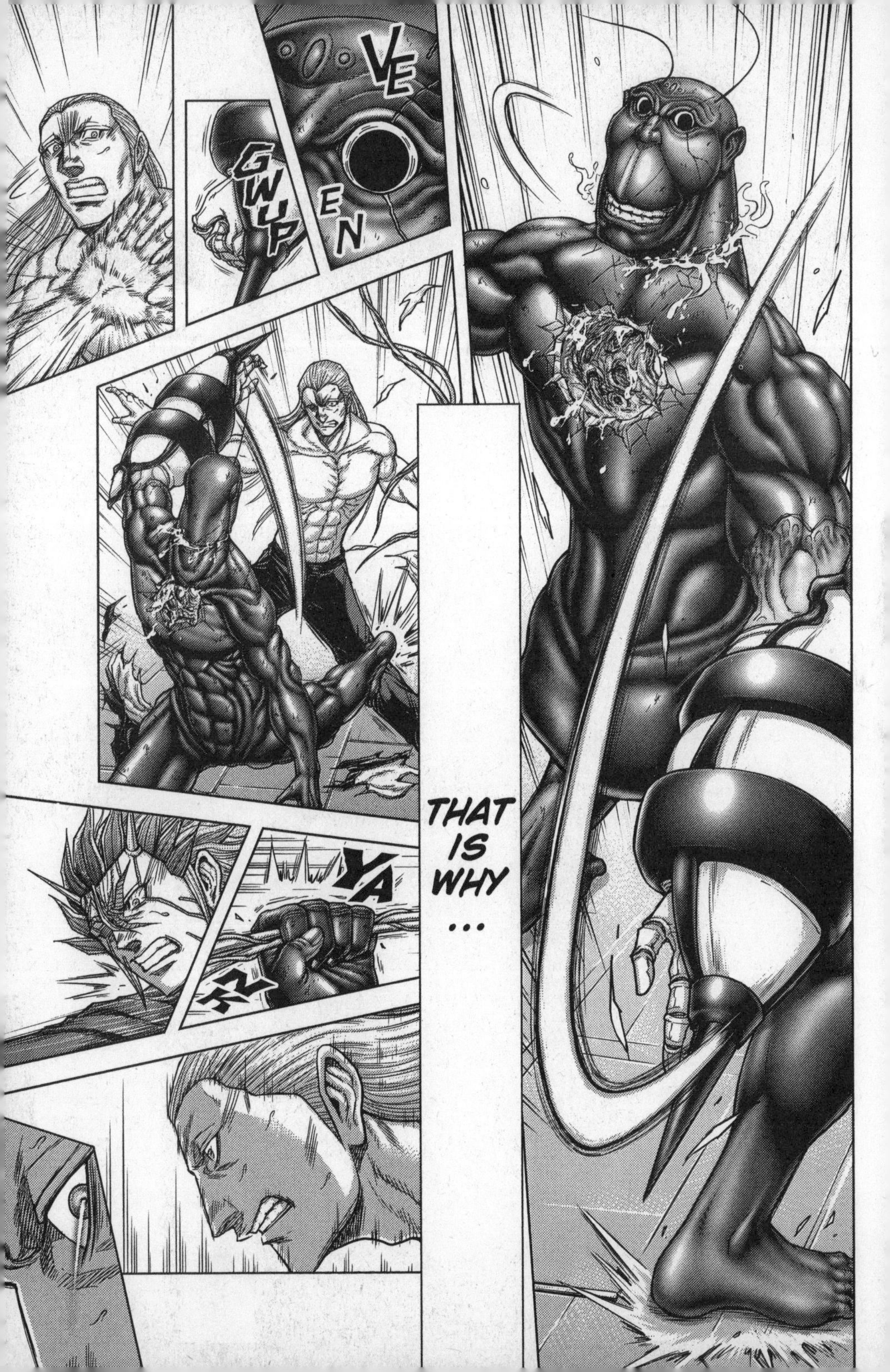

THAT IS WHY ...
VE
EN
GWUP
YA
NK

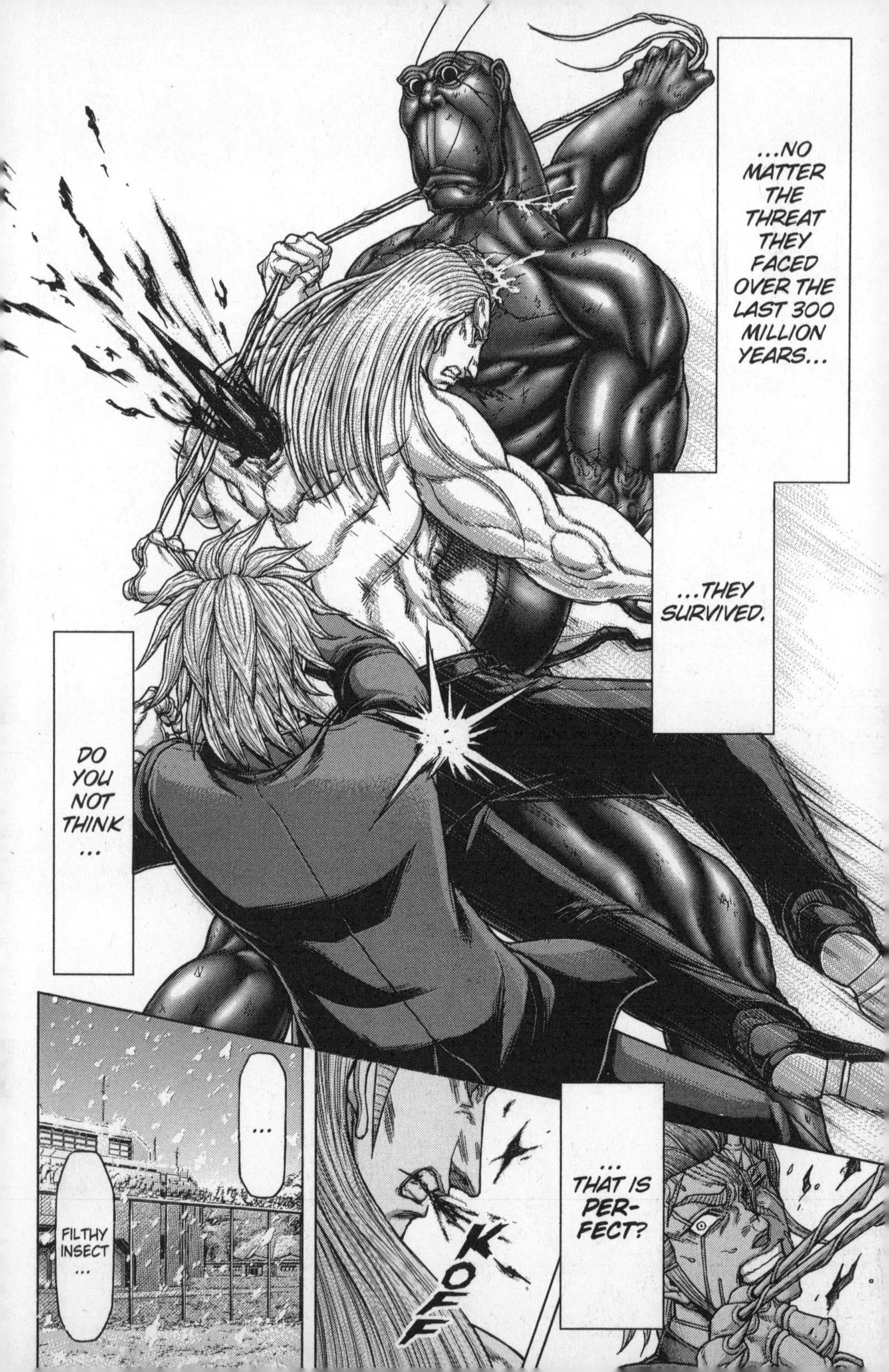
...NO MATTER THE THREAT THEY FACED OVER THE LAST 300 MILLION YEARS...
...THEY SURVIVED.
DO YOU NOT THINK ...
... THAT IS PER-FECT?
KOFF
...
FILTHY INSECT ...

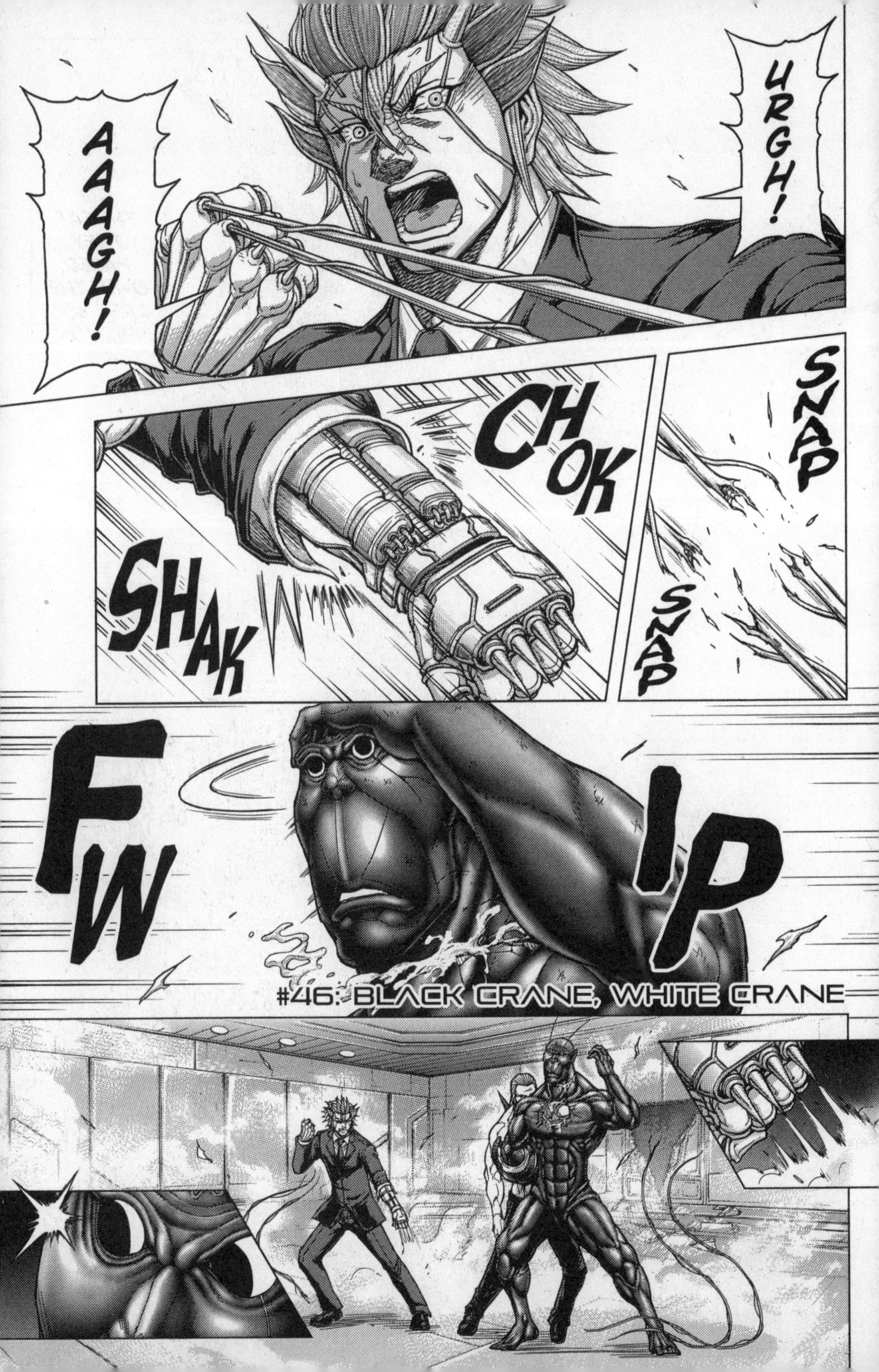
URGH!
AAAGH!
SNAP
SNAP
CHOK
SHAK
FWIP
#46: BLACK CRANE, WHITE CRANE

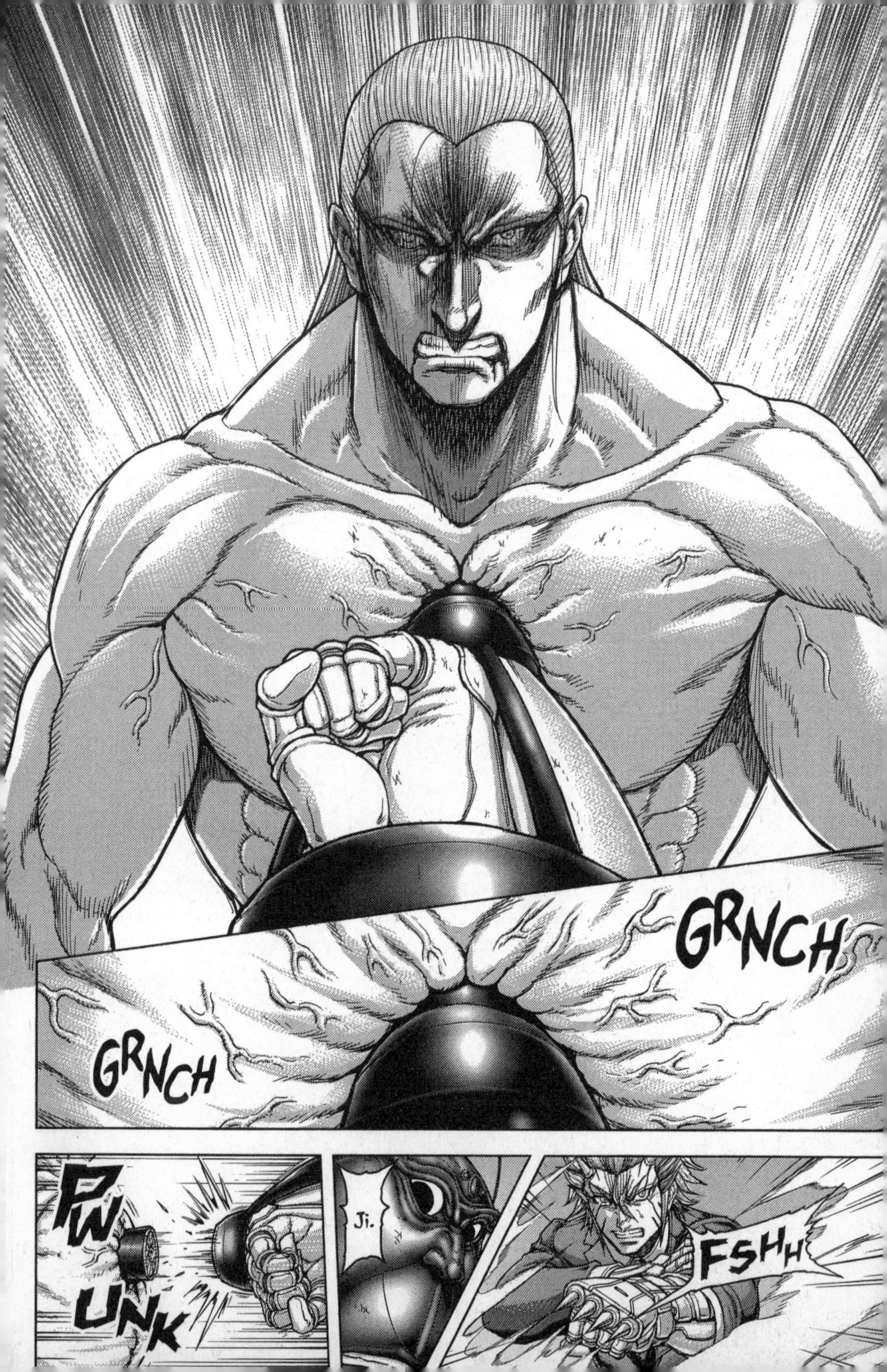
GRNCH
GRNCH
FSHH
Ji.
PWUNK

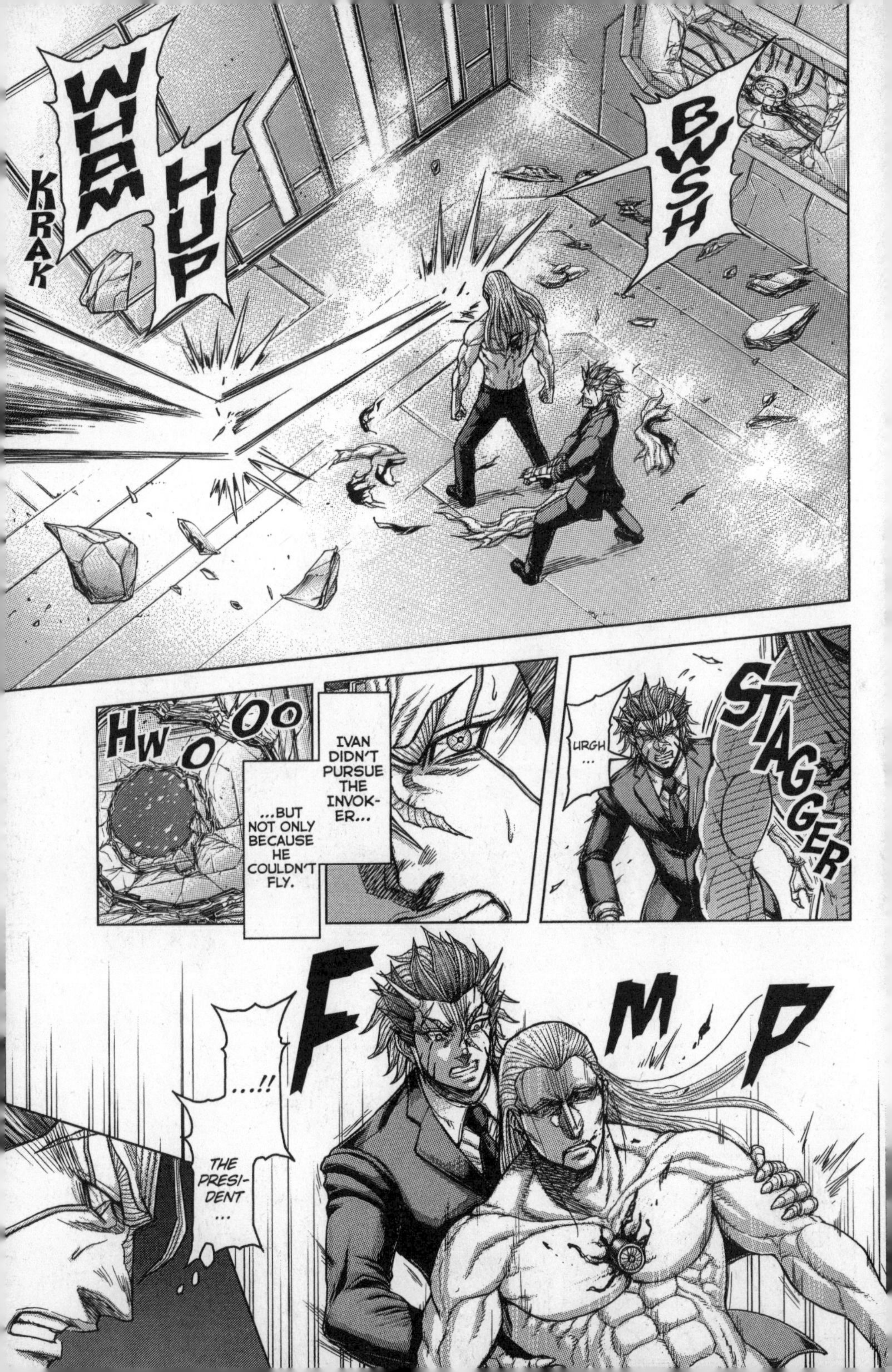
BWSH
HUP
WHAM
KRAK
STAGGER
URGH ...
IVAN DIDN'T PURSUE THE INVOKER...
HWOOO
...BUT NOT ONLY BECAUSE HE COULDN'T FLY.
FMP
...!!
THE PRESIDENT ...

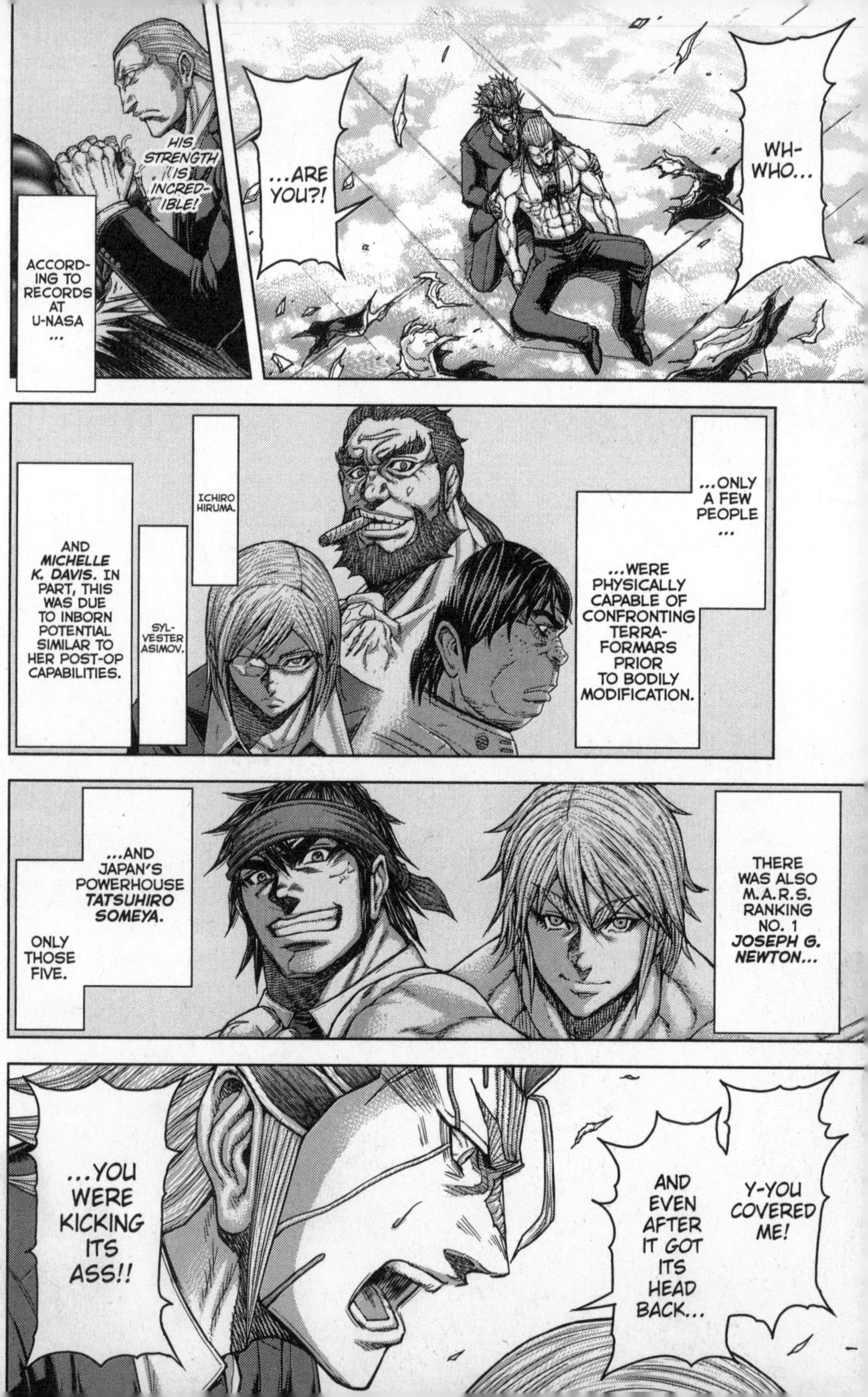
WH-WHO...
...ARE YOU?!
HIS STRENGTH IS INCREDIBLE!
ACCORDING TO RECORDS AT U-NASA...
...ONLY A FEW PEOPLE...
...WERE PHYSICALLY CAPABLE OF CONFRONTING TERRA-FORMARS PRIOR TO BODILY MODIFICATION.
ICHIRO HIRUMA.
SYLVESTER ASIMOV.
AND MICHELLE K. DAVIS. IN PART, THIS WAS DUE TO INBORN POTENTIAL SIMILAR TO HER POST-OP CAPABILITIES.
THERE WAS ALSO M.A.R.S. RANKING NO. 1 JOSEPH G. NEWTON...
...AND JAPAN'S POWERHOUSE TATSUHIRO SOMEYA.
ONLY THOSE FIVE.
Y-YOU COVERED ME!
AND EVEN AFTER IT GOT ITS HEAD BACK...
...YOU WERE KICKING ITS ASS!!

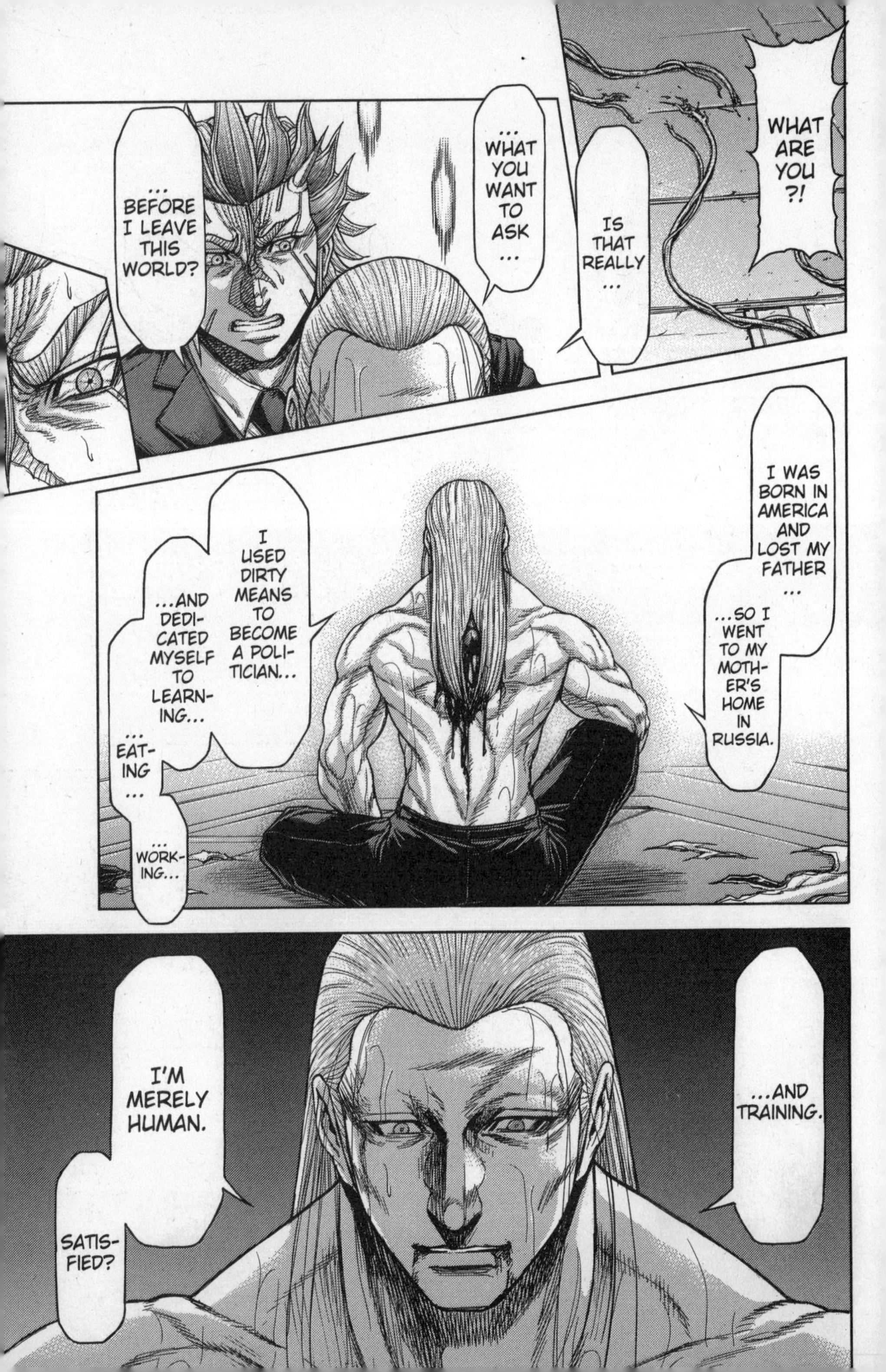
WHAT ARE YOU ?!
IS THAT REALLY ...
... WHAT YOU WANT TO ASK ...
... BEFORE I LEAVE THIS WORLD?
I WAS BORN IN AMERICA AND LOST MY FATHER ...
...SO I WENT TO MY MOTHER'S HOME IN RUSSIA.
I USED DIRTY MEANS TO BECOME A POLITICIAN...
...AND DEDICATED MYSELF TO LEARNING...
... EATING ...
... WORKING...
...AND TRAINING.
I'M MERELY HUMAN.
SATISFIED?

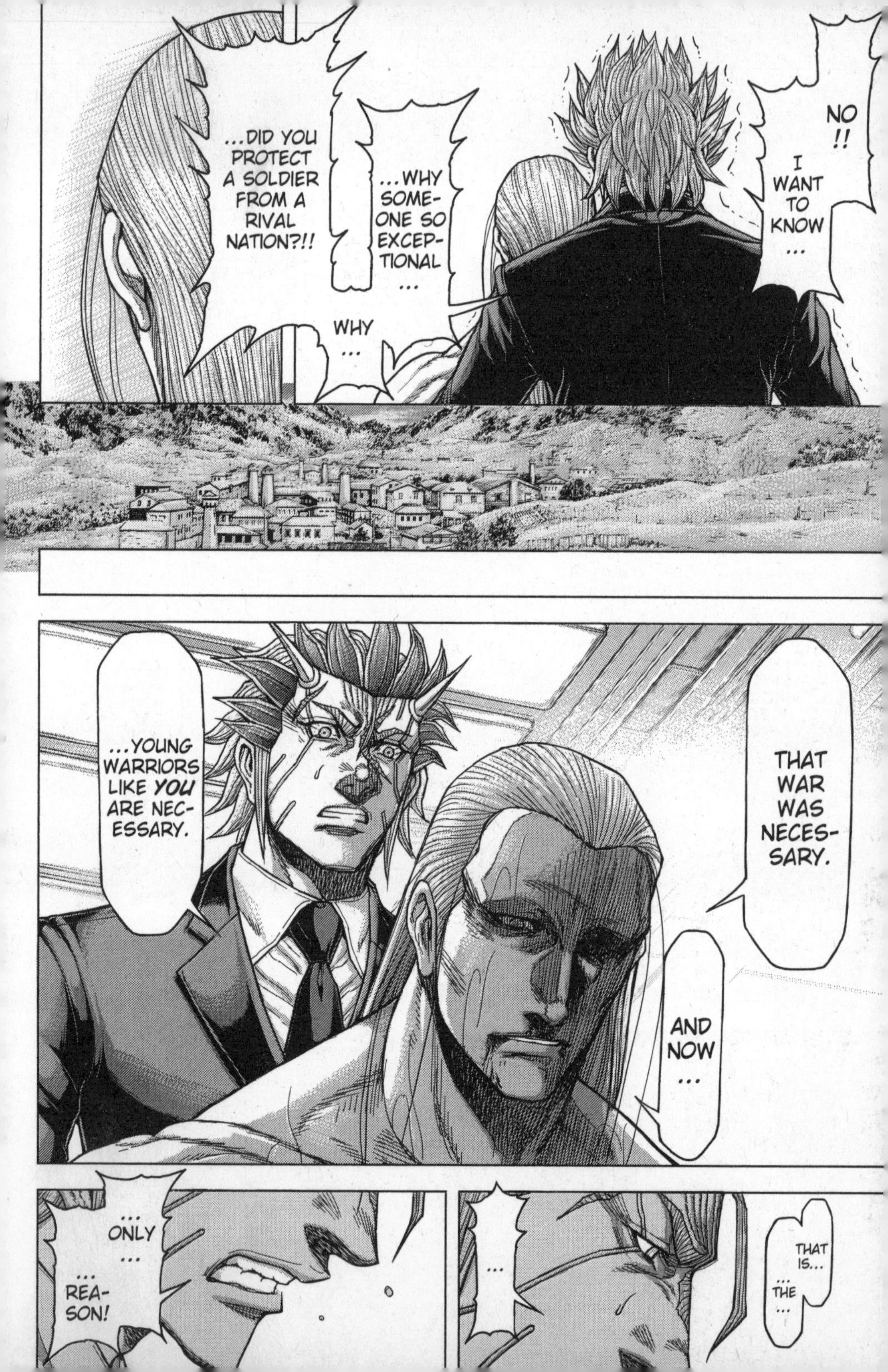
NO!!
I WANT TO KNOW...
...WHY SOMEONE SO EXCEPTIONAL...
WHY...
...DID YOU PROTECT A SOLDIER FROM A RIVAL NATION?!!
THAT WAR WAS NECESSARY.
AND NOW...
...YOUNG WARRIORS LIKE *YOU* ARE NECESSARY.
THAT IS... ...THE...
...
...ONLY...
...REASON!

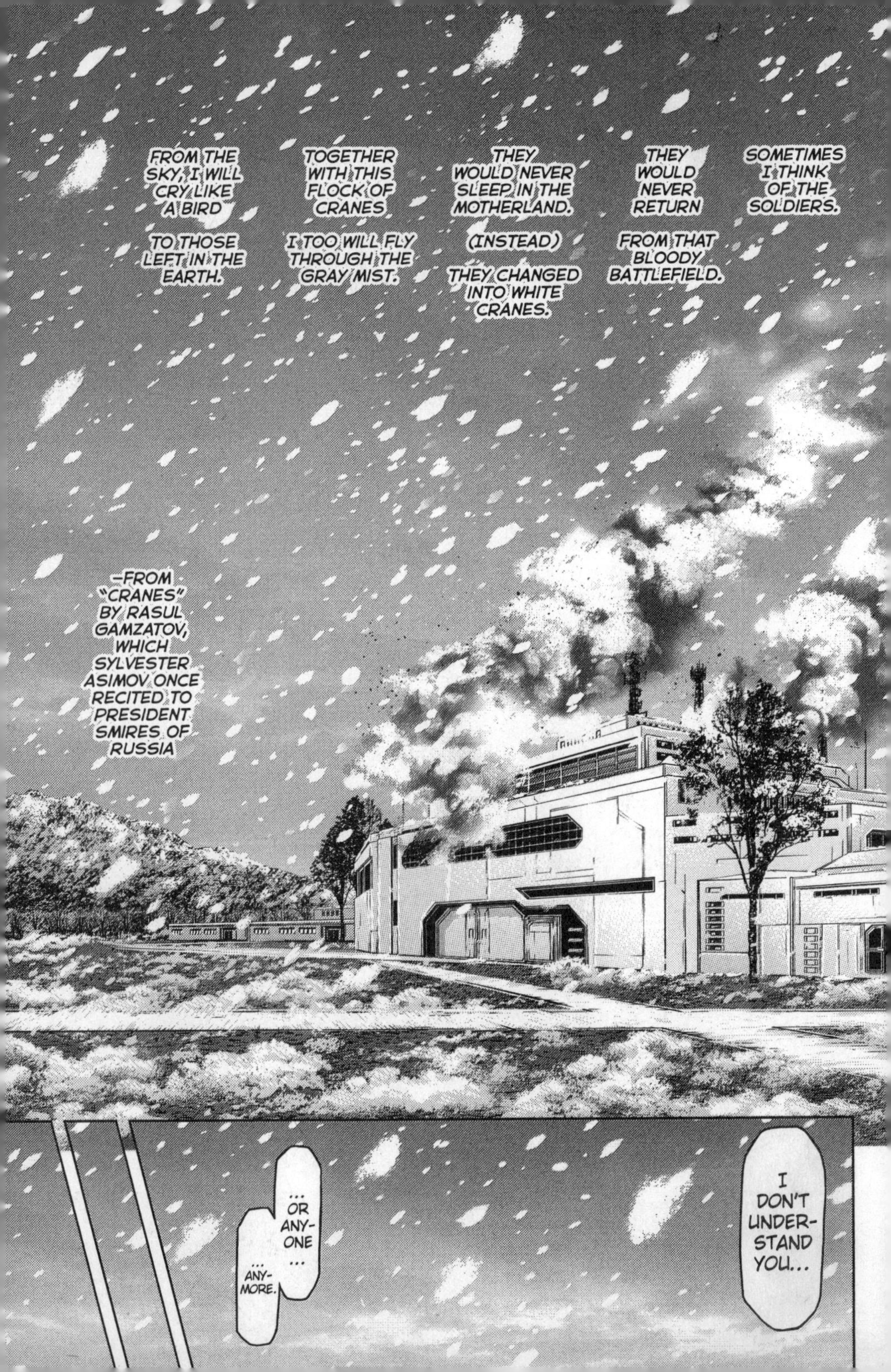
SOMETIMES I THINK OF THE SOLDIERS.
THEY WOULD NEVER RETURN
FROM THAT BLOODY BATTLEFIELD.
THEY WOULD NEVER SLEEP IN THE MOTHERLAND.
(INSTEAD)
THEY CHANGED INTO WHITE CRANES.
TOGETHER WITH THIS FLOCK OF CRANES
I TOO WILL FLY THROUGH THE GRAY MIST.
FROM THE SKY, I WILL CRY LIKE A BIRD
TO THOSE LEFT IN THE EARTH.
—FROM "CRANES" BY RASUL GAMZATOV, WHICH SYLVESTER ASIMOV ONCE RECITED TO PRESIDENT SMIRES OF RUSSIA
I DON'T UNDER-STAND YOU...
...OR ANY-ONE...
...ANY-MORE.

# #46: BLACK CRANE, WHITE CRANE

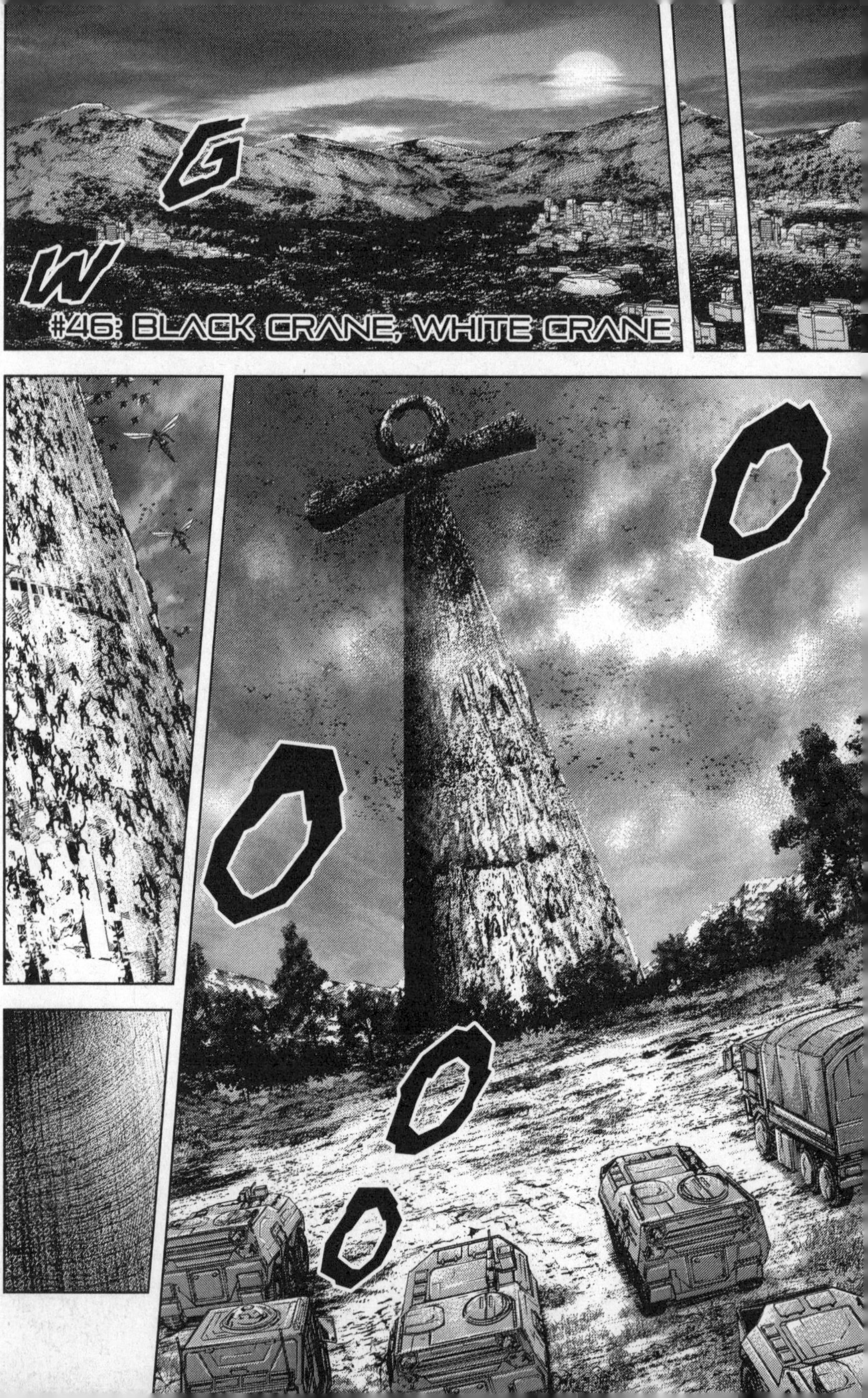
G
W
O
O
O
O

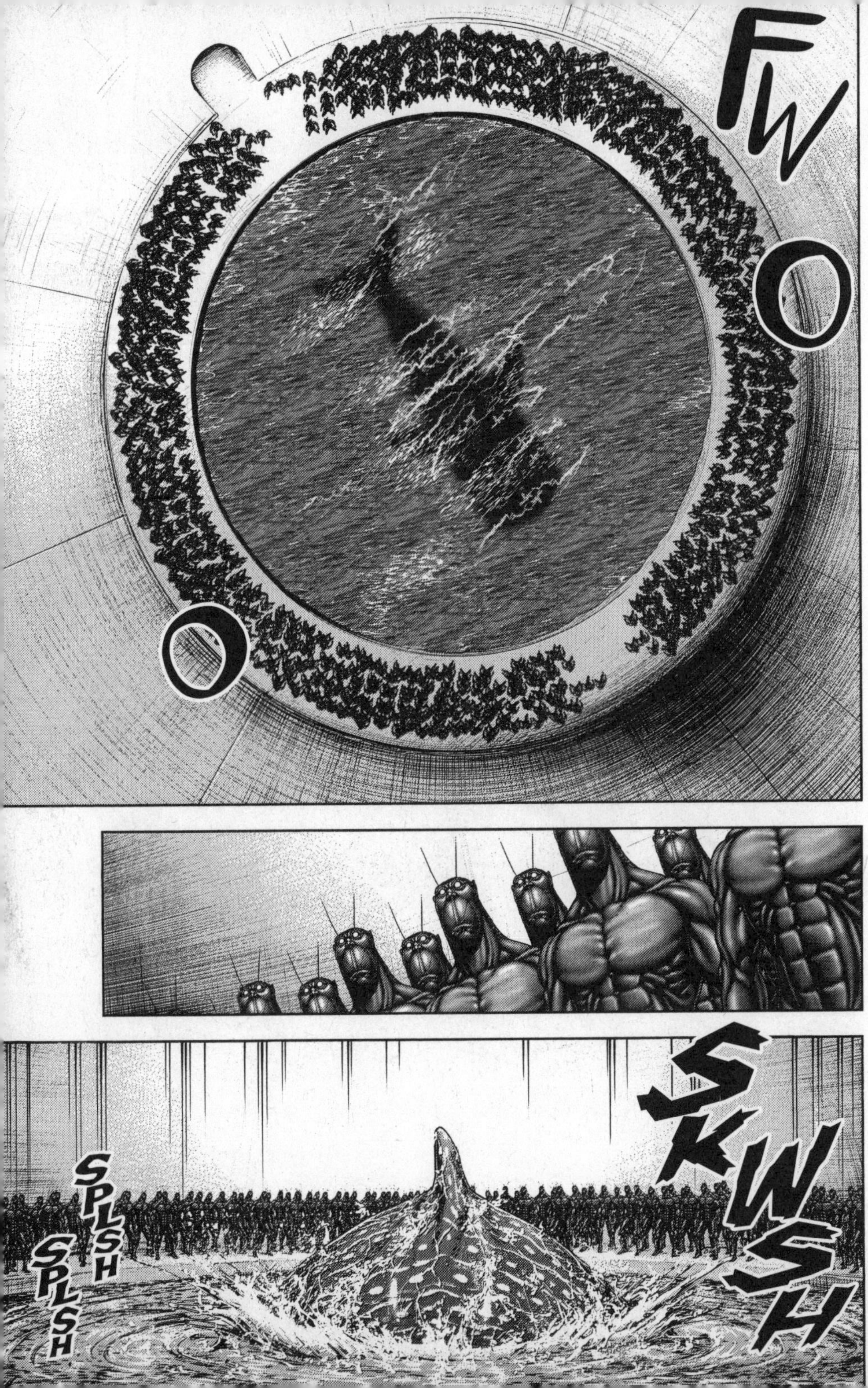
FWOO
SKWSH
SPLSH
SPLSH

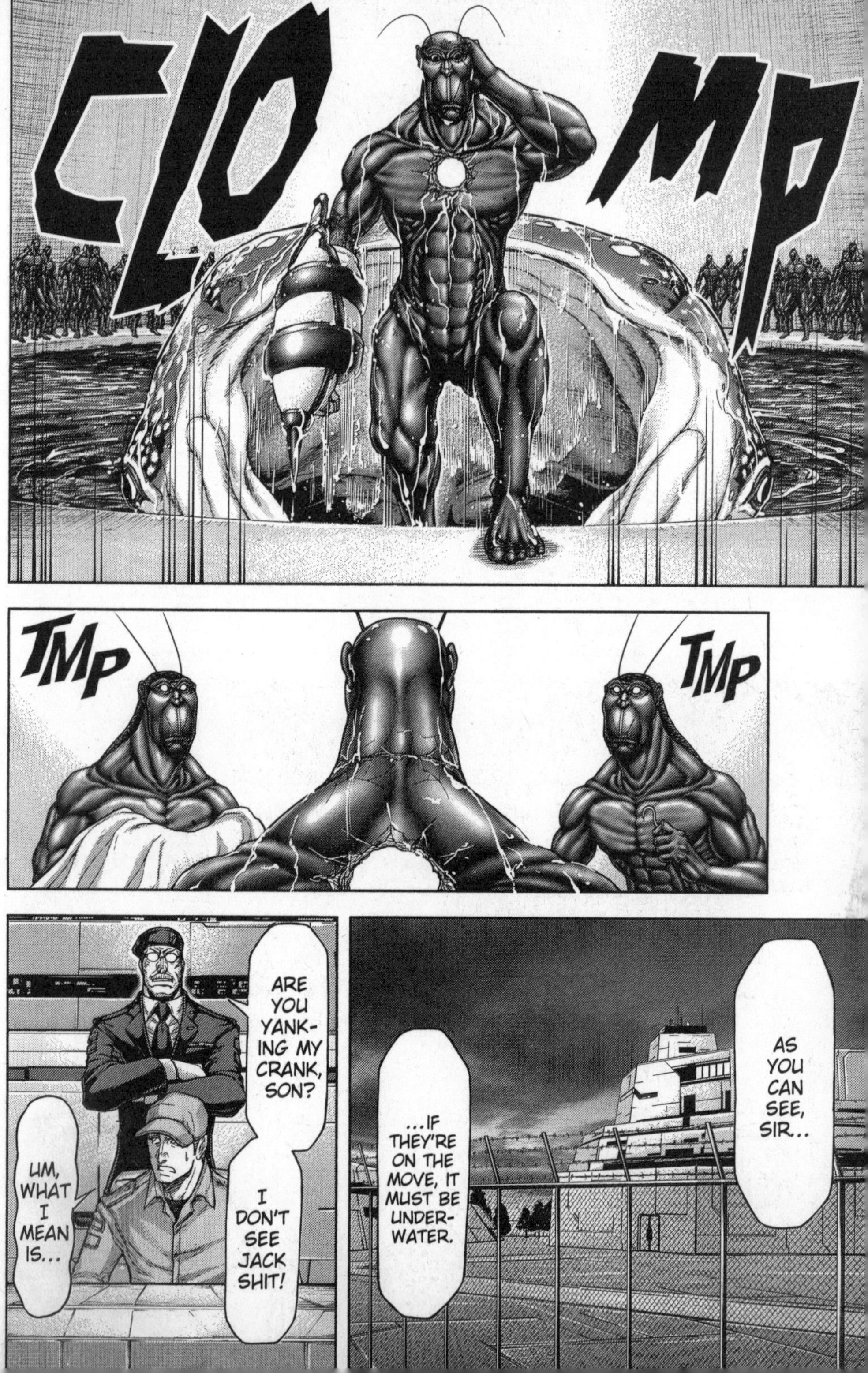
CLOMP
TMP
TMP
AS YOU CAN SEE, SIR...
...IF THEY'RE ON THE MOVE, IT MUST BE UNDER-WATER.
ARE YOU YANK-ING MY CRANK, SON?
I DON'T SEE JACK SHIT!
UM, WHAT I MEAN IS...

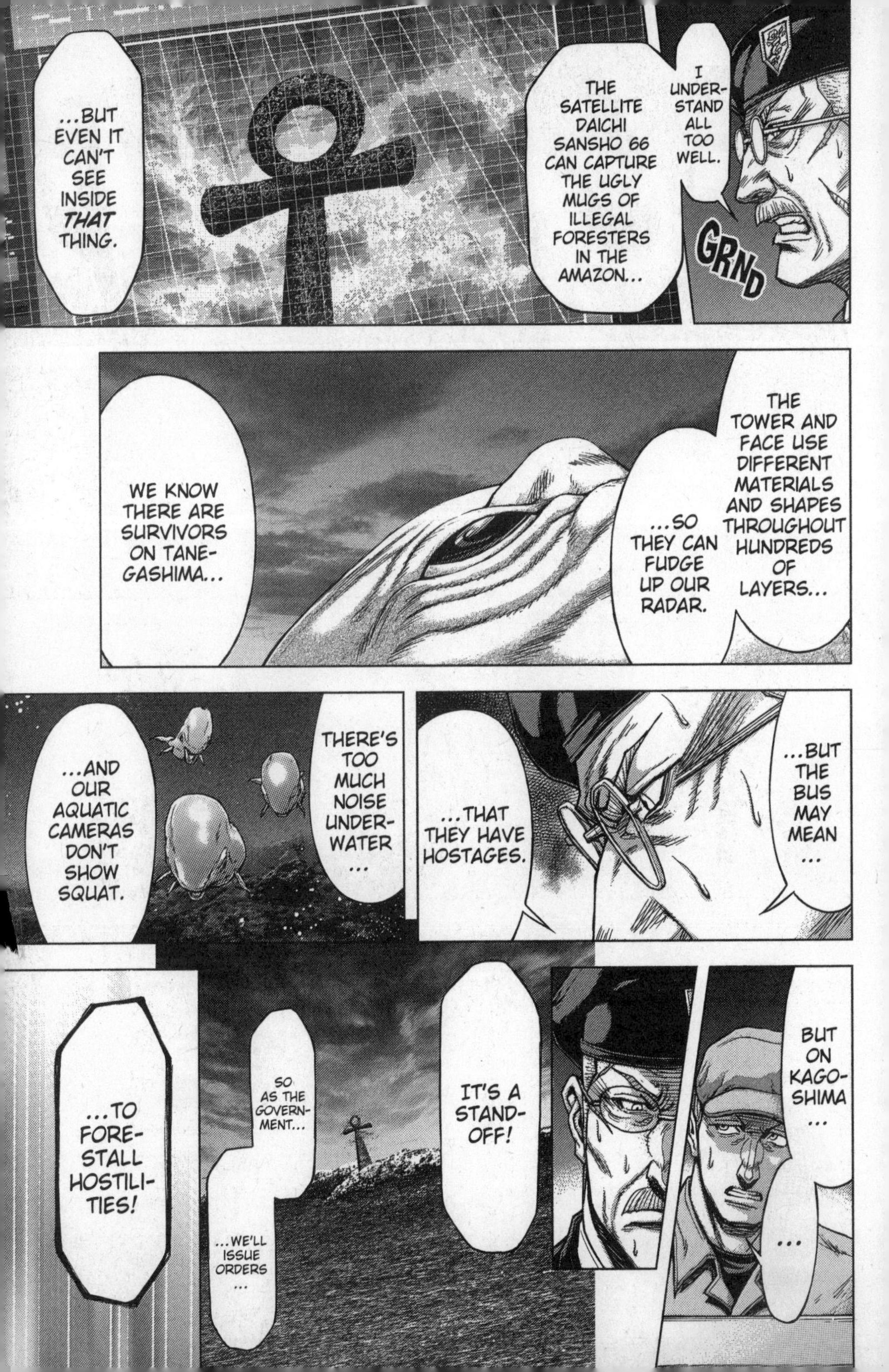
I UNDERSTAND ALL TOO WELL.
THE SATELLITE DAICHI SANSHO 66 CAN CAPTURE THE UGLY MUGS OF ILLEGAL FORESTERS IN THE AMAZON...
GRND
...BUT EVEN IT CAN'T SEE INSIDE *THAT* THING.
THE TOWER AND FACE USE DIFFERENT MATERIALS AND SHAPES THROUGHOUT HUNDREDS OF LAYERS...
...SO THEY CAN FUDGE UP OUR RADAR.
WE KNOW THERE ARE SURVIVORS ON TANEGASHIMA...
...BUT THE BUS MAY MEAN...
...THAT THEY HAVE HOSTAGES.
THERE'S TOO MUCH NOISE UNDERWATER...
...AND OUR AQUATIC CAMERAS DON'T SHOW SQUAT.
BUT ON KAGOSHIMA...
...
IT'S A STANDOFF!
SO AS THE GOVERNMENT...
...WE'LL ISSUE ORDERS...
...TO FORESTALL HOSTILITIES!

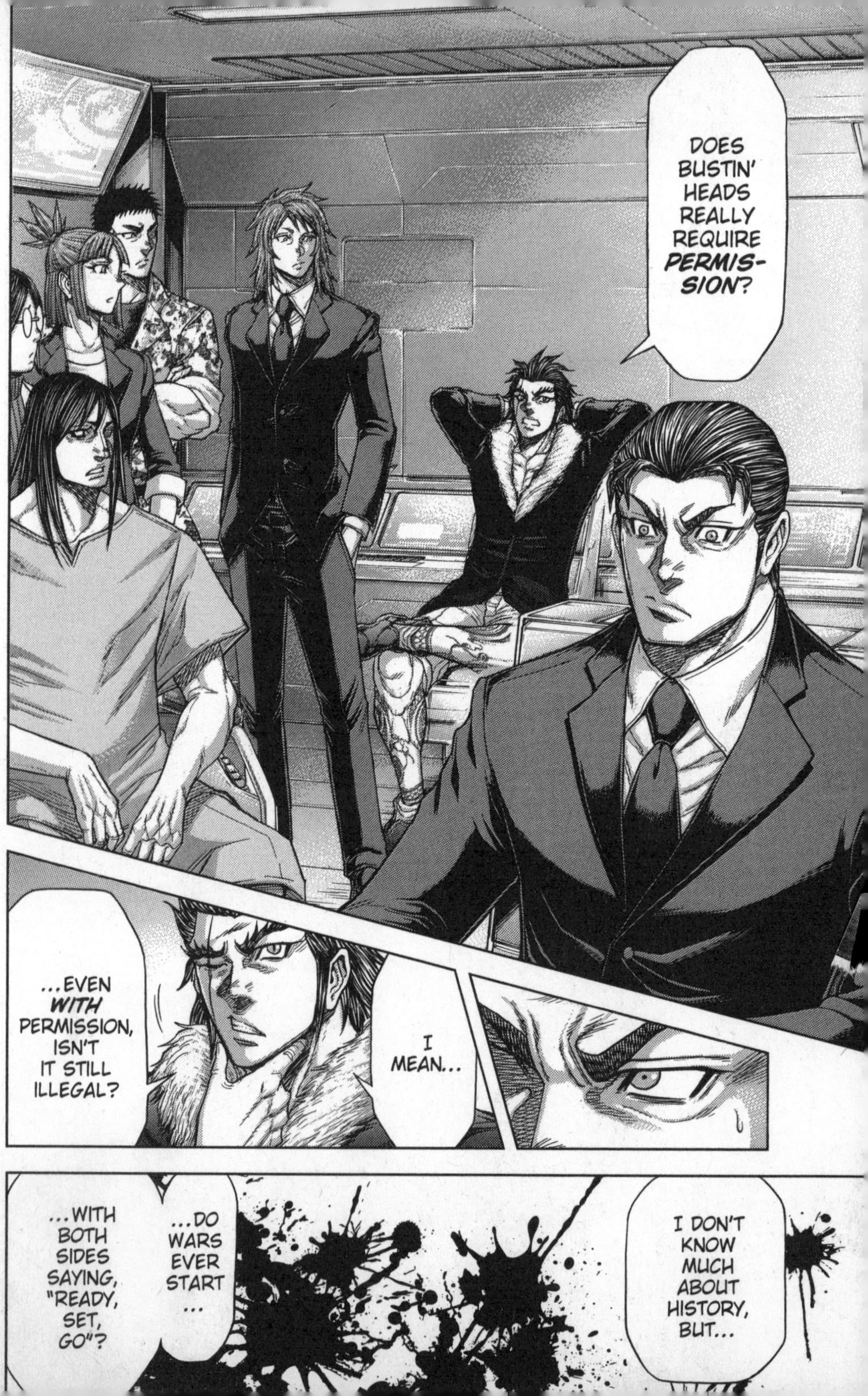
DOES BUSTIN' HEADS REALLY REQUIRE PERMISSION?
I MEAN...
...EVEN WITH PERMISSION, ISN'T IT STILL ILLEGAL?
I DON'T KNOW MUCH ABOUT HISTORY, BUT...
...DO WARS EVER START...
...WITH BOTH SIDES SAYING, "READY, SET, GO"?

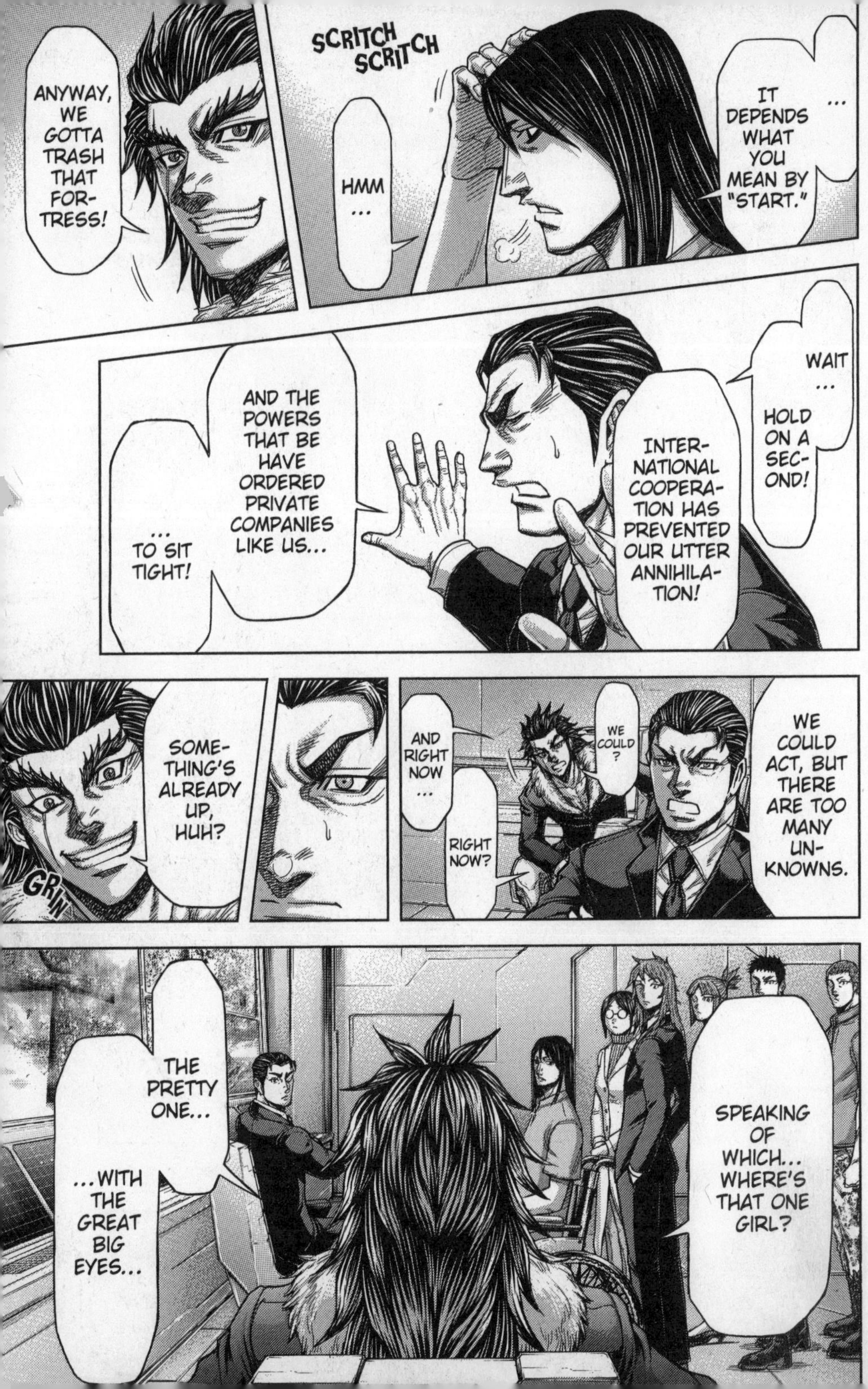
...
IT DEPENDS WHAT YOU MEAN BY "START."
SCRITCH SCRITCH
HMM ...
ANYWAY, WE GOTTA TRASH THAT FORTRESS!
WAIT ... HOLD ON A SECOND!
INTERNATIONAL COOPERATION HAS PREVENTED OUR UTTER ANNIHILATION!
AND THE POWERS THAT BE HAVE ORDERED PRIVATE COMPANIES LIKE US...
... TO SIT TIGHT!
WE COULD ACT, BUT THERE ARE TOO MANY UNKNOWNS.
WE COULD ?
AND RIGHT NOW ...
RIGHT NOW?
SOMETHING'S ALREADY UP, HUH?
GRIN
SPEAKING OF WHICH... WHERE'S THAT ONE GIRL?
THE PRETTY ONE...
...WITH THE GREAT BIG EYES...

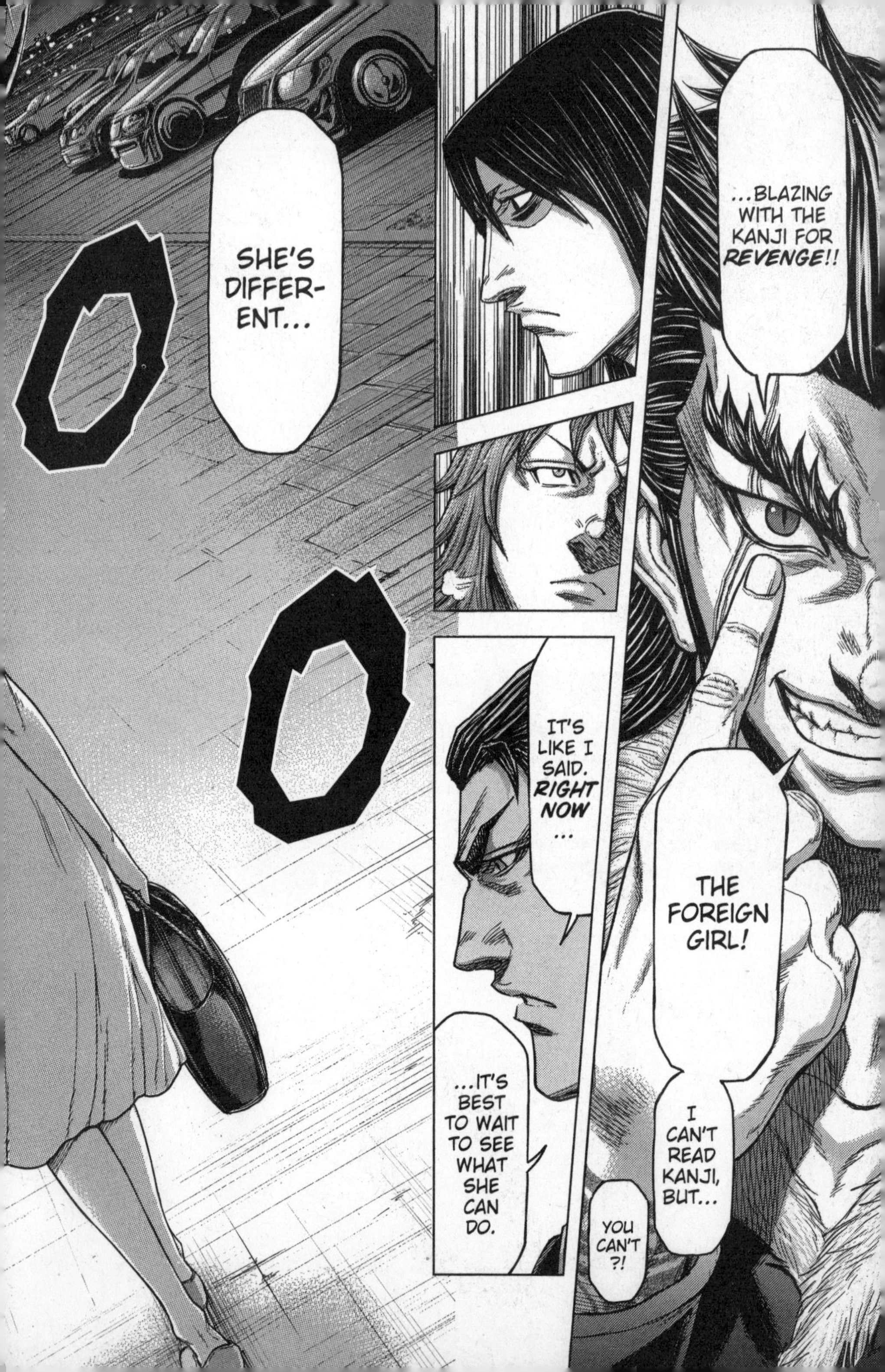
...BLAZING WITH THE KANJI FOR *REVENGE!!*
THE FOREIGN GIRL!
I CAN'T READ KANJI, BUT...
YOU CAN'T?!
IT'S LIKE I SAID. *RIGHT NOW* ...
...IT'S BEST TO WAIT TO SEE WHAT SHE CAN DO.
SHE'S DIFFER-ENT...

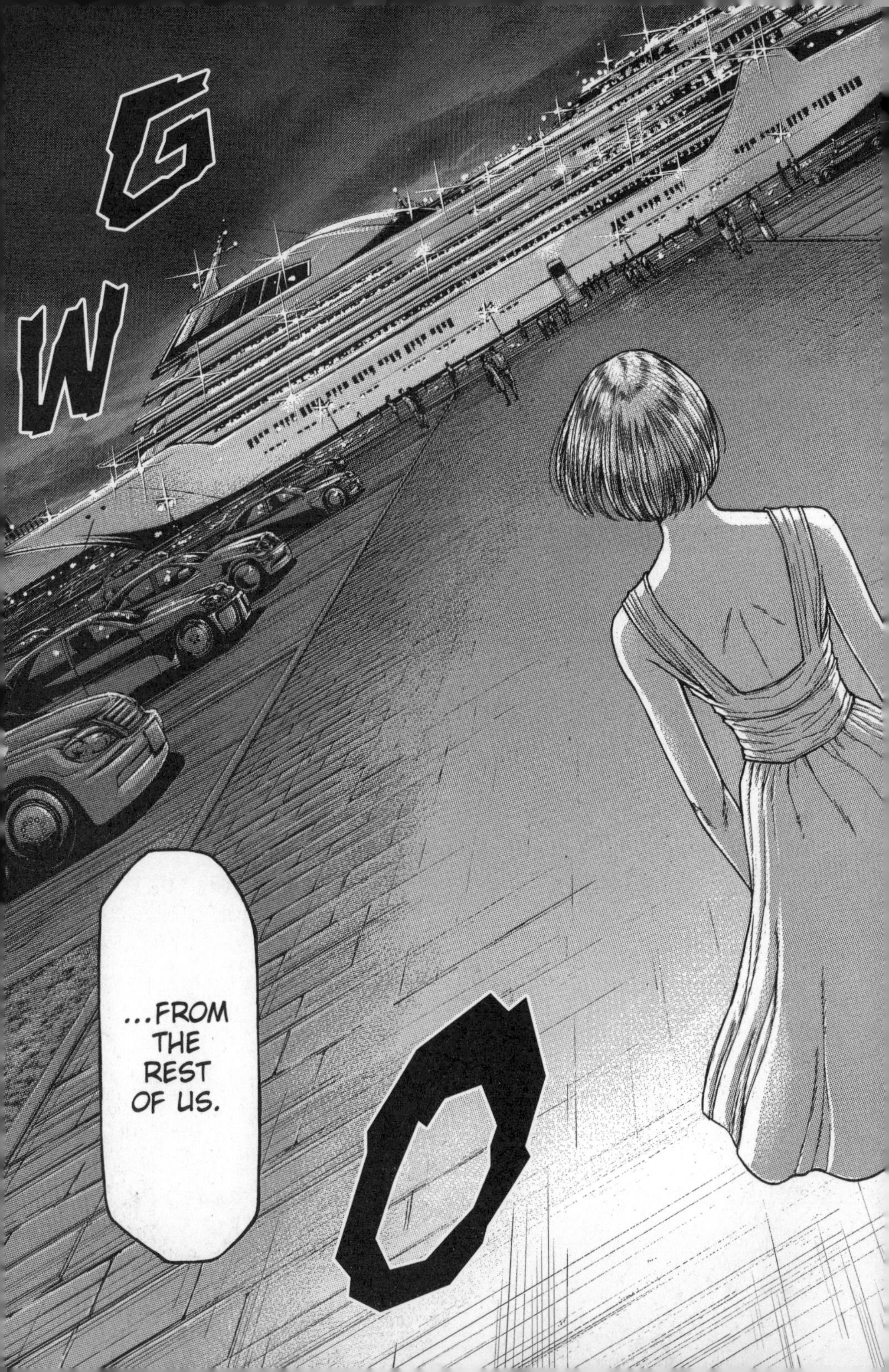

GWO
...FROM THE REST OF US.

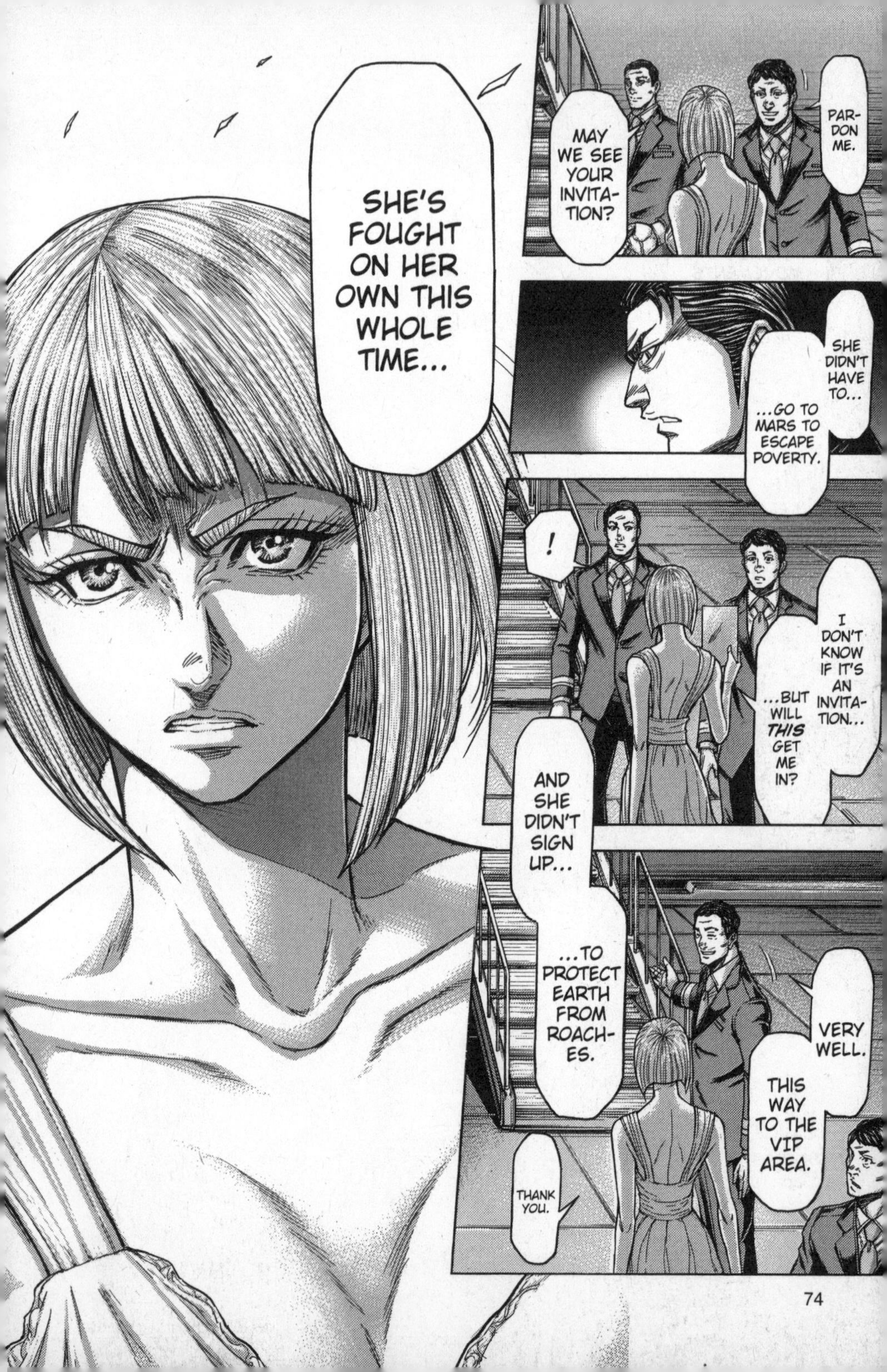
PARDON ME.
MAY WE SEE YOUR INVITATION?
SHE DIDN'T HAVE TO...
...GO TO MARS TO ESCAPE POVERTY.
I DON'T KNOW IF IT'S AN INVITATION...
...BUT WILL *THIS* GET ME IN?
!
AND SHE DIDN'T SIGN UP...
VERY WELL.
THIS WAY TO THE VIP AREA.
...TO PROTECT EARTH FROM ROACHES.
THANK YOU.
SHE'S FOUGHT ON HER OWN THIS WHOLE TIME...

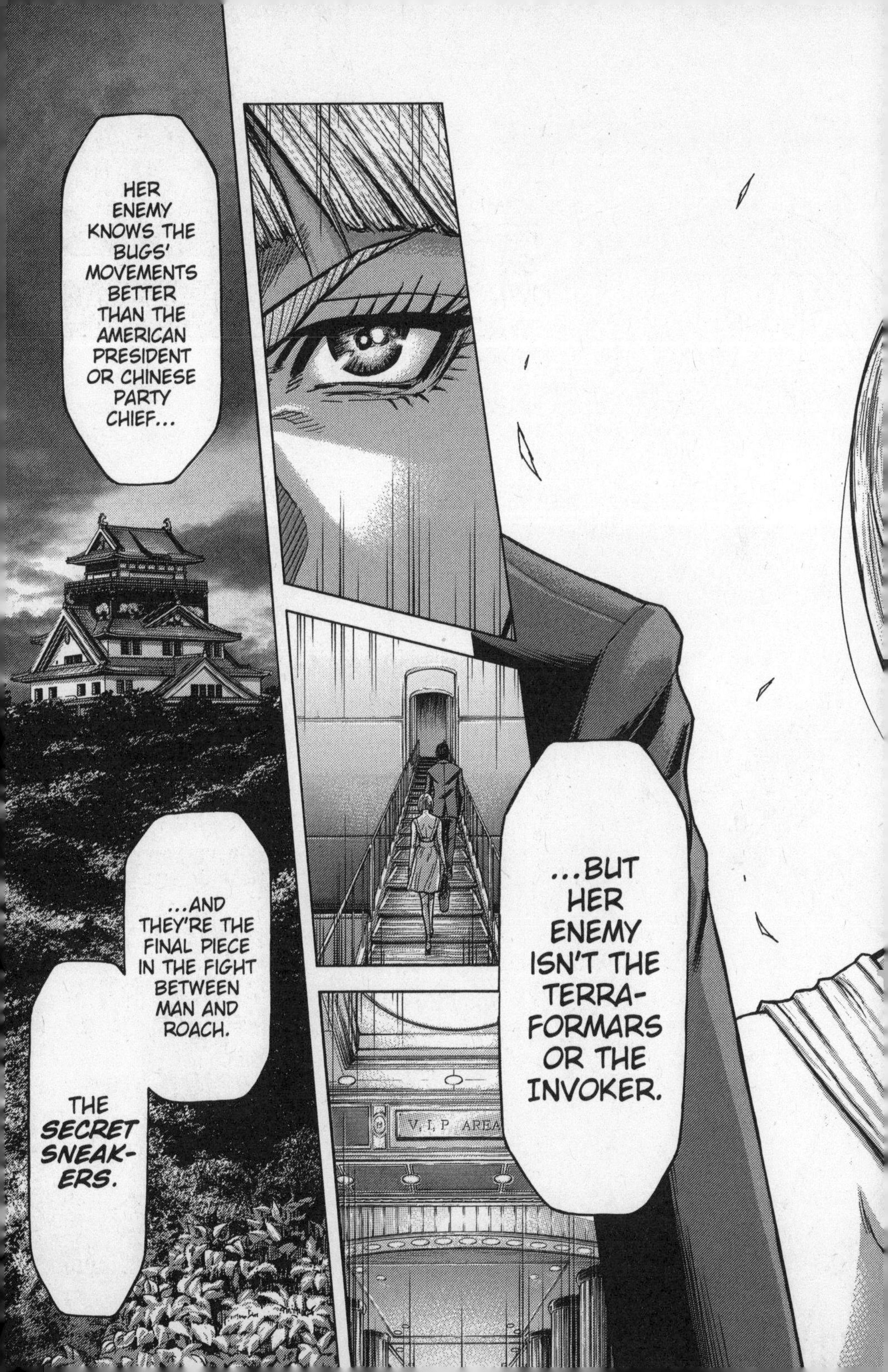

...BUT HER ENEMY ISN'T THE TERRA-FORMARS OR THE INVOKER.
V.I.P AREA
HER ENEMY KNOWS THE BUGS' MOVEMENTS BETTER THAN THE AMERICAN PRESIDENT OR CHINESE PARTY CHIEF...
...AND THEY'RE THE FINAL PIECE IN THE FIGHT BETWEEN MAN AND ROACH.
THE *SECRET SNEAK-ERS.*

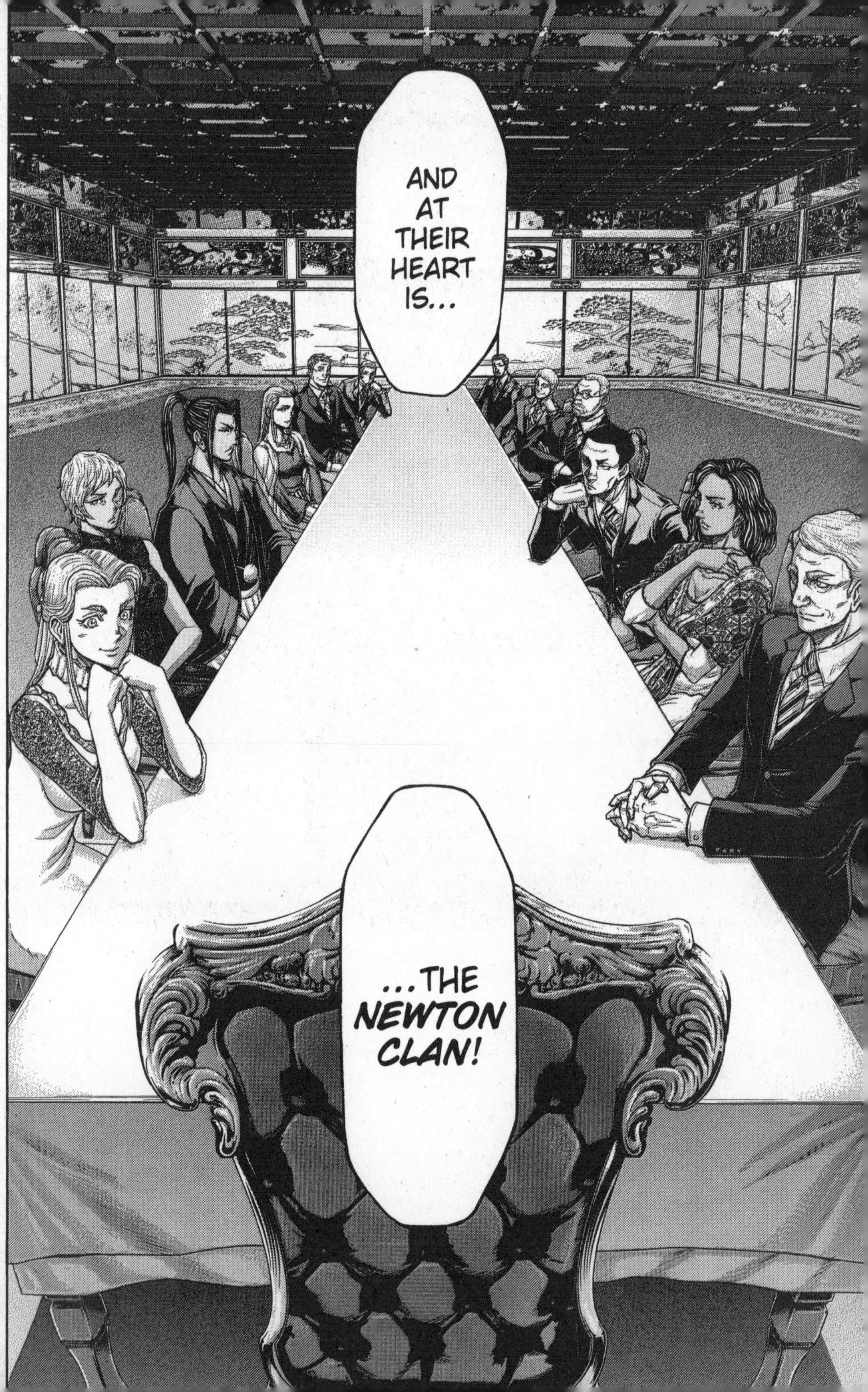
AND AT THEIR HEART IS...
...THE NEWTON CLAN!

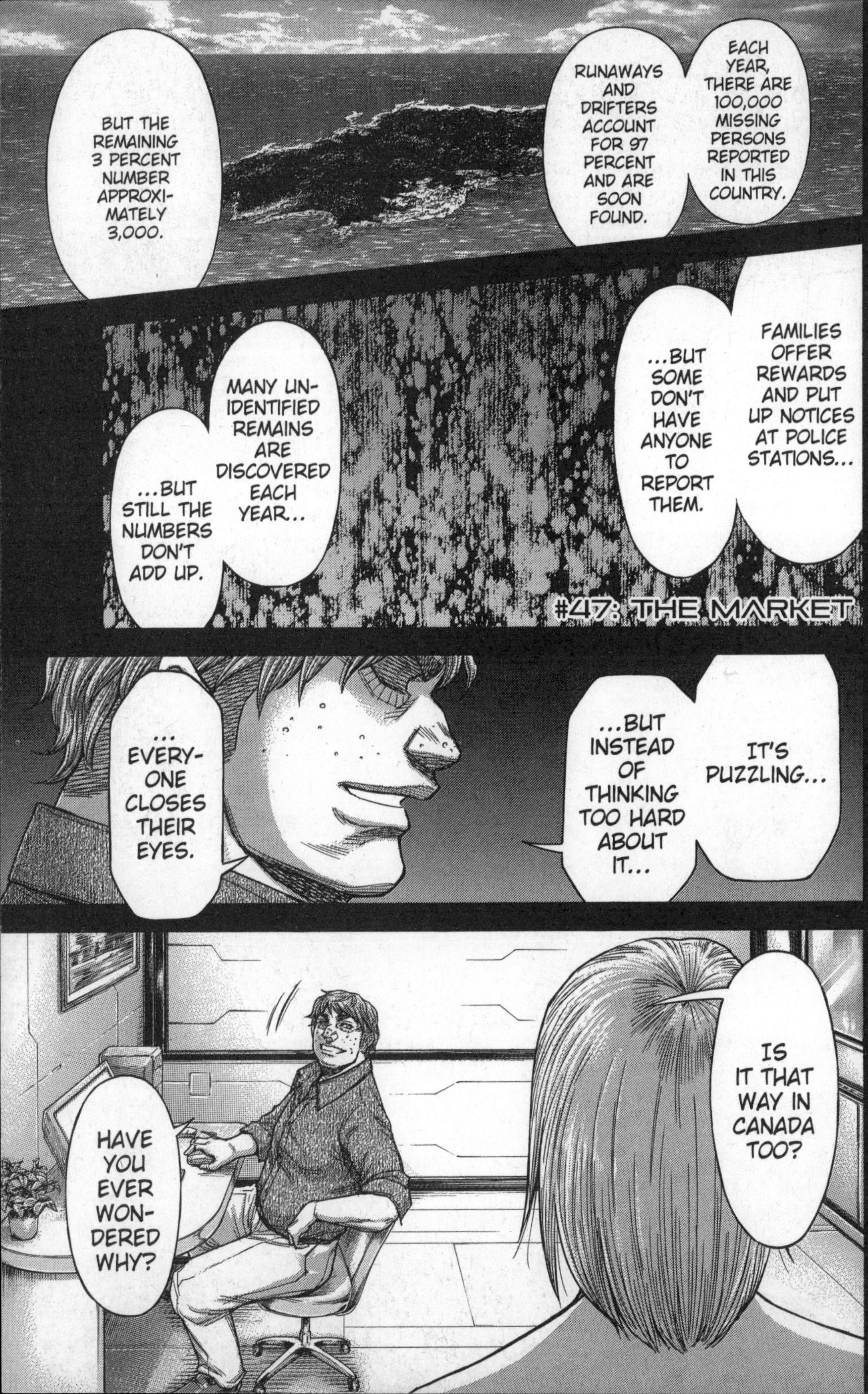
EACH YEAR, THERE ARE 100,000 MISSING PERSONS REPORTED IN THIS COUNTRY.
RUNAWAYS AND DRIFTERS ACCOUNT FOR 97 PERCENT AND ARE SOON FOUND.
BUT THE REMAINING 3 PERCENT NUMBER APPROXI-MATELY 3,000.
FAMILIES OFFER REWARDS AND PUT UP NOTICES AT POLICE STATIONS...
...BUT SOME DON'T HAVE ANYONE TO REPORT THEM.
MANY UN-IDENTIFIED REMAINS ARE DISCOVERED EACH YEAR...
...BUT STILL THE NUMBERS DON'T ADD UP.
#47: THE MARKET
IT'S PUZZLING...
...BUT INSTEAD OF THINKING TOO HARD ABOUT IT...
...EVERY-ONE CLOSES THEIR EYES.
IS IT THAT WAY IN CANADA TOO?
HAVE YOU EVER WON-DERED WHY?

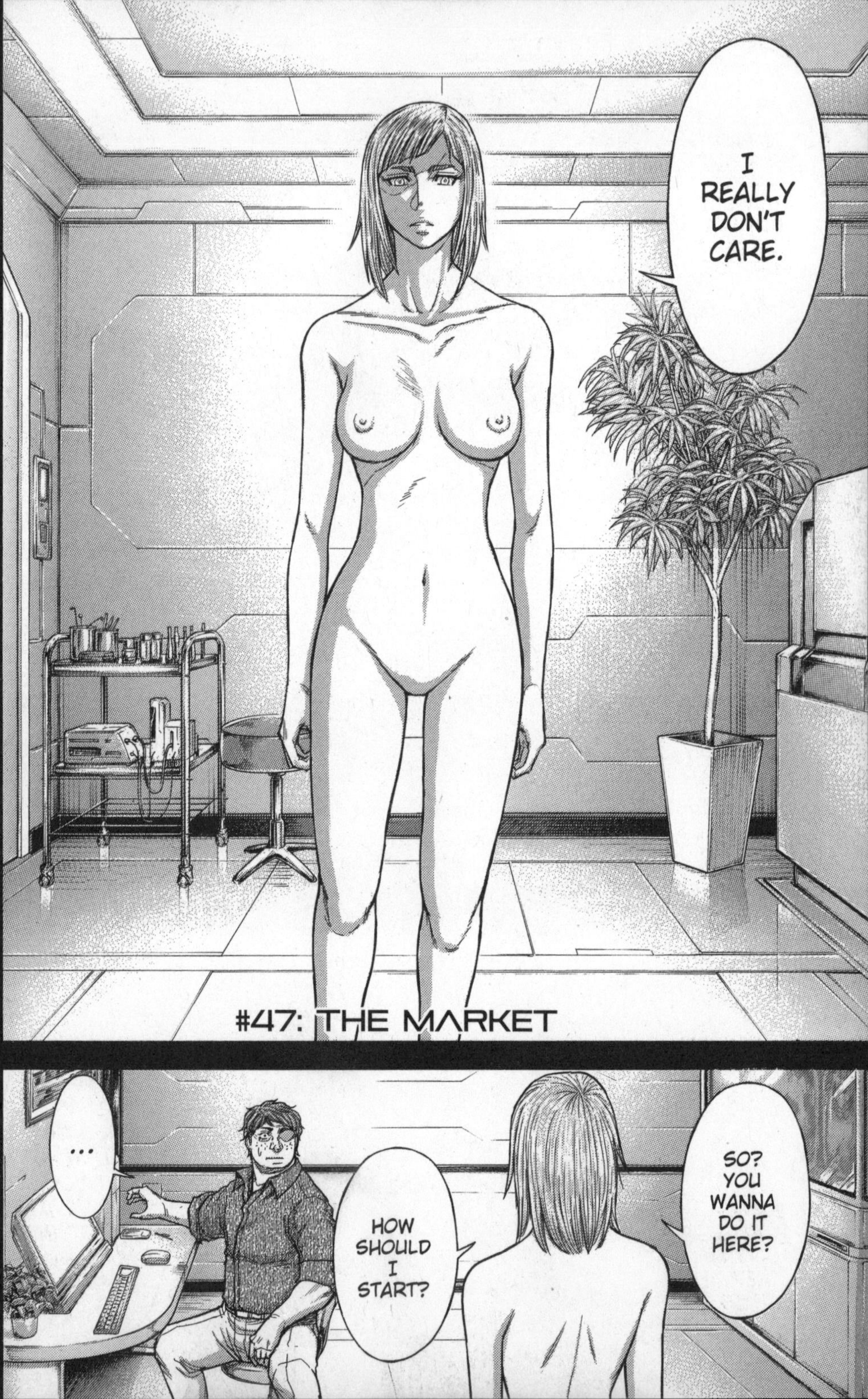
I REALLY DON'T CARE.
#47: THE MARKET
SO? YOU WANNA DO IT HERE?
HOW SHOULD I START?
...

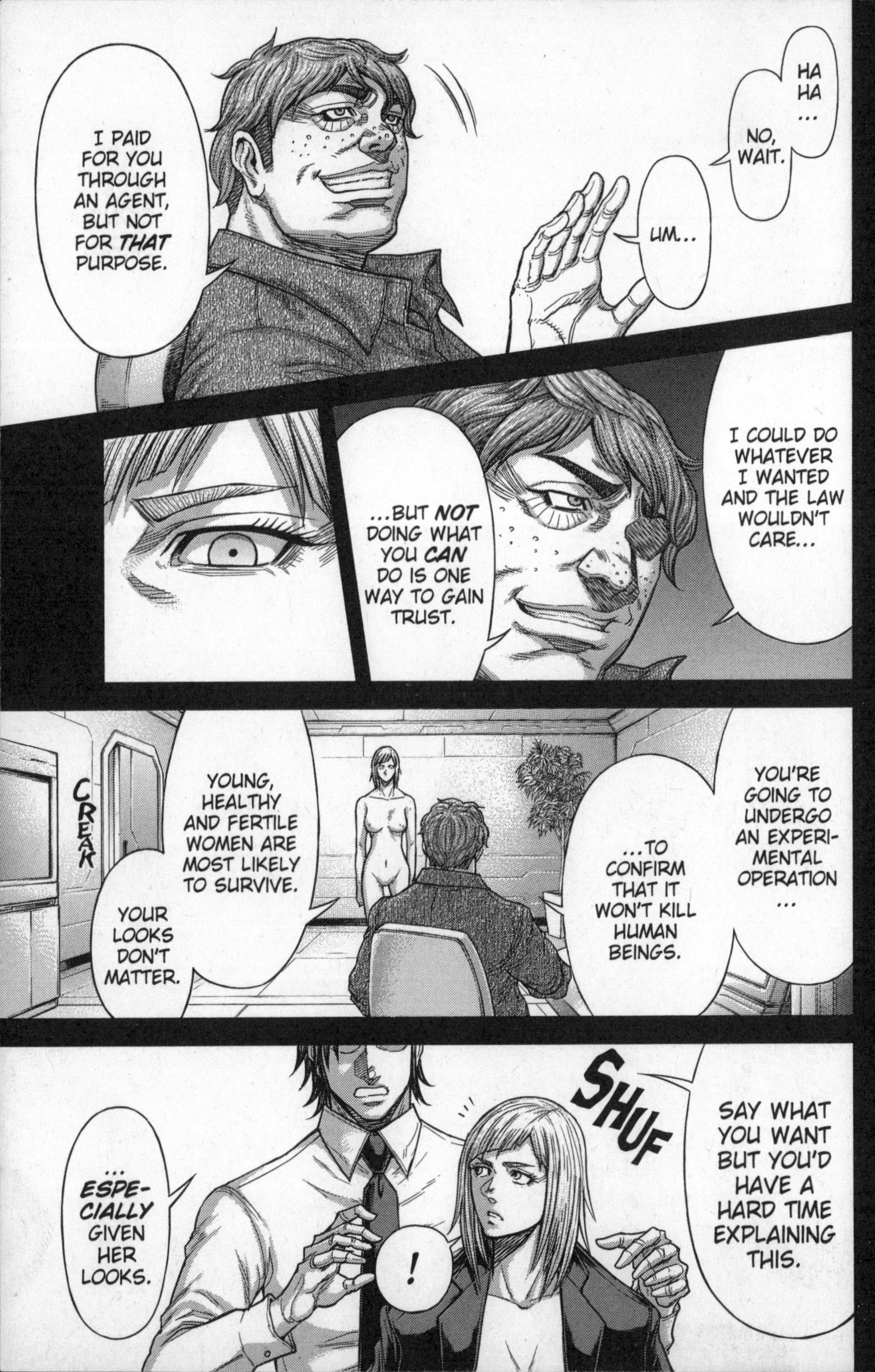
HA HA ... NO, WAIT.
UM...
I PAID FOR YOU THROUGH AN AGENT, BUT NOT FOR *THAT* PURPOSE.
I COULD DO WHATEVER I WANTED AND THE LAW WOULDN'T CARE...
...BUT *NOT* DOING WHAT YOU *CAN* DO IS ONE WAY TO GAIN TRUST.
YOU'RE GOING TO UNDERGO AN EXPERIMENTAL OPERATION ...
...TO CONFIRM THAT IT WON'T KILL HUMAN BEINGS.
YOUNG, HEALTHY AND FERTILE WOMEN ARE MOST LIKELY TO SURVIVE.
YOUR LOOKS DON'T MATTER.
CREAK
SAY WHAT YOU WANT BUT YOU'D HAVE A HARD TIME EXPLAINING THIS.
SHUF
!
... *ESPECIALLY* GIVEN HER LOOKS.

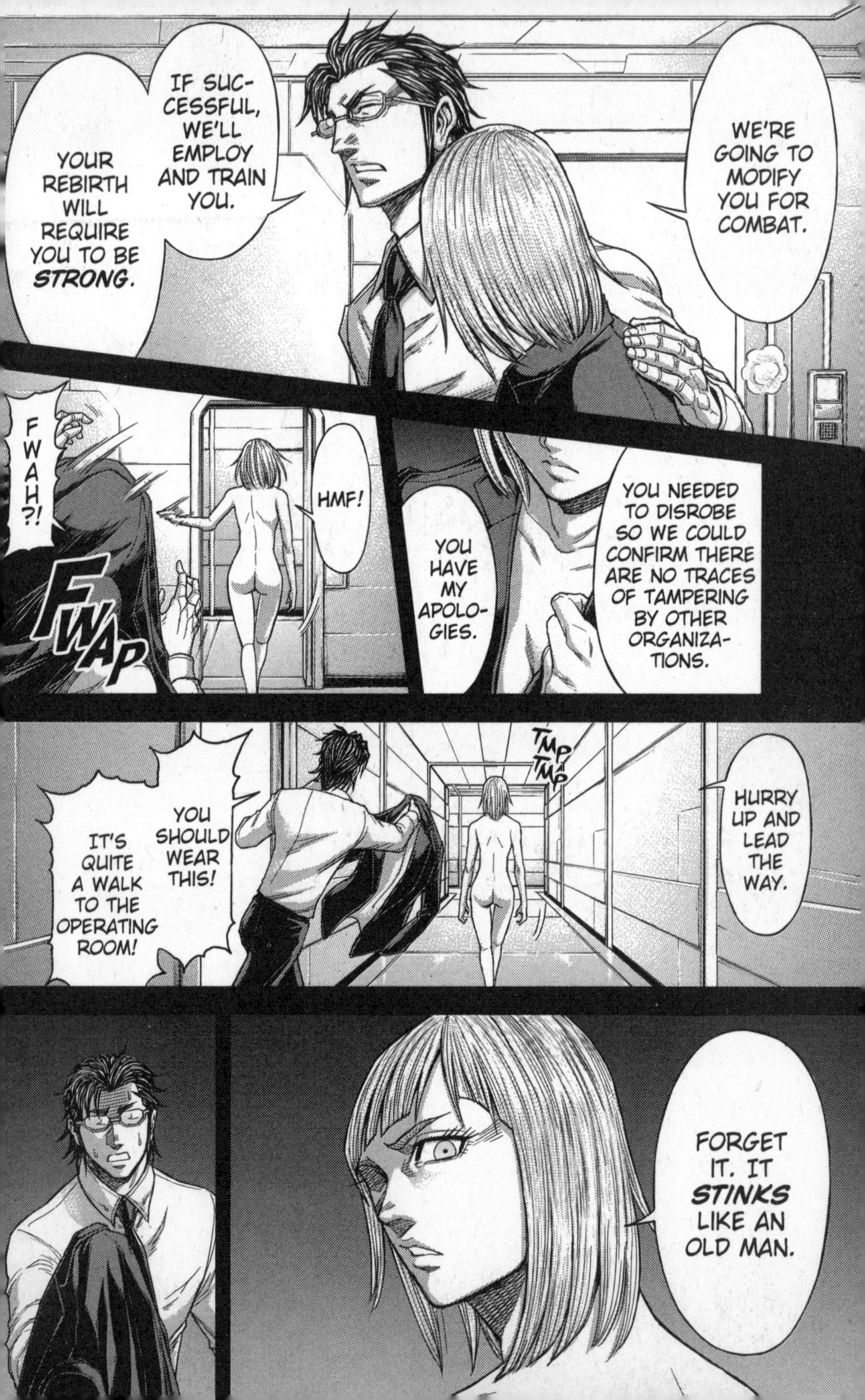
WE'RE GOING TO MODIFY YOU FOR COMBAT.
IF SUCCESSFUL, WE'LL EMPLOY AND TRAIN YOU.
YOUR REBIRTH WILL REQUIRE YOU TO BE STRONG.
YOU NEEDED TO DISROBE SO WE COULD CONFIRM THERE ARE NO TRACES OF TAMPERING BY OTHER ORGANIZATIONS.
YOU HAVE MY APOLOGIES.
HMF!
FWAP
FWAH?!
HURRY UP AND LEAD THE WAY.
TMP TMP
YOU SHOULD WEAR THIS!
IT'S QUITE A WALK TO THE OPERATING ROOM!
FORGET IT. IT STINKS LIKE AN OLD MAN.

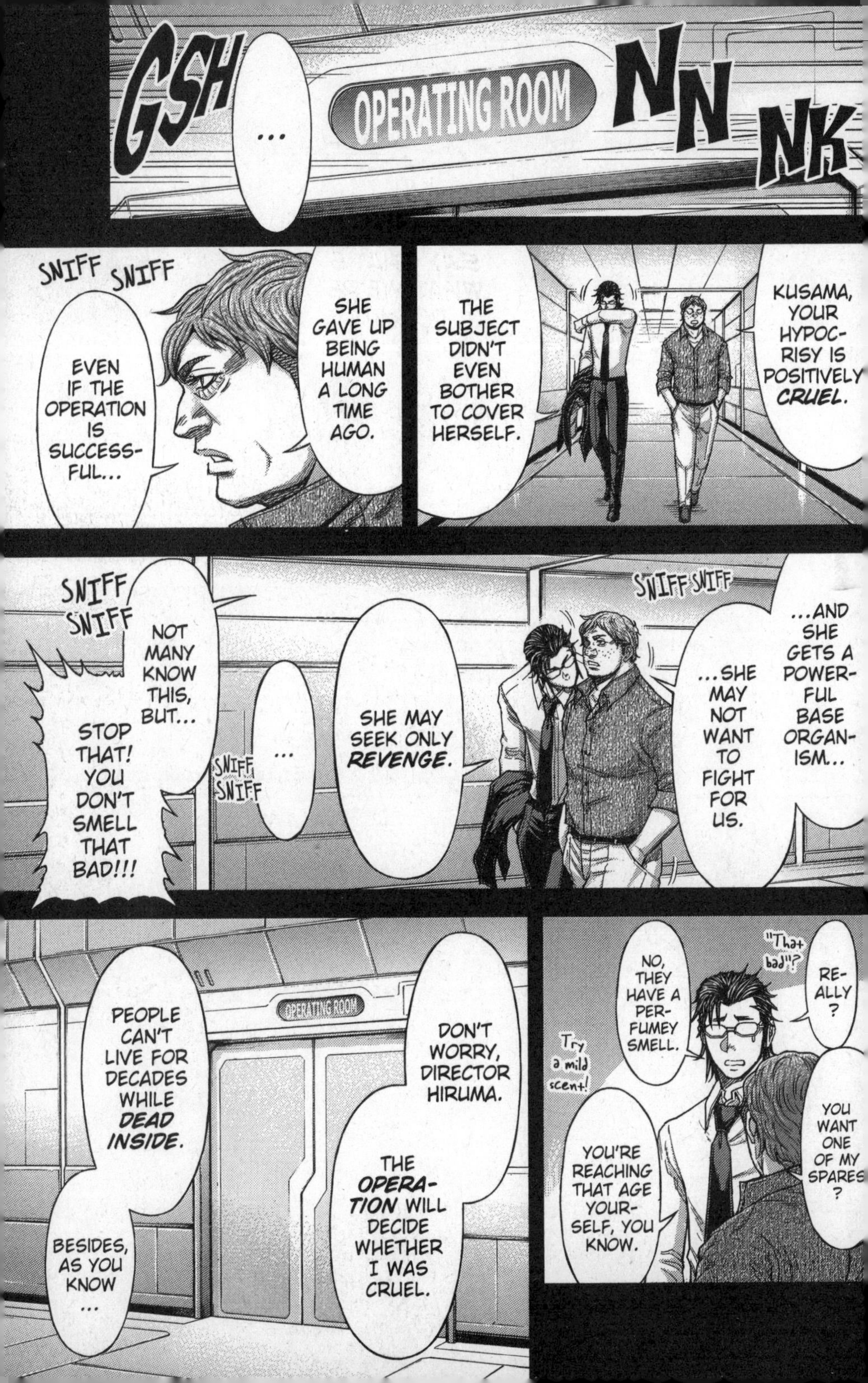
NNNK
OPERATING ROOM
...
GSH
KUSAMA, YOUR HYPOCRISY IS POSITIVELY CRUEL.
THE SUBJECT DIDN'T EVEN BOTHER TO COVER HERSELF.
SHE GAVE UP BEING HUMAN A LONG TIME AGO.
SNIFF SNIFF
EVEN IF THE OPERATION IS SUCCESSFUL...
...AND SHE GETS A POWERFUL BASE ORGANISM...
...SHE MAY NOT WANT TO FIGHT FOR US.
SNIFF SNIFF
SHE MAY SEEK ONLY REVENGE.
...
SNIFF SNIFF
NOT MANY KNOW THIS, BUT...
SNIFF SNIFF
STOP THAT! YOU DON'T SMELL THAT BAD!!!
REALLY?
"That bad"?
NO, THEY HAVE A PERFUMEY SMELL.
Try a mild scent!
YOU WANT ONE OF MY SPARES?
YOU'RE REACHING THAT AGE YOURSELF, YOU KNOW.
DON'T WORRY, DIRECTOR HIRUMA.
OPERATING ROOM
PEOPLE CAN'T LIVE FOR DECADES WHILE DEAD INSIDE.
THE OPERATION WILL DECIDE WHETHER I WAS CRUEL.
BESIDES, AS YOU KNOW...

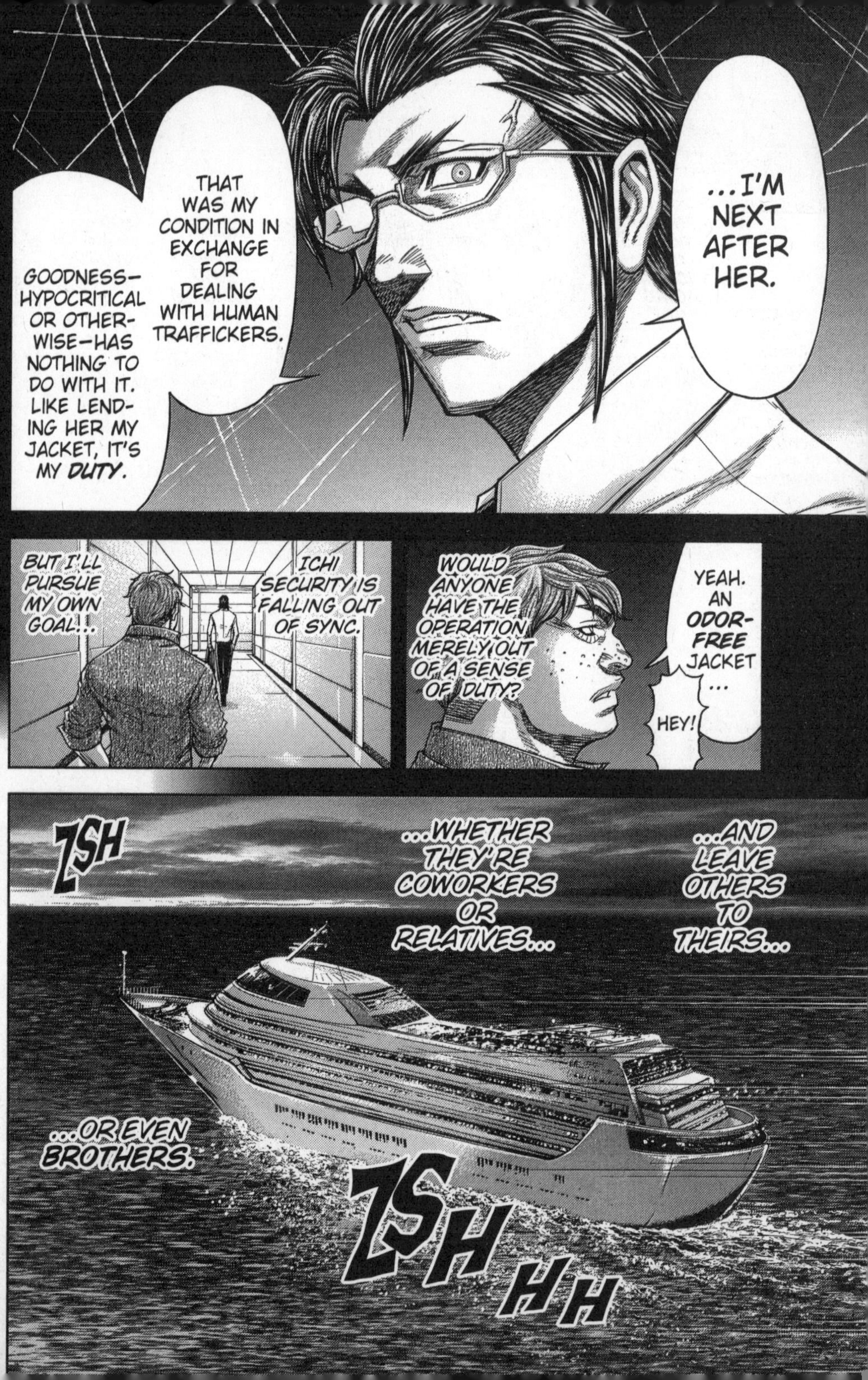
...I'M NEXT AFTER HER.
THAT WAS MY CONDITION IN EXCHANGE FOR DEALING WITH HUMAN TRAFFICKERS.
GOODNESS—HYPOCRITICAL OR OTHER-WISE—HAS NOTHING TO DO WITH IT. LIKE LEND-ING HER MY JACKET, IT'S MY DUTY.
YEAH. AN ODOR-FREE JACKET ...
HEY!
WOULD ANYONE HAVE THE OPERATION MERELY OUT OF A SENSE OF DUTY?
ICHI SECURITY IS FALLING OUT OF SYNC.
BUT I'LL PURSUE MY OWN GOAL...
ZSH
...AND LEAVE OTHERS TO THEIRS...
...WHETHER THEY'RE COWORKERS OR RELATIVES...
...OR EVEN BROTHERS.
ZSHHH

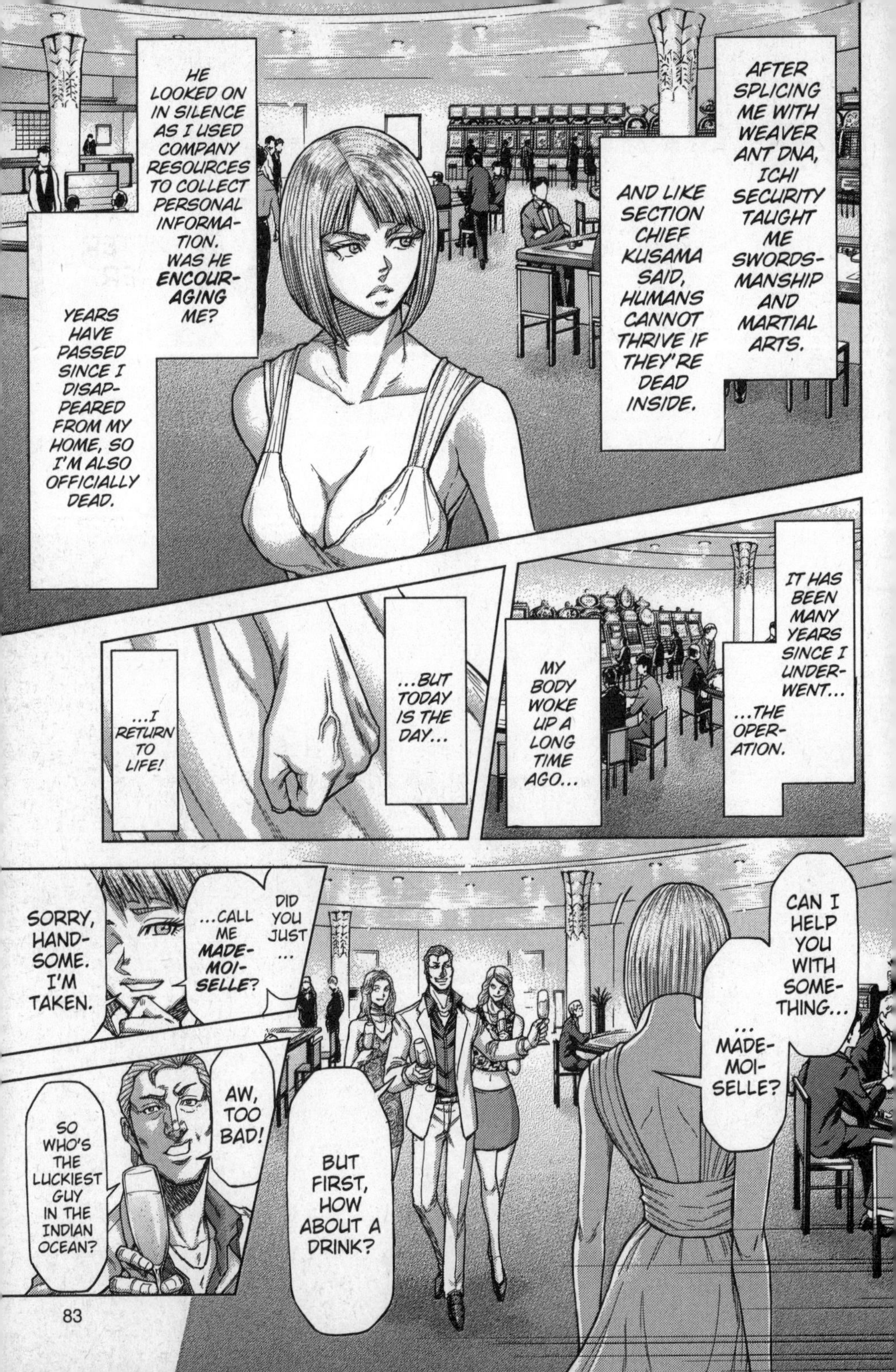
AFTER SPLICING ME WITH WEAVER ANT DNA, ICHI SECURITY TAUGHT ME SWORDSMANSHIP AND MARTIAL ARTS.
AND LIKE SECTION CHIEF KUSAMA SAID, HUMANS CANNOT THRIVE IF THEY'RE DEAD INSIDE.
HE LOOKED ON IN SILENCE AS I USED COMPANY RESOURCES TO COLLECT PERSONAL INFORMATION. WAS HE ENCOURAGING ME?
YEARS HAVE PASSED SINCE I DISAPPEARED FROM MY HOME, SO I'M ALSO OFFICIALLY DEAD.
IT HAS BEEN MANY YEARS SINCE I UNDERWENT...
...THE OPERATION.
MY BODY WOKE UP A LONG TIME AGO...
...BUT TODAY IS THE DAY...
...I RETURN TO LIFE!
CAN I HELP YOU WITH SOMETHING...
...MADEMOISELLE?
DID YOU JUST...
...CALL ME MADEMOISELLE?
SORRY, HANDSOME. I'M TAKEN.
AW, TOO BAD!
SO WHO'S THE LUCKIEST GUY IN THE INDIAN OCEAN?
BUT FIRST, HOW ABOUT A DRINK?

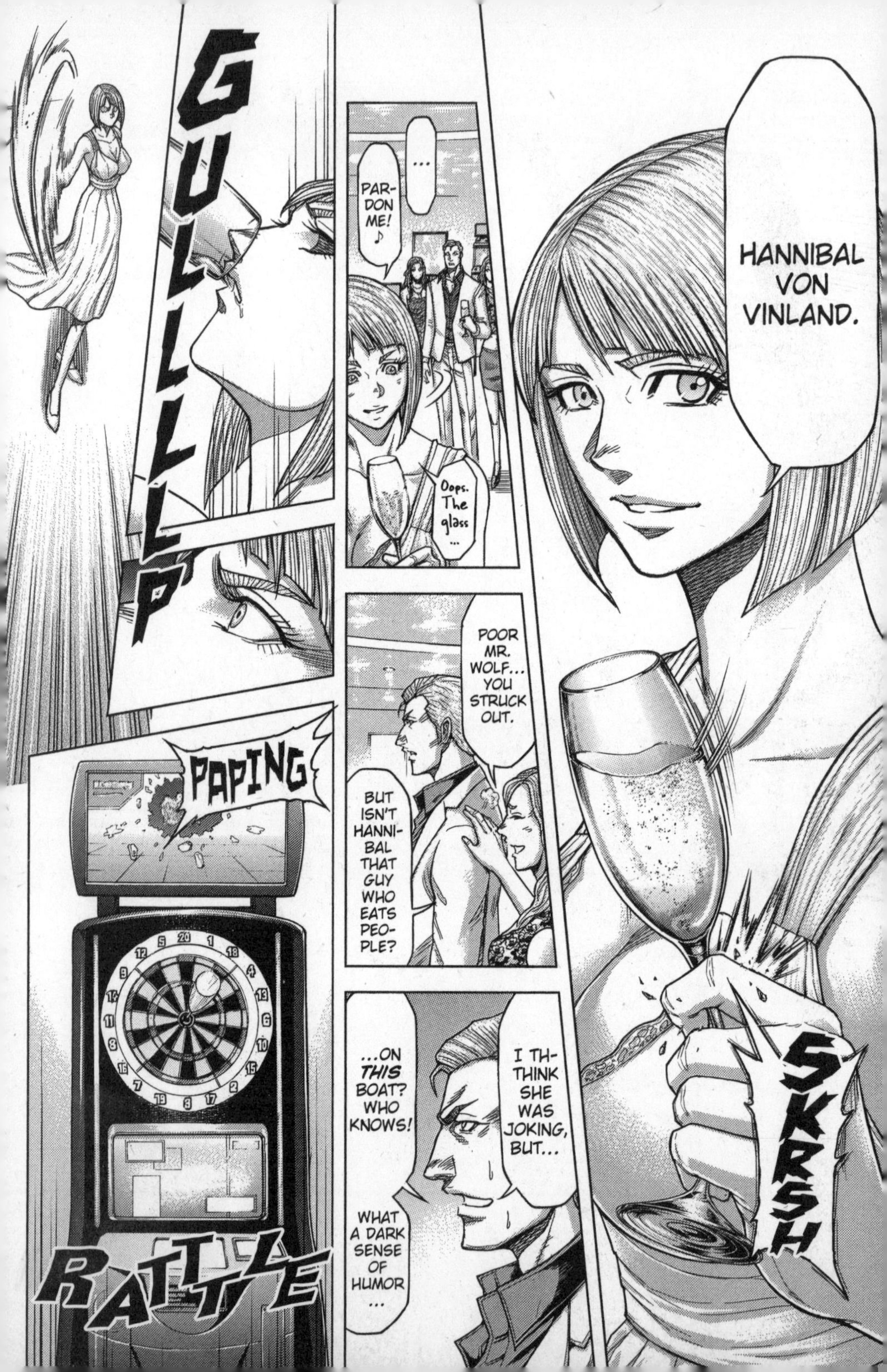
HANNIBAL VON VINLAND.
SKRSH
...
PAR-DON ME! ♪
Oops. The glass...
POOR MR. WOLF... YOU STRUCK OUT.
BUT ISN'T HANNI-BAL THAT GUY WHO EATS PEO-PLE?
I TH-THINK SHE WAS JOKING, BUT...
...ON *THIS* BOAT? WHO KNOWS!
WHAT A DARK SENSE OF HUMOR...
GULLLLP
PAPING
RATTLE

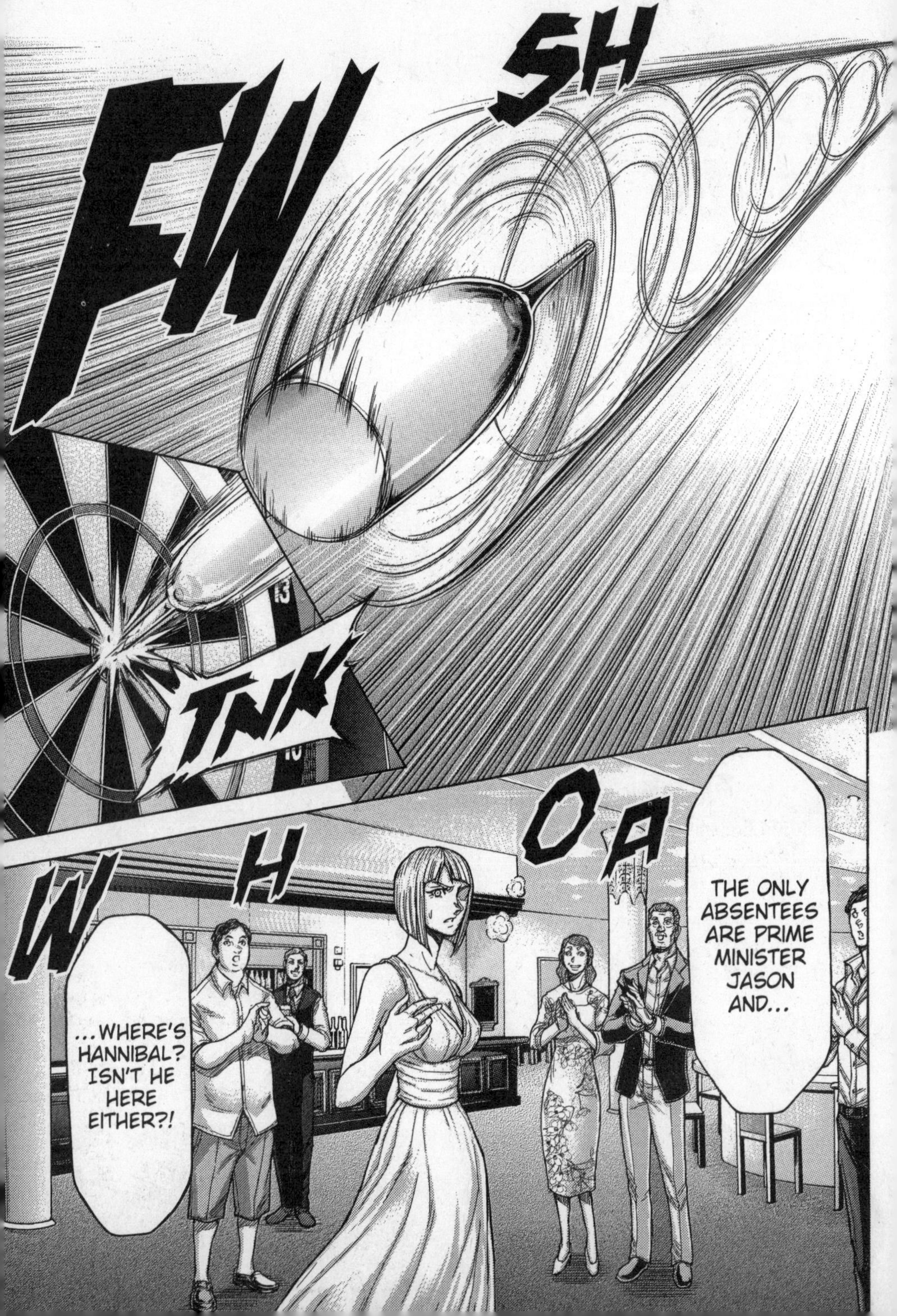
FWSH
TNK
WHOA
THE ONLY ABSENTEES ARE PRIME MINISTER JASON AND...
...WHERE'S HANNIBAL? ISN'T HE HERE EITHER?!

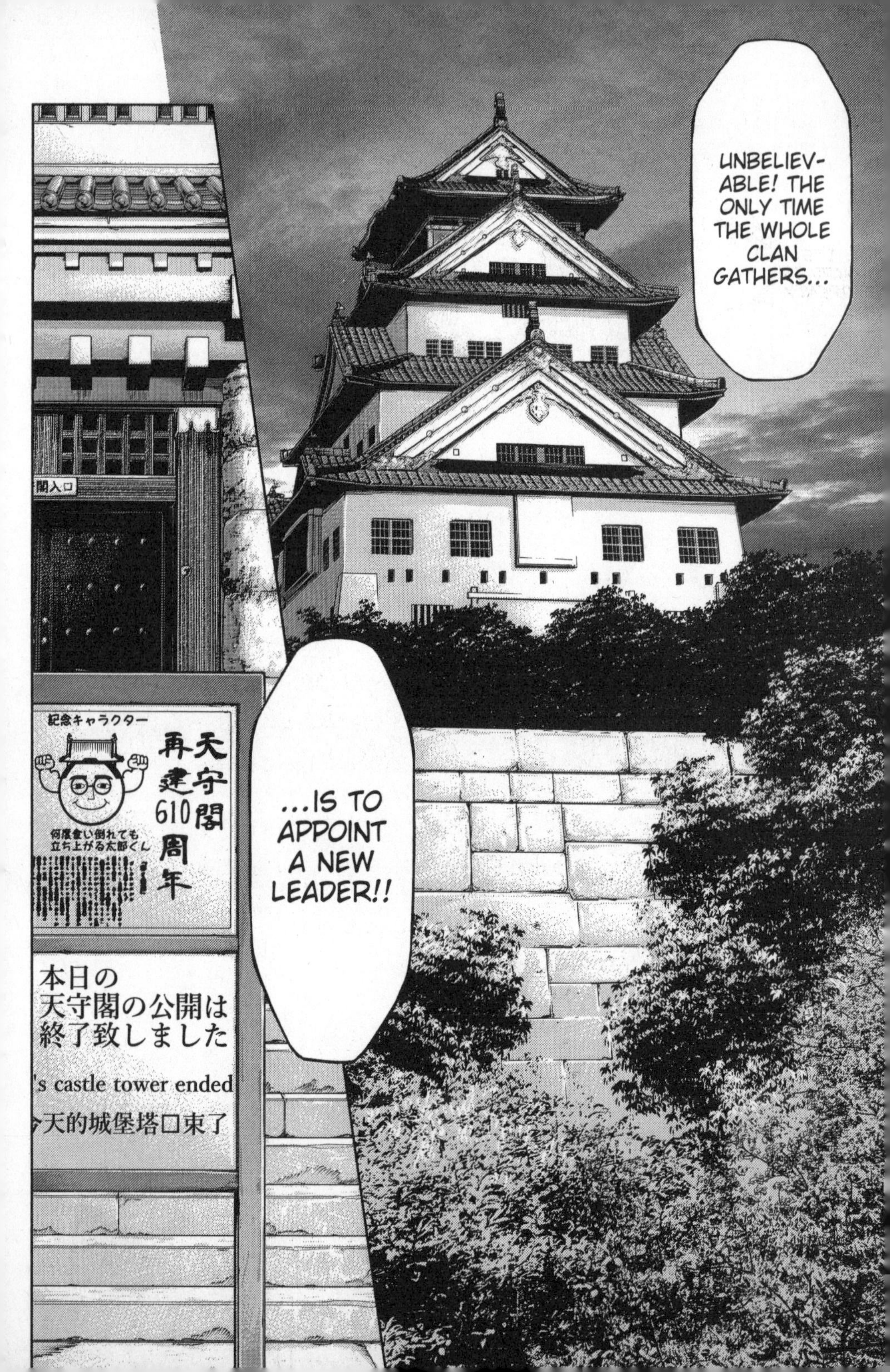
UNBELIEVABLE! THE ONLY TIME THE WHOLE CLAN GATHERS...
...IS TO APPOINT A NEW LEADER!!
閣入口
天守閣再建610周年
記念キャラクター
何度食い倒れても立ち上がる太郎くん
本日の天守閣の公開は終了致しました
's castle tower ended
今天的城堡塔口束了

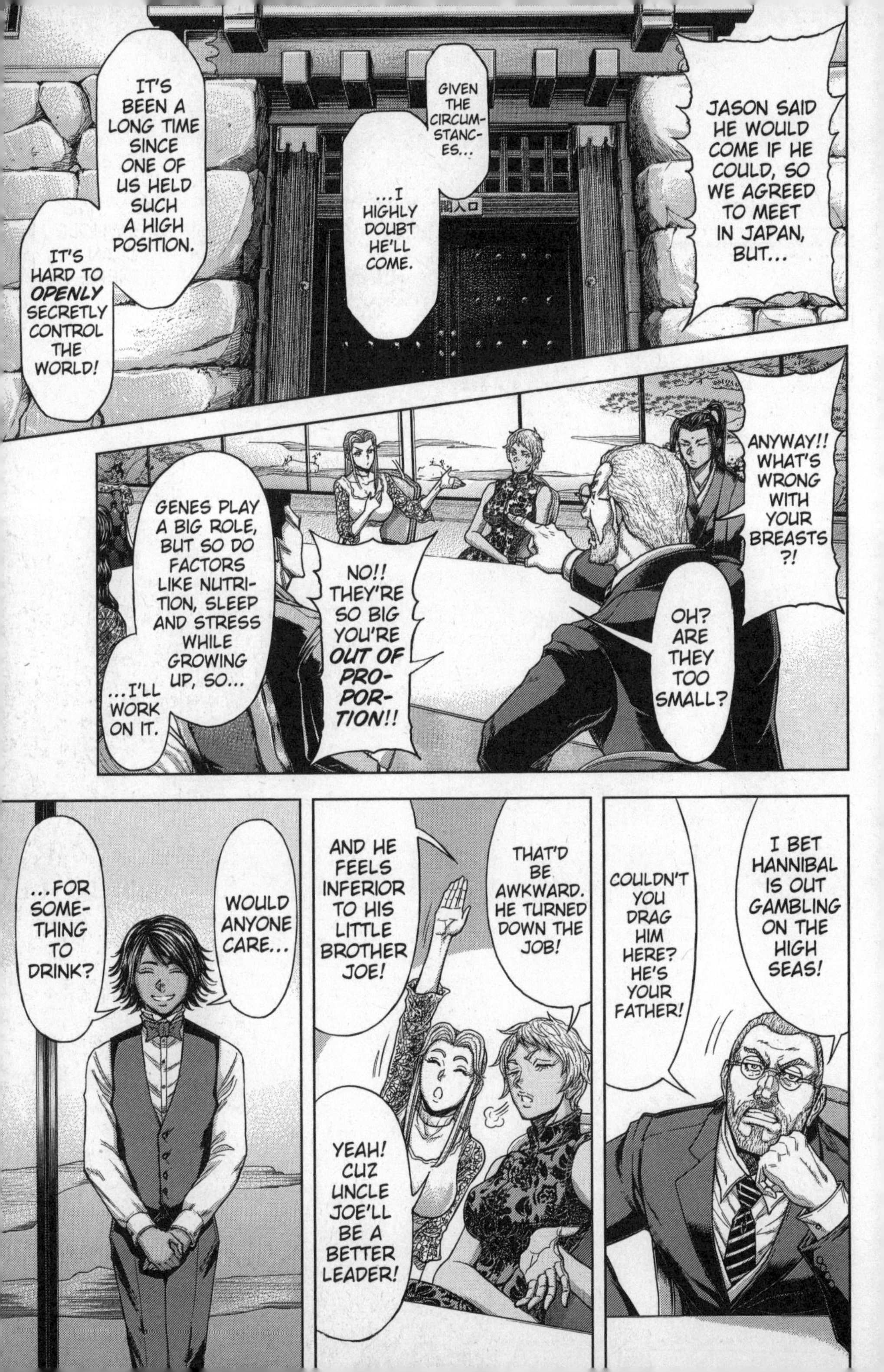
JASON SAID HE WOULD COME IF HE COULD, SO WE AGREED TO MEET IN JAPAN, BUT...
GIVEN THE CIRCUM-STANC-ES...
...I HIGHLY DOUBT HE'LL COME.
IT'S BEEN A LONG TIME SINCE ONE OF US HELD SUCH A HIGH POSITION.
IT'S HARD TO *OPENLY* SECRETLY CONTROL THE WORLD!
ANYWAY!! WHAT'S WRONG WITH YOUR BREASTS?!
OH? ARE THEY TOO SMALL?
NO!! THEY'RE SO BIG YOU'RE *OUT OF PRO-POR-TION*!!
GENES PLAY A BIG ROLE, BUT SO DO FACTORS LIKE NUTRI-TION, SLEEP AND STRESS WHILE GROWING UP, SO...
...I'LL WORK ON IT.
I BET HANNIBAL IS OUT GAMBLING ON THE HIGH SEAS!
COULDN'T YOU DRAG HIM HERE? HE'S YOUR FATHER!
THAT'D BE AWKWARD. HE TURNED DOWN THE JOB!
AND HE FEELS INFERIOR TO HIS LITTLE BROTHER JOE!
YEAH! CUZ UNCLE JOE'LL BE A BETTER LEADER!
WOULD ANYONE CARE...
...FOR SOME-THING TO DRINK?

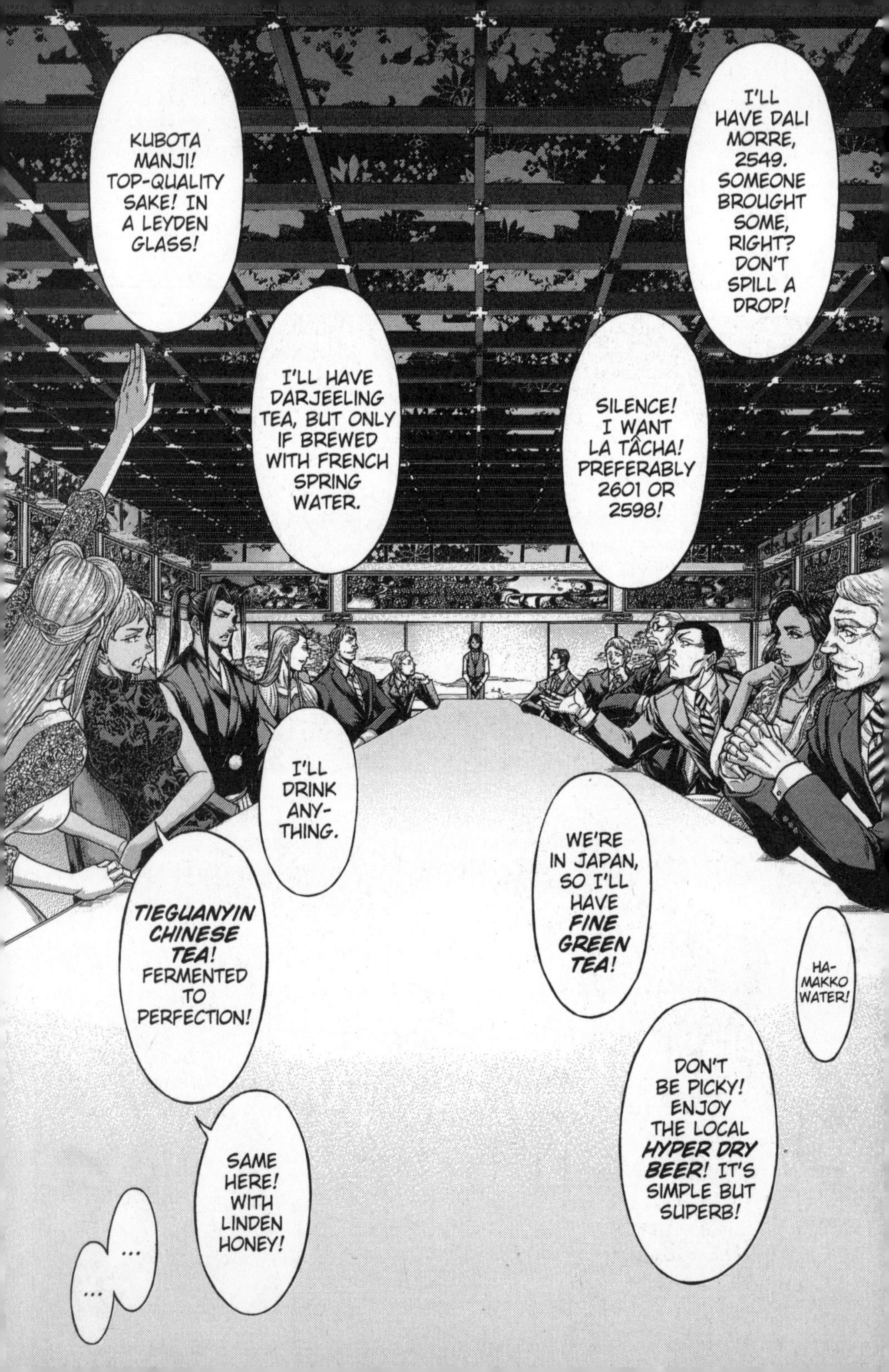
I'LL HAVE DALI MORRE, 2549. SOMEONE BROUGHT SOME, RIGHT? DON'T SPILL A DROP!
KUBOTA MANJI! TOP-QUALITY SAKE! IN A LEYDEN GLASS!
SILENCE! I WANT LA TÂCHA! PREFERABLY 2601 OR 2598!
I'LL HAVE DARJEELING TEA, BUT ONLY IF BREWED WITH FRENCH SPRING WATER.
WE'RE IN JAPAN, SO I'LL HAVE *FINE GREEN TEA*!
I'LL DRINK ANY-THING.
*TIEGUANYIN CHINESE TEA*! FERMENTED TO PERFECTION!
HA-MAKKO WATER!
DON'T BE PICKY! ENJOY THE LOCAL *HYPER DRY BEER*! IT'S SIMPLE BUT SUPERB!
SAME HERE! WITH LINDEN HONEY!
...
...

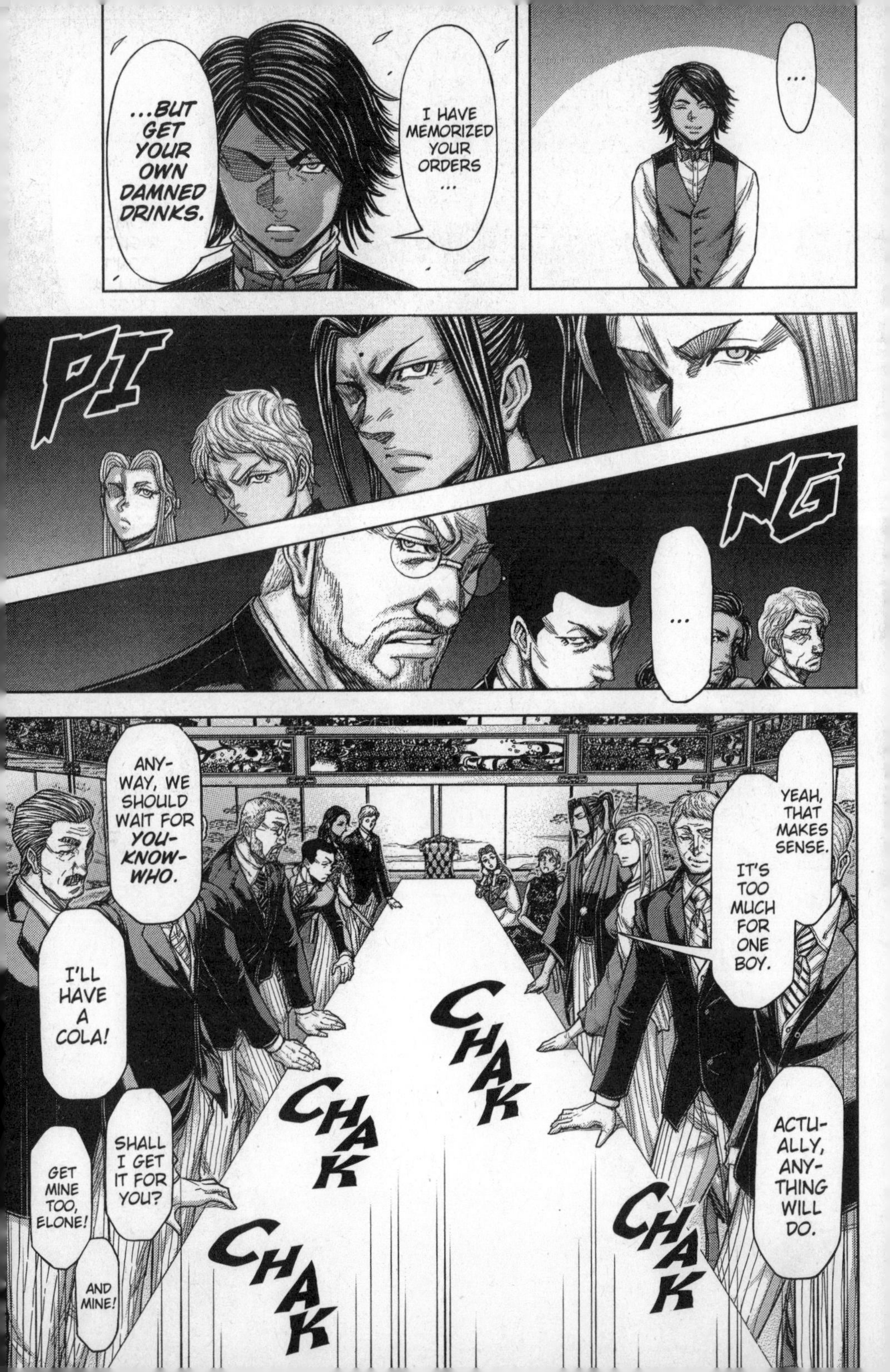
...
I HAVE MEMORIZED YOUR ORDERS ...
...BUT GET YOUR OWN DAMNED DRINKS.
PING
...
YEAH, THAT MAKES SENSE.
IT'S TOO MUCH FOR ONE BOY.
ANYWAY, WE SHOULD WAIT FOR YOU-KNOW-WHO.
I'LL HAVE A COLA!
CHAK
CHAK
ACTUALLY, ANYTHING WILL DO.
CHAK
SHALL I GET IT FOR YOU?
GET MINE TOO, ELONE!
CHAK
AND MINE!

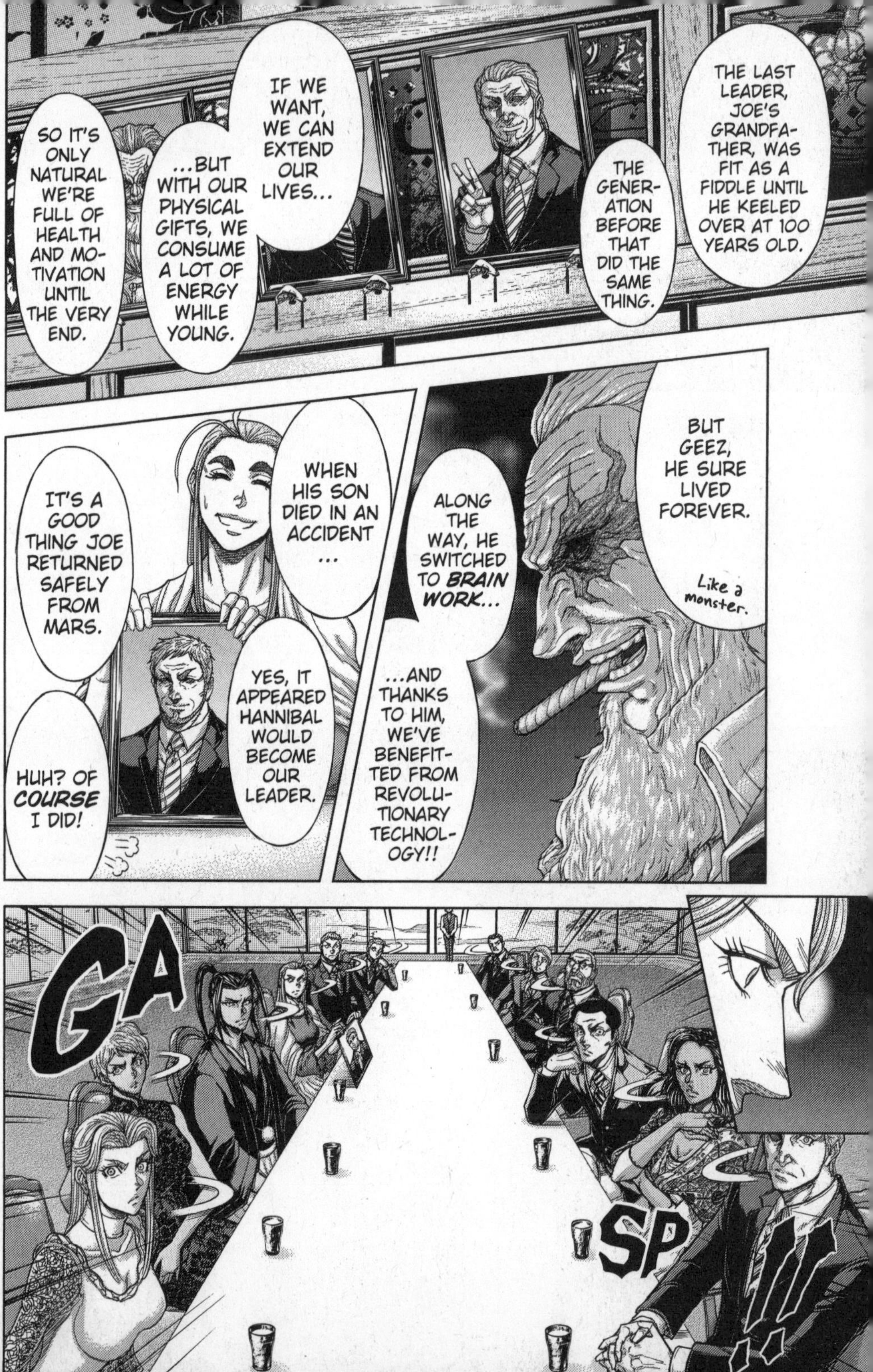
THE LAST LEADER, JOE'S GRANDFATHER, WAS FIT AS A FIDDLE UNTIL HE KEELED OVER AT 100 YEARS OLD.
THE GENERATION BEFORE THAT DID THE SAME THING.
IF WE WANT, WE CAN EXTEND OUR LIVES...
...BUT WITH OUR PHYSICAL GIFTS, WE CONSUME A LOT OF ENERGY WHILE YOUNG.
SO IT'S ONLY NATURAL WE'RE FULL OF HEALTH AND MOTIVATION UNTIL THE VERY END.
BUT GEEZ, HE SURE LIVED FOREVER.
Like a monster.
ALONG THE WAY, HE SWITCHED TO ***BRAIN WORK***...
...AND THANKS TO HIM, WE'VE BENEFITTED FROM REVOLUTIONARY TECHNOLOGY!!
WHEN HIS SON DIED IN AN ACCIDENT...
IT'S A GOOD THING JOE RETURNED SAFELY FROM MARS.
YES, IT APPEARED HANNIBAL WOULD BECOME OUR LEADER.
HUH? OF ***COURSE*** I DID!
GA
SP
!!

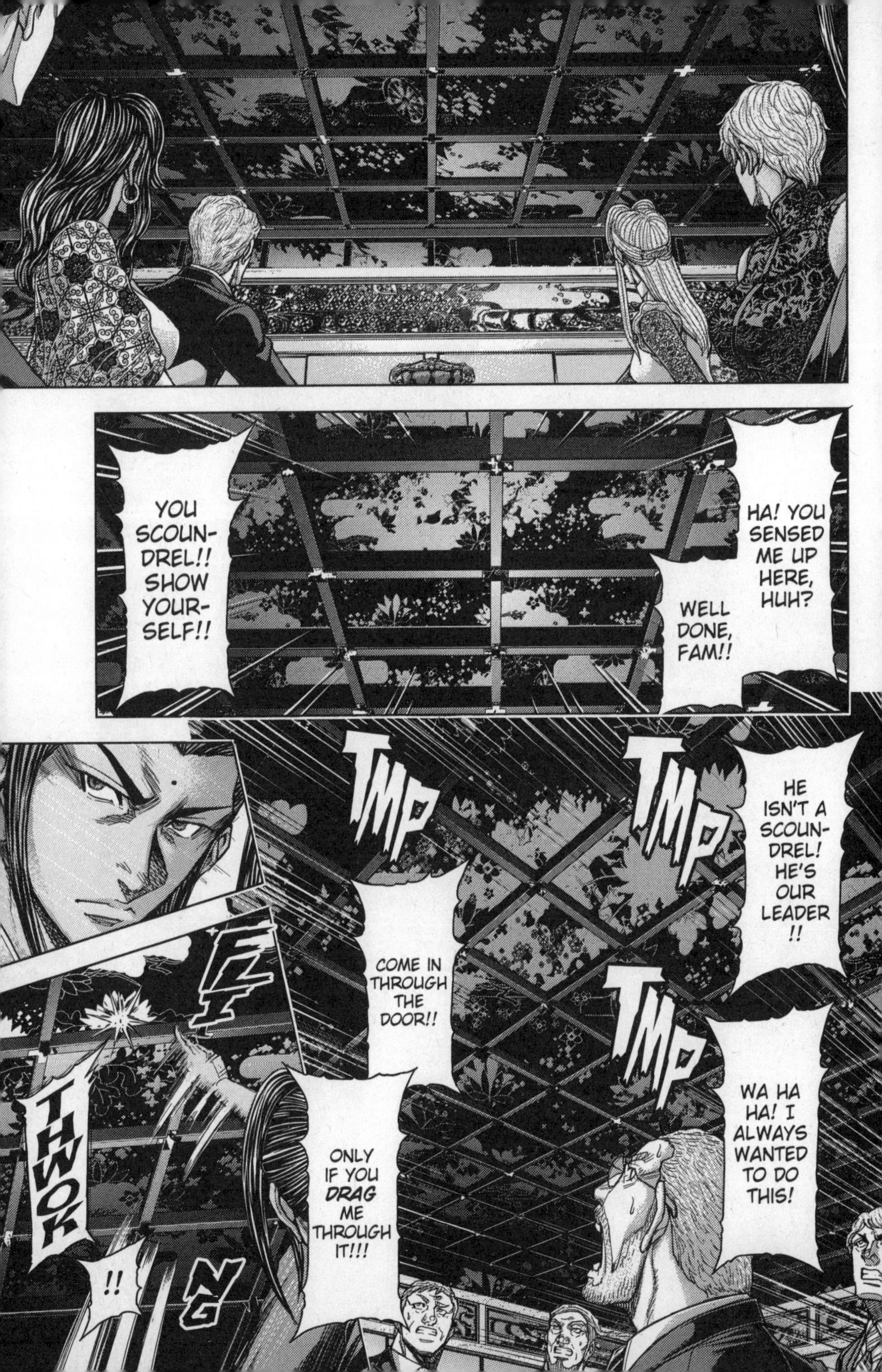
HA! YOU SENSED ME UP HERE, HUH?
WELL DONE, FAM!!
YOU SCOUNDREL!! SHOW YOURSELF!!
TMP
TMP
HE ISN'T A SCOUNDREL! HE'S OUR LEADER!!
COME IN THROUGH THE DOOR!!
TMP
WA HA HA! I ALWAYS WANTED TO DO THIS!
ONLY IF YOU *DRAG* ME THROUGH IT!!!
THWOK
!!
NG

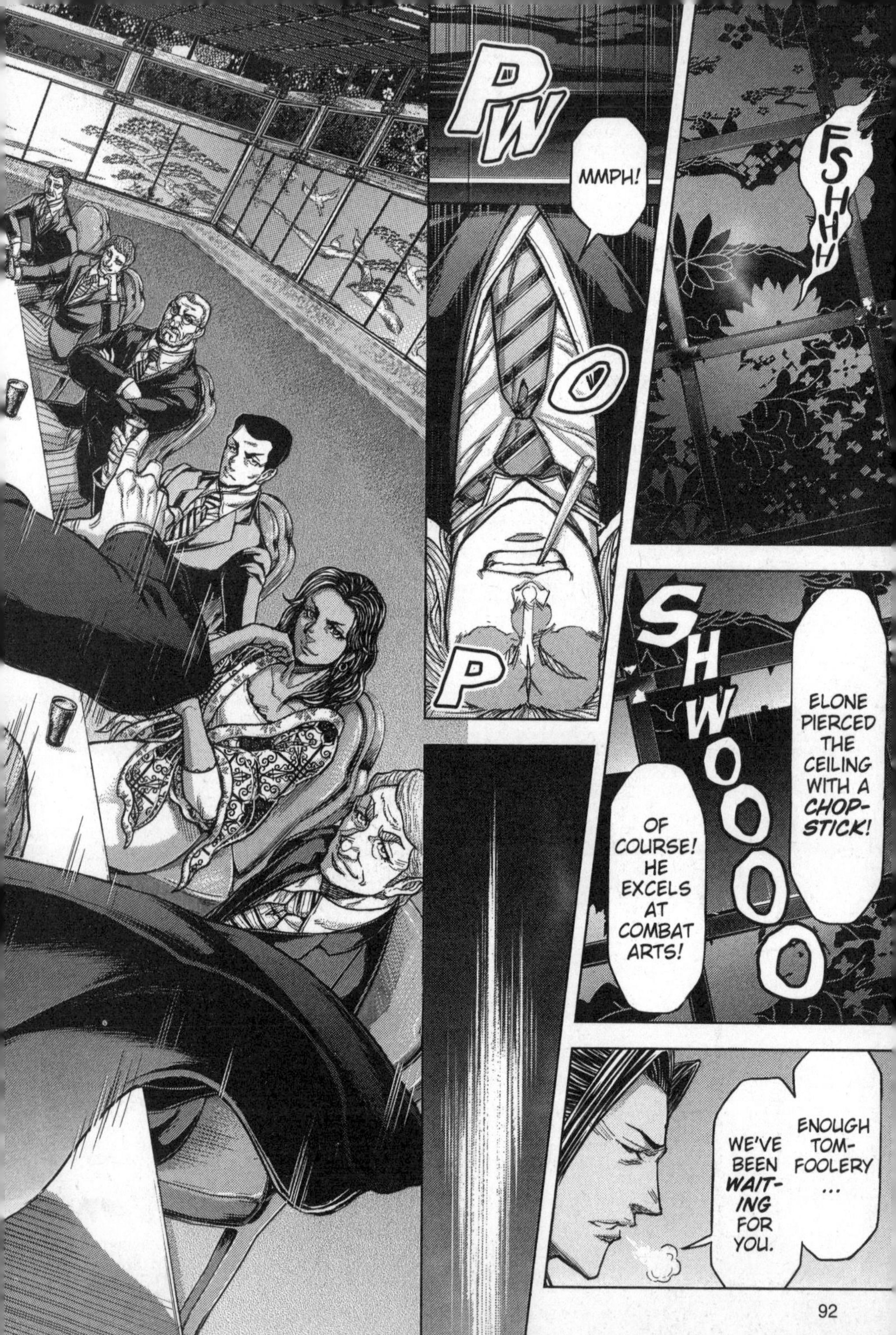
FSHHHH
PWOOP
MMPH!
SHWOOOOO
ELONE PIERCED THE CEILING WITH A *CHOP-STICK!*
OF COURSE! HE EXCELS AT COMBAT ARTS!
ENOUGH TOM-FOOLERY ...
WE'VE BEEN *WAIT-ING* FOR YOU.

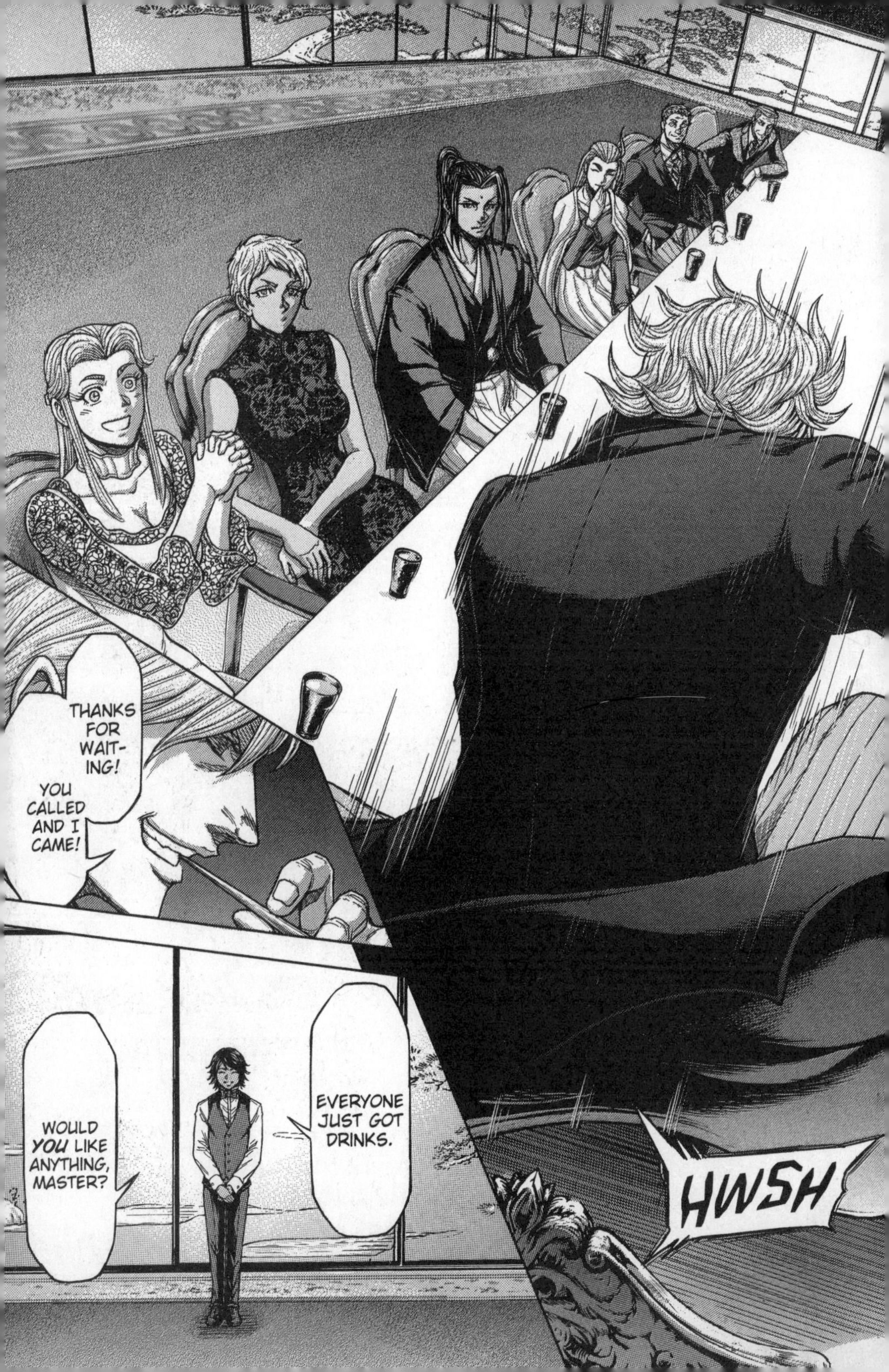
THANKS FOR WAIT-ING!
YOU CALLED AND I CAME!
HWSH
EVERYONE JUST GOT DRINKS.
WOULD *YOU* LIKE ANYTHING, MASTER?

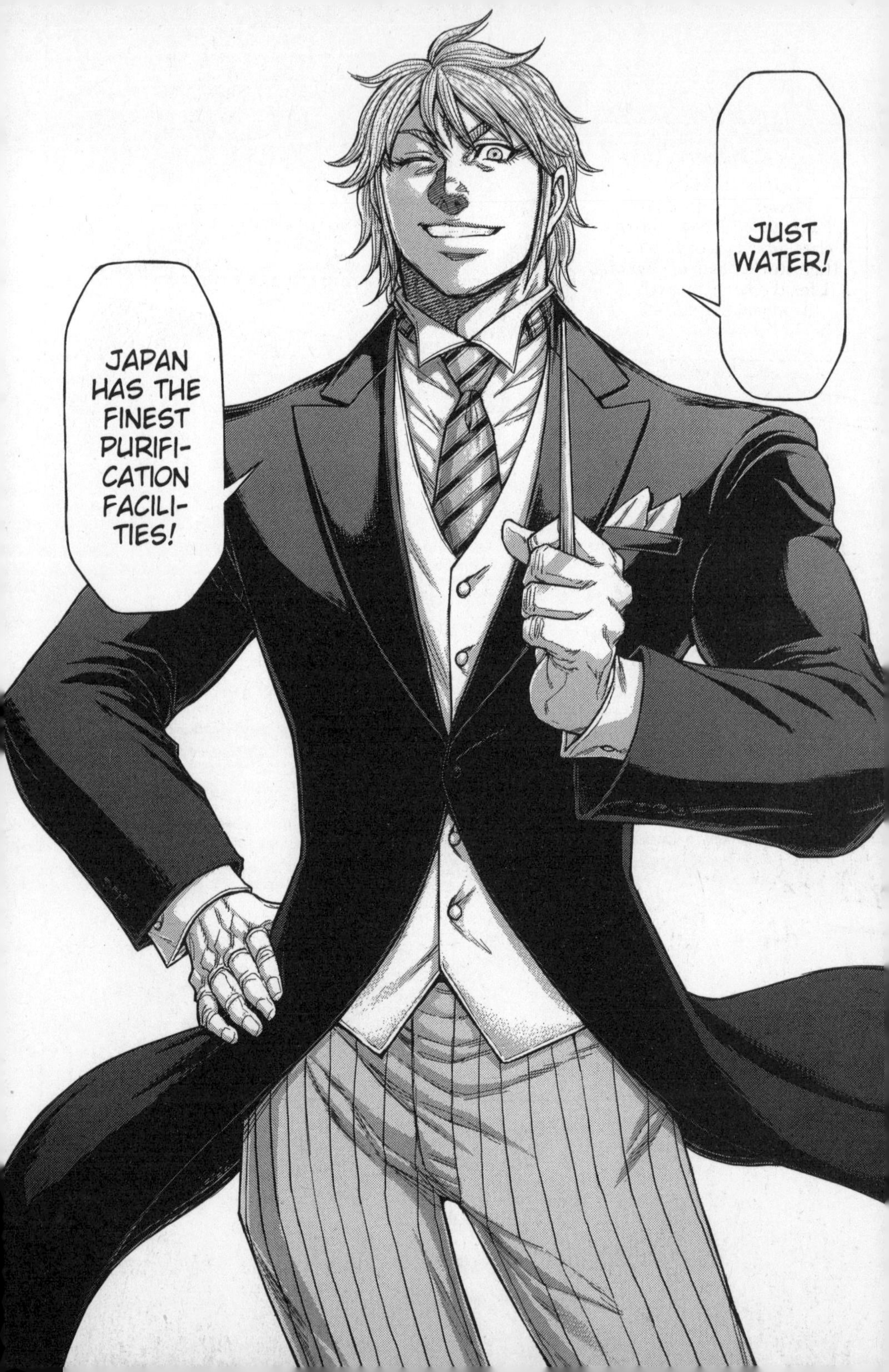
JUST WATER!
JAPAN HAS THE FINEST PURIFI-CATION FACILI-TIES!

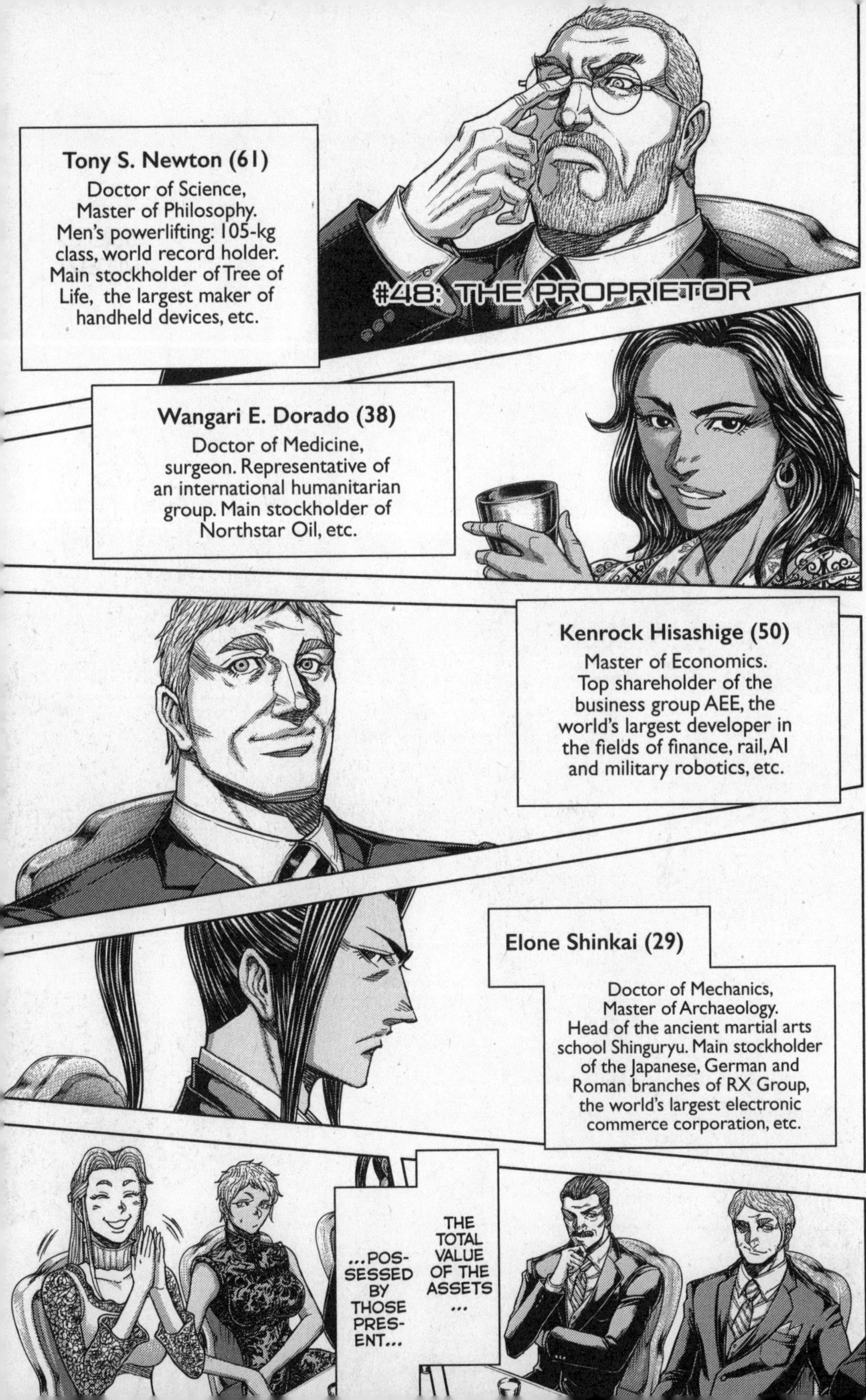
#48: THE PROPRIETOR
Tony S. Newton (61)
Doctor of Science, Master of Philosophy. Men's powerlifting: 105-kg class, world record holder. Main stockholder of Tree of Life, the largest maker of handheld devices, etc.
Wangari E. Dorado (38)
Doctor of Medicine, surgeon. Representative of an international humanitarian group. Main stockholder of Northstar Oil, etc.
Kenrock Hisashige (50)
Master of Economics. Top shareholder of the business group AEE, the world's largest developer in the fields of finance, rail, AI and military robotics, etc.
Elone Shinkai (29)
Doctor of Mechanics, Master of Archaeology. Head of the ancient martial arts school Shinguryu. Main stockholder of the Japanese, German and Roman branches of RX Group, the world's largest electronic commerce corporation, etc.
THE TOTAL VALUE OF THE ASSETS...
...POSSESSED BY THOSE PRESENT...

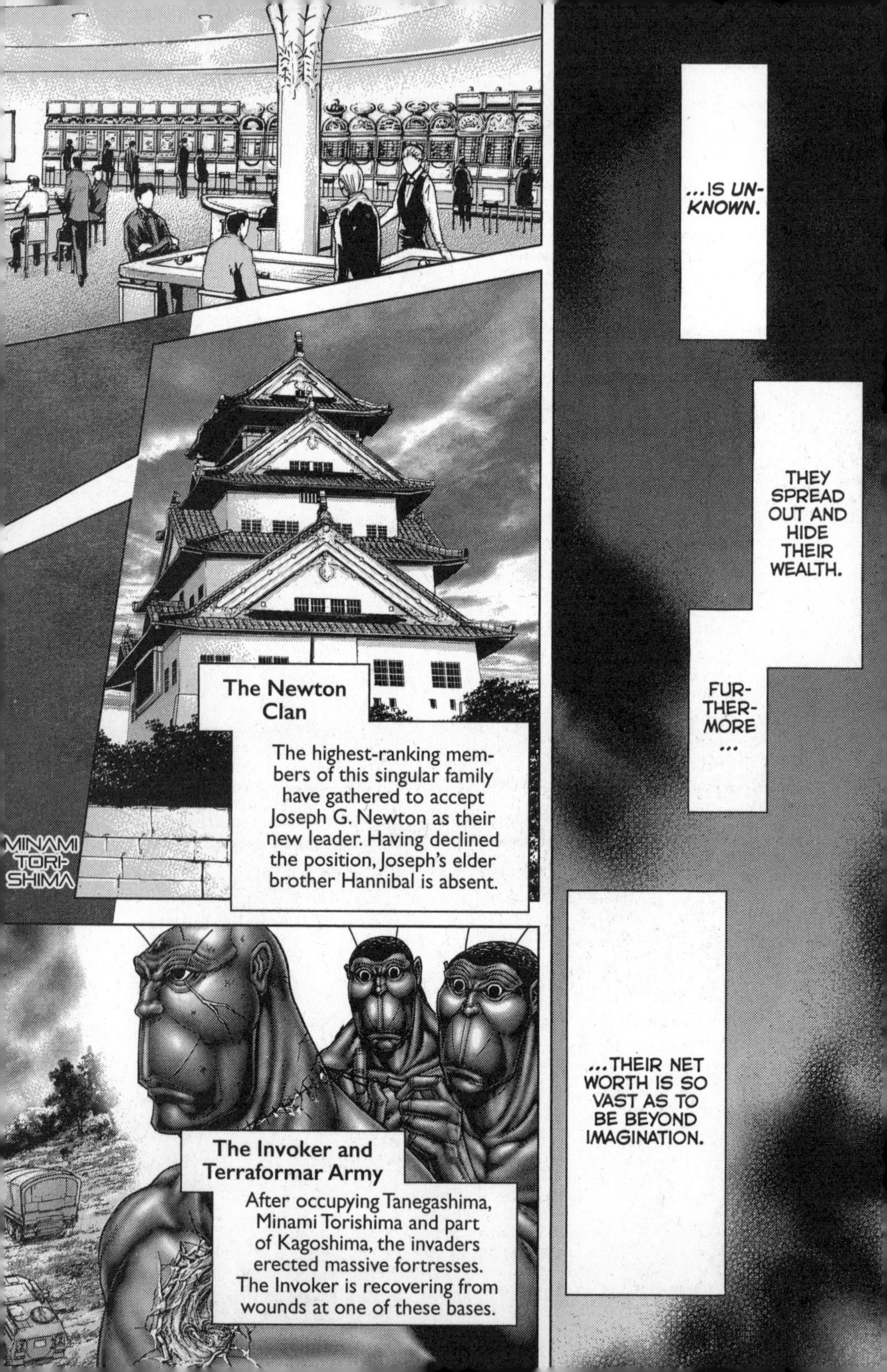

...IS UN-KNOWN.
THEY SPREAD OUT AND HIDE THEIR WEALTH.
FUR-THER-MORE...
...THEIR NET WORTH IS SO VAST AS TO BE BEYOND IMAGINATION.
The Newton Clan
The highest-ranking members of this singular family have gathered to accept Joseph G. Newton as their new leader. Having declined the position, Joseph's elder brother Hannibal is absent.
MINAMI TORI-SHIMA
The Invoker and Terraformar Army
After occupying Tanegashima, Minami Torishima and part of Kagoshima, the invaders erected massive fortresses. The Invoker is recovering from wounds at one of these bases.

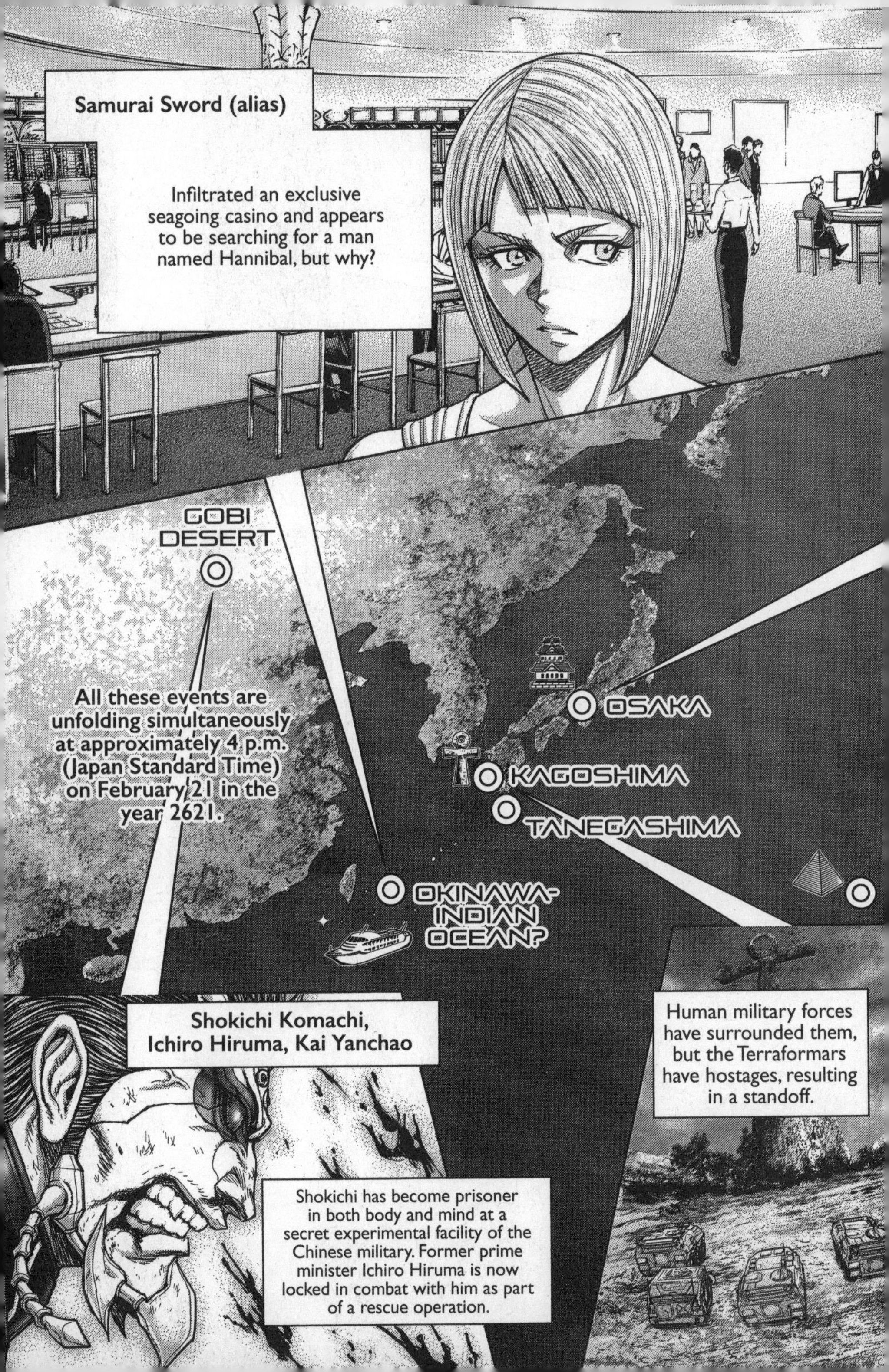
Samurai Sword (alias)
Infiltrated an exclusive seagoing casino and appears to be searching for a man named Hannibal, but why?
GOBI DESERT
OSAKA
KAGOSHIMA
TANEGASHIMA
All these events are unfolding simultaneously at approximately 4 p.m. (Japan Standard Time) on February 21 in the year 2621.
OKINAWA-INDIAN OCEAN?
Human military forces have surrounded them, but the Terraformars have hostages, resulting in a standoff.
Shokichi Komachi, Ichiro Hiruma, Kai Yanchao
Shokichi has become prisoner in both body and mind at a secret experimental facility of the Chinese military. Former prime minister Ichiro Hiruma is now locked in combat with him as part of a rescue operation.

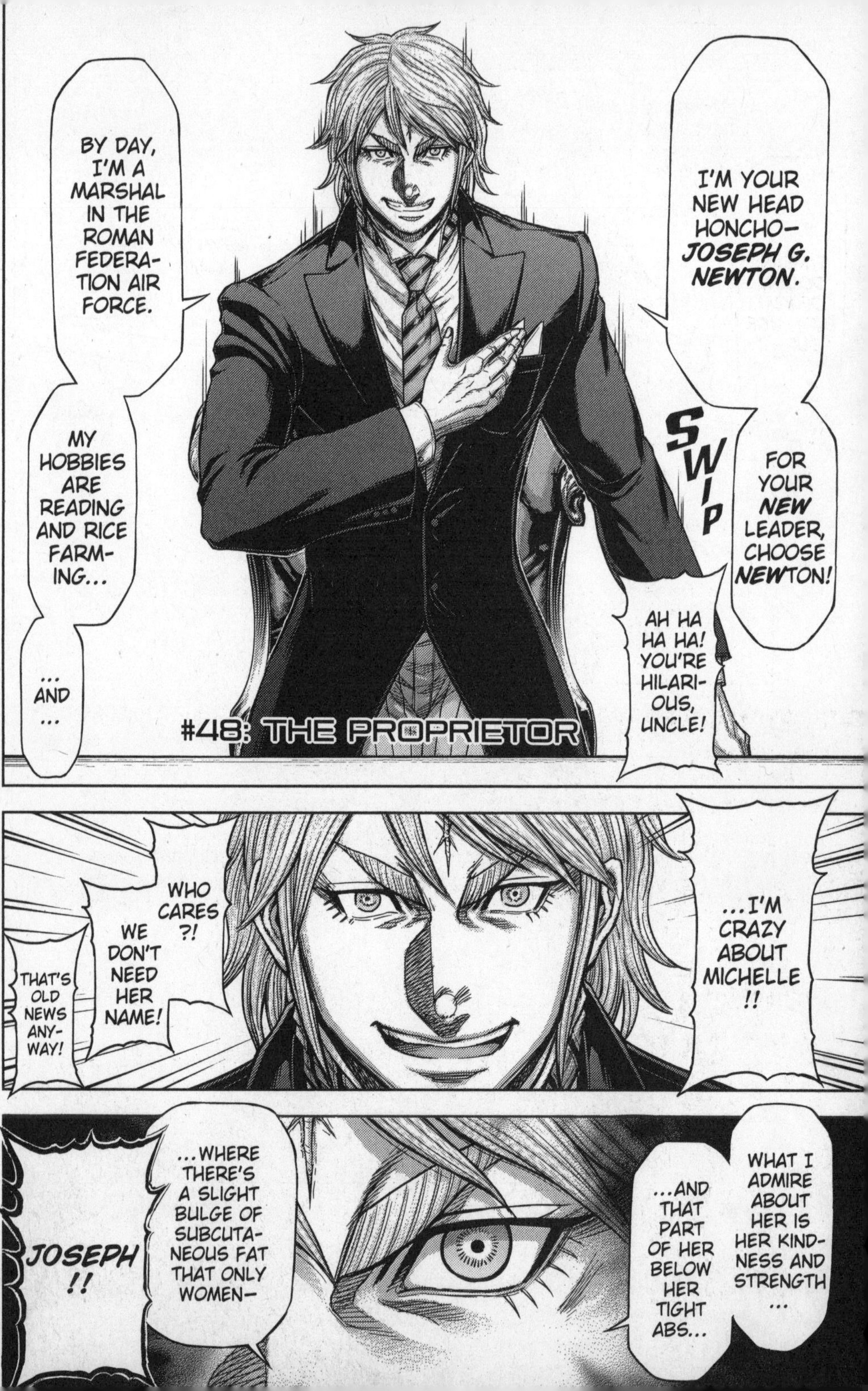
I'M YOUR NEW HEAD HONCHO—JOSEPH G. NEWTON.
BY DAY, I'M A MARSHAL IN THE ROMAN FEDERATION AIR FORCE.
SWIP
FOR YOUR NEW LEADER, CHOOSE NEWTON!
MY HOBBIES ARE READING AND RICE FARMING...
AH HA HA HA! YOU'RE HILARIOUS, UNCLE!
... AND ...
#48: THE PROPRIETOR
...I'M CRAZY ABOUT MICHELLE!!
WHO CARES?!
WE DON'T NEED HER NAME!
THAT'S OLD NEWS ANYWAY!
WHAT I ADMIRE ABOUT HER IS HER KINDNESS AND STRENGTH...
...AND THAT PART OF HER BELOW HER TIGHT ABS...
...WHERE THERE'S A SLIGHT BULGE OF SUBCUTANEOUS FAT THAT ONLY WOMEN—
JOSEPH!!

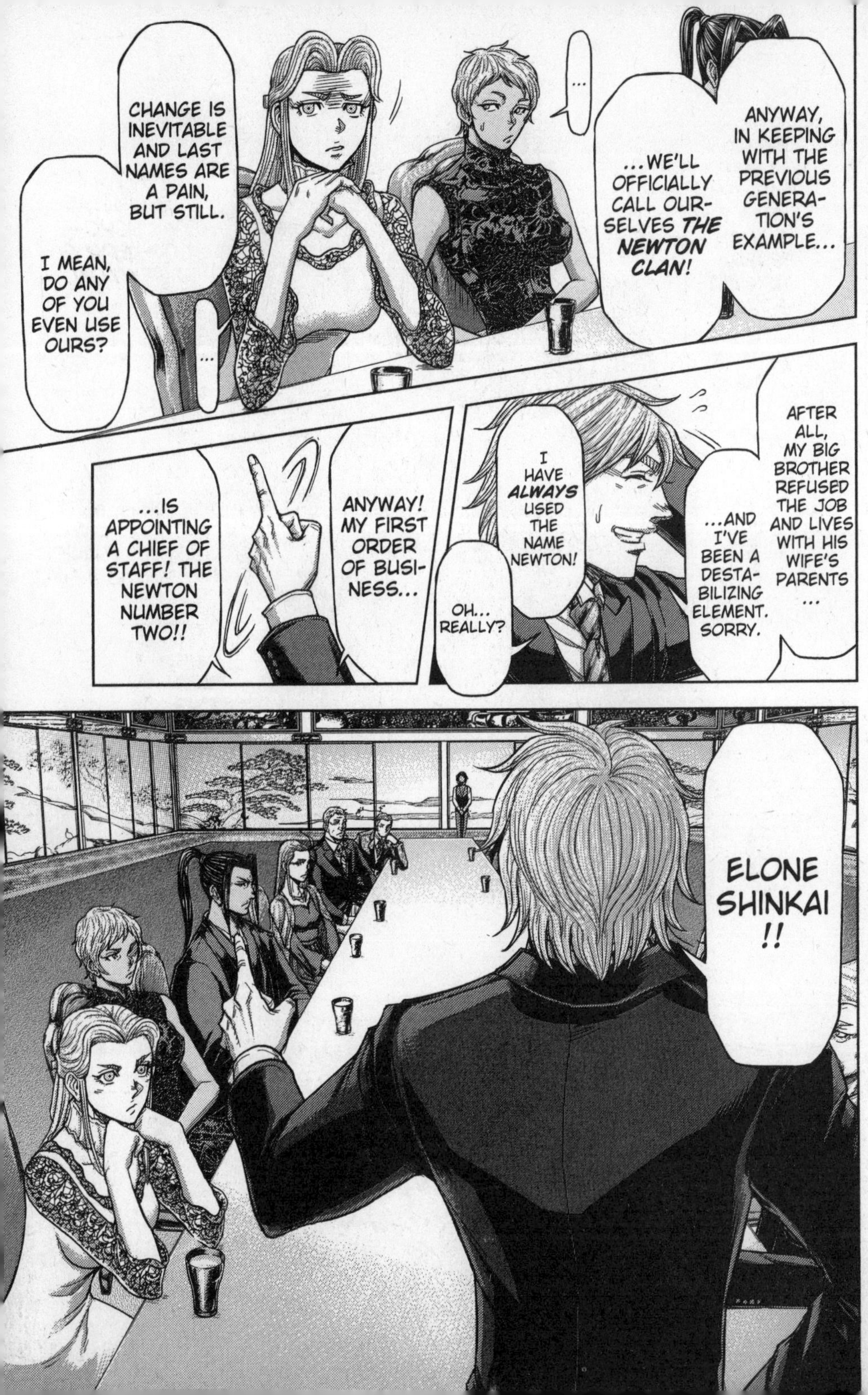
ANYWAY, IN KEEPING WITH THE PREVIOUS GENERATION'S EXAMPLE...
...WE'LL OFFICIALLY CALL OURSELVES ***THE NEWTON CLAN***!
...
CHANGE IS INEVITABLE AND LAST NAMES ARE A PAIN, BUT STILL.
I MEAN, DO ANY OF YOU EVEN USE OURS?
...
AFTER ALL, MY BIG BROTHER REFUSED THE JOB AND LIVES WITH HIS WIFE'S PARENTS...
...AND I'VE BEEN A DESTABILIZING ELEMENT. SORRY.
I HAVE ***ALWAYS*** USED THE NAME NEWTON!
OH... REALLY?
ANYWAY! MY FIRST ORDER OF BUSINESS...
...IS APPOINTING A CHIEF OF STAFF! THE NEWTON NUMBER TWO!!
ELONE SHINKAI !!

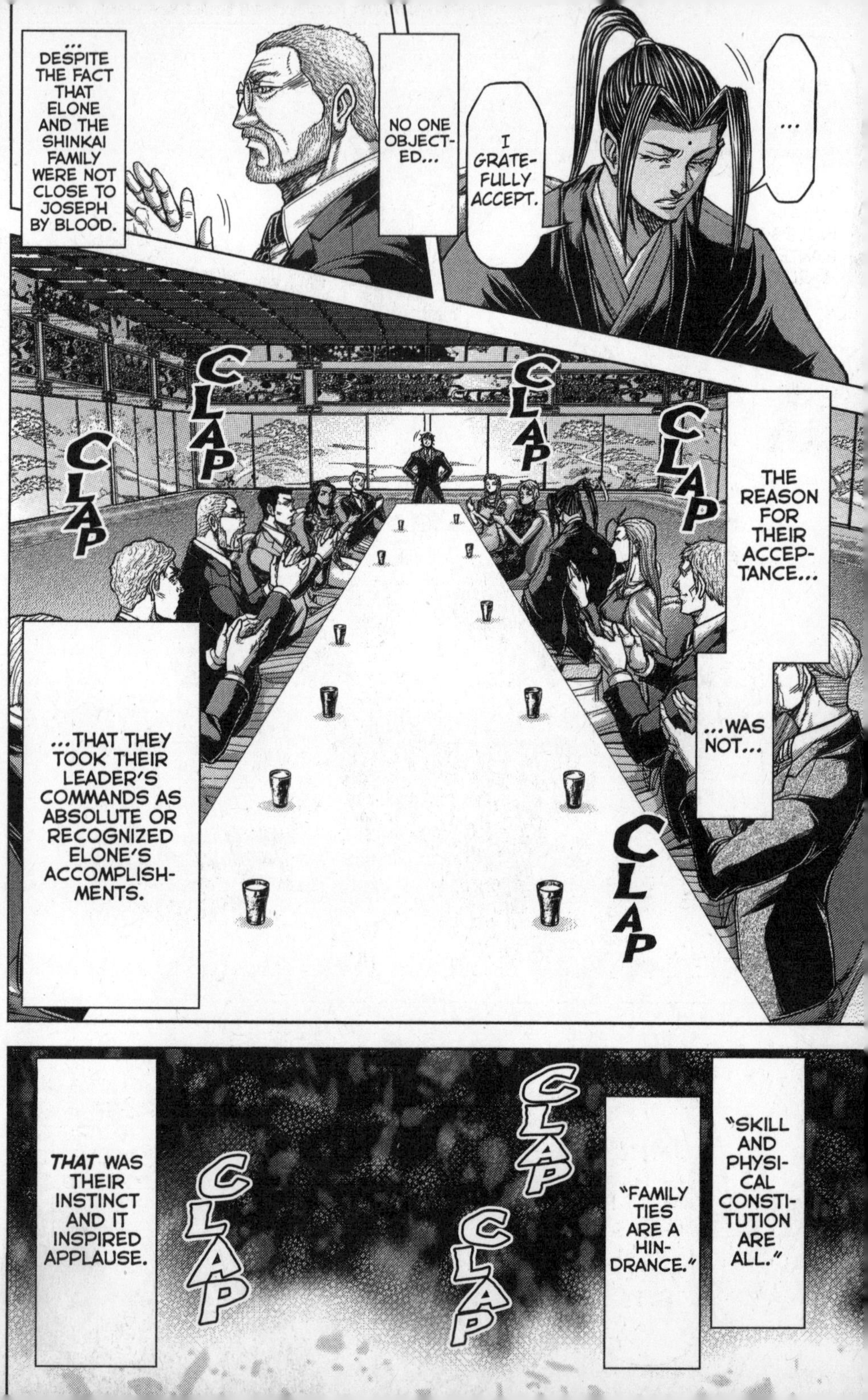
...
I GRATEFULLY ACCEPT.
NO ONE OBJECTED...
...DESPITE THE FACT THAT ELONE AND THE SHINKAI FAMILY WERE NOT CLOSE TO JOSEPH BY BLOOD.
CLAP CLAP CLAP CLAP CLAP CLAP
THE REASON FOR THEIR ACCEPTANCE...
...WAS NOT...
...THAT THEY TOOK THEIR LEADER'S COMMANDS AS ABSOLUTE OR RECOGNIZED ELONE'S ACCOMPLISHMENTS.
"SKILL AND PHYSICAL CONSTITUTION ARE ALL."
"FAMILY TIES ARE A HINDRANCE."
CLAP CLAP CLAP
*THAT* WAS THEIR INSTINCT AND IT INSPIRED APPLAUSE.

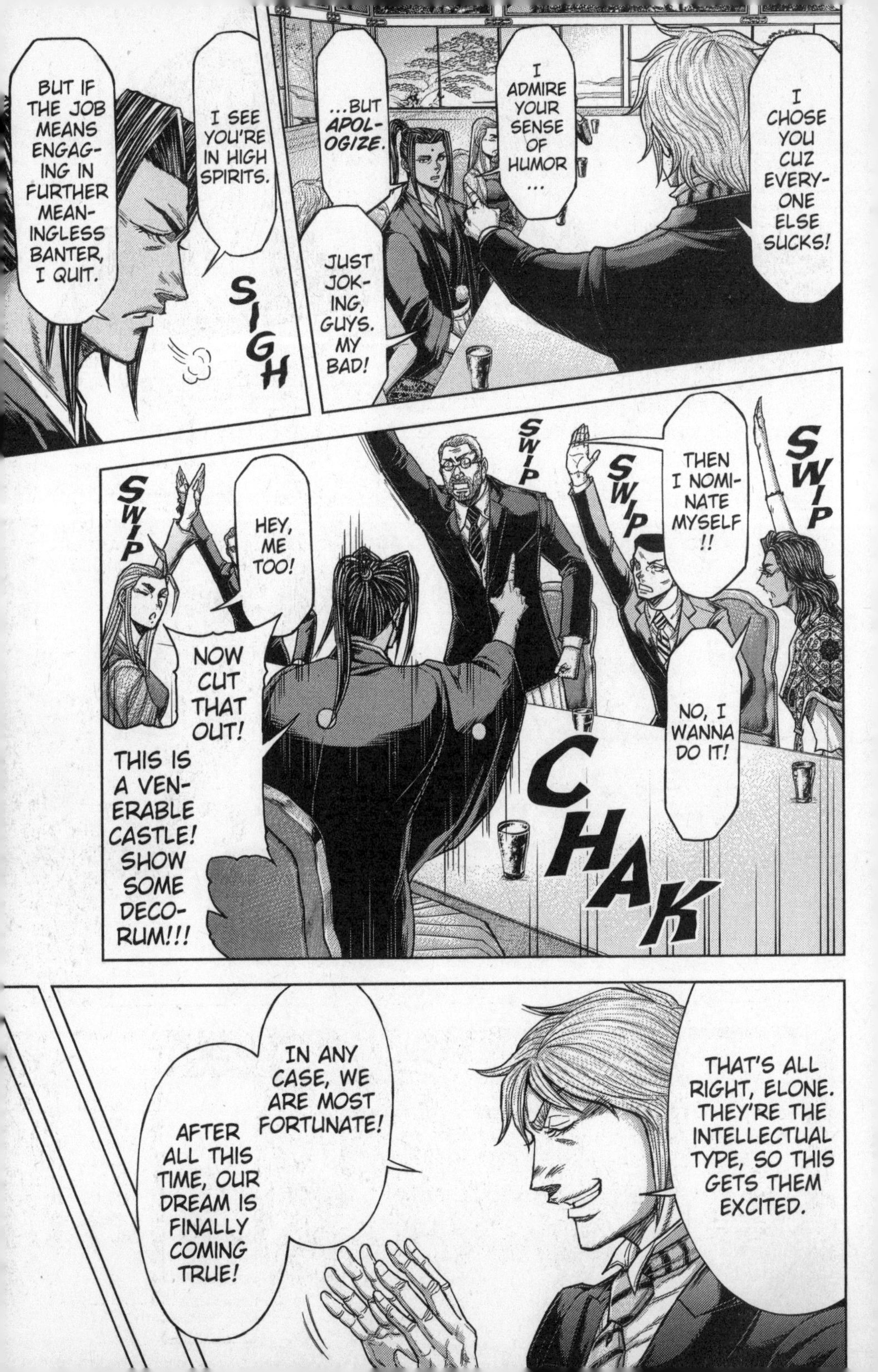

I CHOSE YOU CUZ EVERYONE ELSE SUCKS!
I ADMIRE YOUR SENSE OF HUMOR...
...BUT APOLOGIZE.
JUST JOKING, GUYS. MY BAD!
I SEE YOU'RE IN HIGH SPIRITS.
SIGH
BUT IF THE JOB MEANS ENGAGING IN FURTHER MEANINGLESS BANTER, I QUIT.
SWIP
THEN I NOMINATE MYSELF!!
SWIP
SWIP
NO, I WANNA DO IT!
HEY, ME TOO!
SWIP
CHAK
NOW CUT THAT OUT!
THIS IS A VENERABLE CASTLE! SHOW SOME DECORUM!!!
THAT'S ALL RIGHT, ELONE. THEY'RE THE INTELLECTUAL TYPE, SO THIS GETS THEM EXCITED.
IN ANY CASE, WE ARE MOST FORTUNATE!
AFTER ALL THIS TIME, OUR DREAM IS FINALLY COMING TRUE!

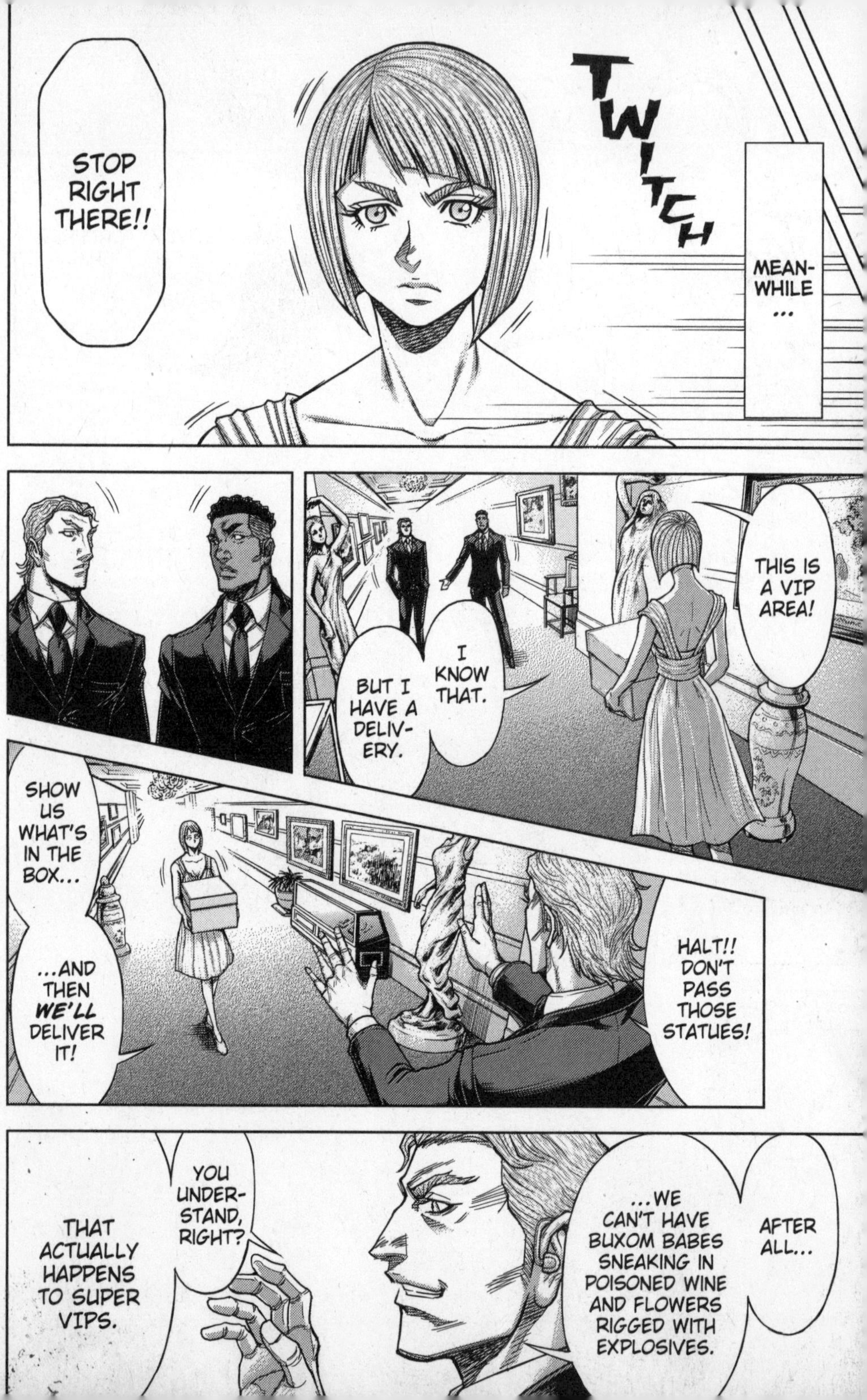
MEAN-WHILE...
TWITCH
STOP RIGHT THERE!!
THIS IS A VIP AREA!
I KNOW THAT.
BUT I HAVE A DELIV-ERY.
HALT!! DON'T PASS THOSE STATUES!
SHOW US WHAT'S IN THE BOX...
...AND THEN *WE'LL* DELIVER IT!
AFTER ALL...
...WE CAN'T HAVE BUXOM BABES SNEAKING IN POISONED WINE AND FLOWERS RIGGED WITH EXPLOSIVES.
YOU UNDER-STAND, RIGHT?
THAT ACTUALLY HAPPENS TO SUPER VIPS.

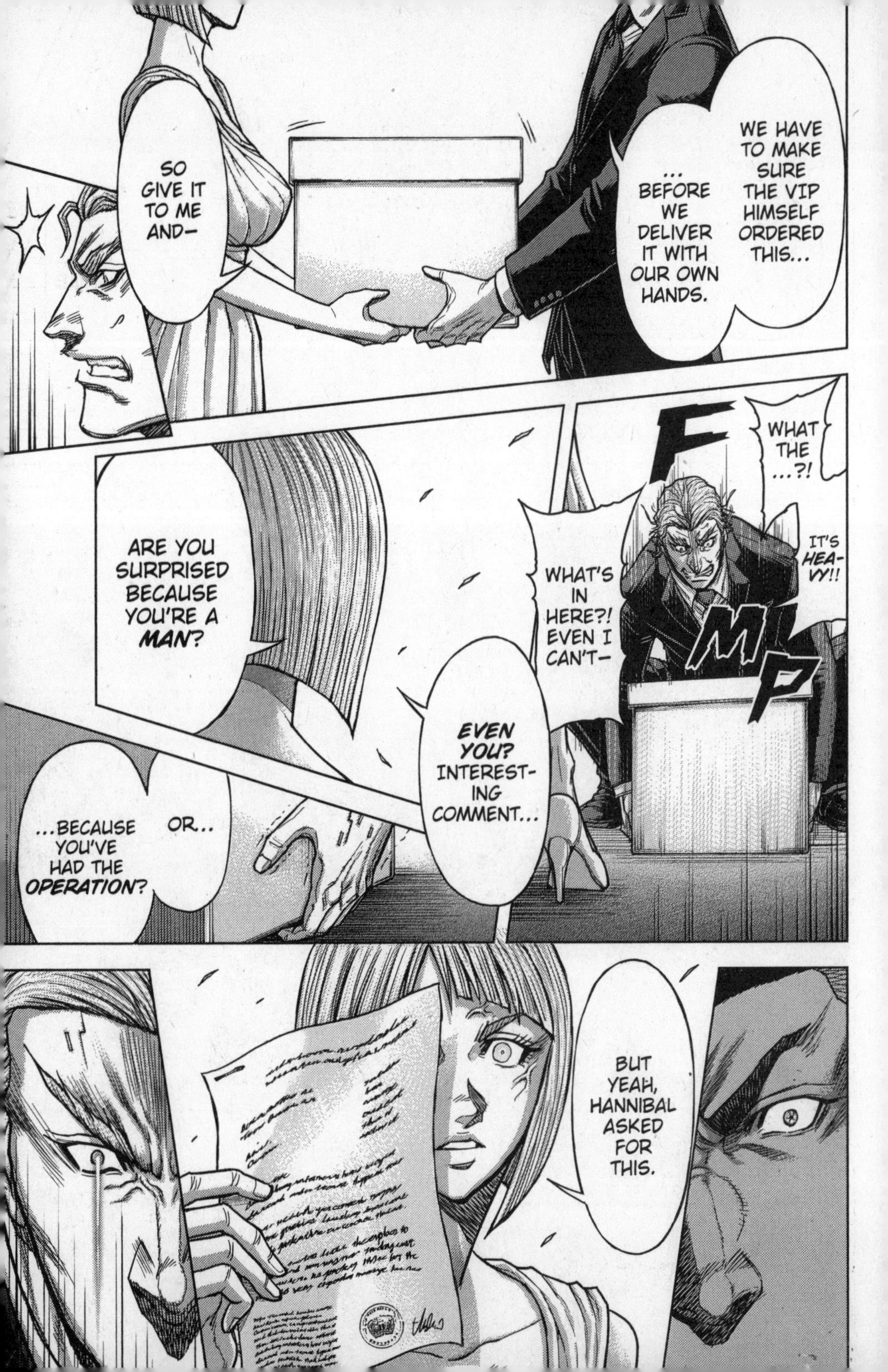
WE HAVE TO MAKE SURE THE VIP HIMSELF ORDERED THIS...
...BEFORE WE DELIVER IT WITH OUR OWN HANDS.
SO GIVE IT TO ME AND—
WHAT THE ...?!
FMP
IT'S HEAVY!!
WHAT'S IN HERE?! EVEN I CAN'T—
EVEN YOU? INTERESTING COMMENT...
ARE YOU SURPRISED BECAUSE YOU'RE A MAN?
OR...
...BECAUSE YOU'VE HAD THE OPERATION?
BUT YEAH, HANNIBAL ASKED FOR THIS.

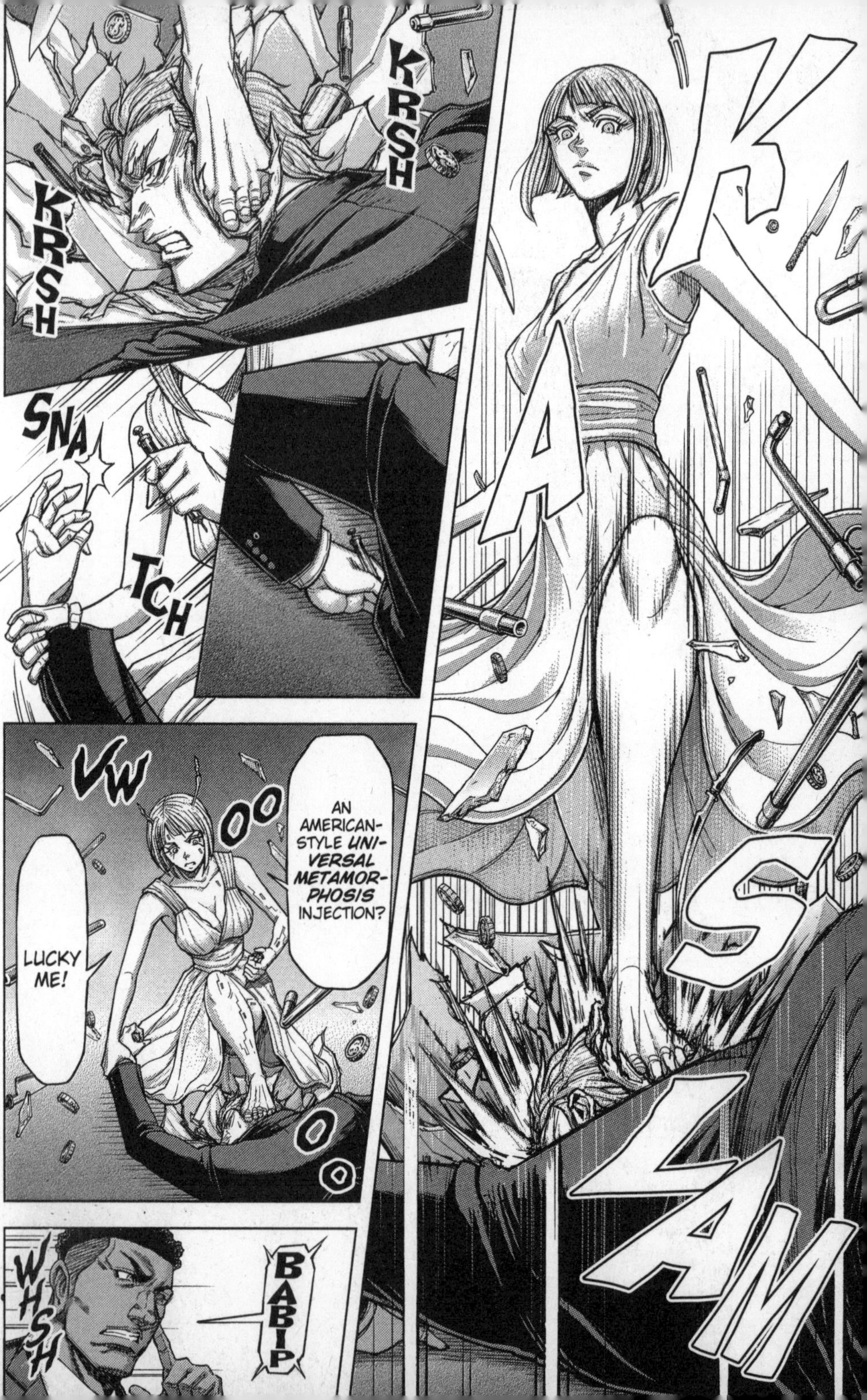
KA
SLAM
KRSH
KRSH
SNATCH
VWOOO
AN AMERICAN-STYLE UNIVERSAL METAMORPHOSIS INJECTION?
LUCKY ME!
BABIP
WHSH

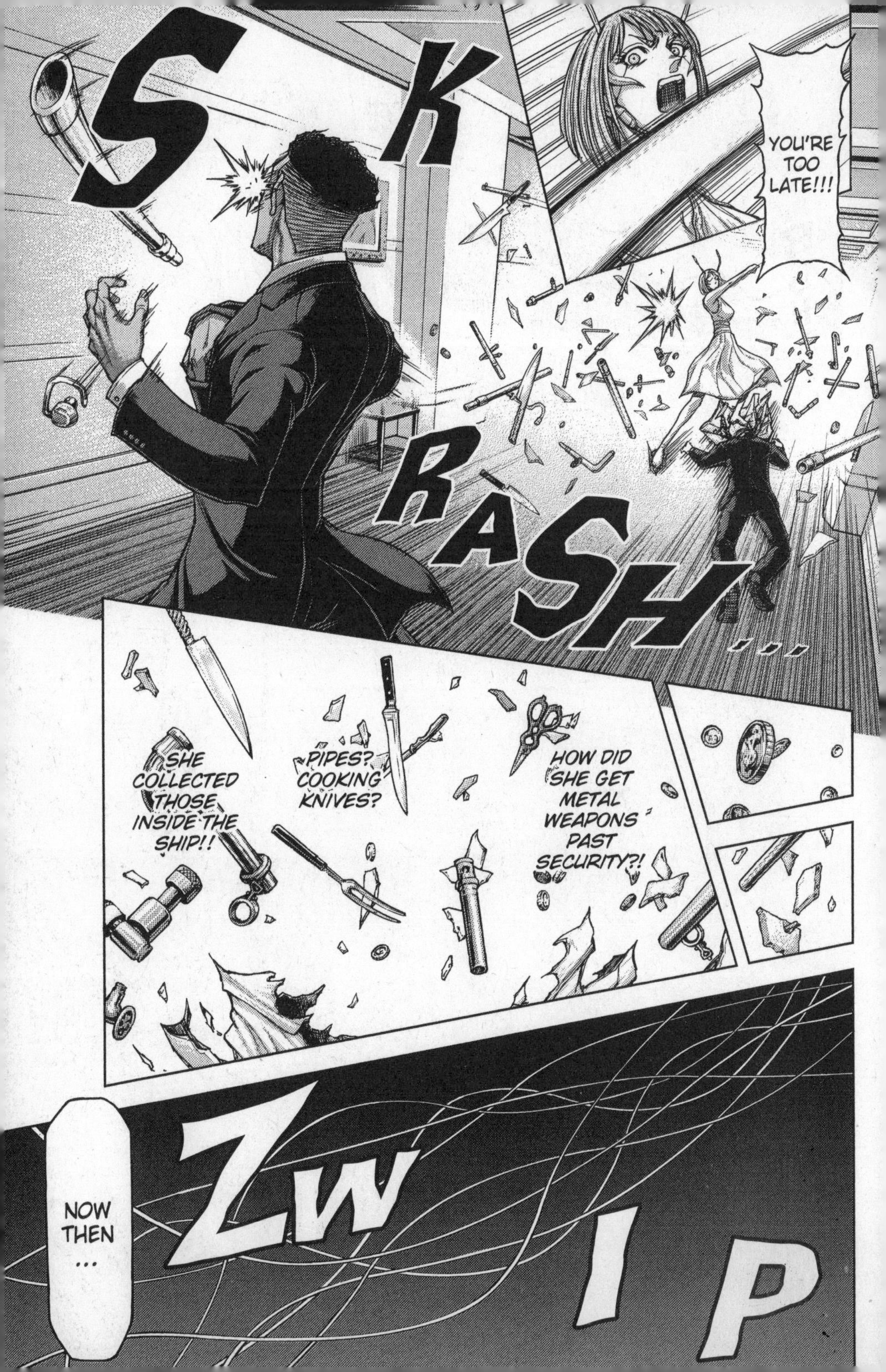
YOU'RE TOO LATE!!!
SKRASH...
HOW DID SHE GET METAL WEAPONS PAST SECURITY?!
PIPES? COOKING KNIVES?
SHE COLLECTED THOSE INSIDE THE SHIP!!
ZWIP
NOW THEN ...

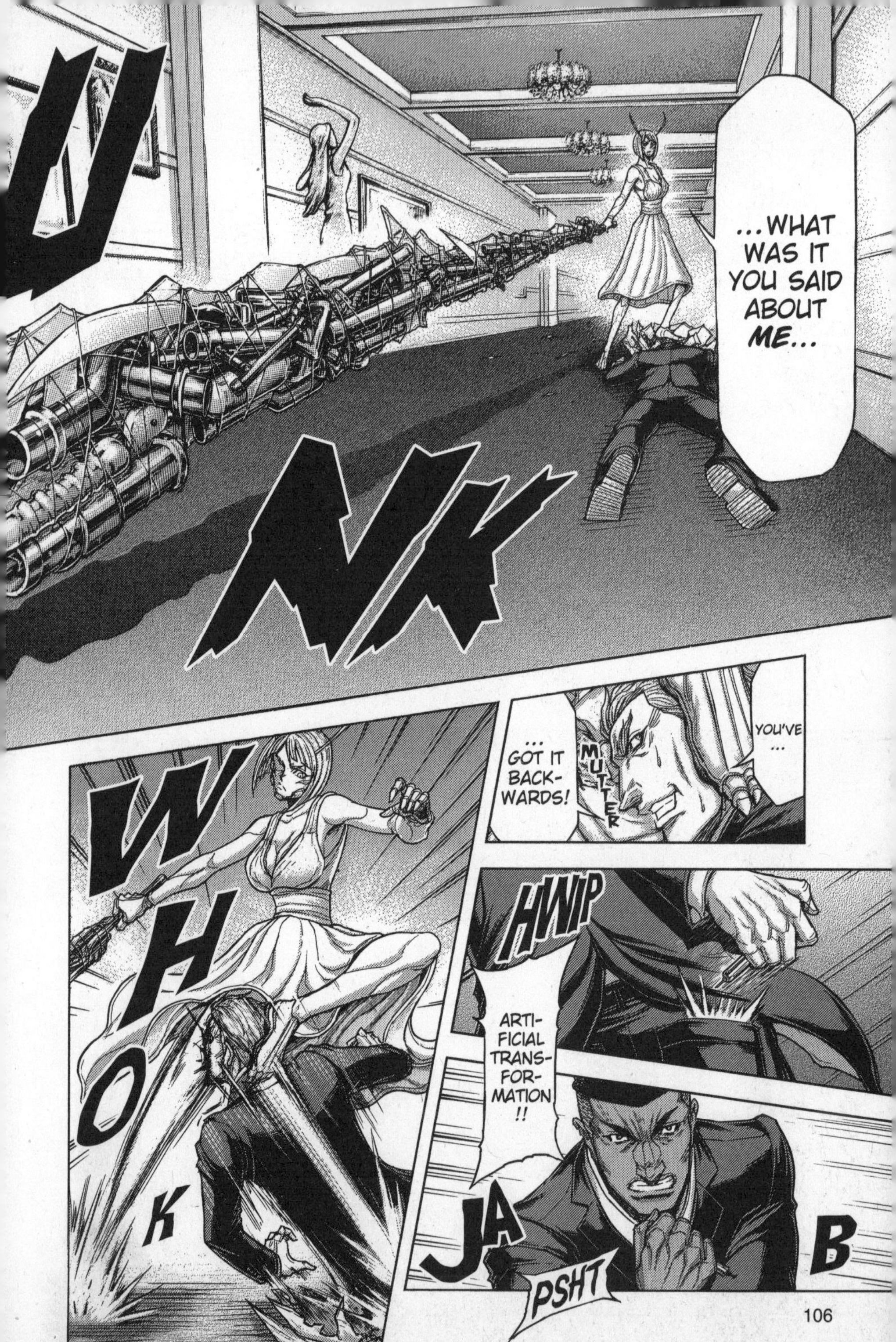
...WHAT WAS IT YOU SAID ABOUT ME...
U
NK
YOU'VE ...
MUTTER
... GOT IT BACKWARDS!
HWIP
ARTIFICIAL TRANSFORMATION!!
JAB
PSHT
WHOK

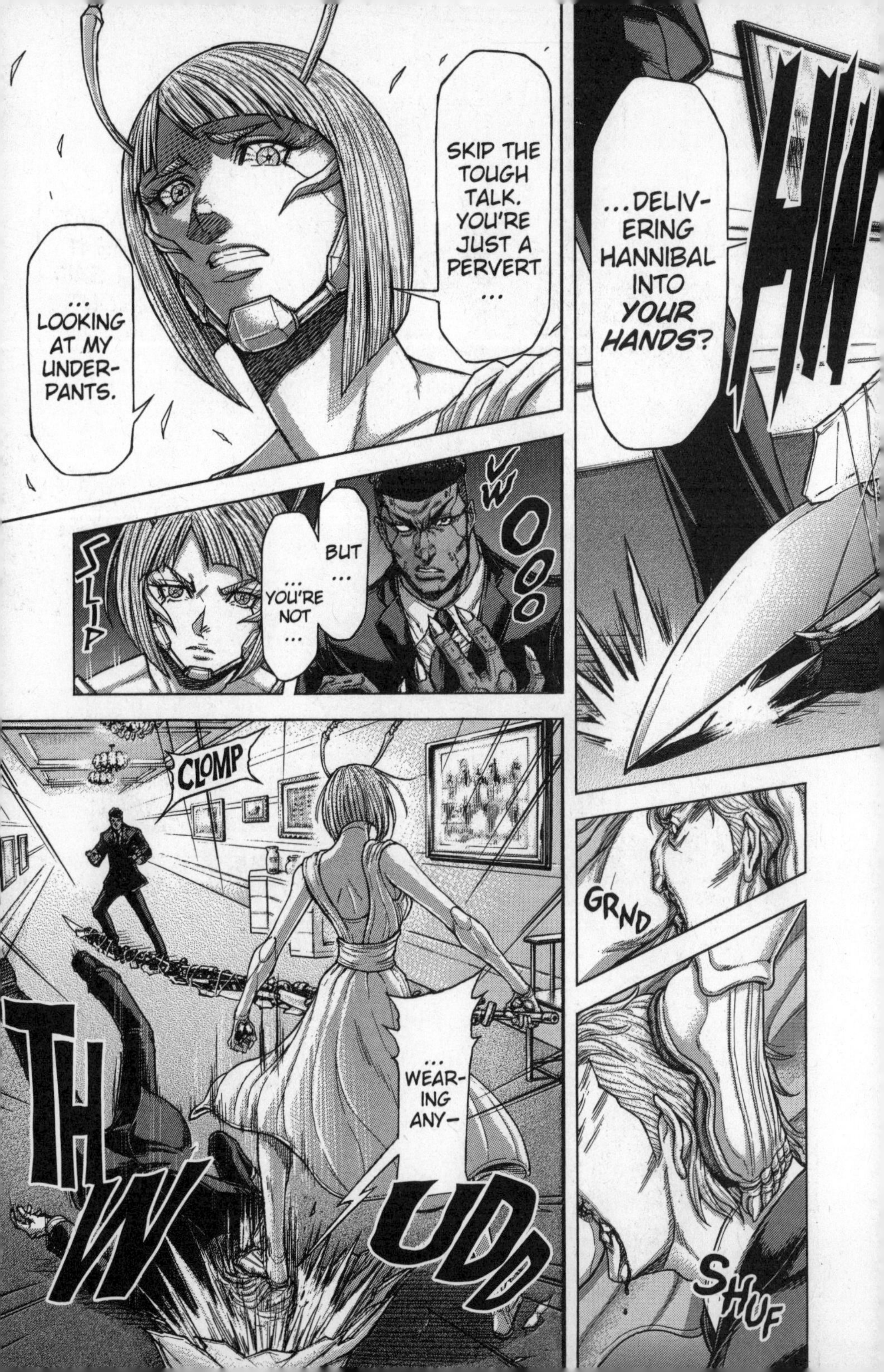
...DELIV-ERING HANNIBAL INTO *YOUR HANDS*?
SKIP THE TOUGH TALK. YOU'RE JUST A PERVERT ...
... LOOKING AT MY UNDER-PANTS.
VWOOO
BUT ...
... YOU'RE NOT ...
SLIP
CLOMP
... WEAR-ING ANY-
THWUDD
GRND
SHUF

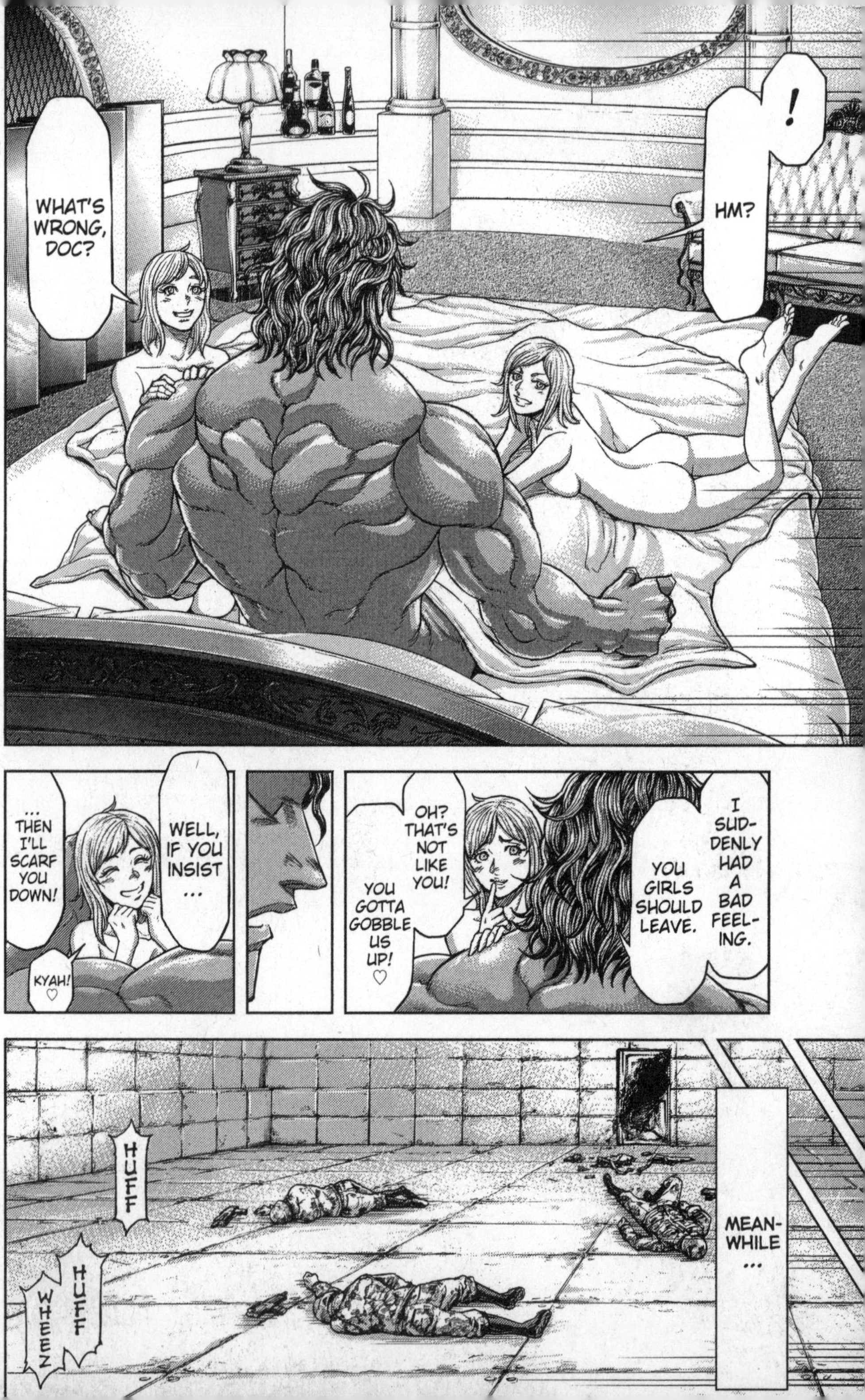
!
HM?
WHAT'S WRONG, DOC?
I SUDDENLY HAD A BAD FEELING.
YOU GIRLS SHOULD LEAVE.
OH? THAT'S NOT LIKE YOU!
YOU GOTTA GOBBLE US UP! ♡
WELL, IF YOU INSIST...
...THEN I'LL SCARF YOU DOWN!
KYAH! ♡
MEANWHILE...
HUFF
HUFF
WHEEZ

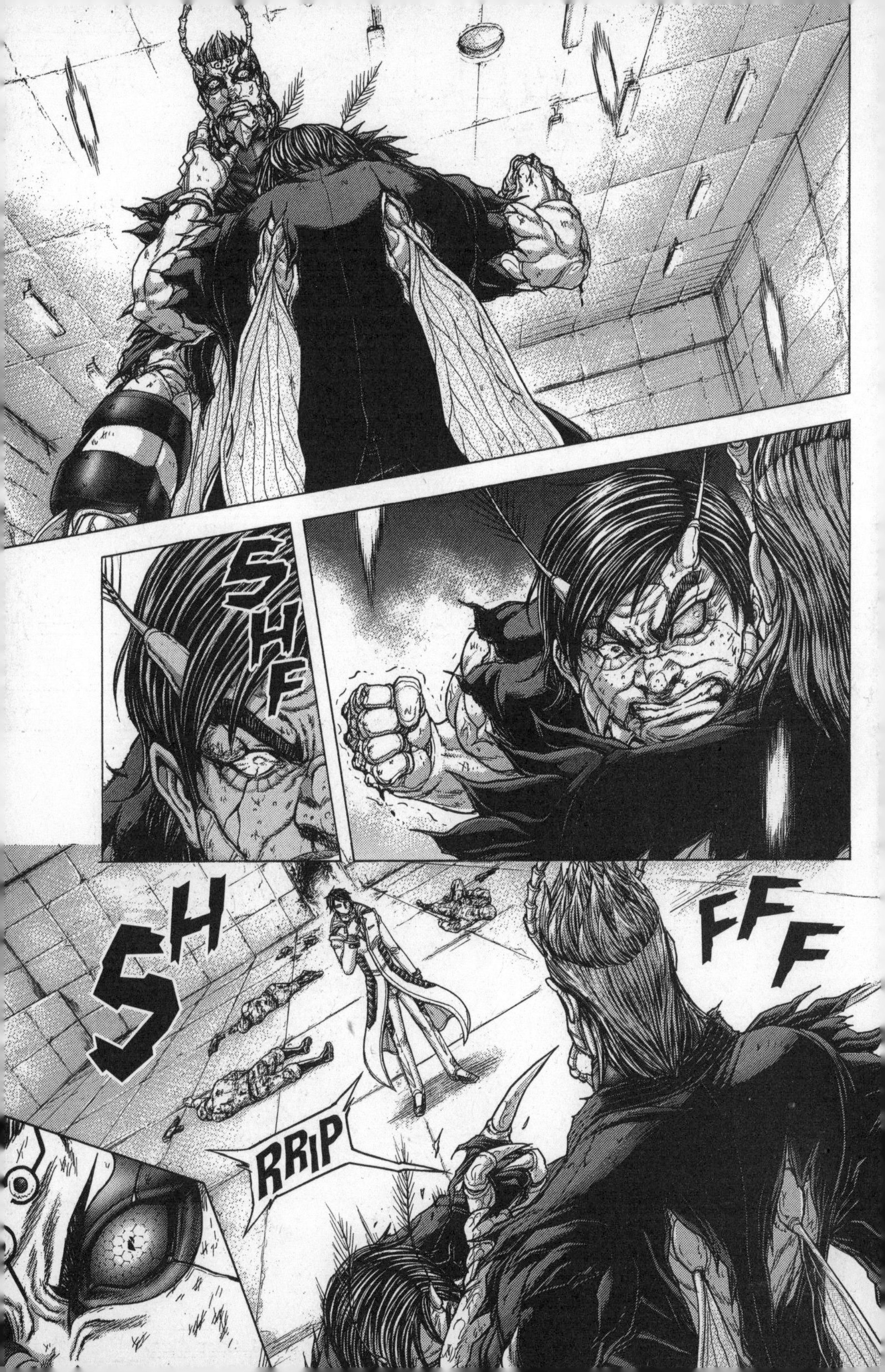
SHF
FFF
SH
RRIP

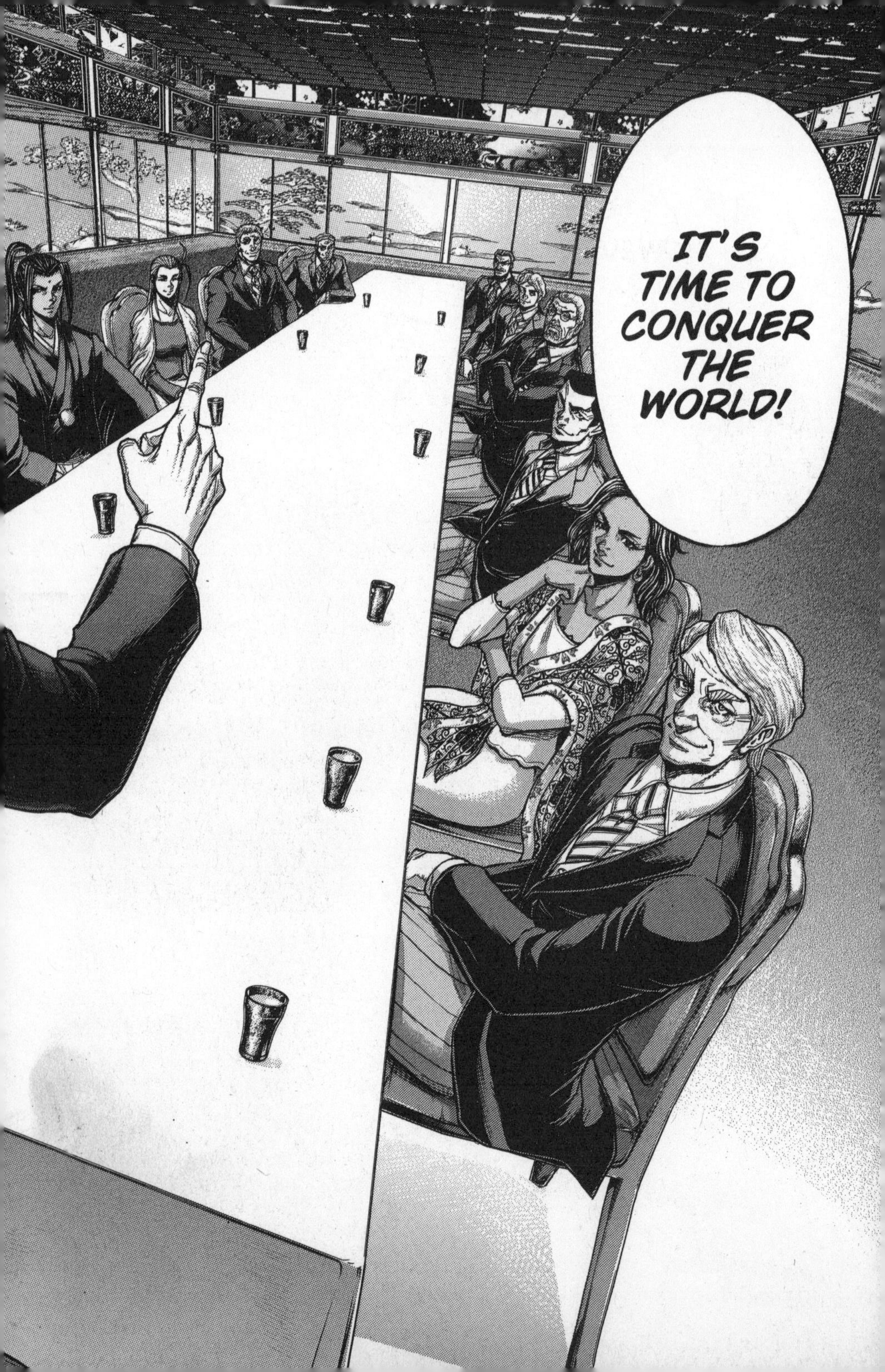
IT'S TIME TO CONQUER THE WORLD!

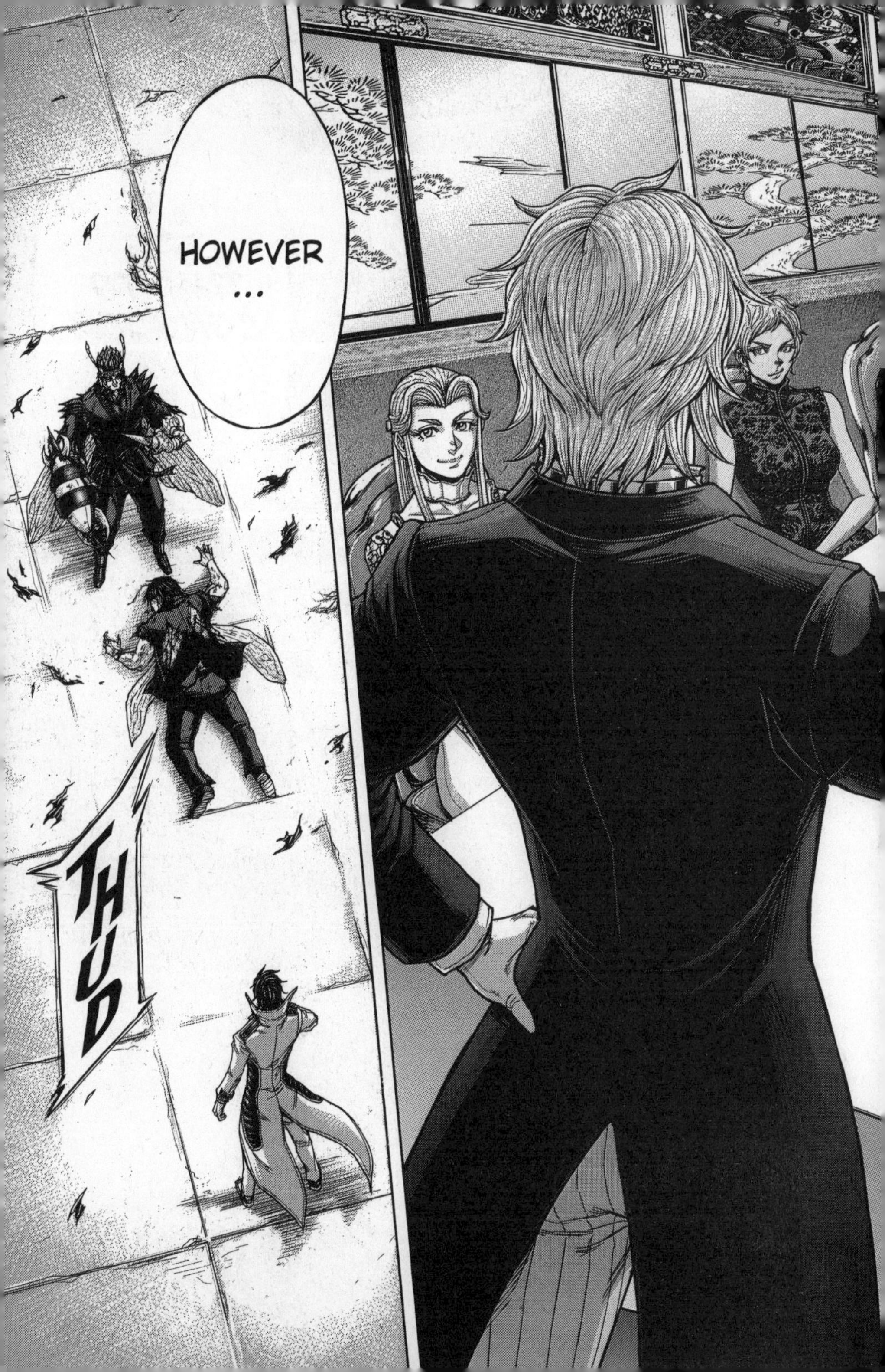
HOWEVER ...
THUD

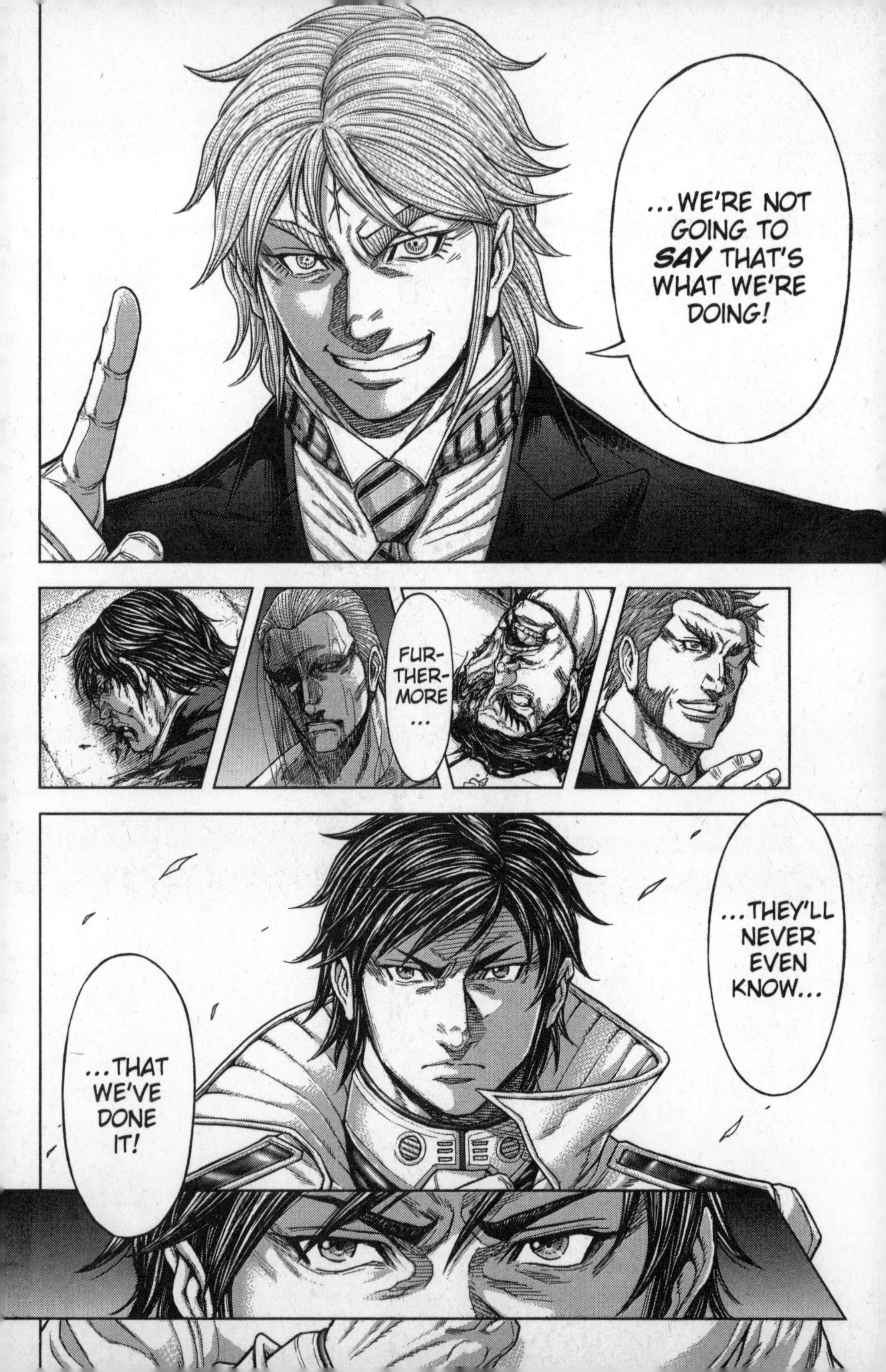
...WE'RE NOT GOING TO ***SAY*** THAT'S WHAT WE'RE DOING!
FUR-THER-MORE ...
...THEY'LL NEVER EVEN KNOW...
...THAT WE'VE DONE IT!

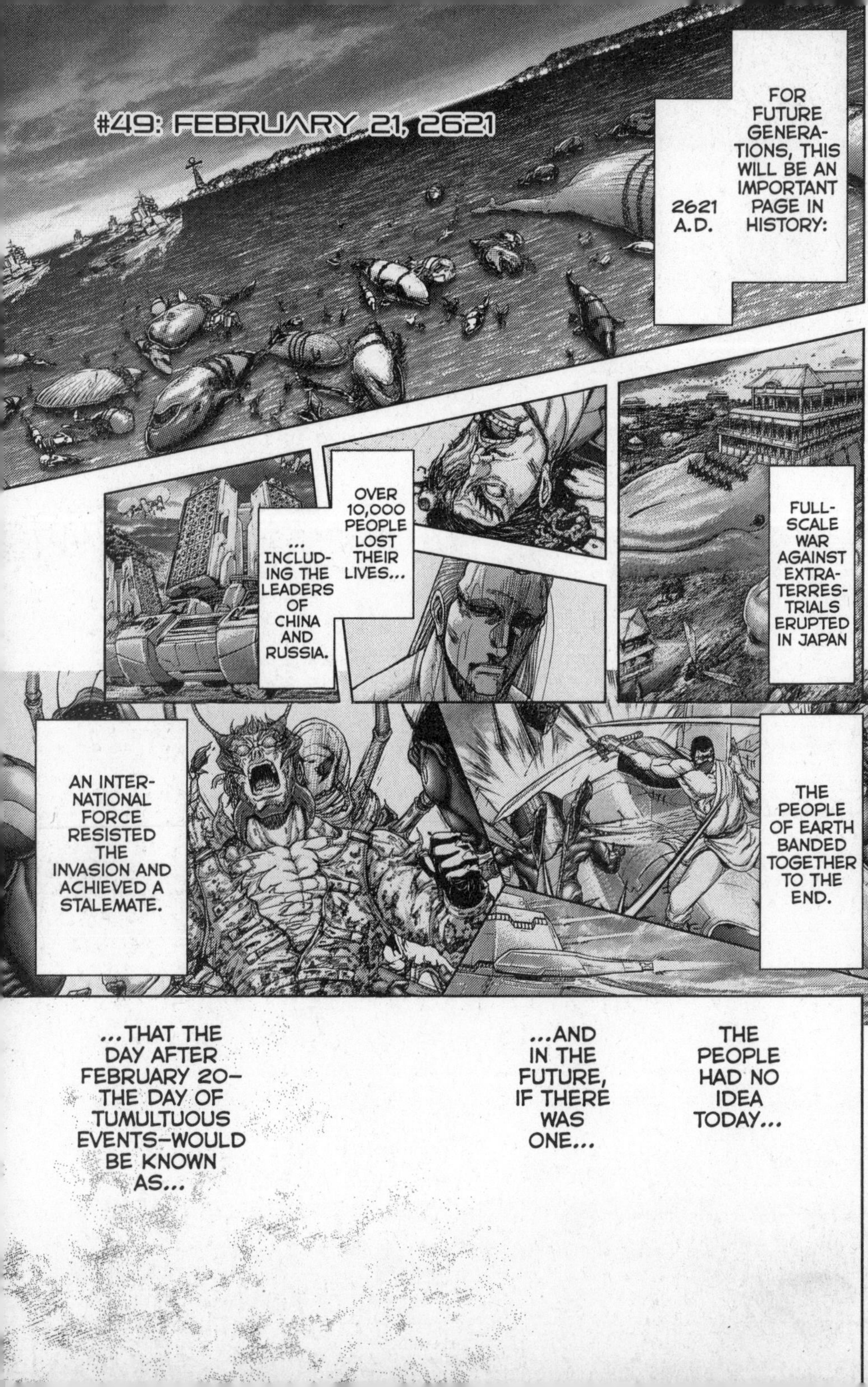
#49: FEBRUARY 21, 2621
FOR FUTURE GENERATIONS, THIS WILL BE AN IMPORTANT PAGE IN HISTORY:
2621 A.D.
FULL-SCALE WAR AGAINST EXTRATERRESTRIALS ERUPTED IN JAPAN
OVER 10,000 PEOPLE LOST THEIR LIVES...
...INCLUDING THE LEADERS OF CHINA AND RUSSIA.
THE PEOPLE OF EARTH BANDED TOGETHER TO THE END.
AN INTERNATIONAL FORCE RESISTED THE INVASION AND ACHIEVED A STALEMATE.
THE PEOPLE HAD NO IDEA TODAY...
...AND IN THE FUTURE, IF THERE WAS ONE...
...THAT THE DAY AFTER FEBRUARY 20—THE DAY OF TUMULTUOUS EVENTS—WOULD BE KNOWN AS...

# #49: FEBRUARY 21, 2621

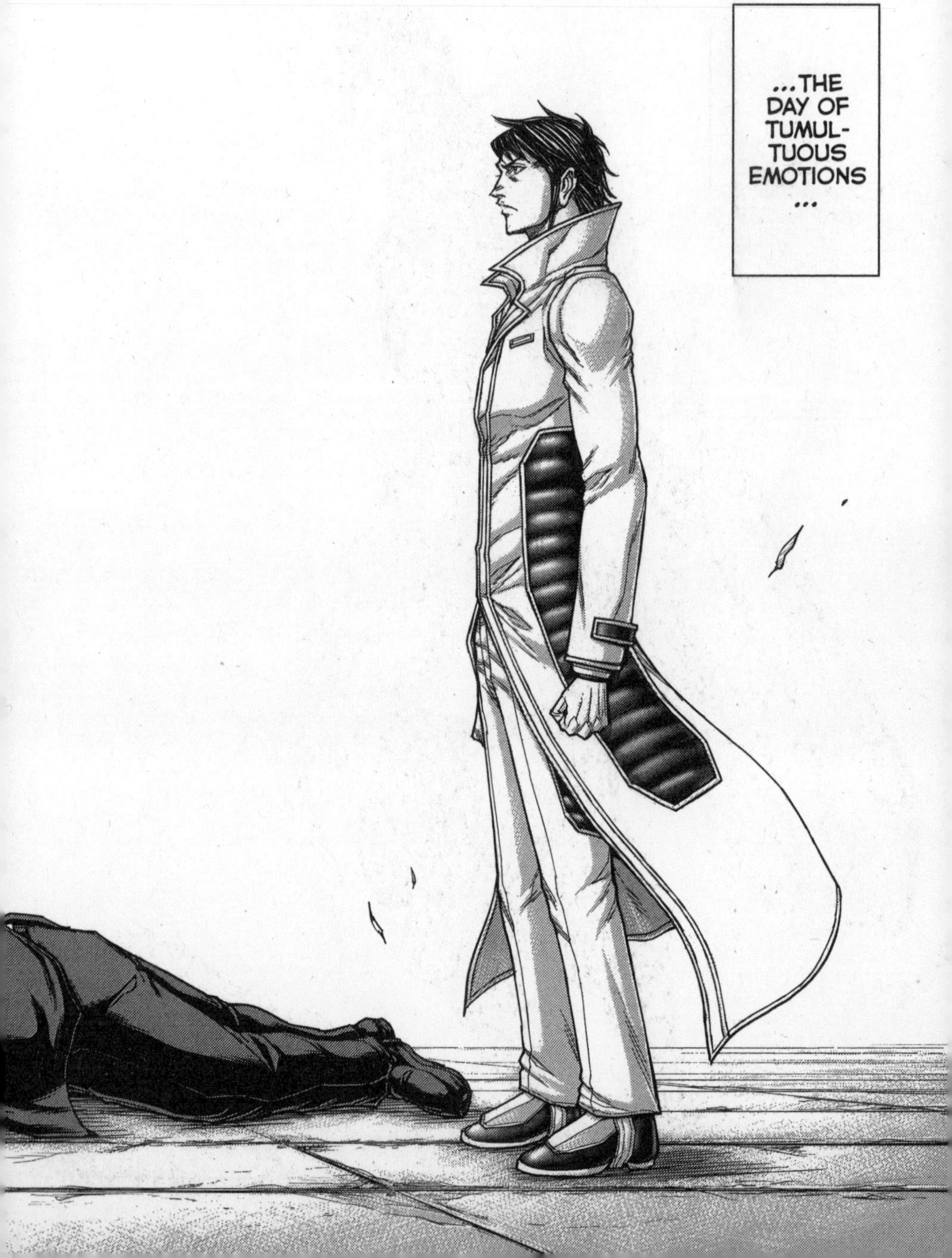
...THE DAY OF TUMUL-TUOUS EMOTIONS ...

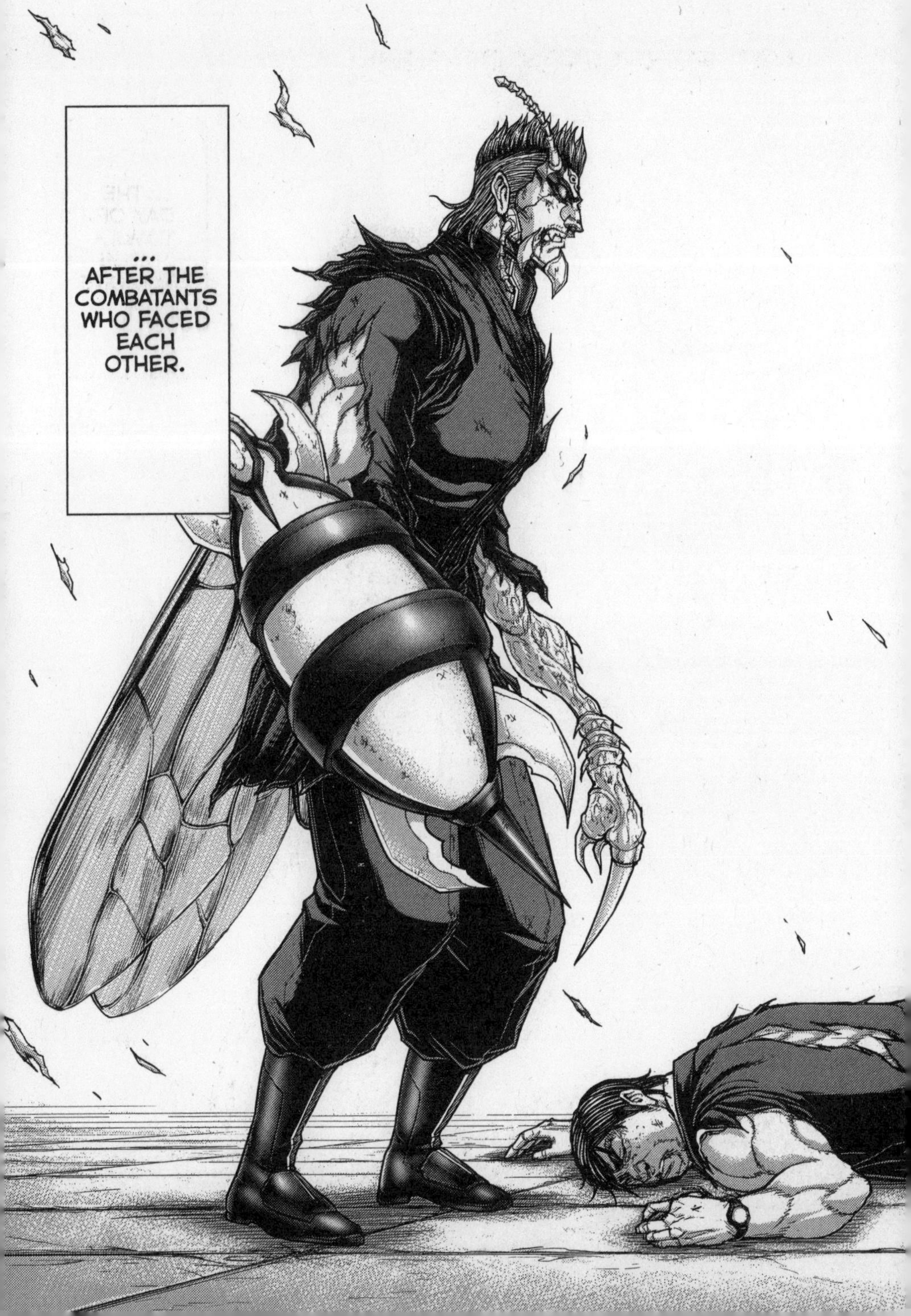
... AFTER THE COMBATANTS WHO FACED EACH OTHER.

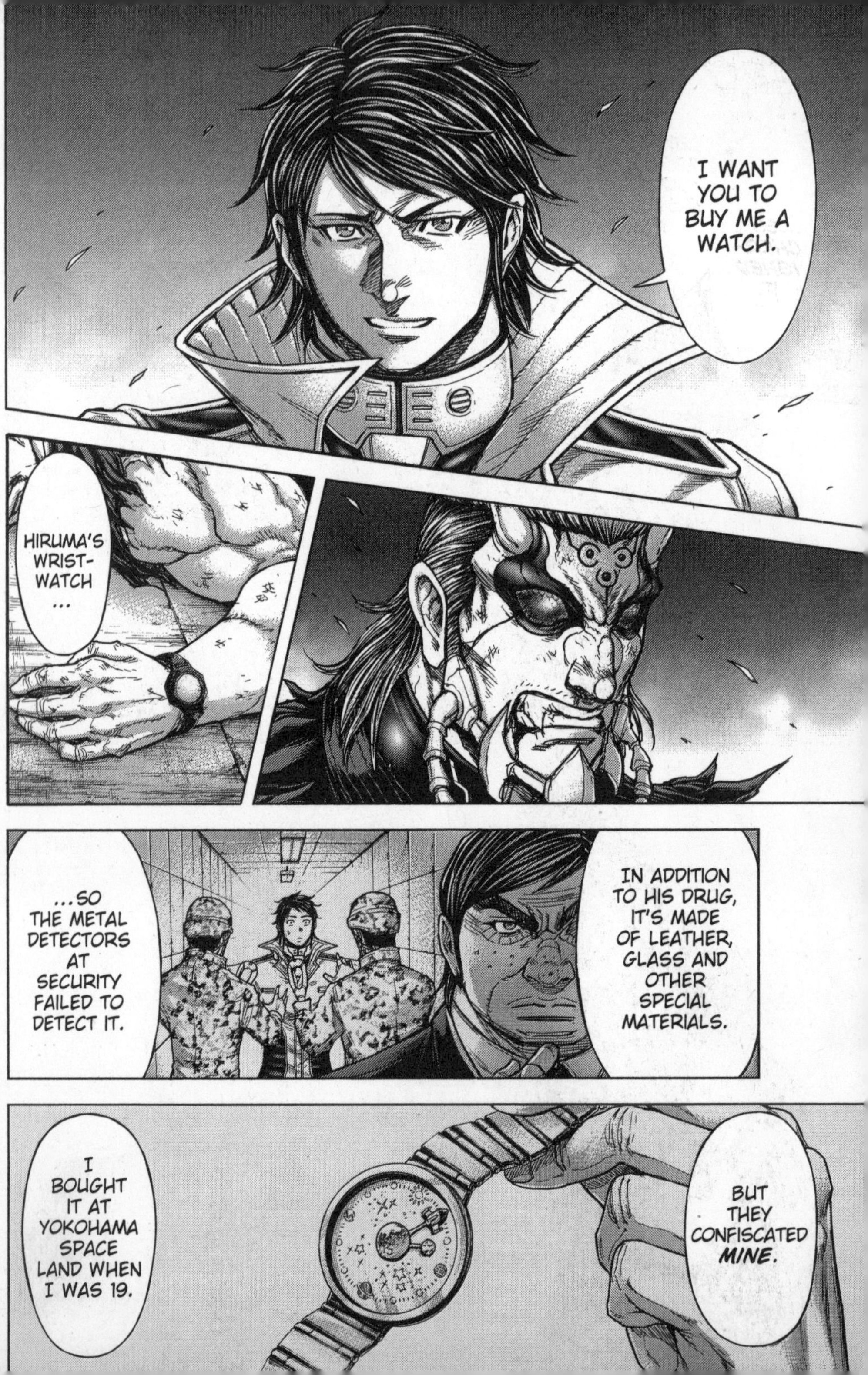
I WANT YOU TO BUY ME A WATCH.
HIRUMA'S WRIST-WATCH...
IN ADDITION TO HIS DRUG, IT'S MADE OF LEATHER, GLASS AND OTHER SPECIAL MATERIALS.
...SO THE METAL DETECTORS AT SECURITY FAILED TO DETECT IT.
BUT THEY CONFISCATED *MINE.*
I BOUGHT IT AT YOKOHAMA SPACE LAND WHEN I WAS 19.

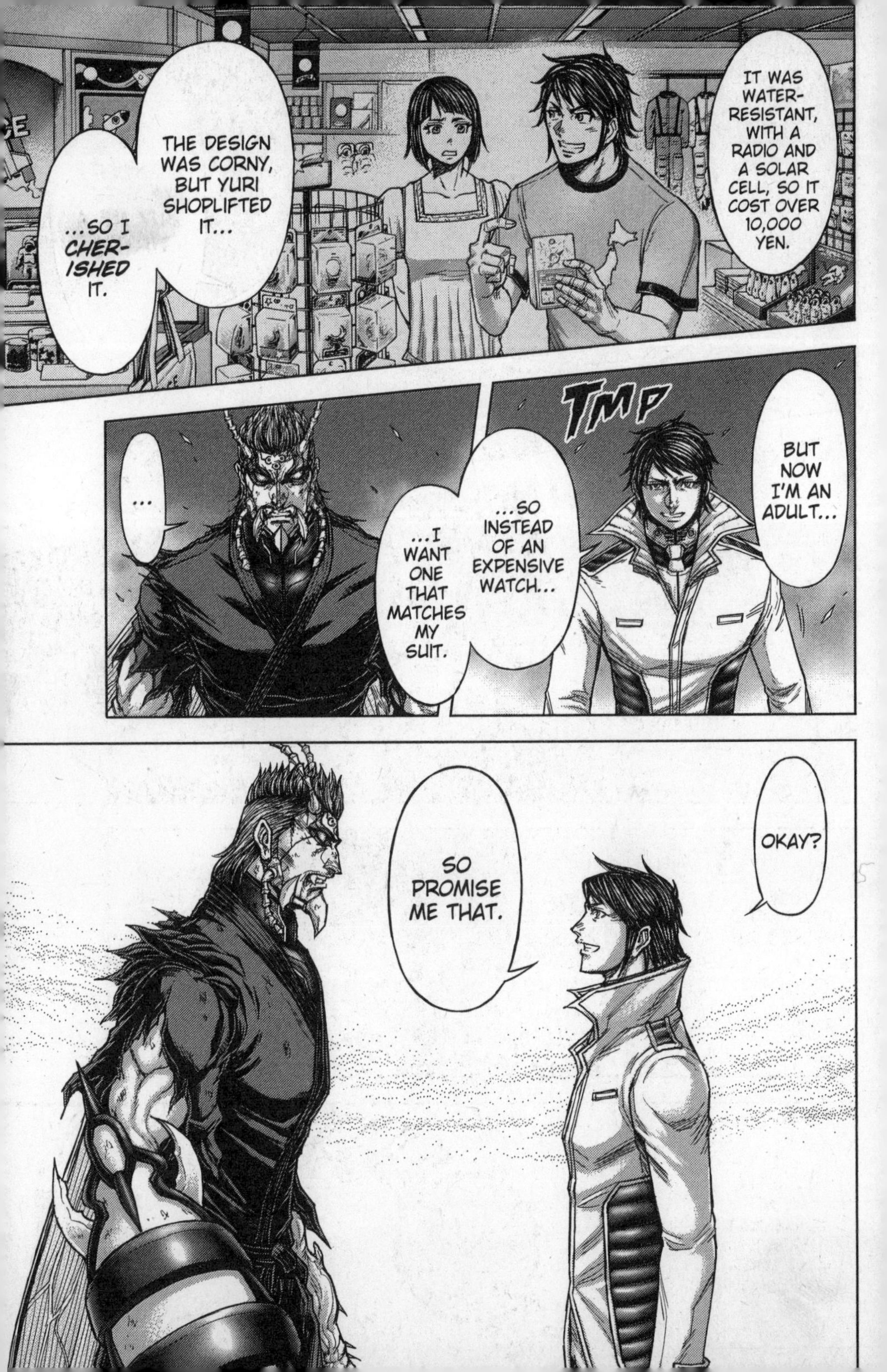
IT WAS WATER-RESISTANT, WITH A RADIO AND A SOLAR CELL, SO IT COST OVER 10,000 YEN.
THE DESIGN WAS CORNY, BUT YURI SHOPLIFTED IT...
...SO I CHERISHED IT.
TMP
BUT NOW I'M AN ADULT...
...SO INSTEAD OF AN EXPENSIVE WATCH...
...I WANT ONE THAT MATCHES MY SUIT.
...
OKAY?
SO PROMISE ME THAT.

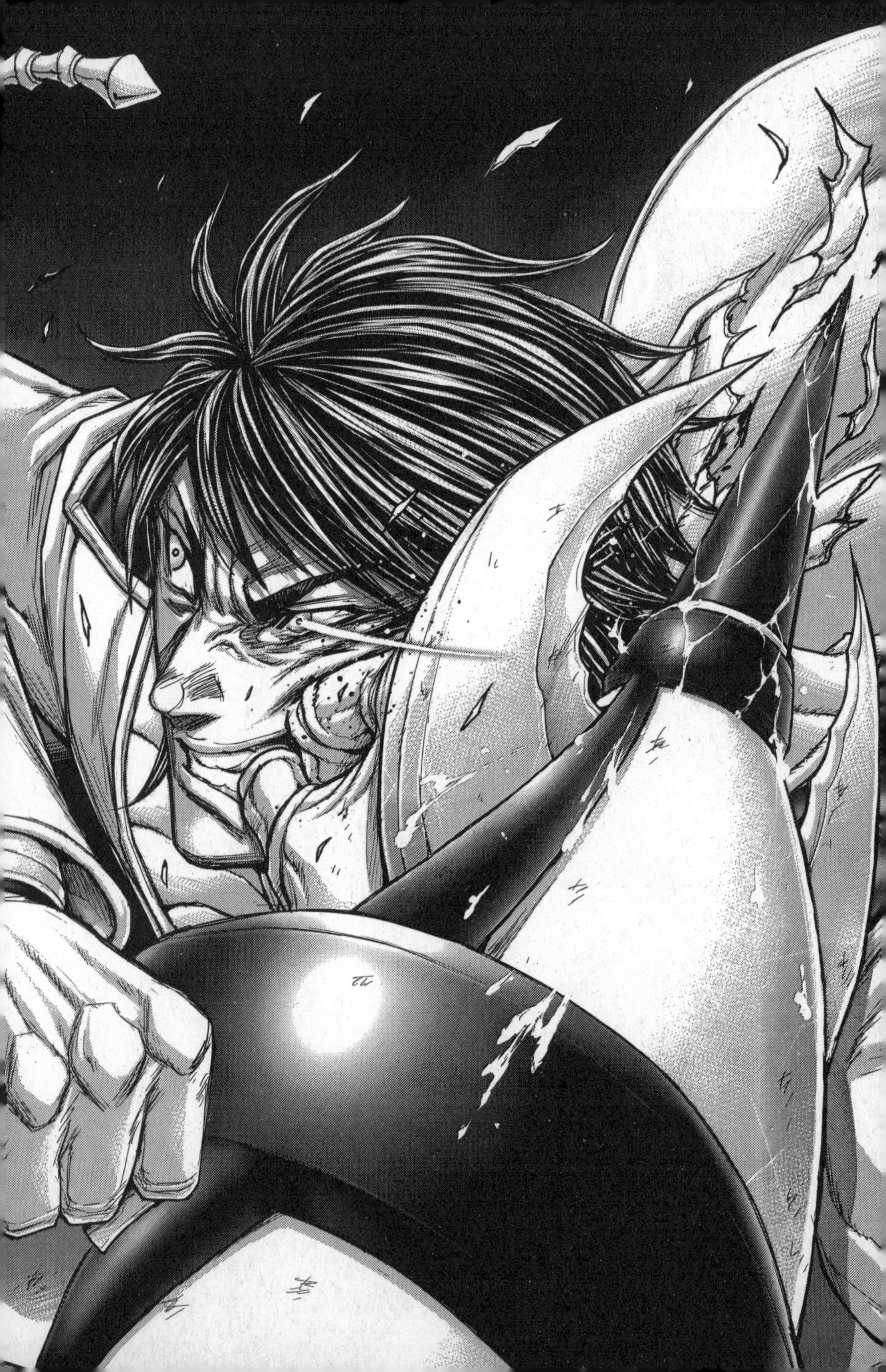

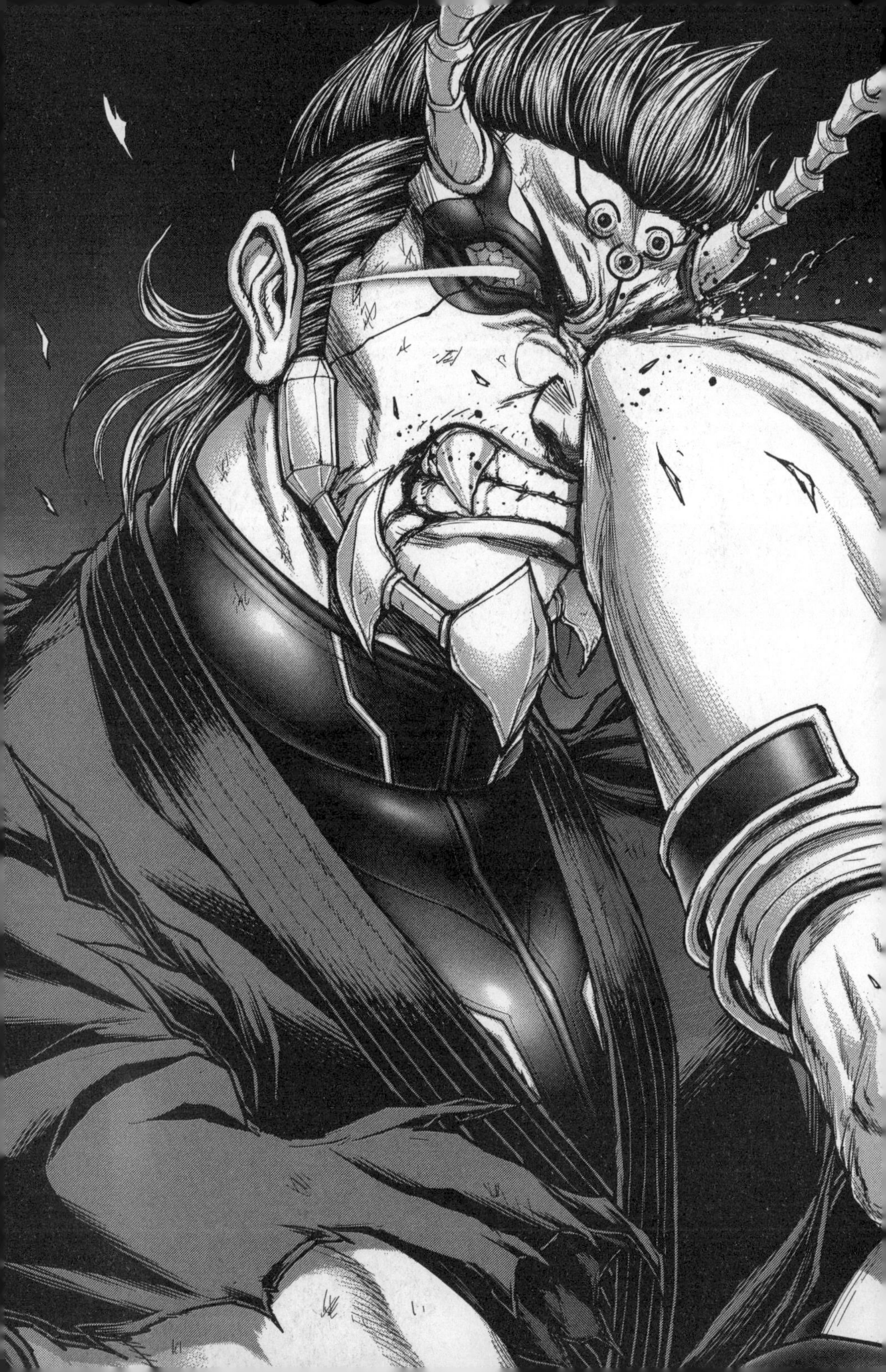

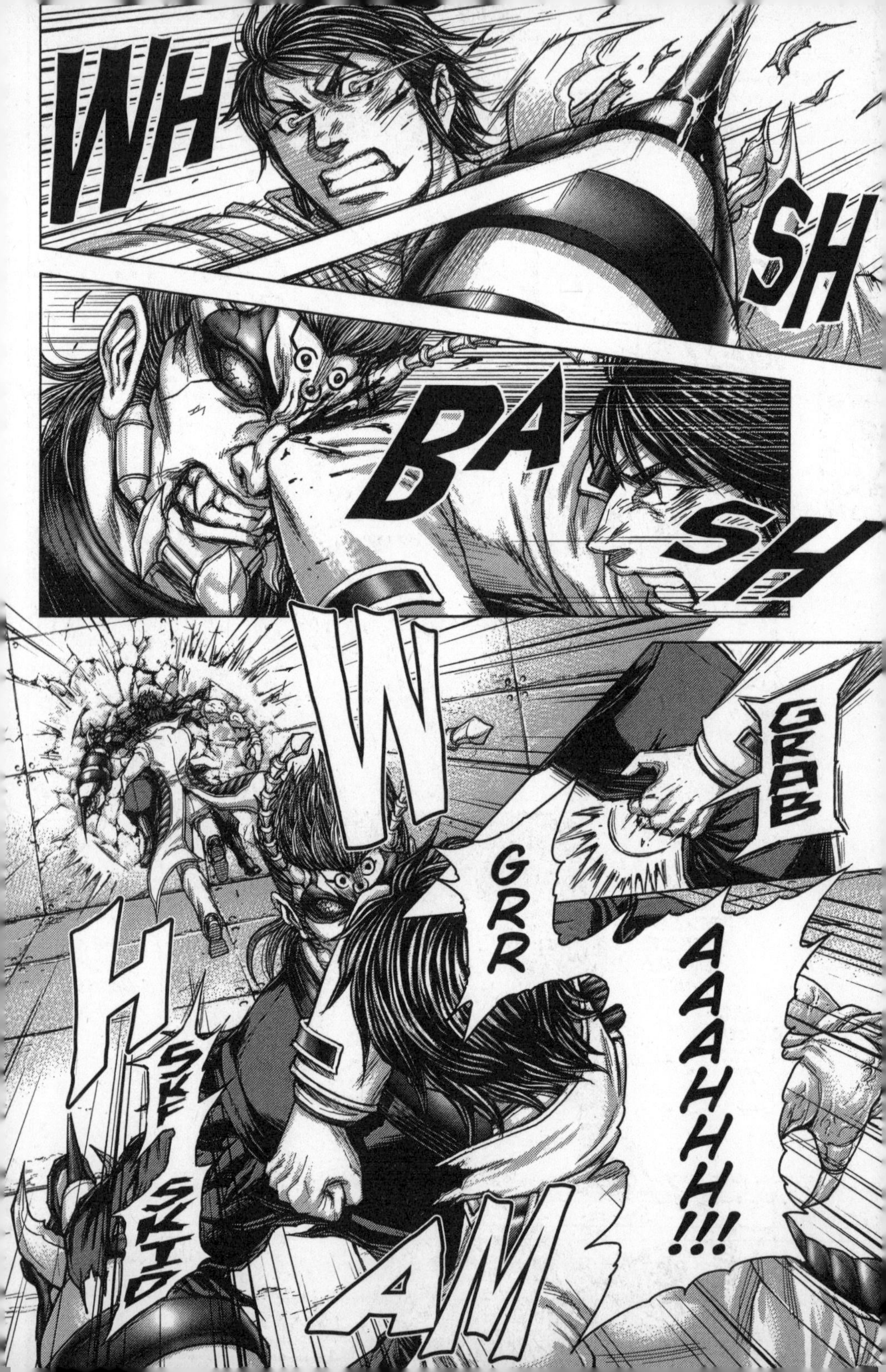
WH
SH
BA
SH
GRAB
W
H
AM
AAAAHHH!!!
GRR
SKF
SKID

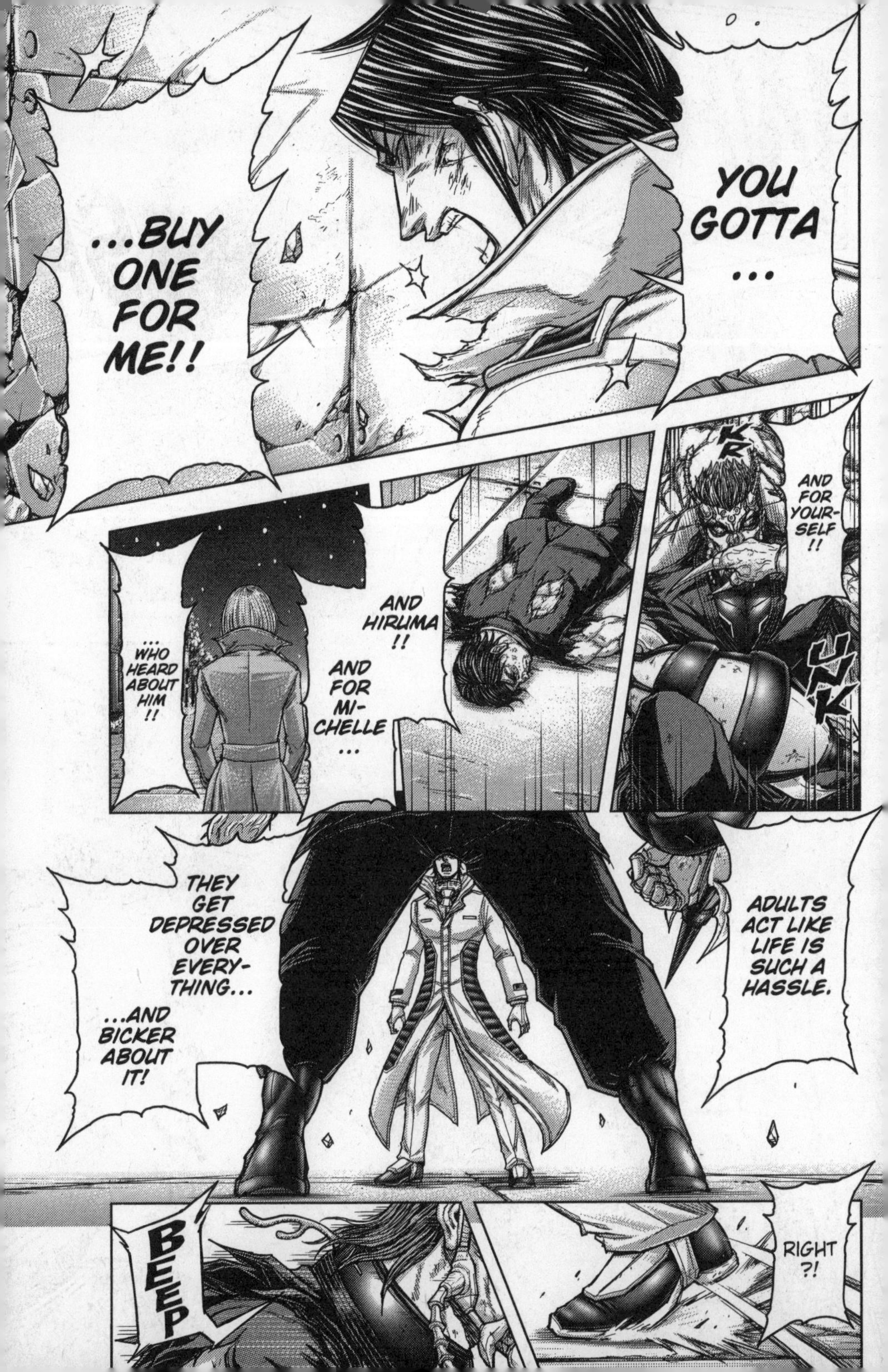
YOU GOTTA...
...BUY ONE FOR ME!!
KR
AND FOR YOUR-SELF!!
UNK
AND HIRUMA!!
AND FOR MI-CHELLE...
...WHO HEARD ABOUT HIM!!
ADULTS ACT LIKE LIFE IS SUCH A HASSLE.
THEY GET DEPRESSED OVER EVERY-THING...
...AND BICKER ABOUT IT!
RIGHT?!
BEEP

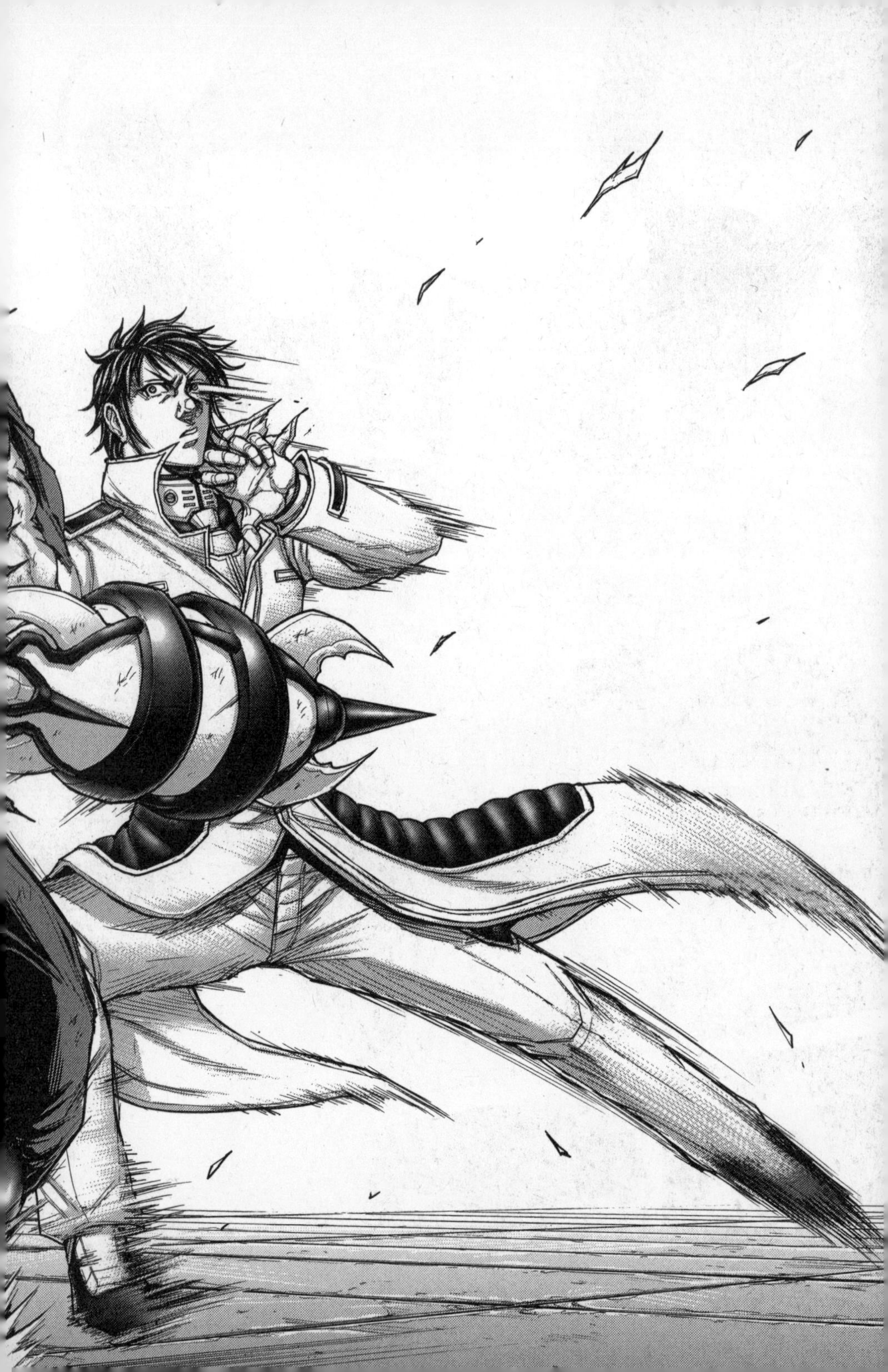

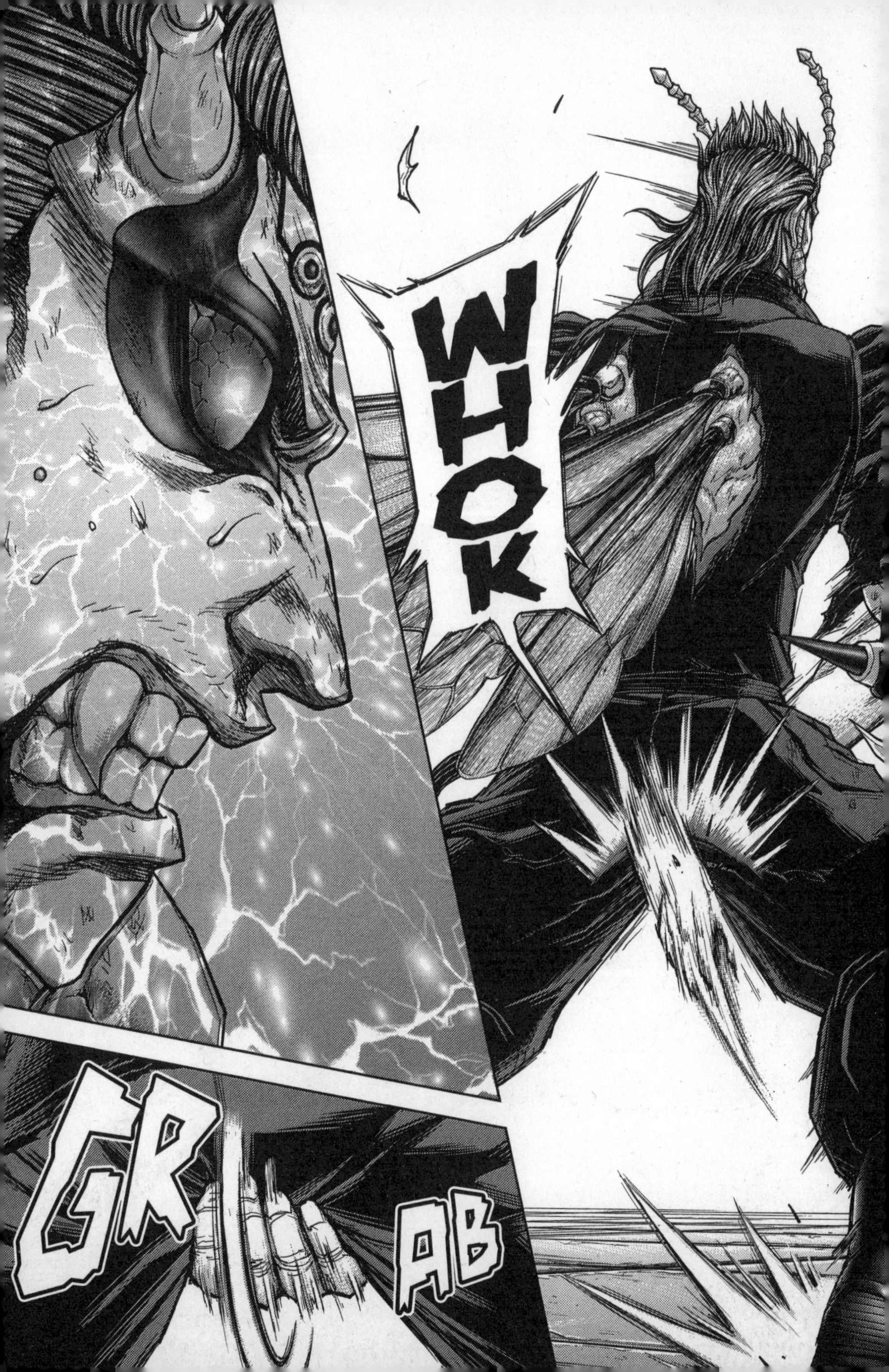
WHOK
GR AB

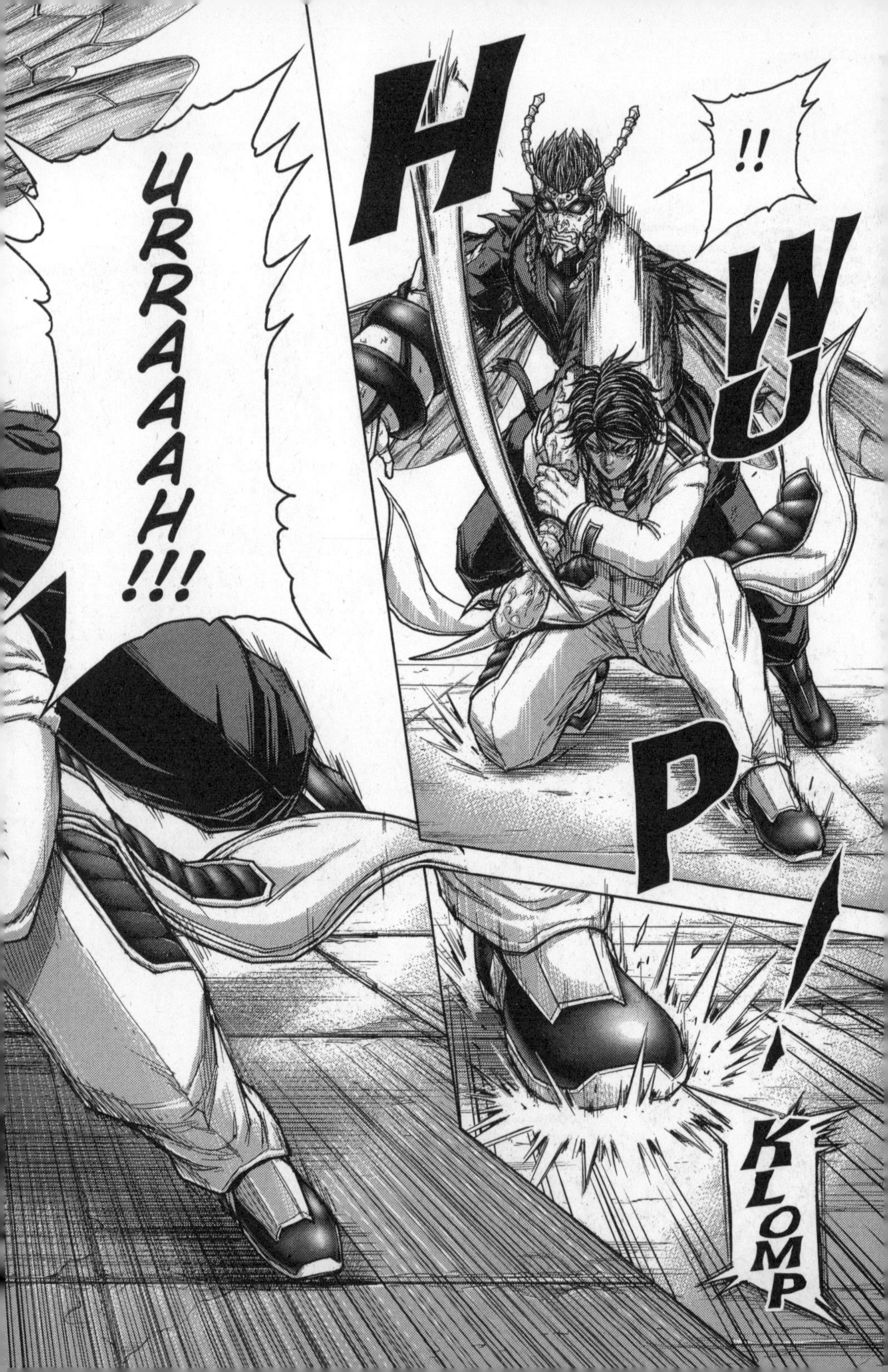
!!
HWUP!
KLOMP
URRAAAH!!!

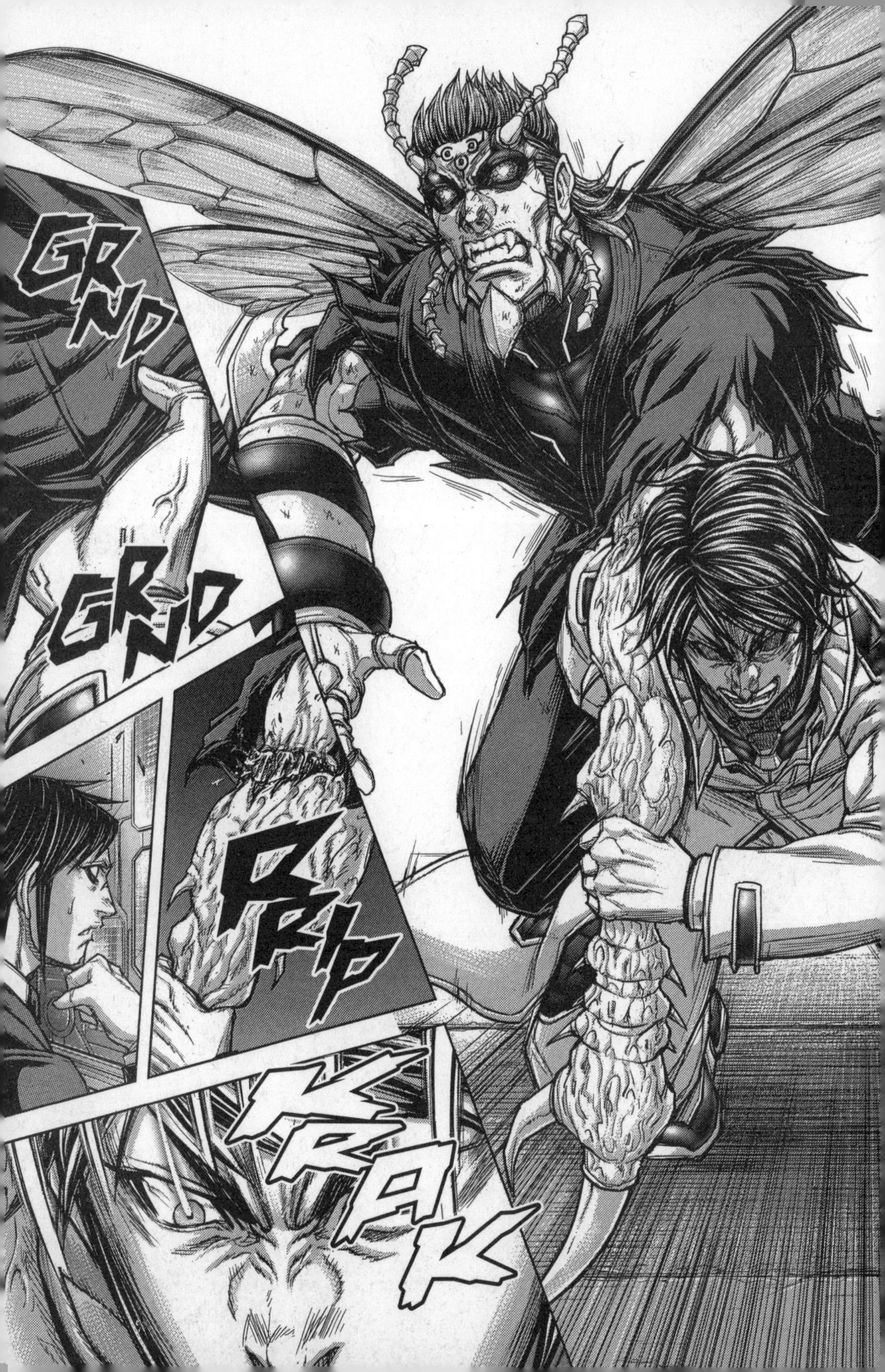
GRND
GRND
RRIP
KRAK

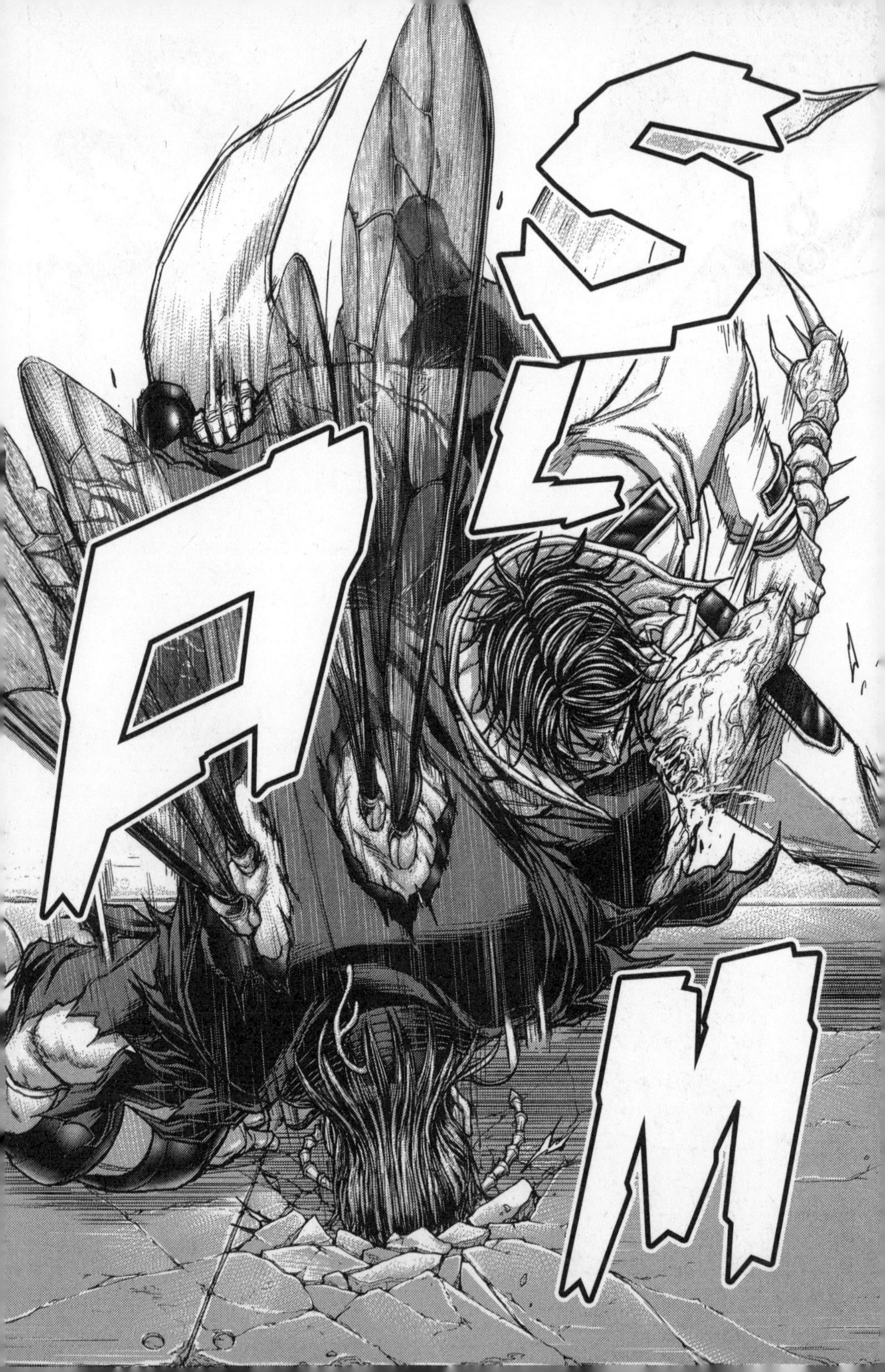
SLAM

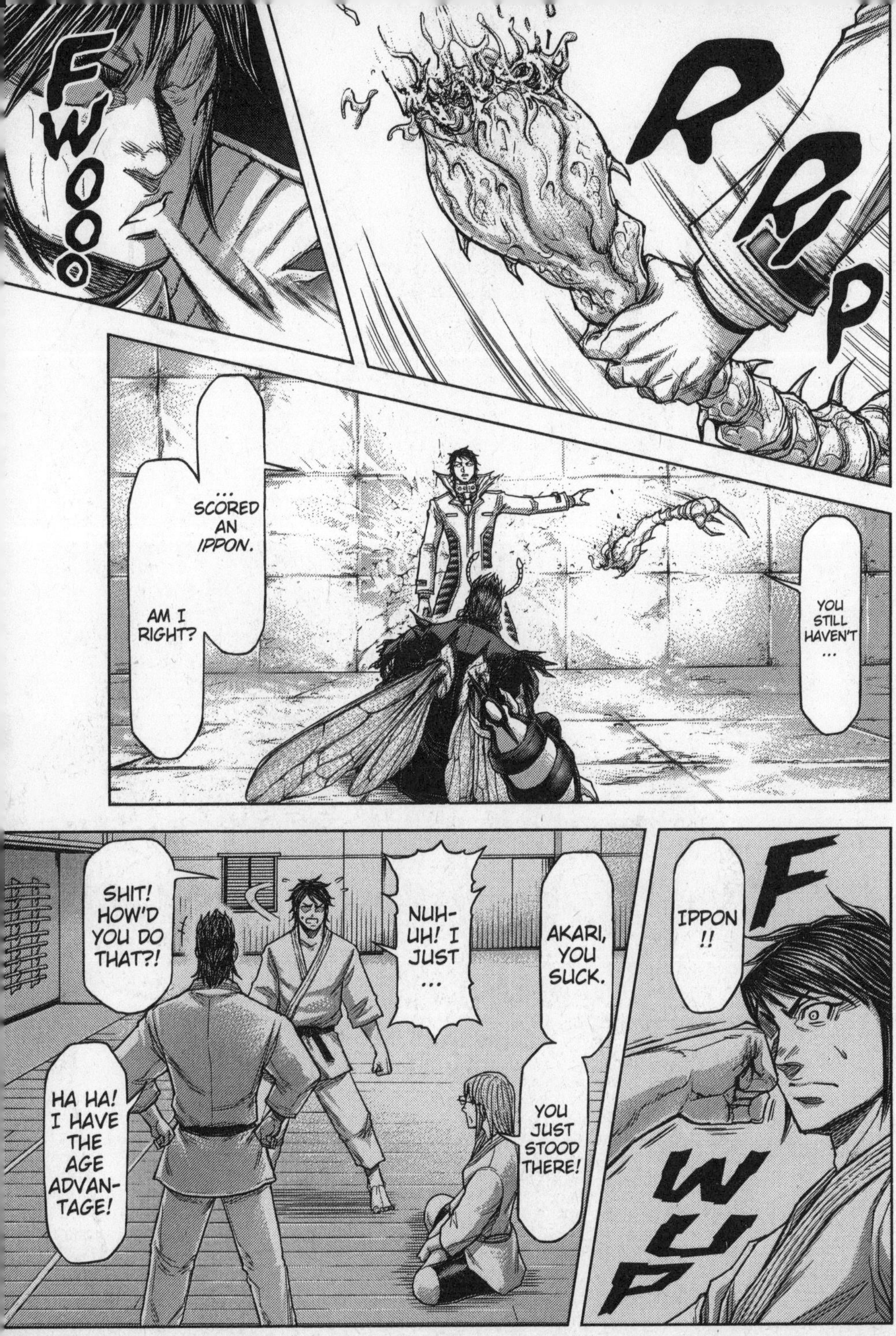
RAAP
FWOOO
YOU STILL HAVEN'T ...
... SCORED AN IPPON.
AM I RIGHT?
FWUP
IPPON !!
AKARI, YOU SUCK.
YOU JUST STOOD THERE!
NUH-UH! I JUST ...
SHIT! HOW'D YOU DO THAT?!
HA HA! I HAVE THE AGE ADVAN-TAGE!

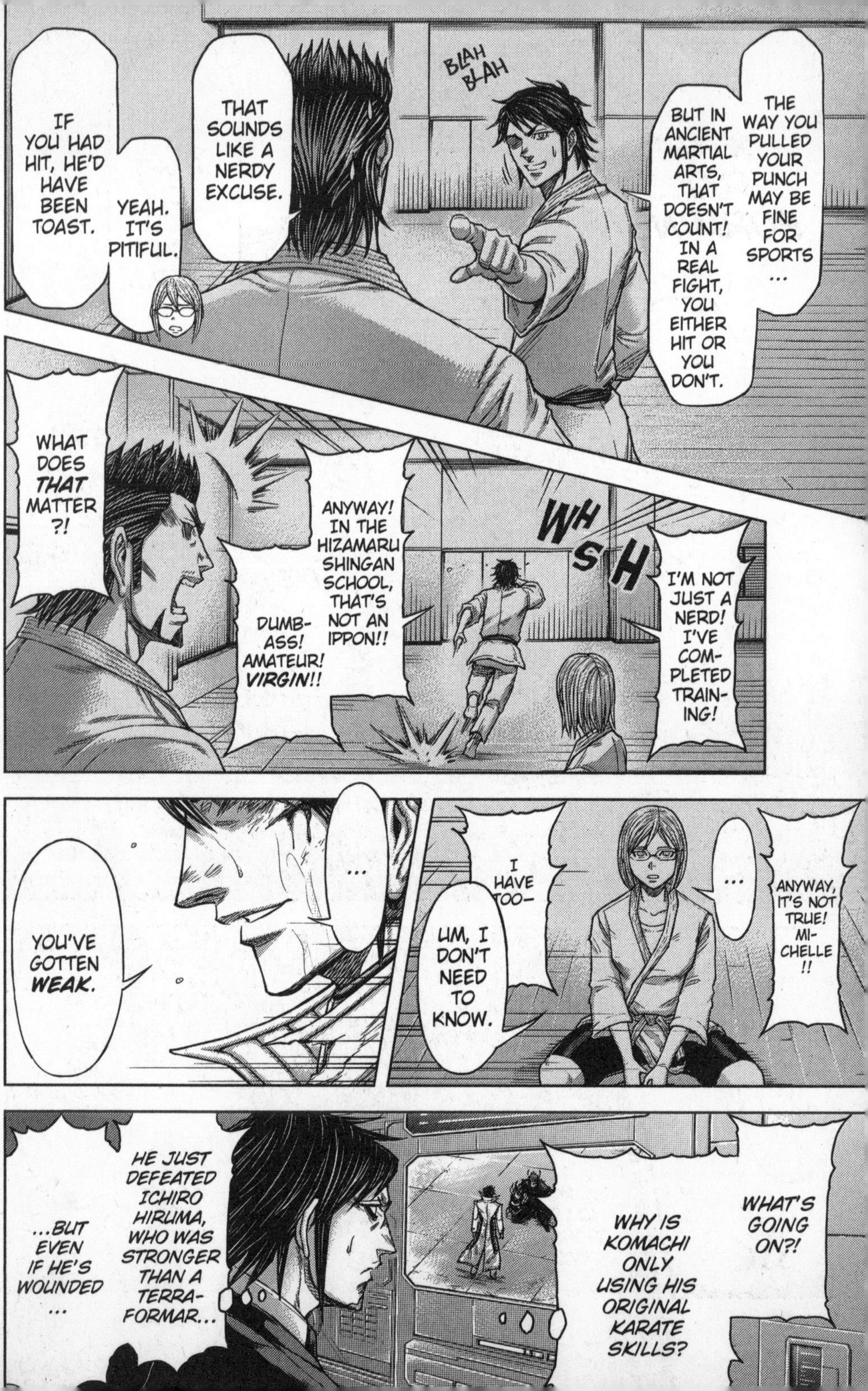
THE WAY YOU PULLED YOUR PUNCH MAY BE FINE FOR SPORTS...
BUT IN ANCIENT MARTIAL ARTS, THAT DOESN'T COUNT! IN A REAL FIGHT, YOU EITHER HIT OR YOU DON'T.
BLAH BLAH
THAT SOUNDS LIKE A NERDY EXCUSE.
YEAH. IT'S PITIFUL.
IF YOU HAD HIT, HE'D HAVE BEEN TOAST.
I'M NOT JUST A NERD! I'VE COM-PLETED TRAIN-ING!
WHSH
ANYWAY! IN THE HIZAMARU SHINGAN SCHOOL, THAT'S NOT AN IPPON!!
DUMB-ASS! AMATEUR! VIRGIN!!
WHAT DOES THAT MATTER?!
ANYWAY, IT'S NOT TRUE! MI-CHELLE!!
...
I HAVE TOO—
UM, I DON'T NEED TO KNOW.
...
YOU'VE GOTTEN WEAK.
WHAT'S GOING ON?!
WHY IS KOMACHI ONLY USING HIS ORIGINAL KARATE SKILLS?
HE JUST DEFEATED ICHIRO HIRUMA, WHO WAS STRONGER THAN A TERRA-FORMAR...
...BUT EVEN IF HE'S WOUNDED...

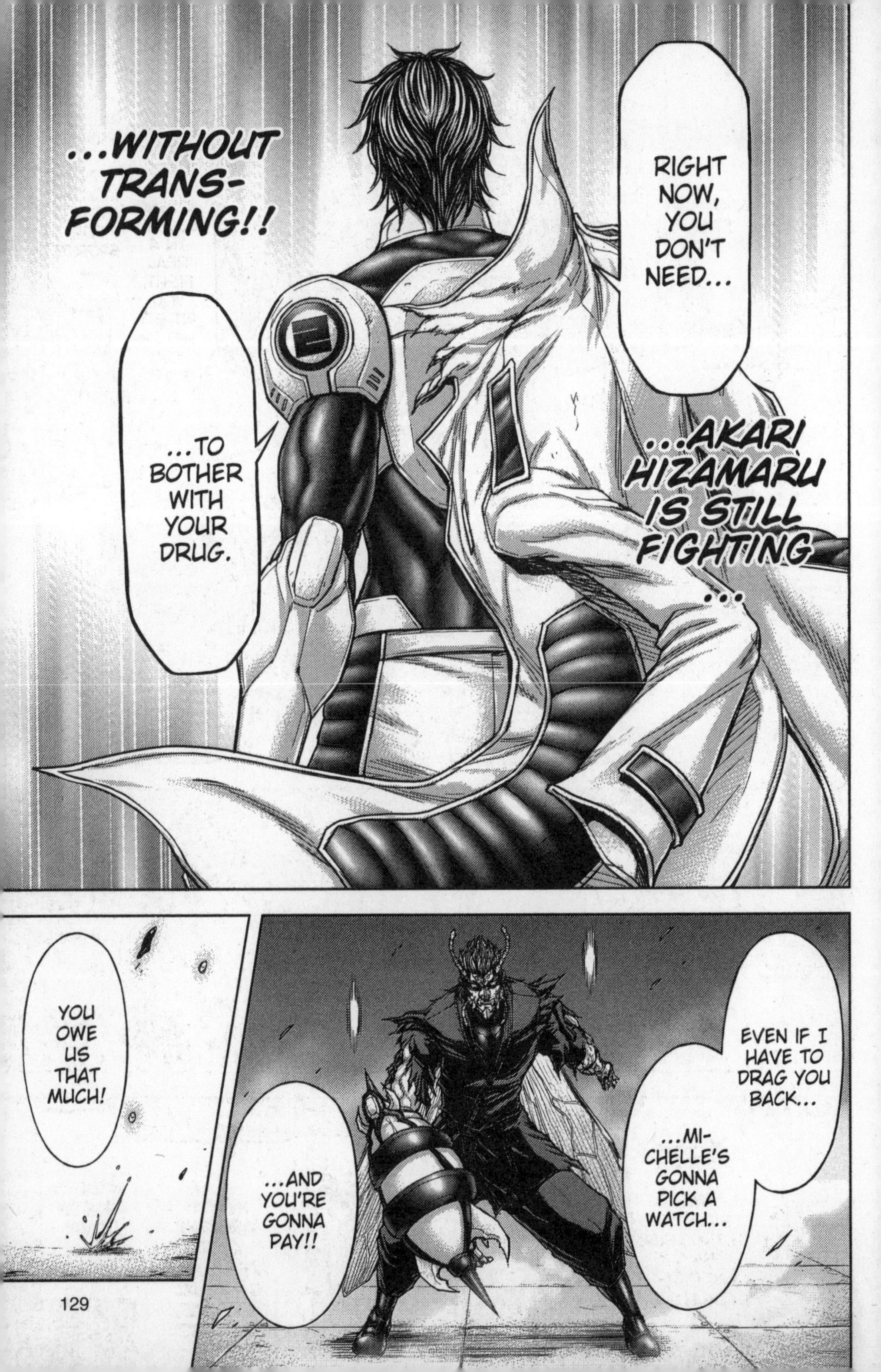
RIGHT NOW, YOU DON'T NEED...
...TO BOTHER WITH YOUR DRUG.
...AKARI HIZAMARU IS STILL FIGHTING...
...WITHOUT TRANS-FORMING!!
EVEN IF I HAVE TO DRAG YOU BACK...
...MI-CHELLE'S GONNA PICK A WATCH...
...AND YOU'RE GONNA PAY!!
YOU OWE US THAT MUCH!

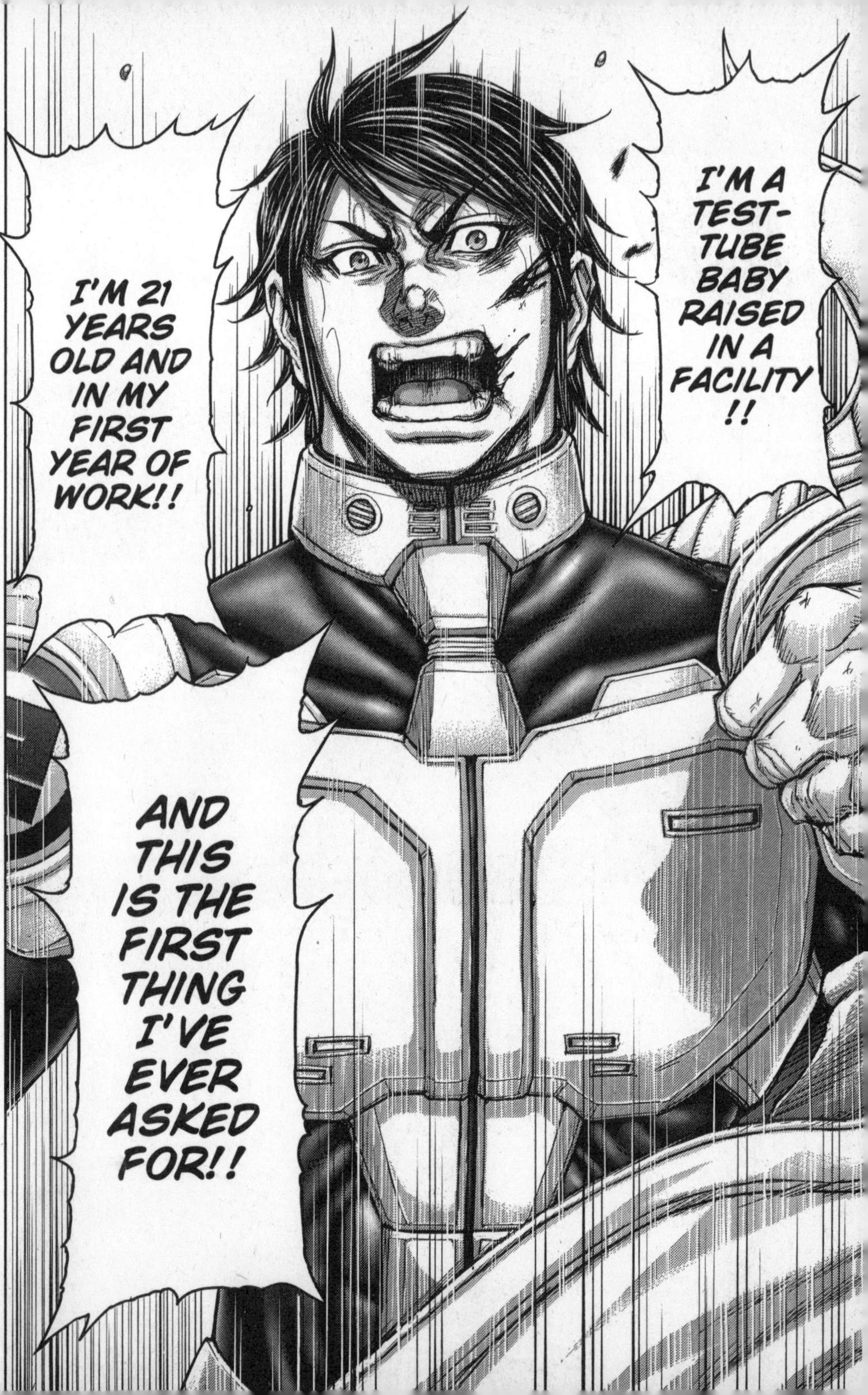
I'M A TEST-TUBE BABY RAISED IN A FACILITY!!
I'M 21 YEARS OLD AND IN MY FIRST YEAR OF WORK!!
AND THIS IS THE FIRST THING I'VE EVER ASKED FOR!!

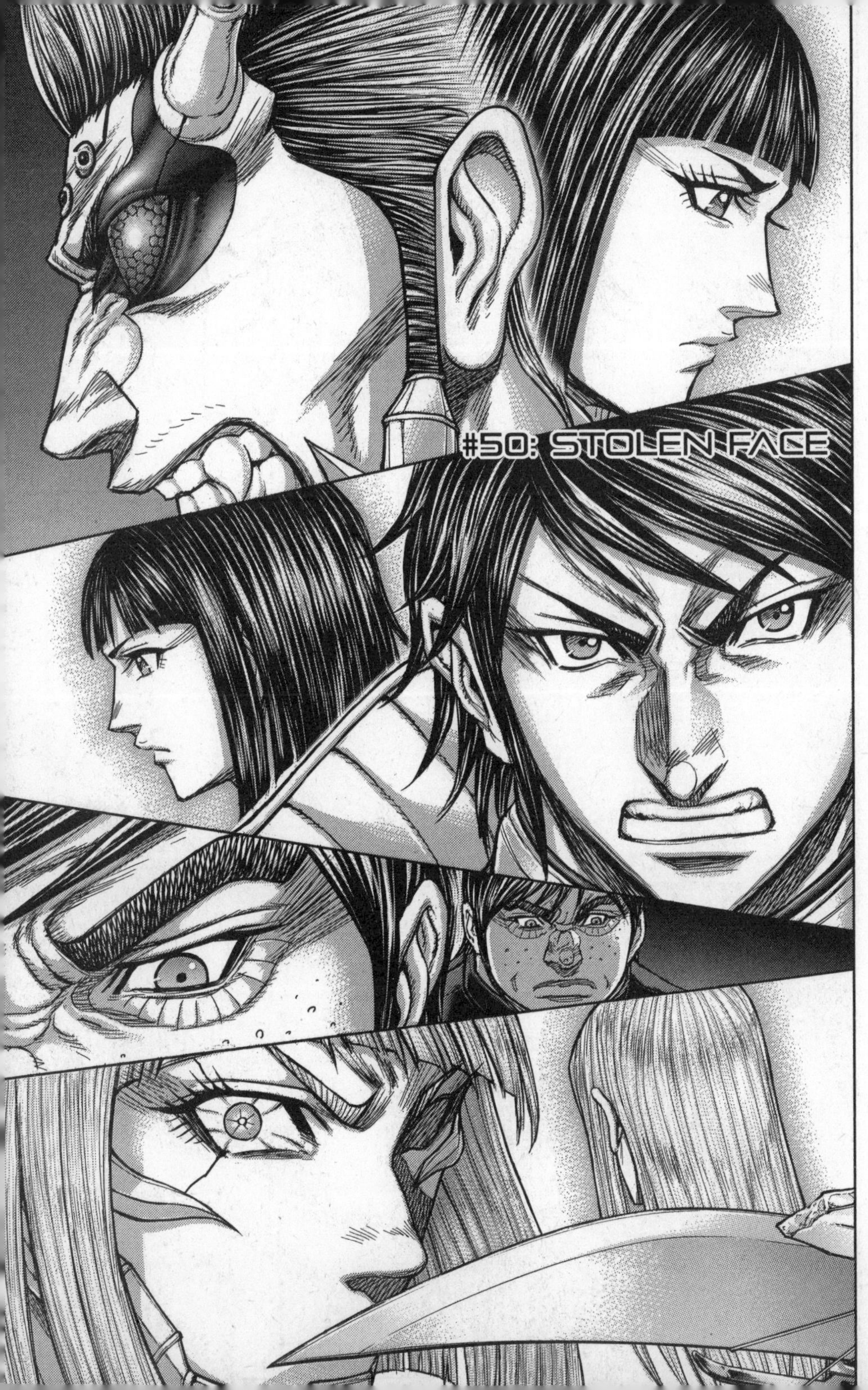
#50: STOLEN FACE

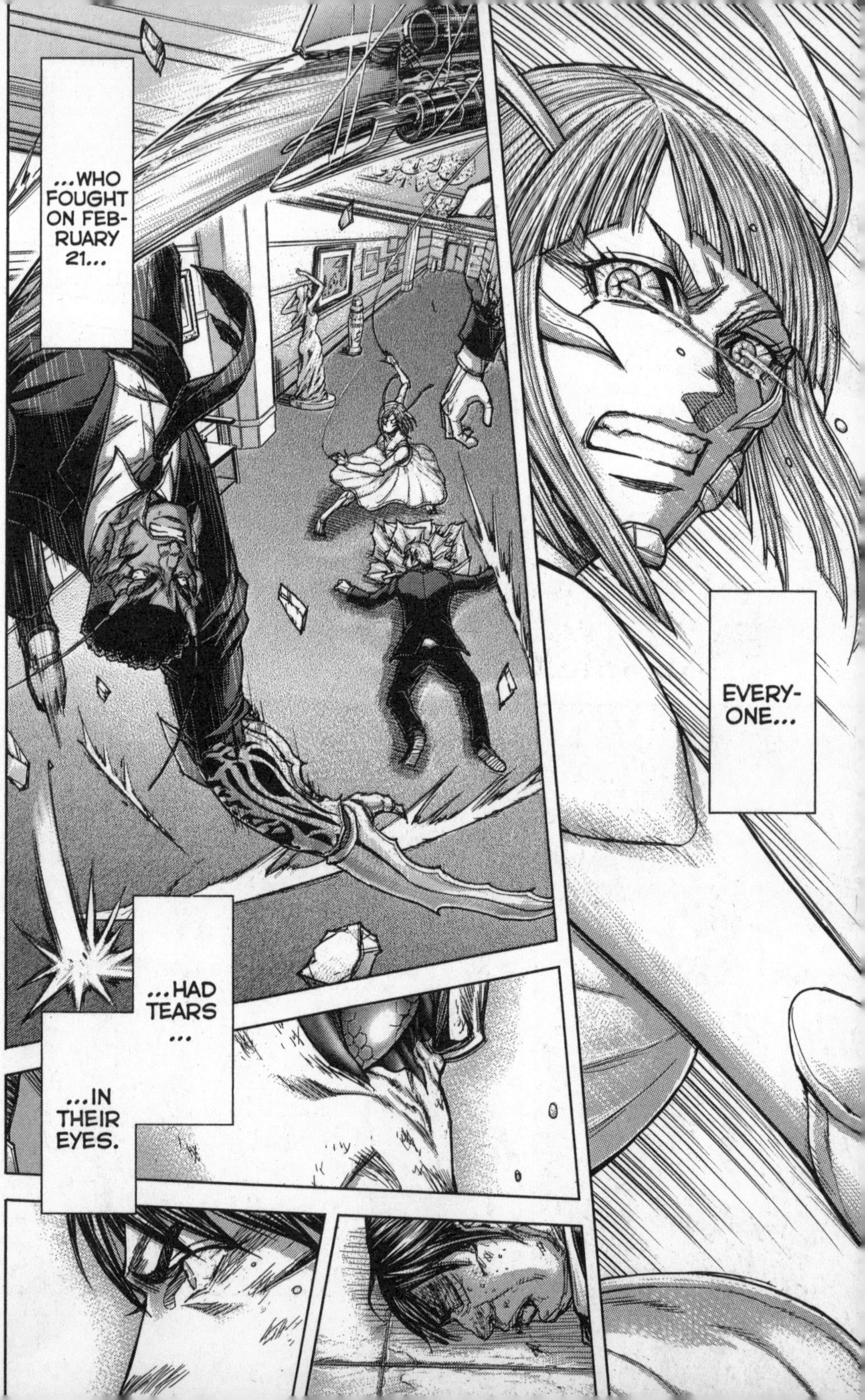
EVERY-ONE...
...WHO FOUGHT ON FEB-RUARY 21...
...HAD TEARS ...
...IN THEIR EYES.

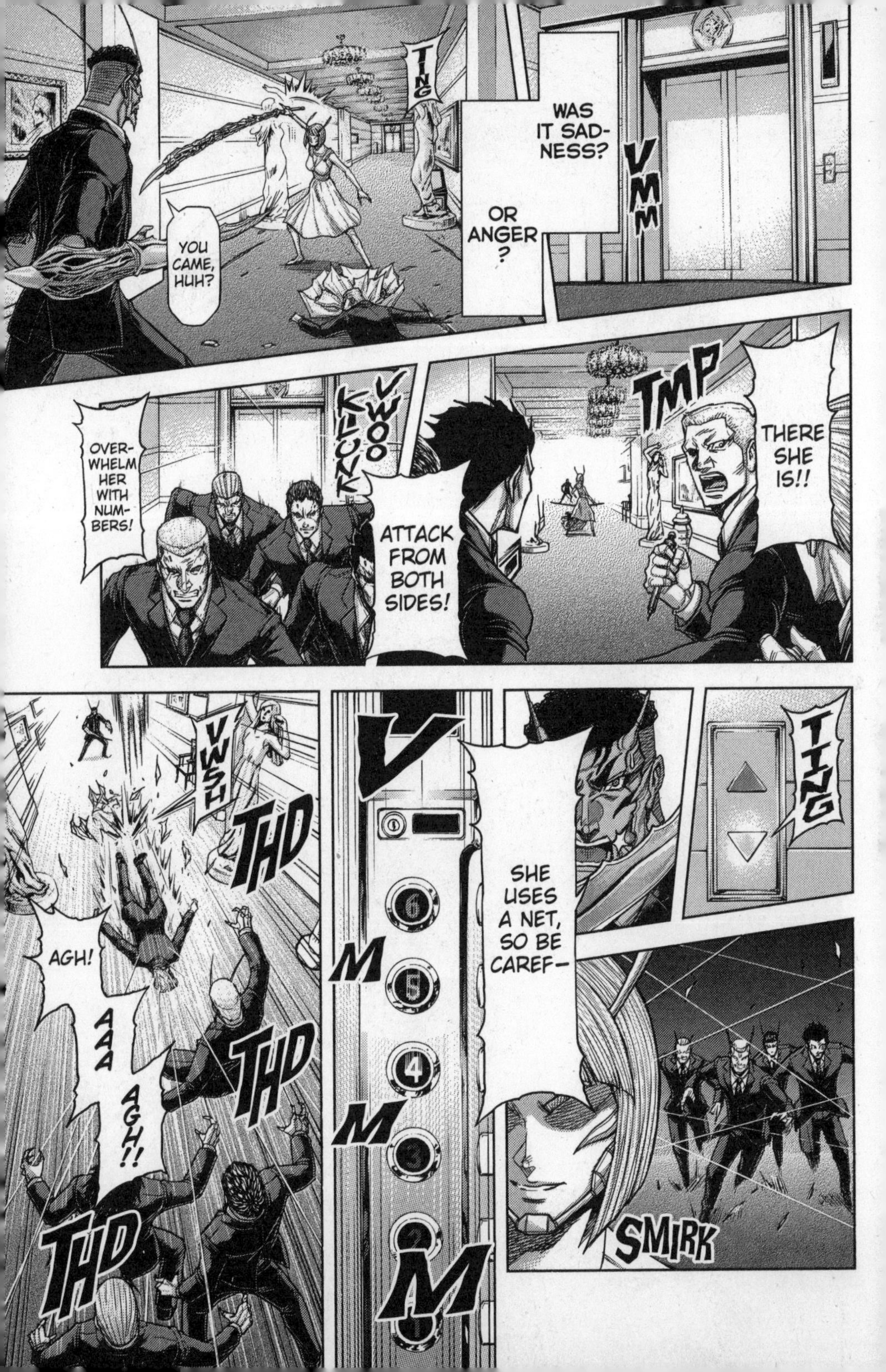
WAS IT SADNESS?
OR ANGER?
VMM
TING
YOU CAME, HUH?
TMP
THERE SHE IS!!
ATTACK FROM BOTH SIDES!
VWOO
KLUNK
OVERWHELM HER WITH NUMBERS!
TING
SHE USES A NET, SO BE CAREF—
SMIRK
V
M
M
M
VWSH
THD
AGH!
THD
AAAAGH!!
THD

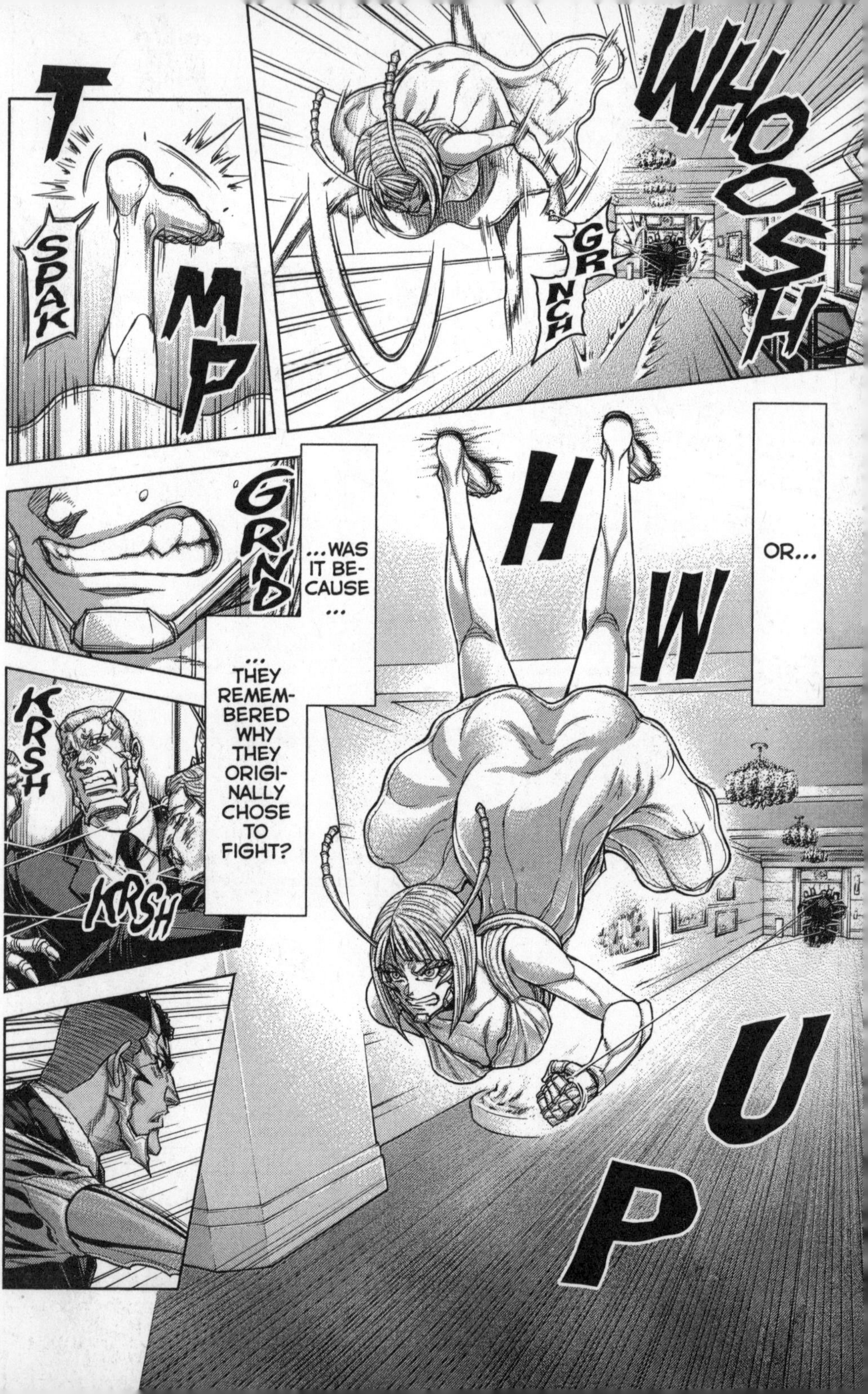
WHOOSH
GRNCH
TMP
SPAK
OR...
HWUP
...WAS IT BECAUSE...
GRND
...THEY REMEMBERED WHY THEY ORIGINALLY CHOSE TO FIGHT?
KRSH
KRSH

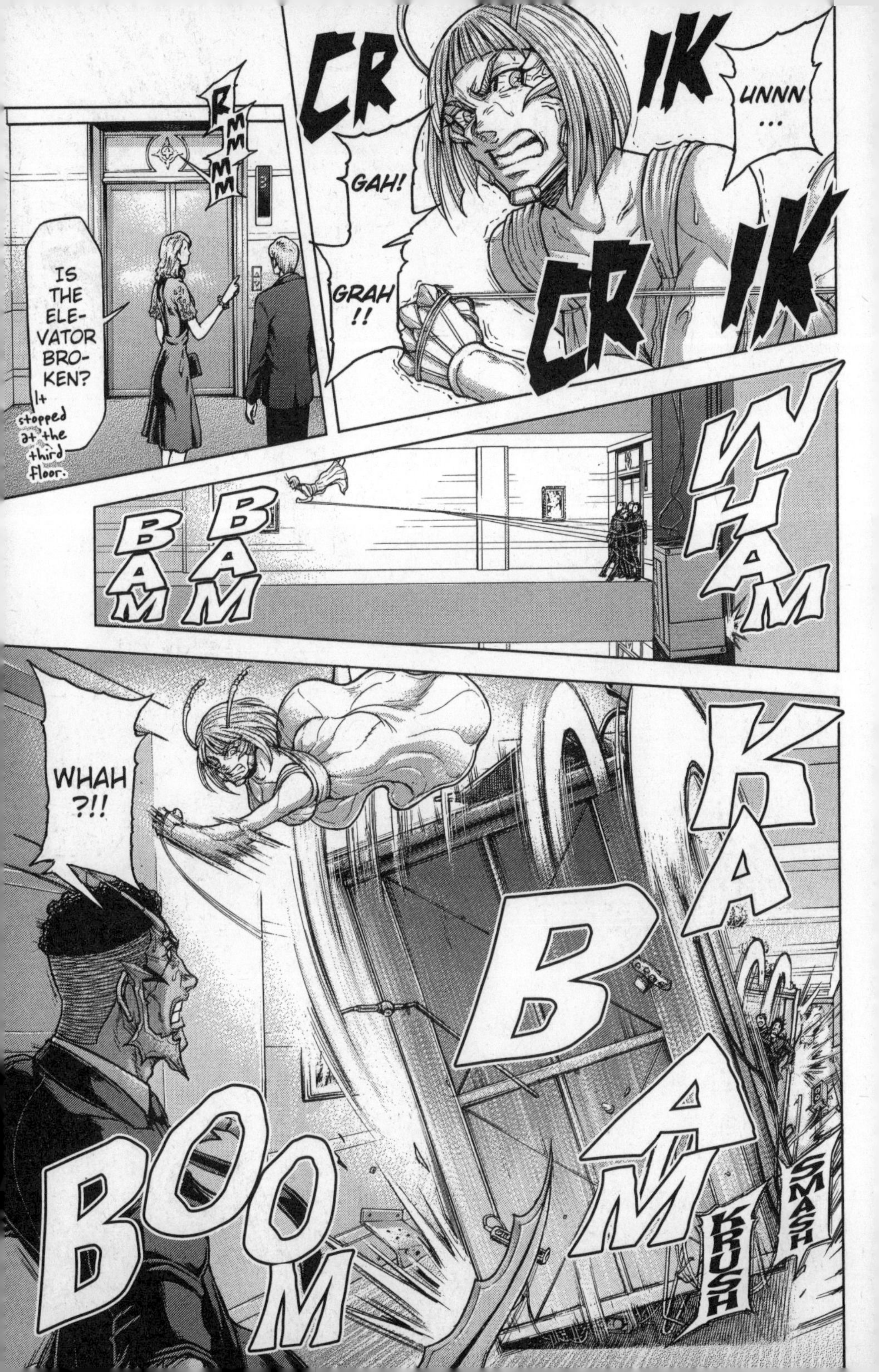
CRIK
UNNN...
GAH!
CRIK
GRAH!!
RMMMM
IS THE ELEVATOR BROKEN?
It stopped at the third floor.
WHAM
BAM
BAM
KABAM
SMASH
KRUSH
WHAH?!!
BOOM

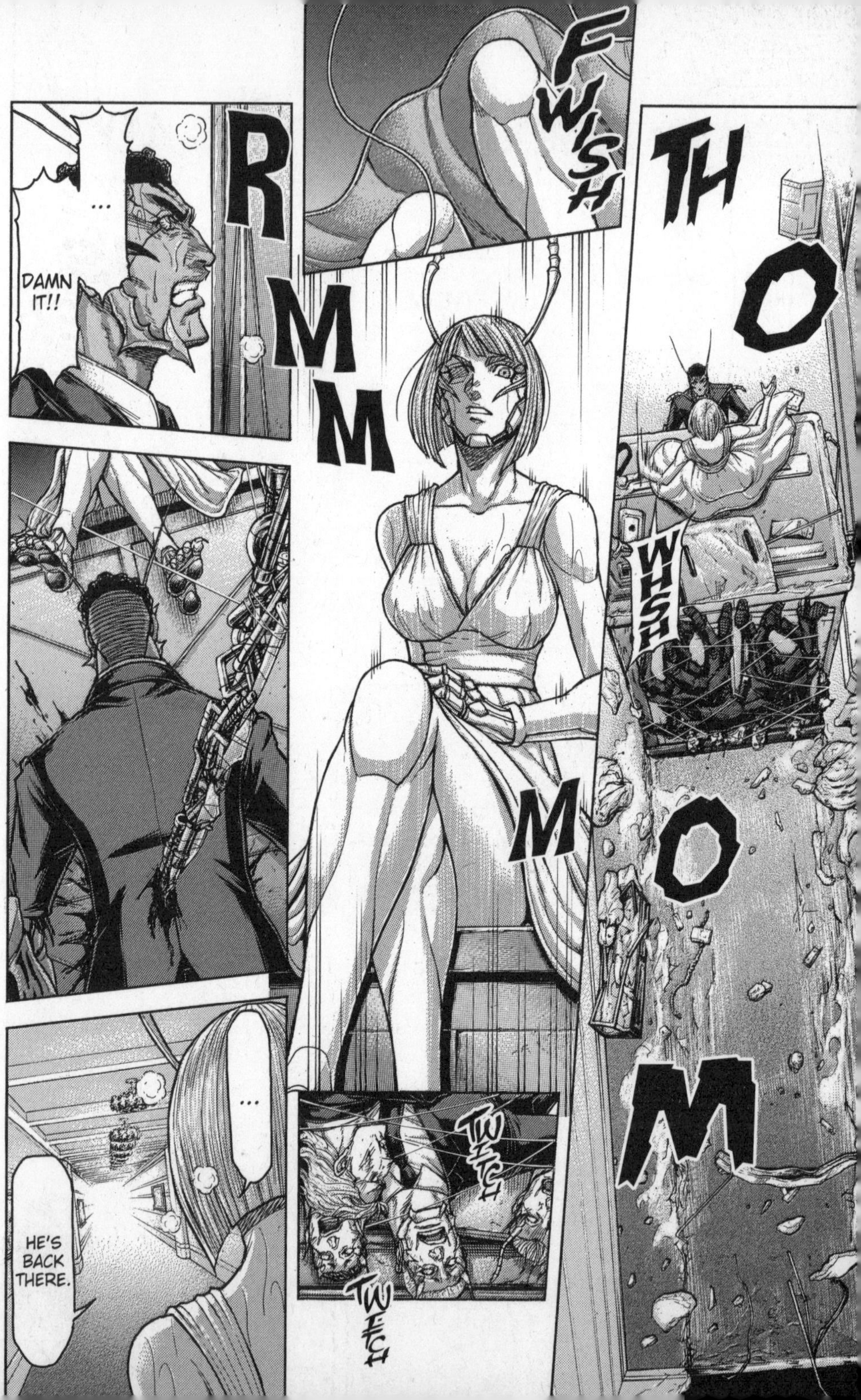
TH
O
O
M
WHSH
FWISH
R
M
M
M
TWITCH
TWITCH
...
DAMN IT!!
...
HE'S BACK THERE.

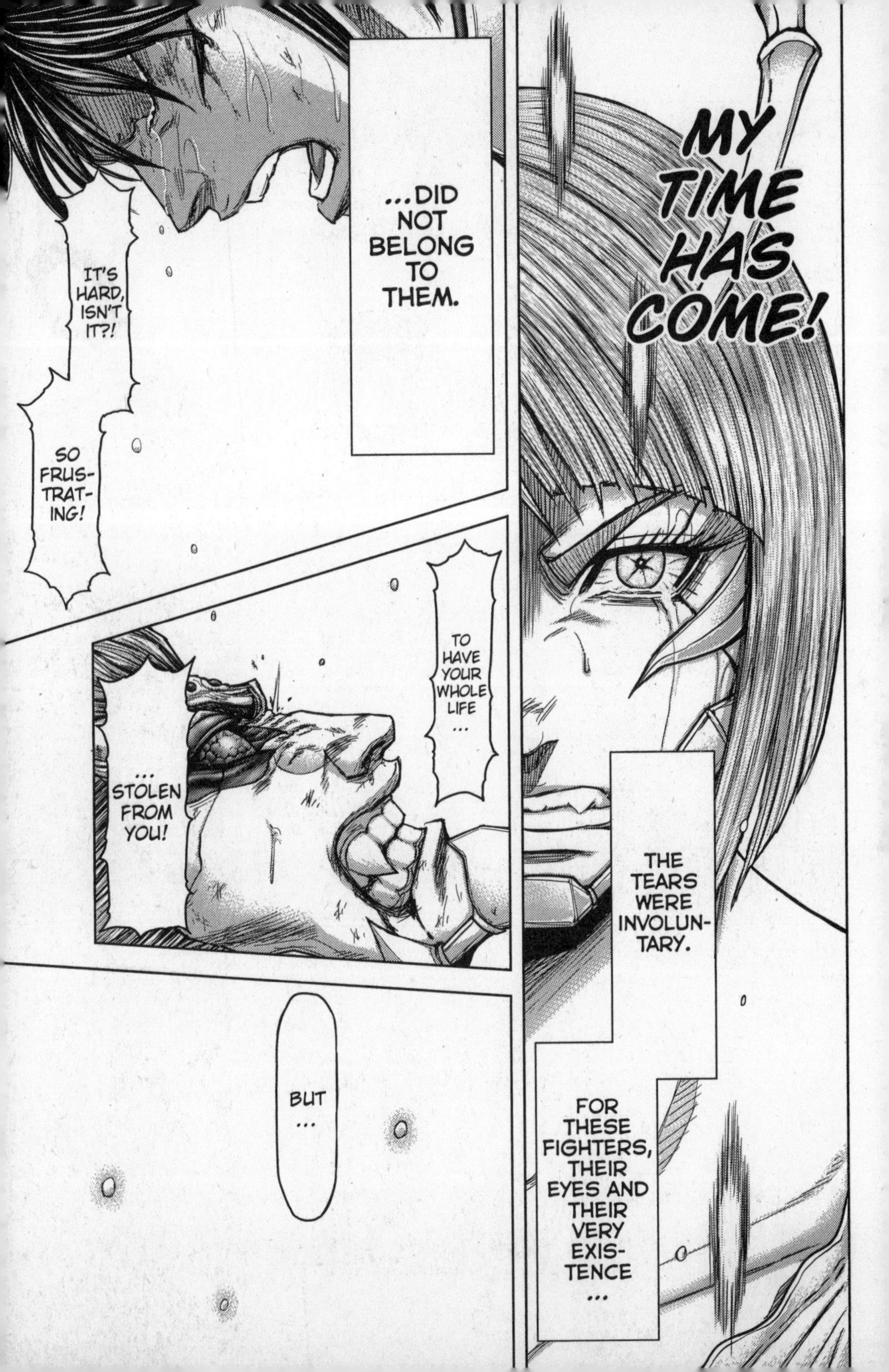
MY TIME HAS COME!
THE TEARS WERE INVOLUN-TARY.
FOR THESE FIGHTERS, THEIR EYES AND THEIR VERY EXIS-TENCE ...
...DID NOT BELONG TO THEM.
IT'S HARD, ISN'T IT?!
SO FRUS-TRAT-ING!
TO HAVE YOUR WHOLE LIFE ...
... STOLEN FROM YOU!
BUT ...

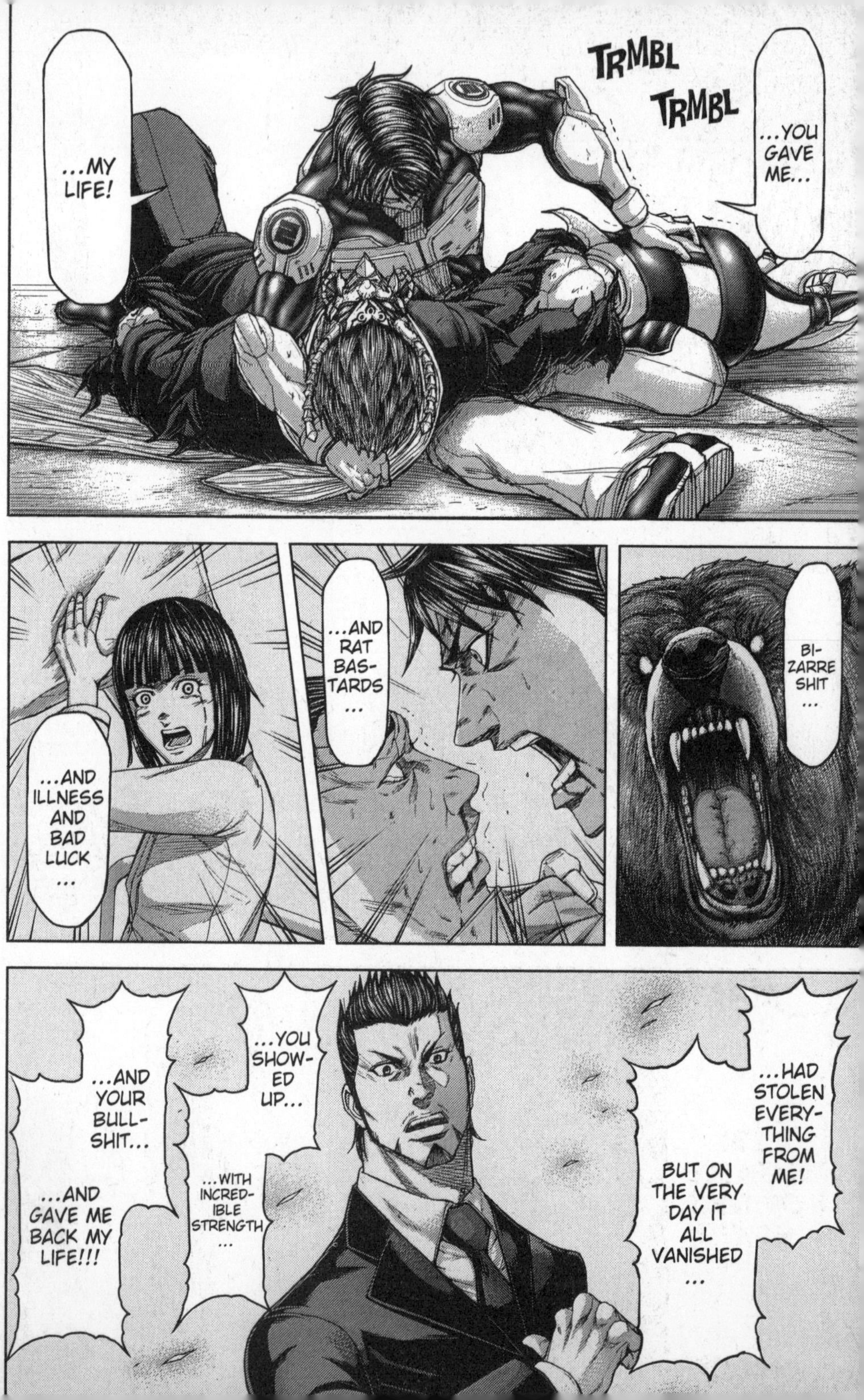
TRMBL TRMBL
...YOU GAVE ME...
...MY LIFE!
BI-ZARRE SHIT ...
...AND RAT BAS-TARDS ...
...AND ILLNESS AND BAD LUCK ...
...HAD STOLEN EVERY-THING FROM ME!
BUT ON THE VERY DAY IT ALL VANISHED ...
...YOU SHOW-ED UP...
...WITH INCRED-IBLE STRENGTH ...
...AND YOUR BULL-SHIT...
...AND GAVE ME BACK MY LIFE!!!

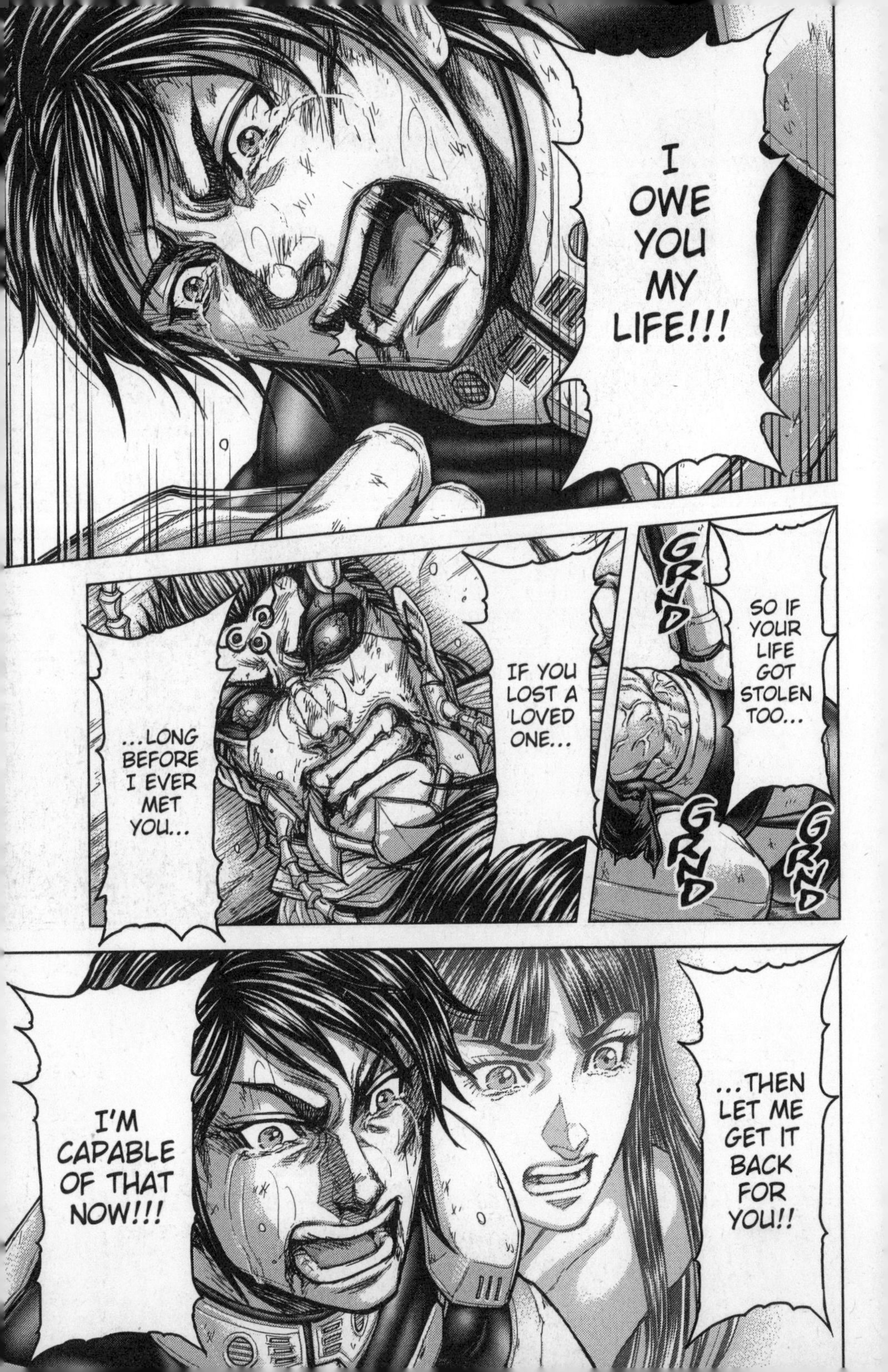
I OWE YOU MY LIFE!!!
GRND
SO IF YOUR LIFE GOT STOLEN TOO...
GRND
GRND
IF YOU LOST A LOVED ONE...
...LONG BEFORE I EVER MET YOU...
...THEN LET ME GET IT BACK FOR YOU!!
I'M CAPABLE OF THAT NOW!!!

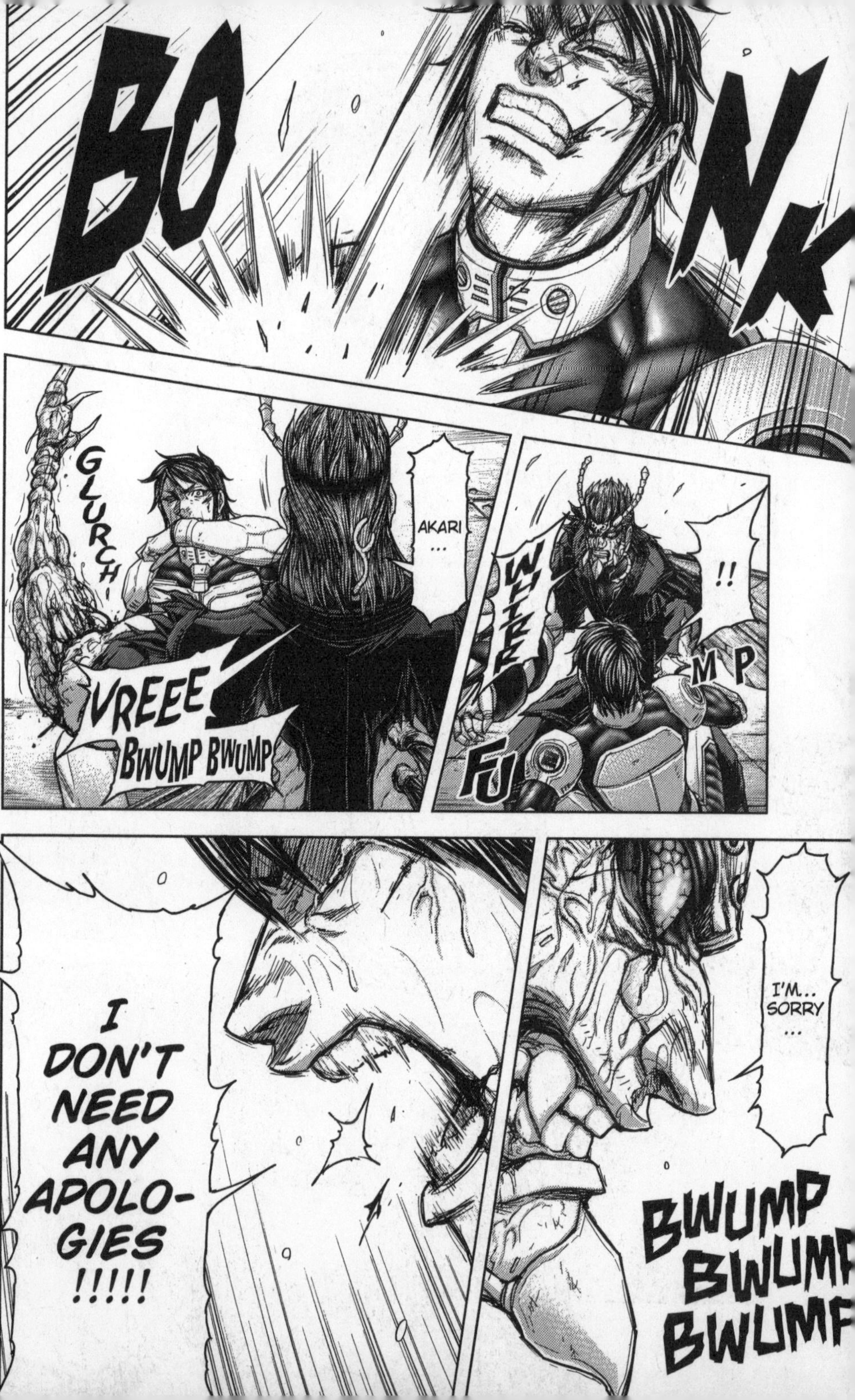
BO
NK
!!
WHIRR
FU
MP
AKARI ...
GLURCH
VREEE
BWUMP BWUMP
I'M... SORRY ...
BWUMP BWUMP BWUMP
I DON'T NEED ANY APOLOGIES !!!!!

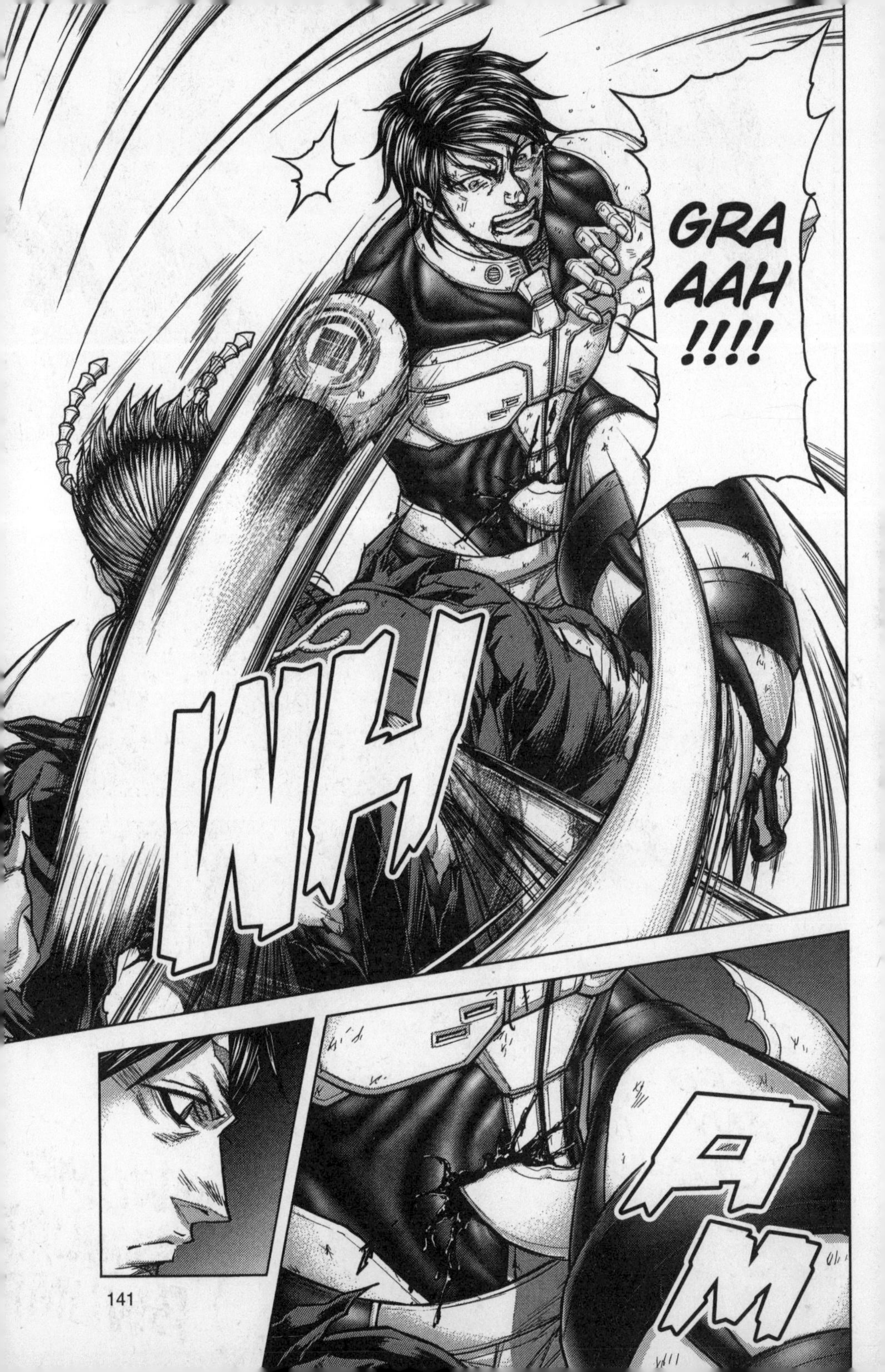
GRA
AAH
!!!!
WH
AM

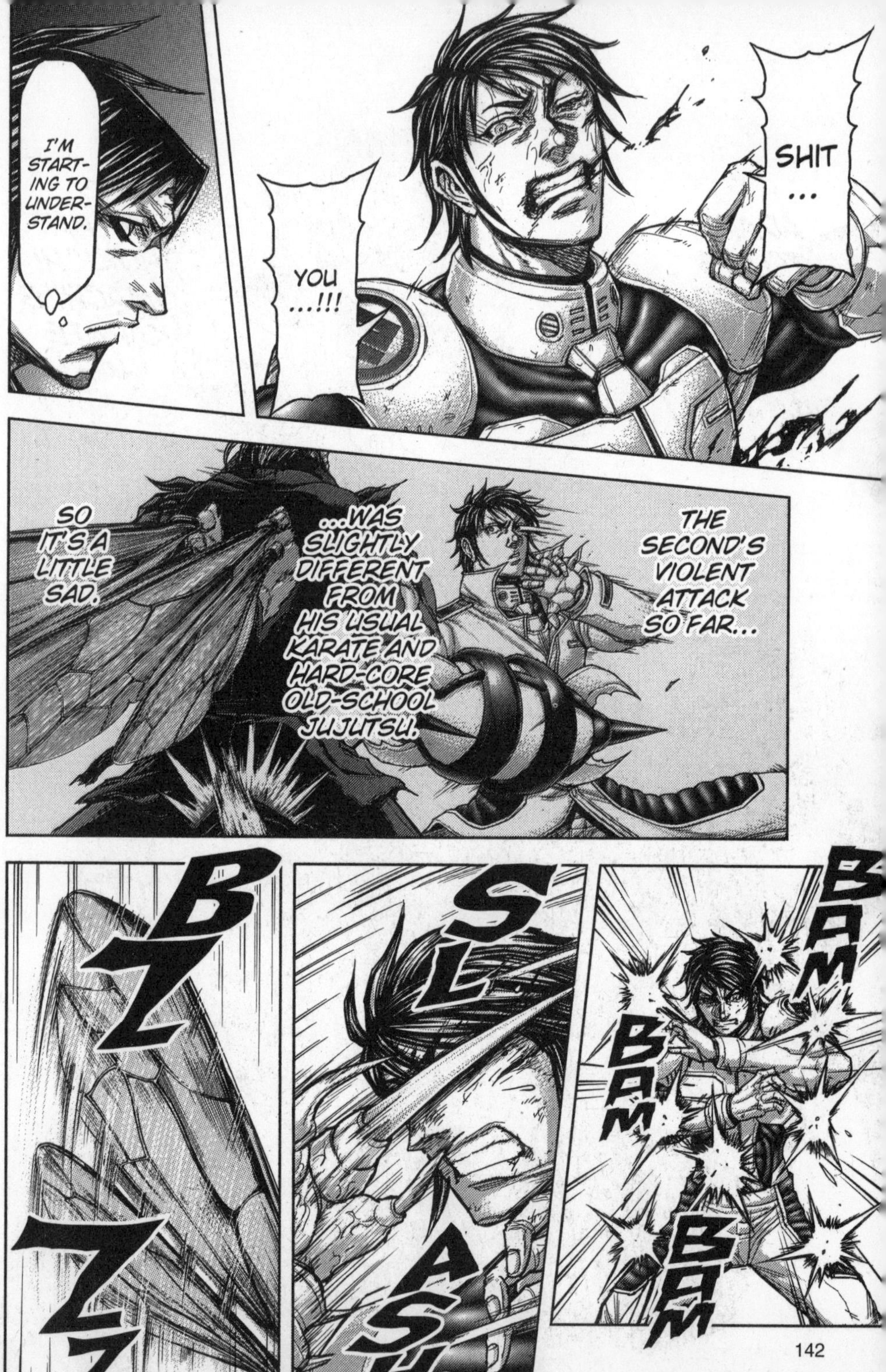
SHIT ...
YOU ...!!!
I'M STARTING TO UNDERSTAND.
THE SECOND'S VIOLENT ATTACK SO FAR...
...WAS SLIGHTLY DIFFERENT FROM HIS USUAL KARATE AND HARD-CORE OLD-SCHOOL JUJUTSU.
SO IT'S A LITTLE SAD.
BAM
BAM
BAM
BAM
SLASH
BZZZ

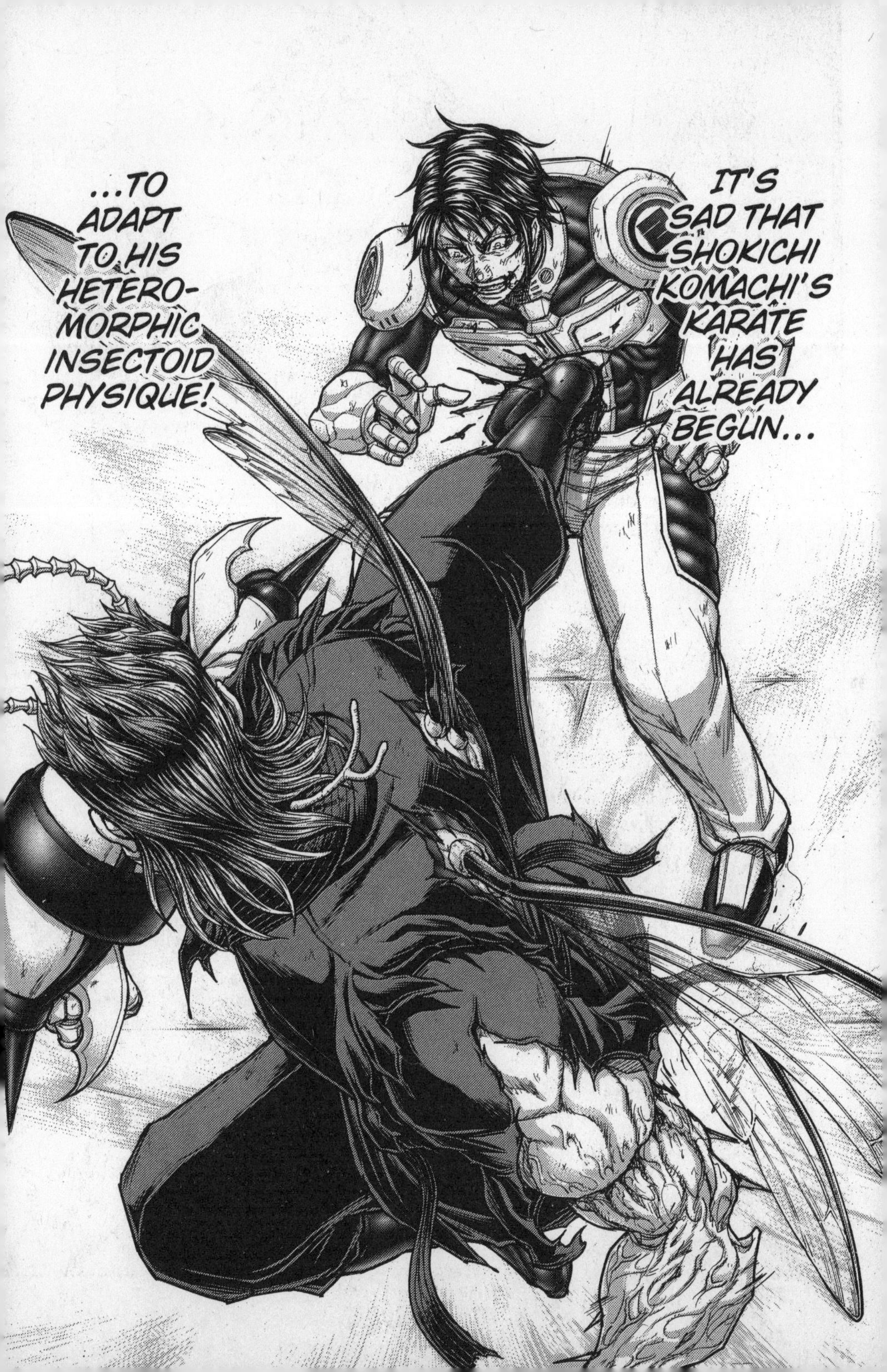
IT'S SAD THAT SHOKICHI KOMACHI'S KARATE HAS ALREADY BEGUN...
...TO ADAPT TO HIS HETERO-MORPHIC INSECTOID PHYSIQUE!

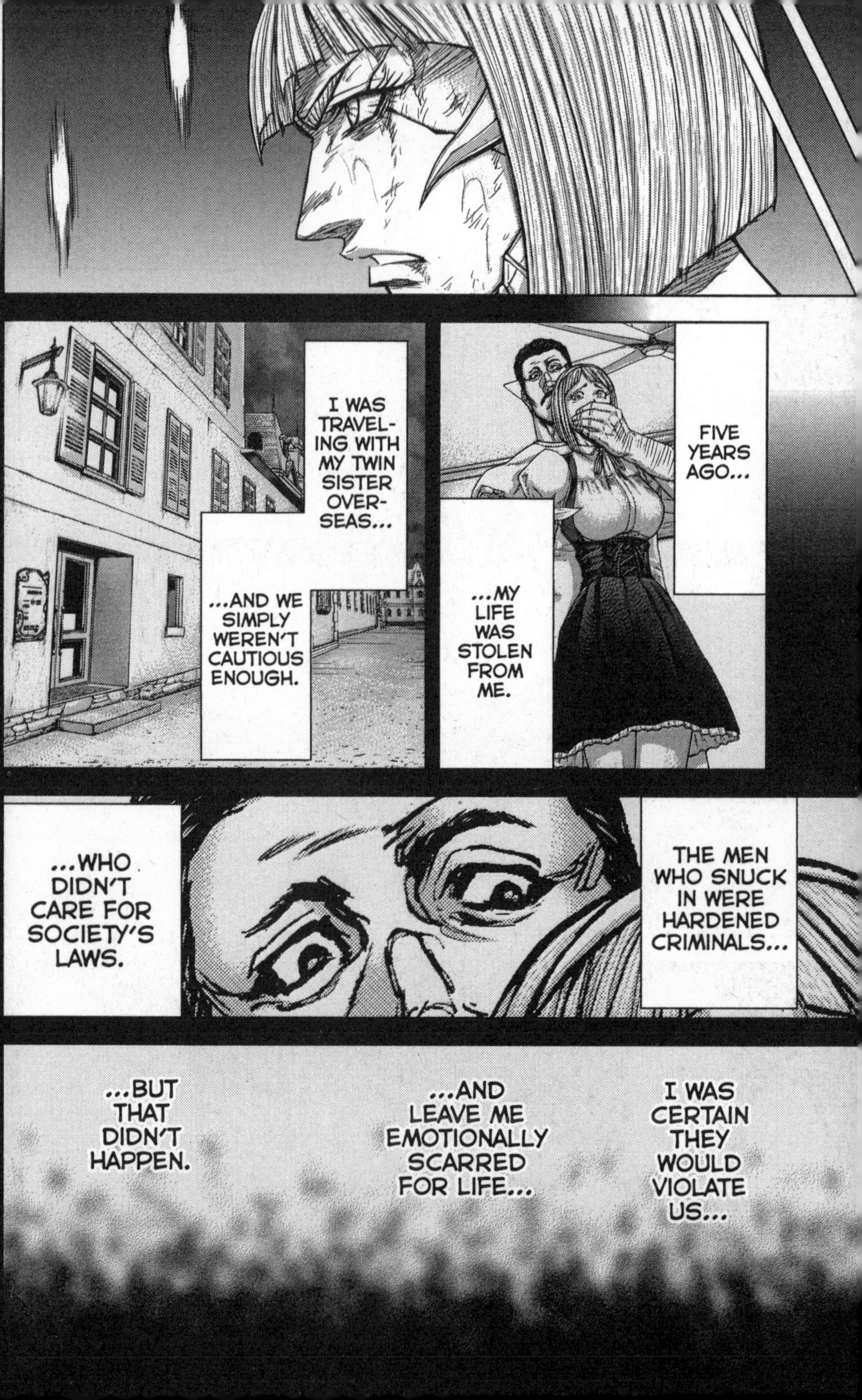
FIVE YEARS AGO...
...MY LIFE WAS STOLEN FROM ME.
I WAS TRAVEL-ING WITH MY TWIN SISTER OVER-SEAS...
...AND WE SIMPLY WEREN'T CAUTIOUS ENOUGH.
THE MEN WHO SNUCK IN WERE HARDENED CRIMINALS...
...WHO DIDN'T CARE FOR SOCIETY'S LAWS.
I WAS CERTAIN THEY WOULD VIOLATE US...
...AND LEAVE ME EMOTIONALLY SCARRED FOR LIFE...
...BUT THAT DIDN'T HAPPEN.

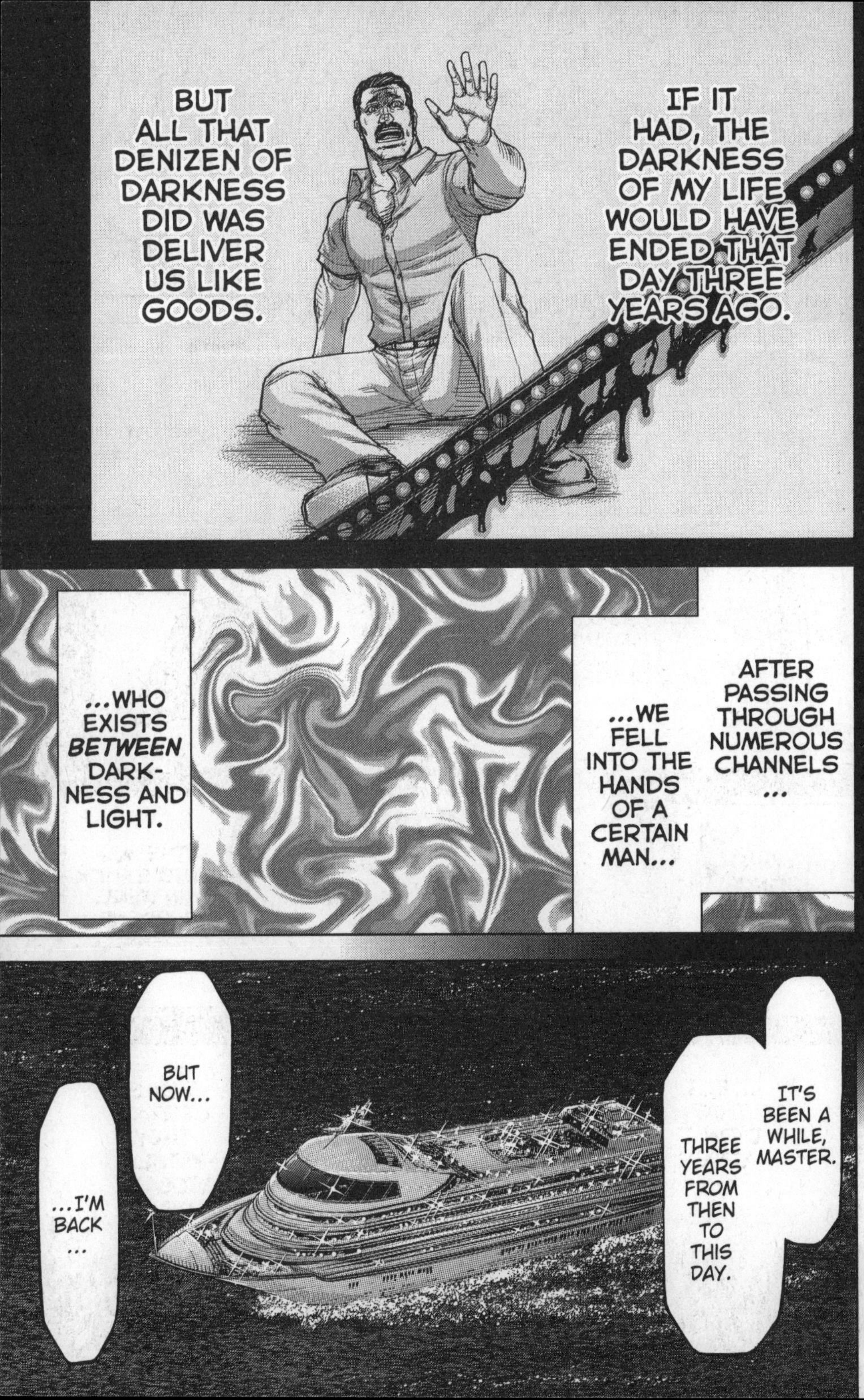
IF IT HAD, THE DARKNESS OF MY LIFE WOULD HAVE ENDED THAT DAY THREE YEARS AGO.
BUT ALL THAT DENIZEN OF DARKNESS DID WAS DELIVER US LIKE GOODS.
AFTER PASSING THROUGH NUMEROUS CHANNELS...
...WE FELL INTO THE HANDS OF A CERTAIN MAN...
...WHO EXISTS *BETWEEN* DARKNESS AND LIGHT.
IT'S BEEN A WHILE, MASTER.
THREE YEARS FROM THEN TO THIS DAY.
BUT NOW...
...I'M BACK...

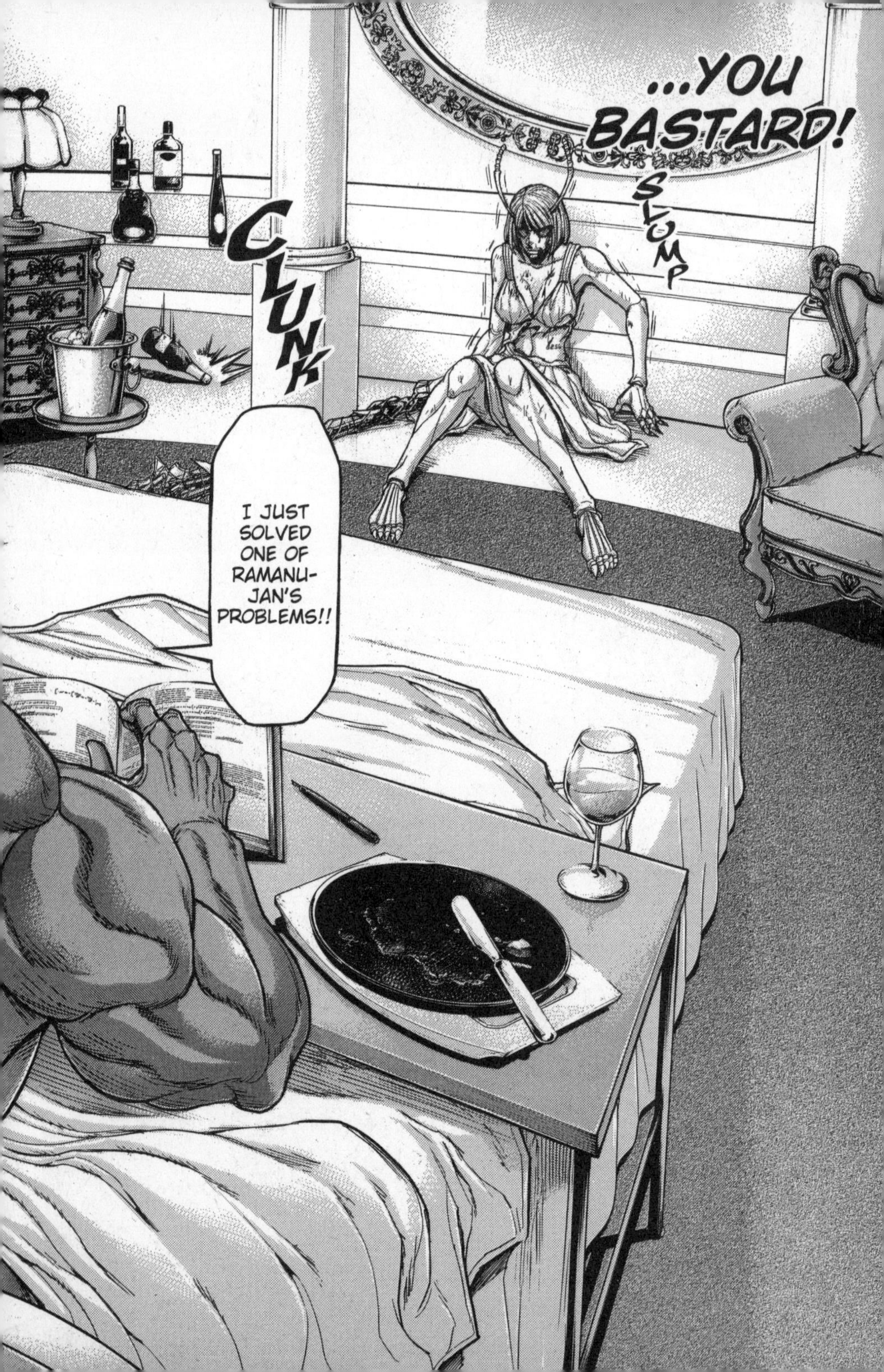
...YOU BASTARD!
SLOMP
CLUNK
I JUST SOLVED ONE OF RAMANUJAN'S PROBLEMS!!

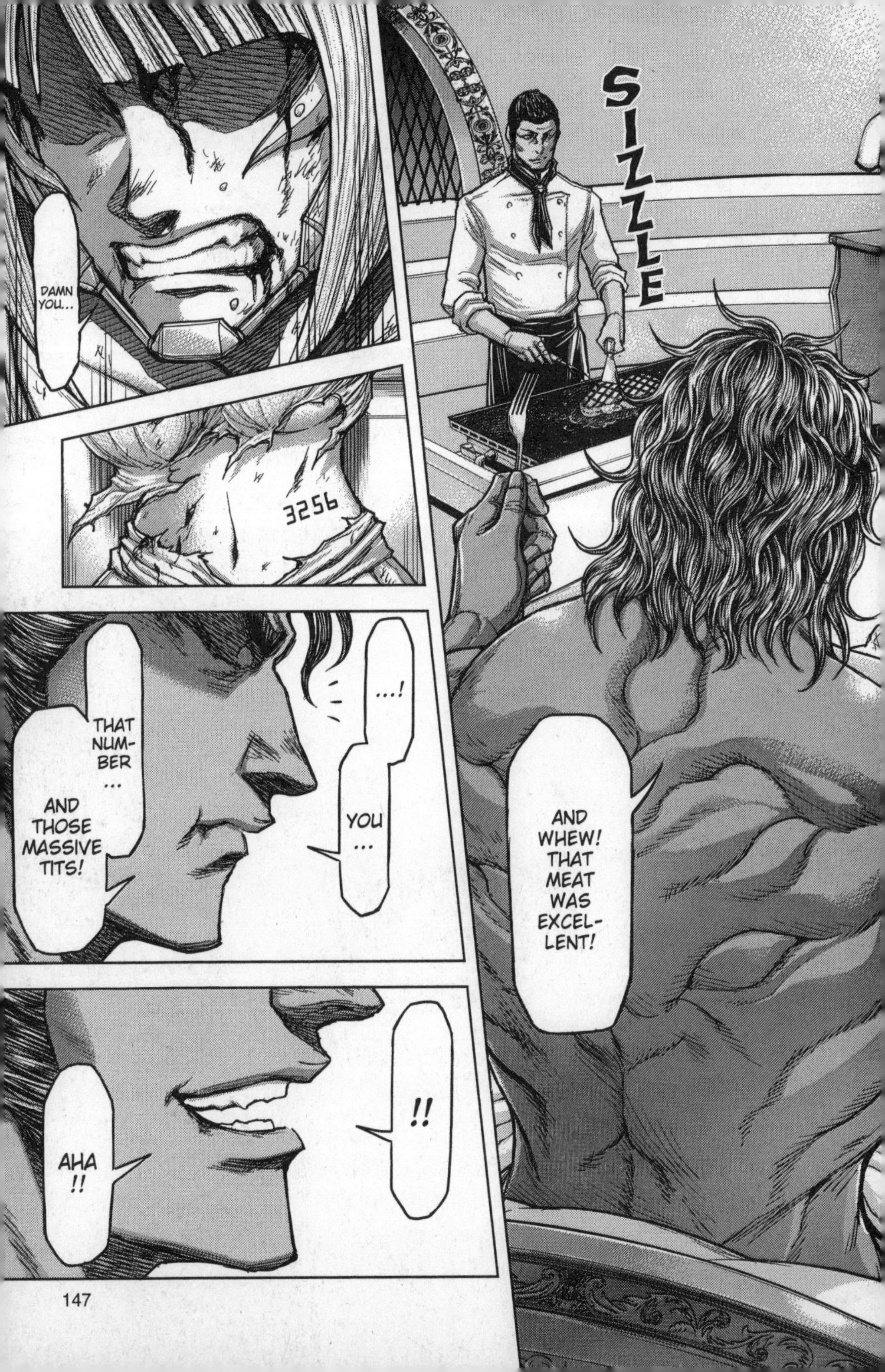
SIZZLE
AND WHEW! THAT MEAT WAS EXCEL-LENT!
DAMN YOU...
3256
...!
YOU...
THAT NUM-BER... AND THOSE MASSIVE TITS!
!!
AHA!!

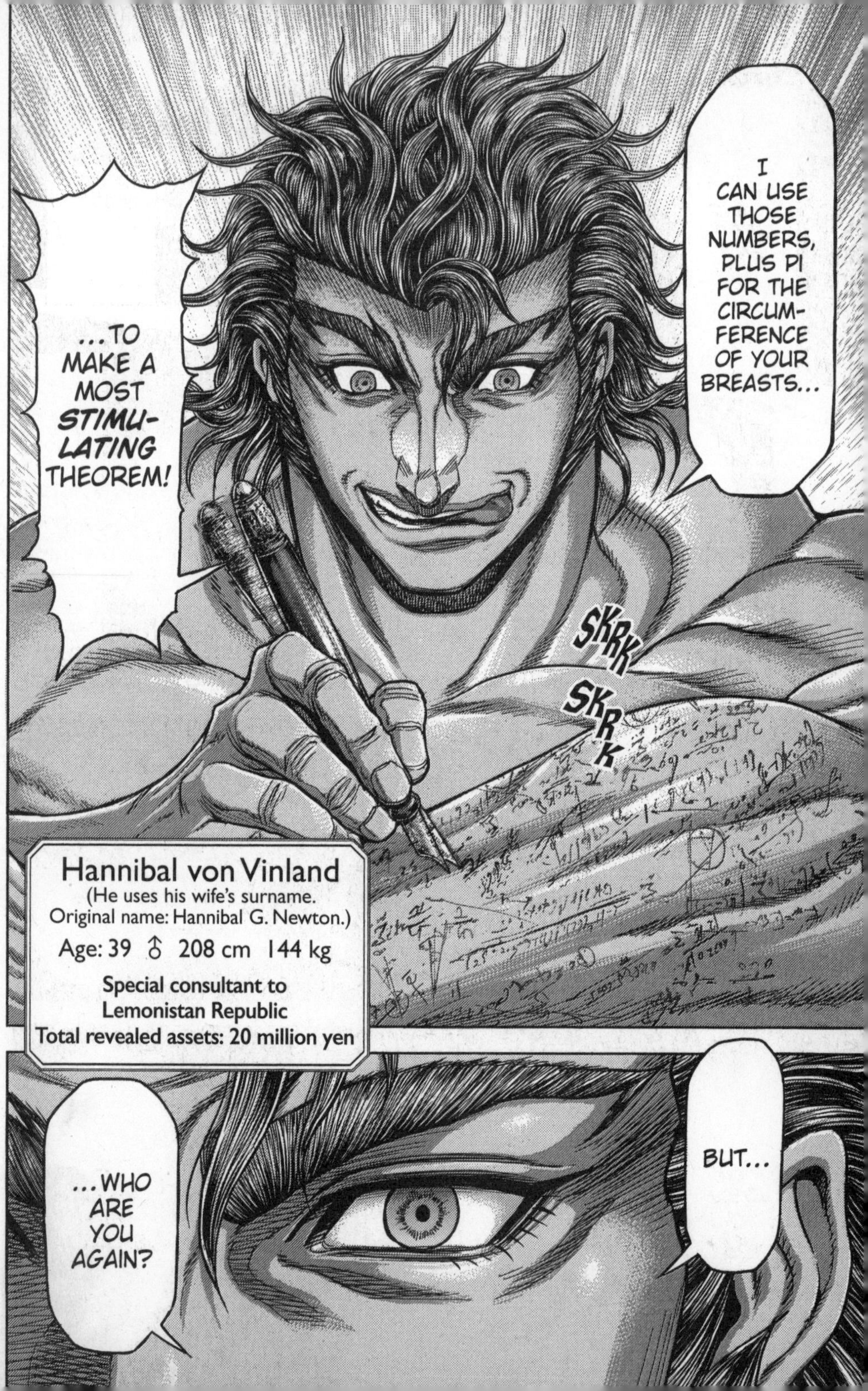
I CAN USE THOSE NUMBERS, PLUS PI FOR THE CIRCUMFERENCE OF YOUR BREASTS...
...TO MAKE A MOST STIMULATING THEOREM!
SKRK
SKRK
Hannibal von Vinland
(He uses his wife's surname. Original name: Hannibal G. Newton.)
Age: 39 ♂ 208 cm 144 kg
Special consultant to Lemonistan Republic
Total revealed assets: 20 million yen
BUT...
...WHO ARE YOU AGAIN?

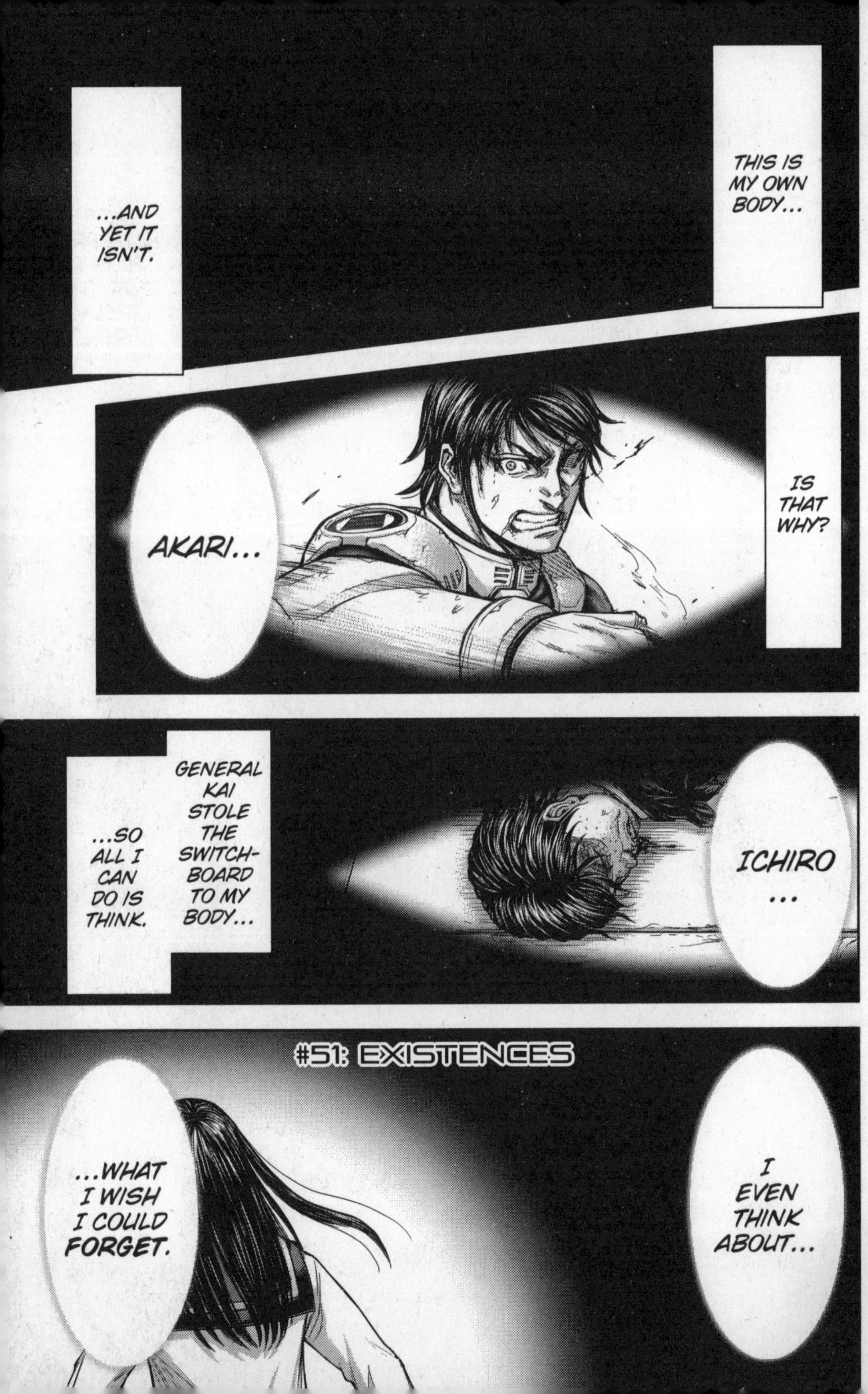
THIS IS MY OWN BODY...
...AND YET IT ISN'T.
IS THAT WHY?
AKARI...
ICHIRO ...
GENERAL KAI STOLE THE SWITCH-BOARD TO MY BODY...
...SO ALL I CAN DO IS THINK.
#51: EXISTENCES
I EVEN THINK ABOUT...
...WHAT I WISH I COULD FORGET.

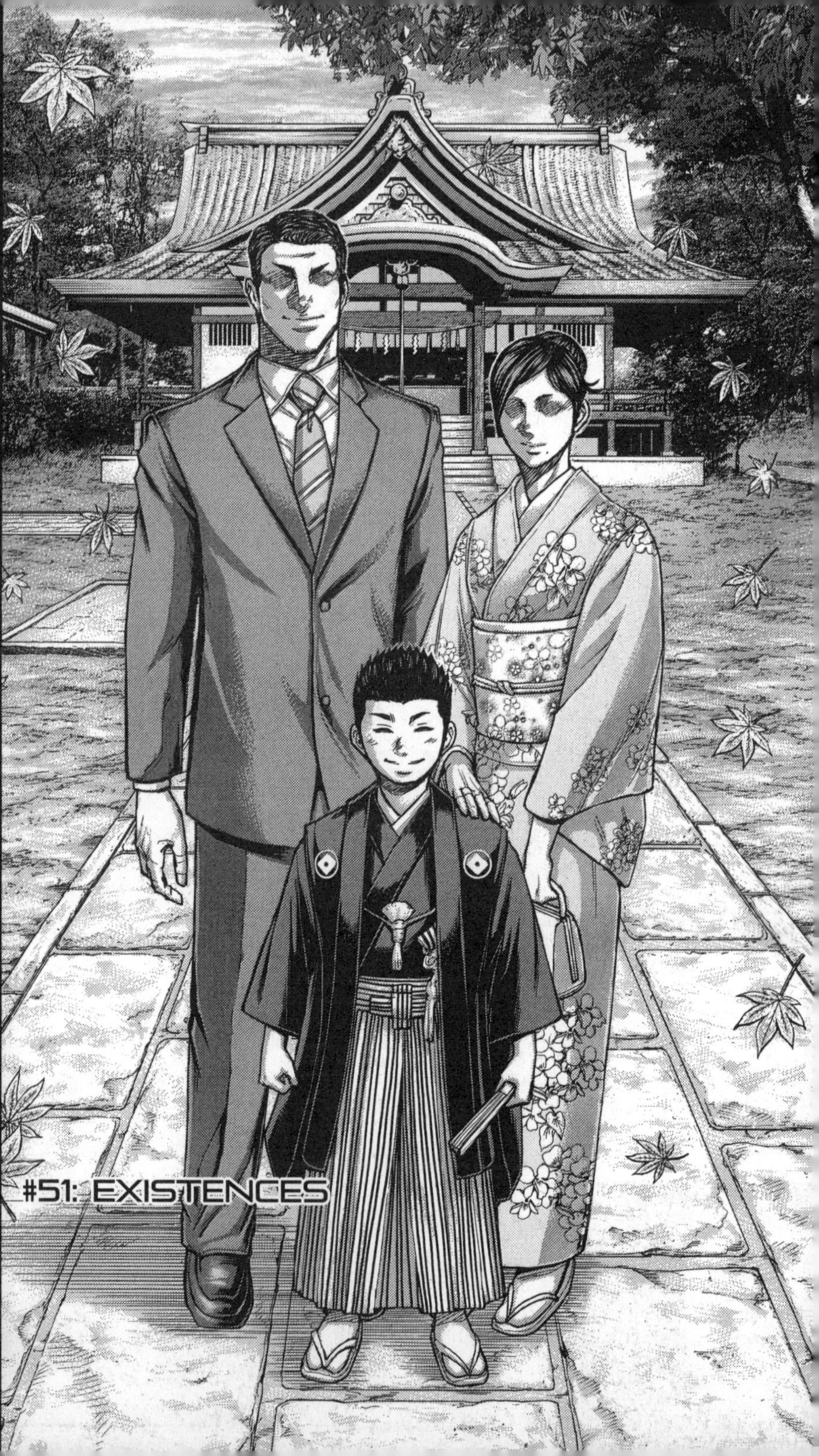
#51: EXISTENCES

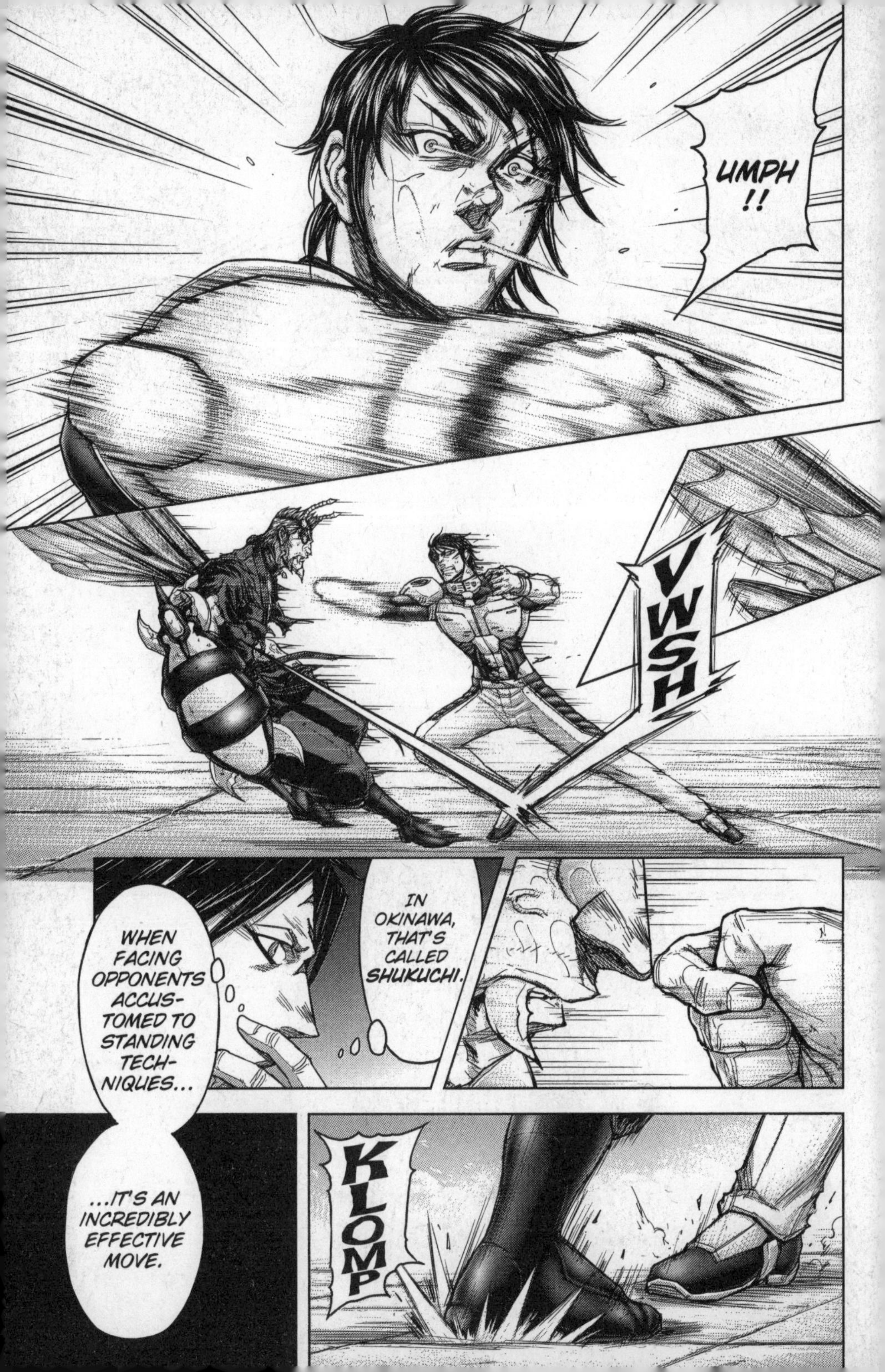
UMPH !!
VWSH
IN OKINAWA, THAT'S CALLED SHUKUCHI.
WHEN FACING OPPONENTS ACCUSTOMED TO STANDING TECHNIQUES...
KLOMP
...IT'S AN INCREDIBLY EFFECTIVE MOVE.

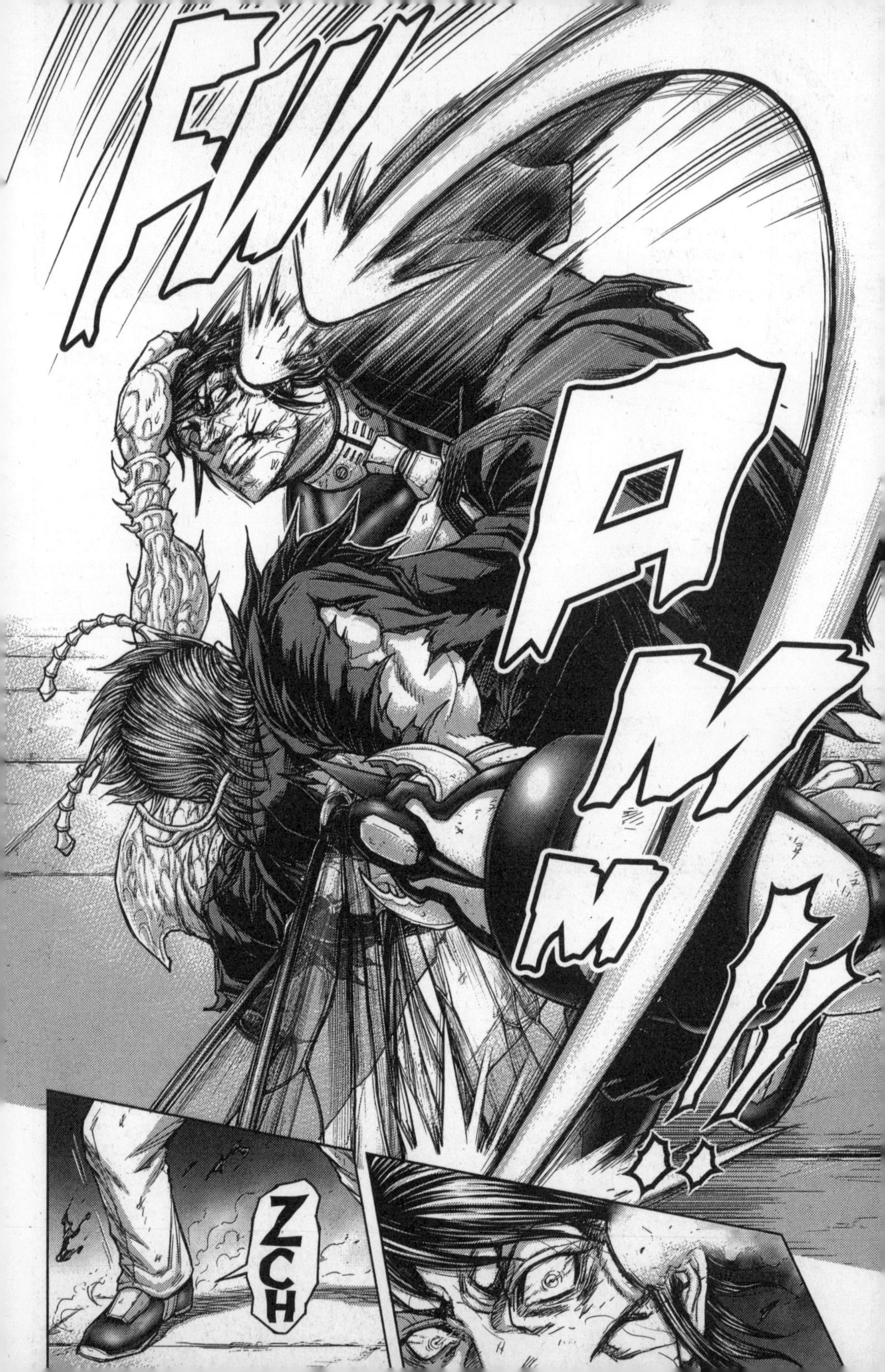
FWAMM!!
ZCH

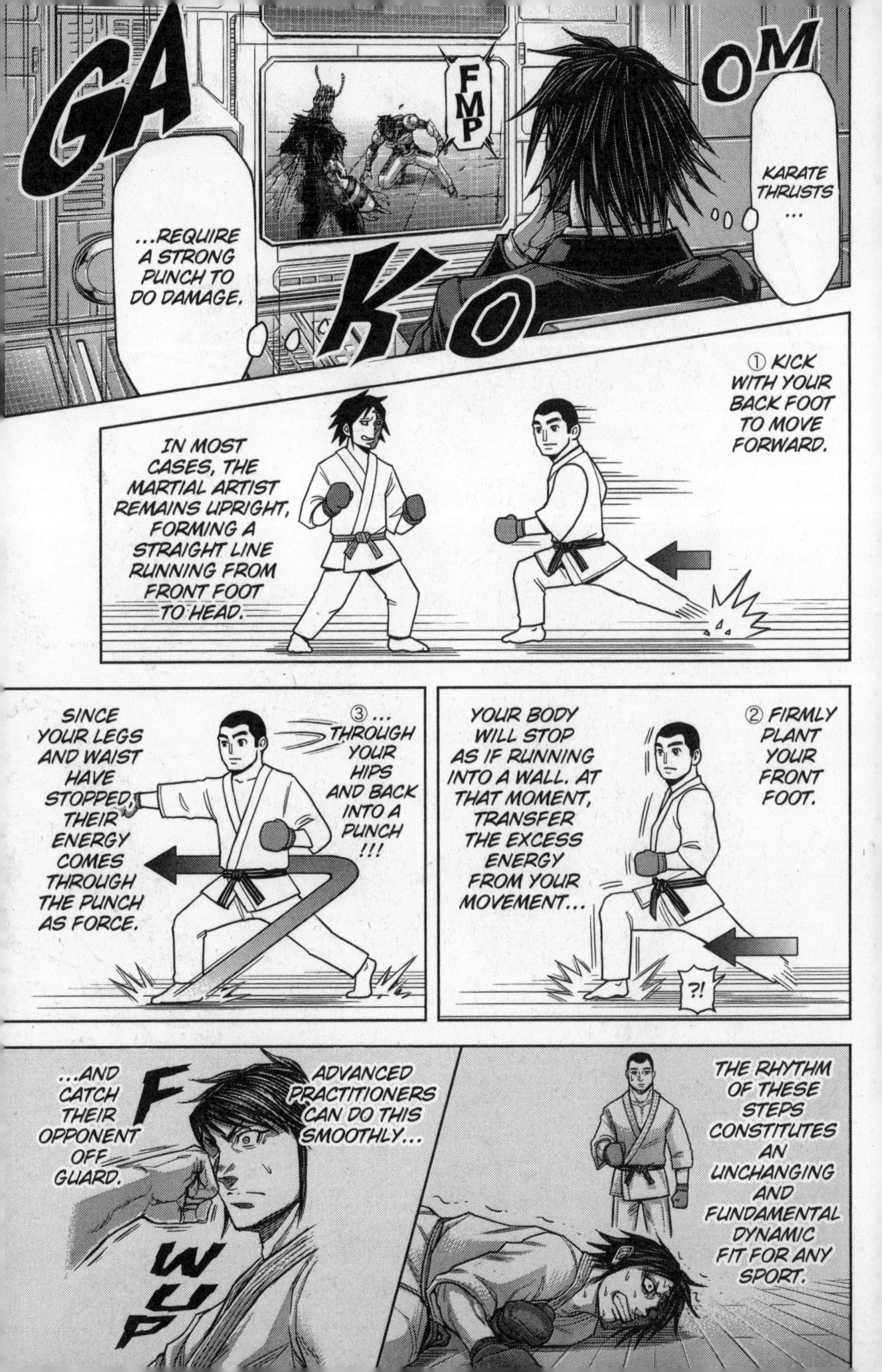

GA
KO
OM
KARATE THRUSTS ...
FMP
...REQUIRE A STRONG PUNCH TO DO DAMAGE.
① KICK WITH YOUR BACK FOOT TO MOVE FORWARD.
IN MOST CASES, THE MARTIAL ARTIST REMAINS UPRIGHT, FORMING A STRAIGHT LINE RUNNING FROM FRONT FOOT TO HEAD.
② FIRMLY PLANT YOUR FRONT FOOT.
YOUR BODY WILL STOP AS IF RUNNING INTO A WALL. AT THAT MOMENT, TRANSFER THE EXCESS ENERGY FROM YOUR MOVEMENT...
?!
③... THROUGH YOUR HIPS AND BACK INTO A PUNCH!!!
SINCE YOUR LEGS AND WAIST HAVE STOPPED, THEIR ENERGY COMES THROUGH THE PUNCH AS FORCE.
THE RHYTHM OF THESE STEPS CONSTITUTES AN UNCHANGING AND FUNDAMENTAL DYNAMIC FIT FOR ANY SPORT.
ADVANCED PRACTITIONERS CAN DO THIS SMOOTHLY...
...AND CATCH THEIR OPPONENT OFF GUARD.
F
WUP

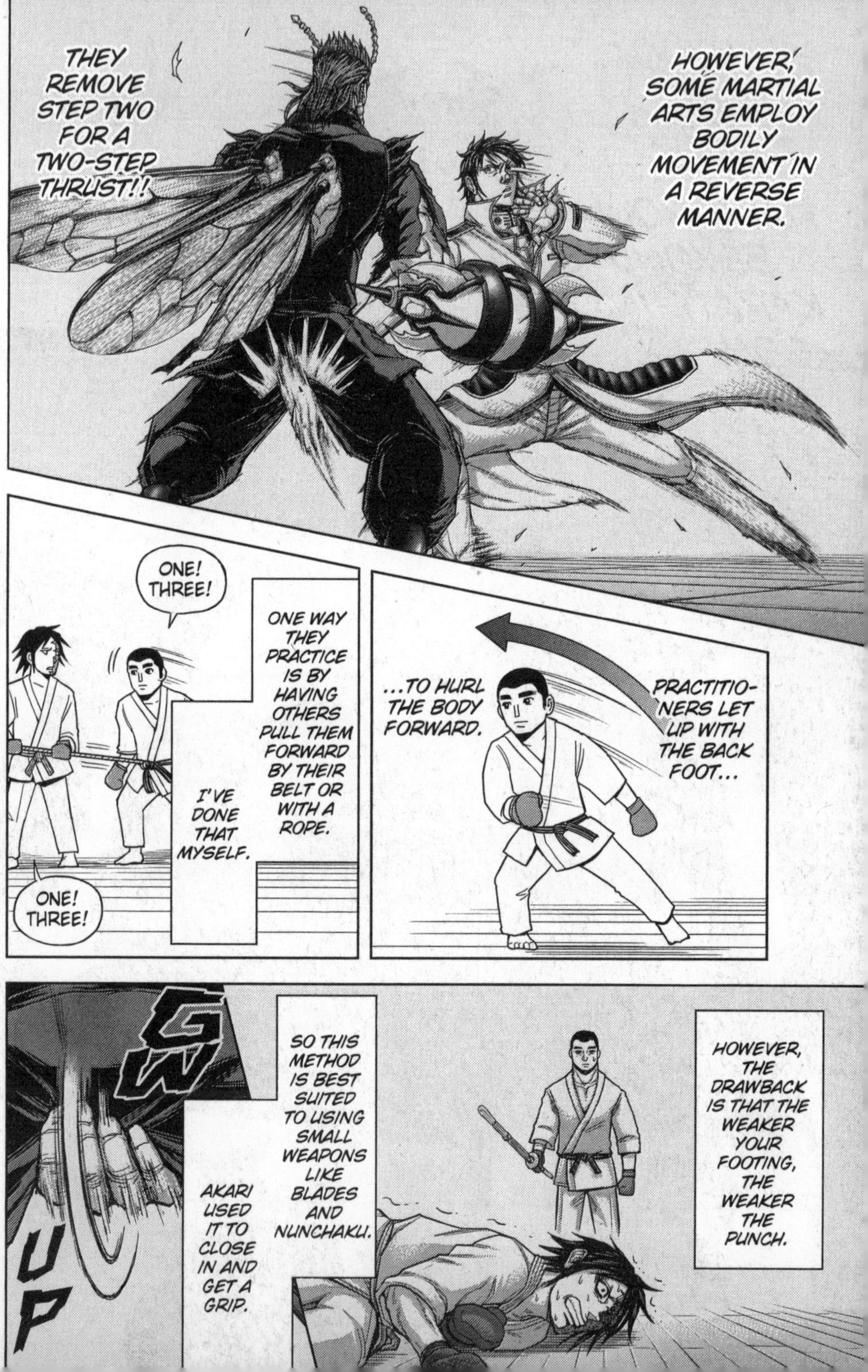

HOWEVER, SOME MARTIAL ARTS EMPLOY BODILY MOVEMENT IN A REVERSE MANNER.
THEY REMOVE STEP TWO FOR A TWO-STEP THRUST!!
PRACTITIONERS LET UP WITH THE BACK FOOT...
...TO HURL THE BODY FORWARD.
ONE WAY THEY PRACTICE IS BY HAVING OTHERS PULL THEM FORWARD BY THEIR BELT OR WITH A ROPE.
ONE! THREE!
I'VE DONE THAT MYSELF.
ONE! THREE!
HOWEVER, THE DRAWBACK IS THAT THE WEAKER YOUR FOOTING, THE WEAKER THE PUNCH.
SO THIS METHOD IS BEST SUITED TO USING SMALL WEAPONS LIKE BLADES AND NUNCHAKU.
AKARI USED IT TO CLOSE IN AND GET A GRIP.
GWUP

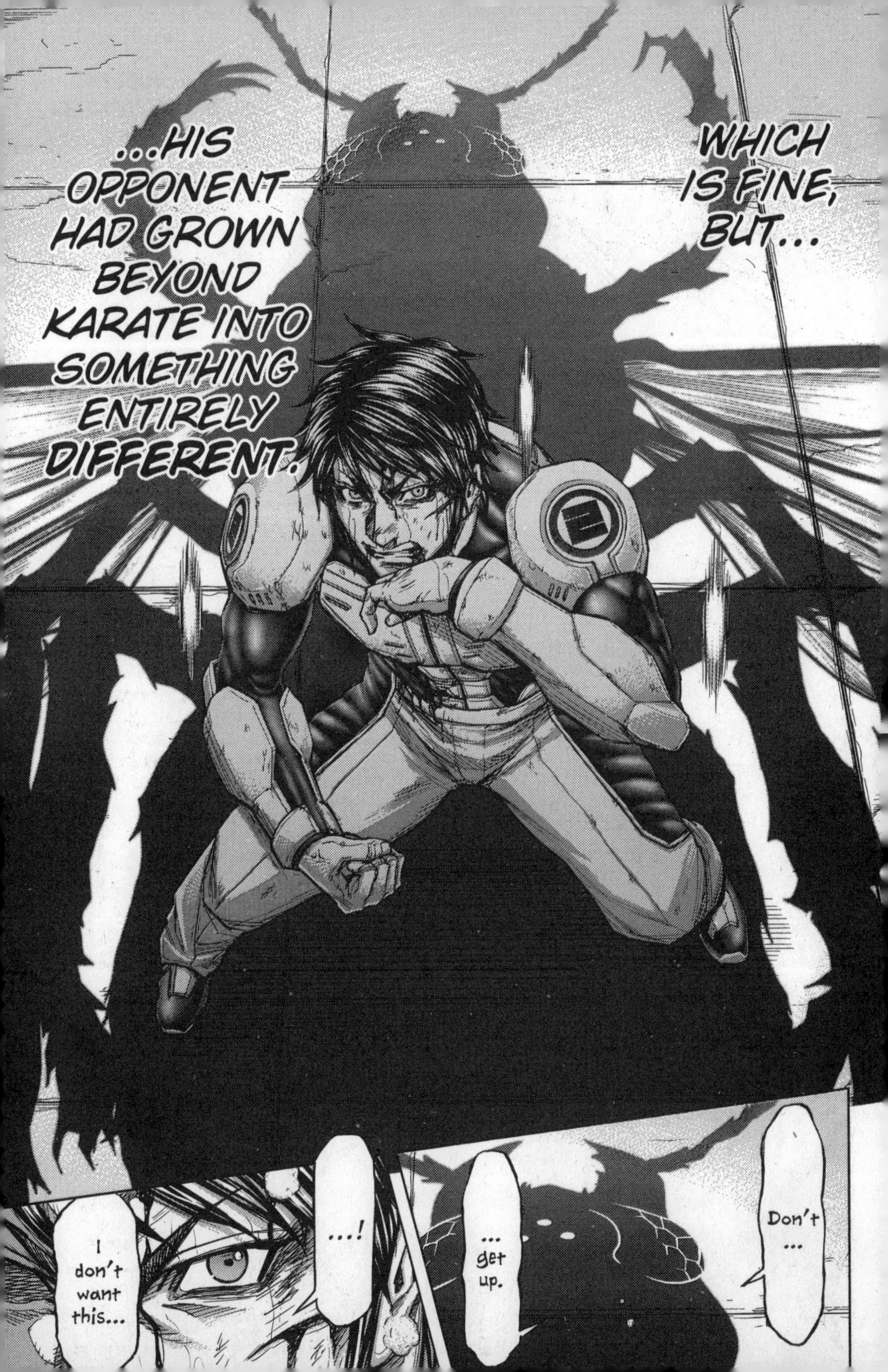
WHICH IS FINE, BUT...
...HIS OPPONENT HAD GROWN BEYOND KARATE INTO SOMETHING ENTIRELY DIFFERENT.
Don't ...
... get up.
...!
I don't want this...

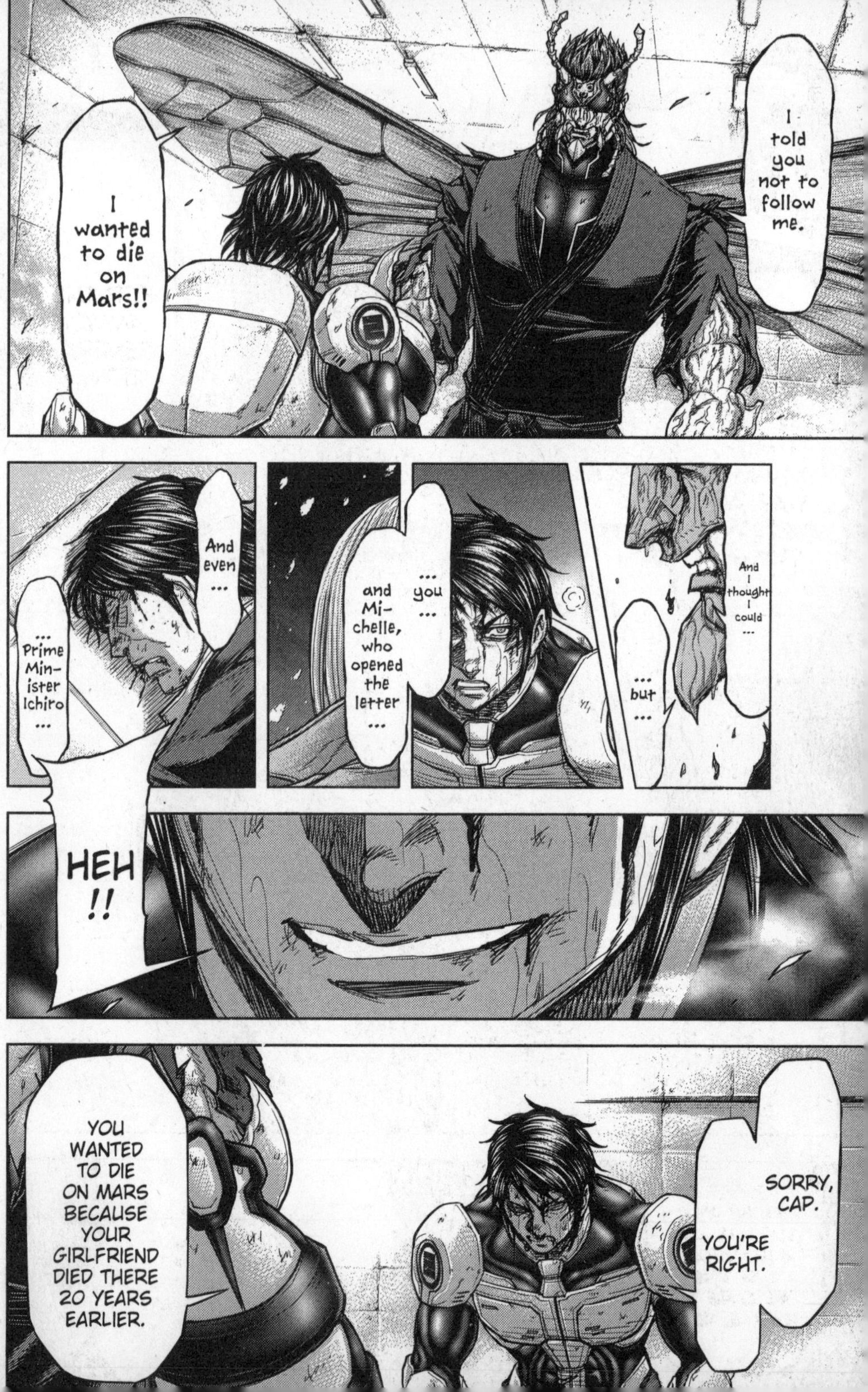
I told you not to follow me.
I wanted to die on Mars!!
And I thought I could ...
... but ...
... you ...
and Michelle, who opened the letter ...
And even ...
... Prime Minister Ichiro ...
HEH!!
SORRY, CAP.
YOU'RE RIGHT.
YOU WANTED TO DIE ON MARS BECAUSE YOUR GIRLFRIEND DIED THERE 20 YEARS EARLIER.

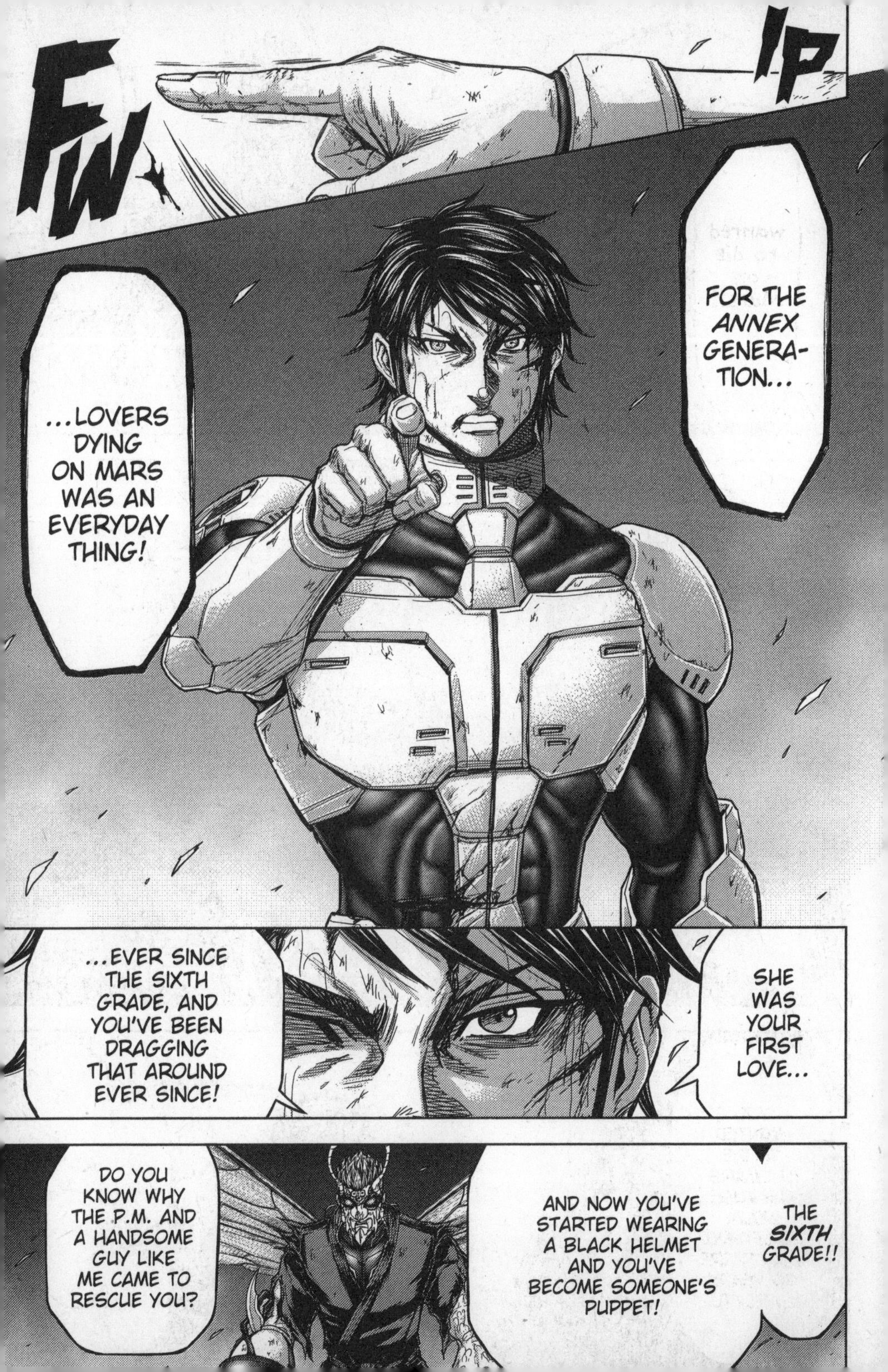
FWIP
FOR THE *ANNEX* GENERATION...
...LOVERS DYING ON MARS WAS AN EVERYDAY THING!
SHE WAS YOUR FIRST LOVE...
...EVER SINCE THE SIXTH GRADE, AND YOU'VE BEEN DRAGGING THAT AROUND EVER SINCE!
THE ***SIXTH*** GRADE!!
AND NOW YOU'VE STARTED WEARING A BLACK HELMET AND YOU'VE BECOME SOMEONE'S PUPPET!
DO YOU KNOW WHY THE P.M. AND A HANDSOME GUY LIKE ME CAME TO RESCUE YOU?

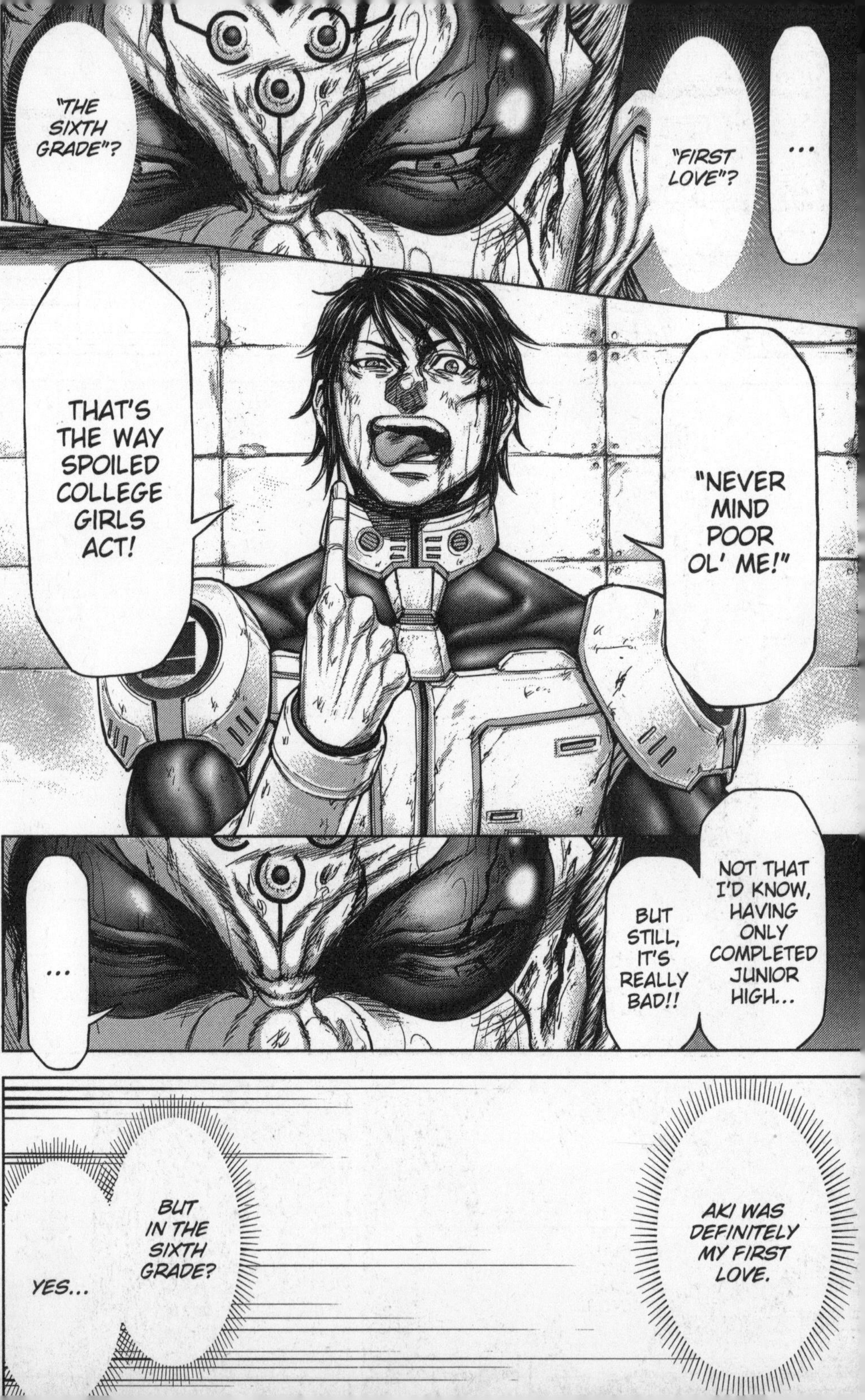
...
"FIRST LOVE"?
"THE SIXTH GRADE"?
"NEVER MIND POOR OL' ME!"
THAT'S THE WAY SPOILED COLLEGE GIRLS ACT!
NOT THAT I'D KNOW, HAVING ONLY COMPLETED JUNIOR HIGH...
BUT STILL, IT'S REALLY BAD!!
...
AKI WAS DEFINITELY MY FIRST LOVE.
BUT IN THE SIXTH GRADE?
YES...

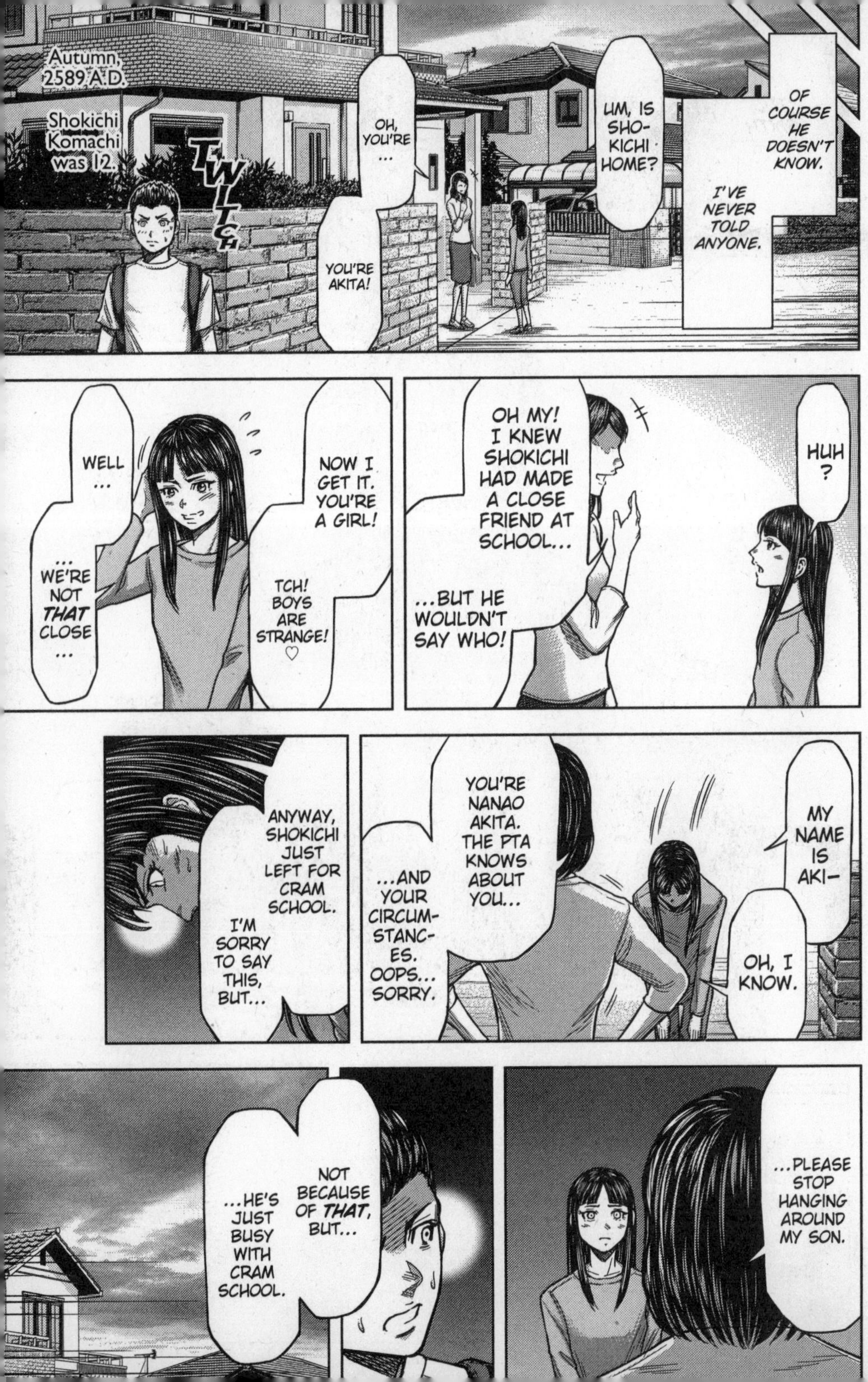

OF COURSE HE DOESN'T KNOW.
I'VE NEVER TOLD ANYONE.
UM, IS SHOKICHI HOME?
OH, YOU'RE ...
YOU'RE AKITA!
TWITCH
Autumn, 2589 A.D.
Shokichi Komachi was 12.
HUH?
OH MY! I KNEW SHOKICHI HAD MADE A CLOSE FRIEND AT SCHOOL...
...BUT HE WOULDN'T SAY WHO!
NOW I GET IT. YOU'RE A GIRL!
TCH! BOYS ARE STRANGE! ♡
WELL...
...WE'RE NOT *THAT* CLOSE...
MY NAME IS AKI-
OH, I KNOW.
YOU'RE NANAO AKITA. THE PTA KNOWS ABOUT YOU...
...AND YOUR CIRCUMSTANCES. OOPS... SORRY.
ANYWAY, SHOKICHI JUST LEFT FOR CRAM SCHOOL.
I'M SORRY TO SAY THIS, BUT...
...PLEASE STOP HANGING AROUND MY SON.
NOT BECAUSE OF *THAT*, BUT...
...HE'S JUST BUSY WITH CRAM SCHOOL.

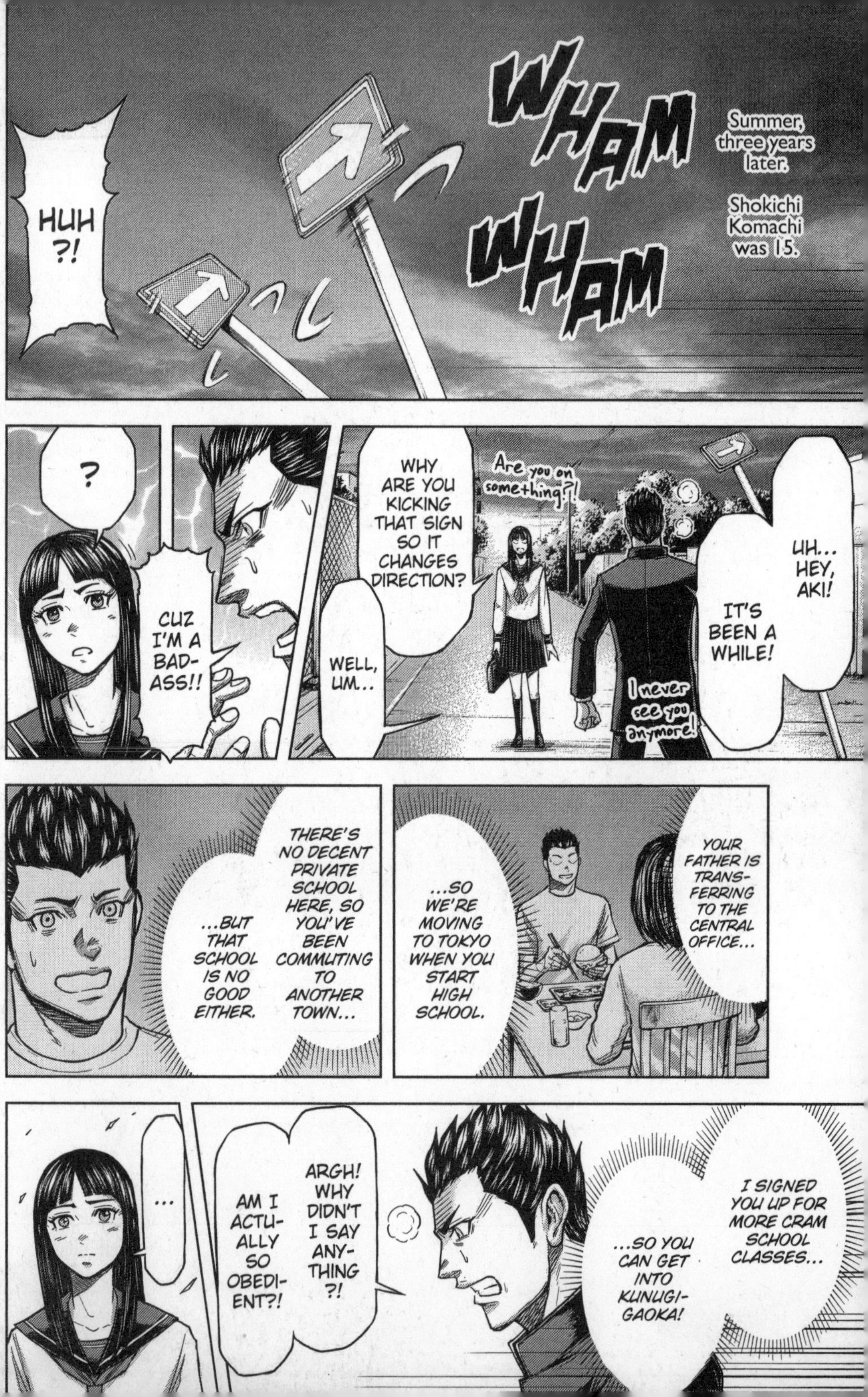

Summer, three years later.
Shokichi Komachi was 15.
WHAM WHAM
HUH?!
UH... HEY, AKI!
IT'S BEEN A WHILE!
I never see you anymore!
Are you on something?!
WHY ARE YOU KICKING THAT SIGN SO IT CHANGES DIRECTION?
WELL, UM...
CUZ I'M A BAD-ASS!!
?
YOUR FATHER IS TRANSFERRING TO THE CENTRAL OFFICE...
...SO WE'RE MOVING TO TOKYO WHEN YOU START HIGH SCHOOL.
THERE'S NO DECENT PRIVATE SCHOOL HERE, SO YOU'VE BEEN COMMUTING TO ANOTHER TOWN...
...BUT THAT SCHOOL IS NO GOOD EITHER.
I SIGNED YOU UP FOR MORE CRAM SCHOOL CLASSES...
...SO YOU CAN GET INTO KUNUGIGAOKA!
ARGH! WHY DIDN'T I SAY ANYTHING?!
AM I ACTUALLY SO OBEDIENT?!
...

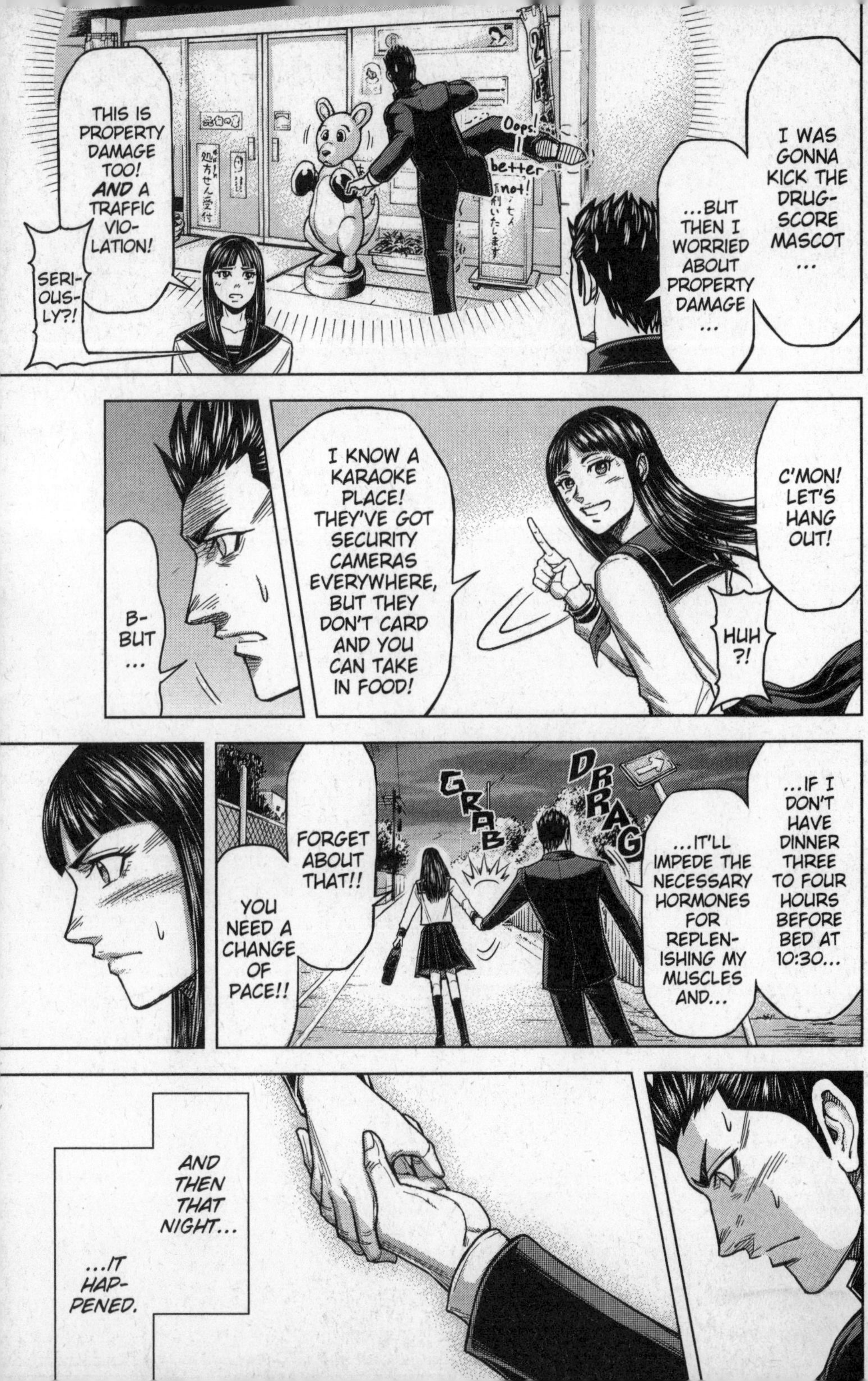
I WAS GONNA KICK THE DRUG-SCORE MASCOT ...
...BUT THEN I WORRIED ABOUT PROPERTY DAMAGE ...
Oops!
better not!
THIS IS PROPERTY DAMAGE TOO! AND A TRAFFIC VIOLATION!
SERIOUSLY?!
C'MON! LET'S HANG OUT!
HUH?!
I KNOW A KARAOKE PLACE! THEY'VE GOT SECURITY CAMERAS EVERYWHERE, BUT THEY DON'T CARD AND YOU CAN TAKE IN FOOD!
B-BUT ...
...IF I DON'T HAVE DINNER THREE TO FOUR HOURS BEFORE BED AT 10:30...
...IT'LL IMPEDE THE NECESSARY HORMONES FOR REPLENISHING MY MUSCLES AND...
DRAG
GRAB
FORGET ABOUT THAT!!
YOU NEED A CHANGE OF PACE!!
AND THEN THAT NIGHT...
...IT HAPPENED.

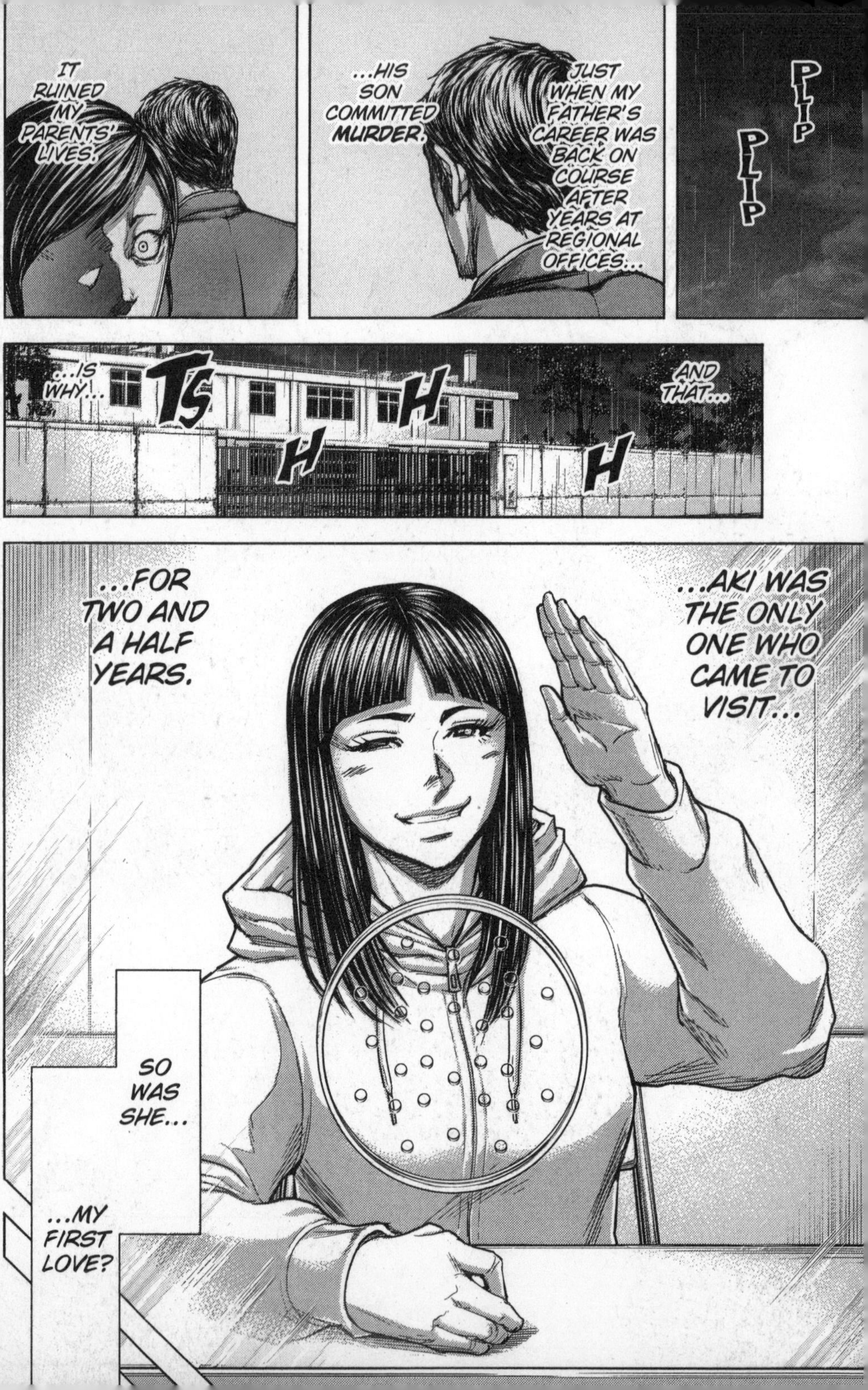
PLIP
PLIP
JUST WHEN MY FATHER'S CAREER WAS BACK ON COURSE AFTER YEARS AT REGIONAL OFFICES...
...HIS SON COMMITTED MURDER.
IT RUINED MY PARENTS' LIVES.
AND THAT...
TSHHH
...IS WHY...
...AKI WAS THE ONLY ONE WHO CAME TO VISIT...
...FOR TWO AND A HALF YEARS.
SO WAS SHE...
...MY FIRST LOVE?

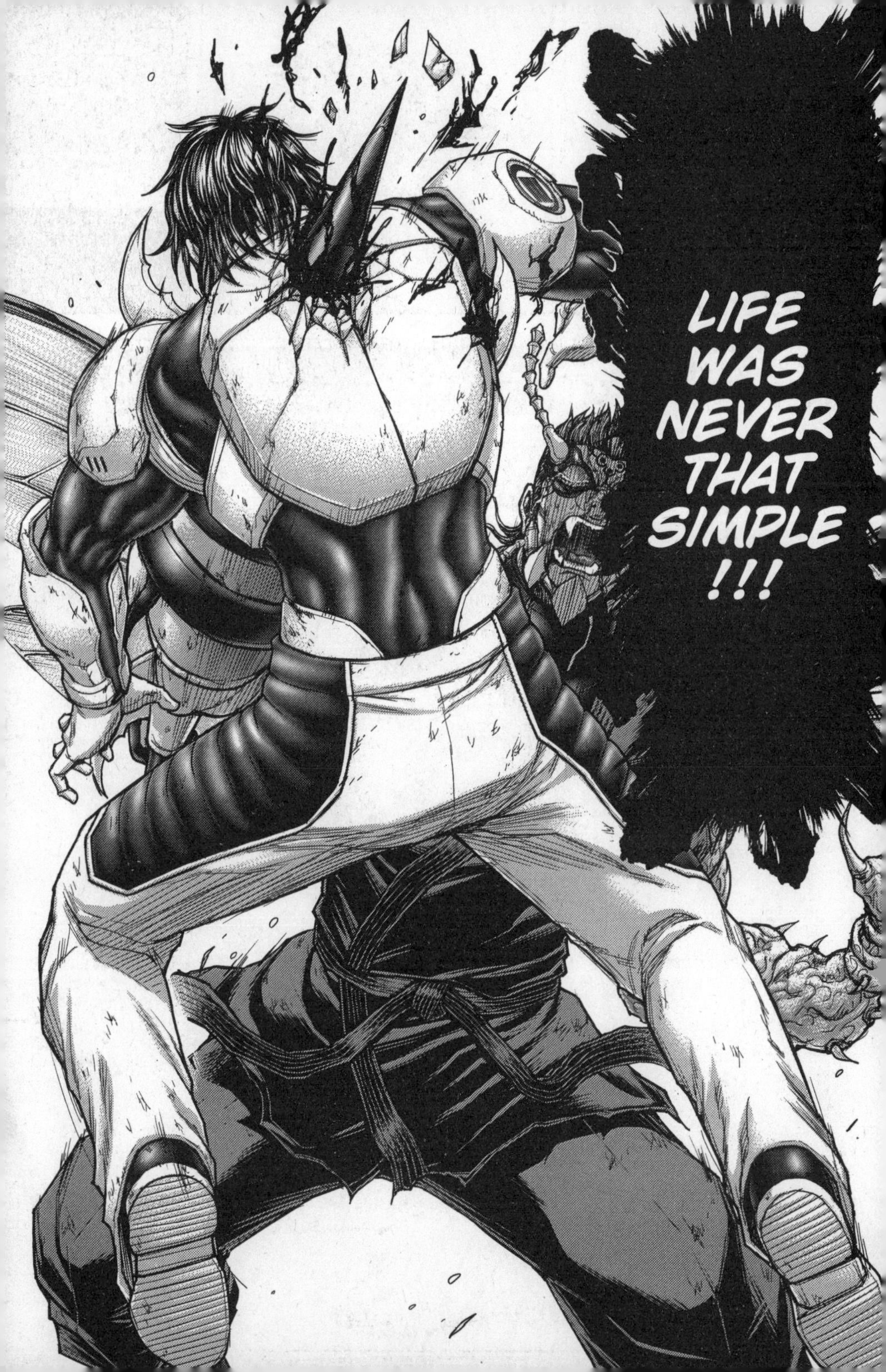
LIFE WAS NEVER THAT SIMPLE !!!

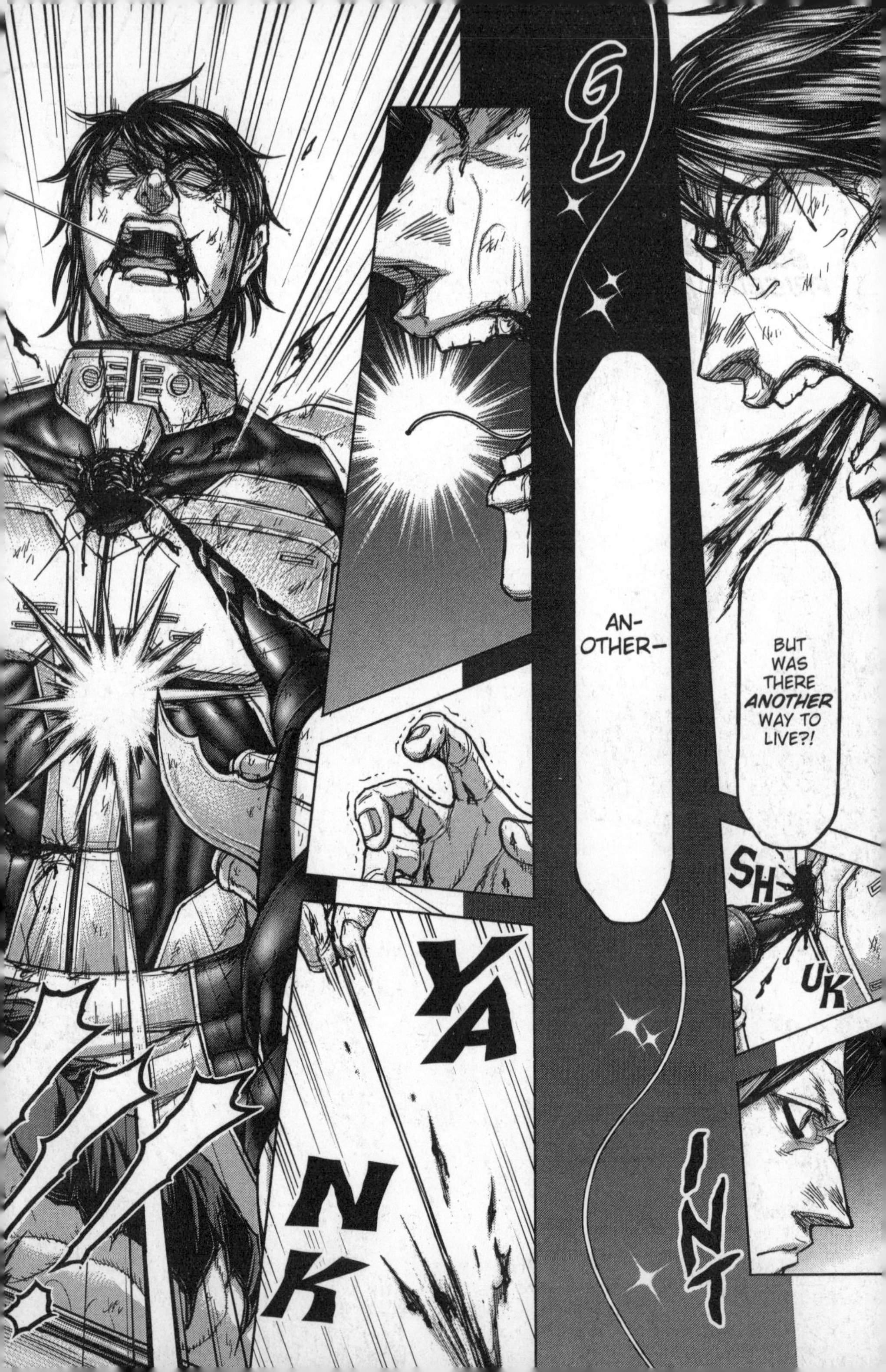
BUT WAS THERE ***ANOTHER*** WAY TO LIVE?!
SH
UK
GL
AN-OTHER-
INK
YA
NK

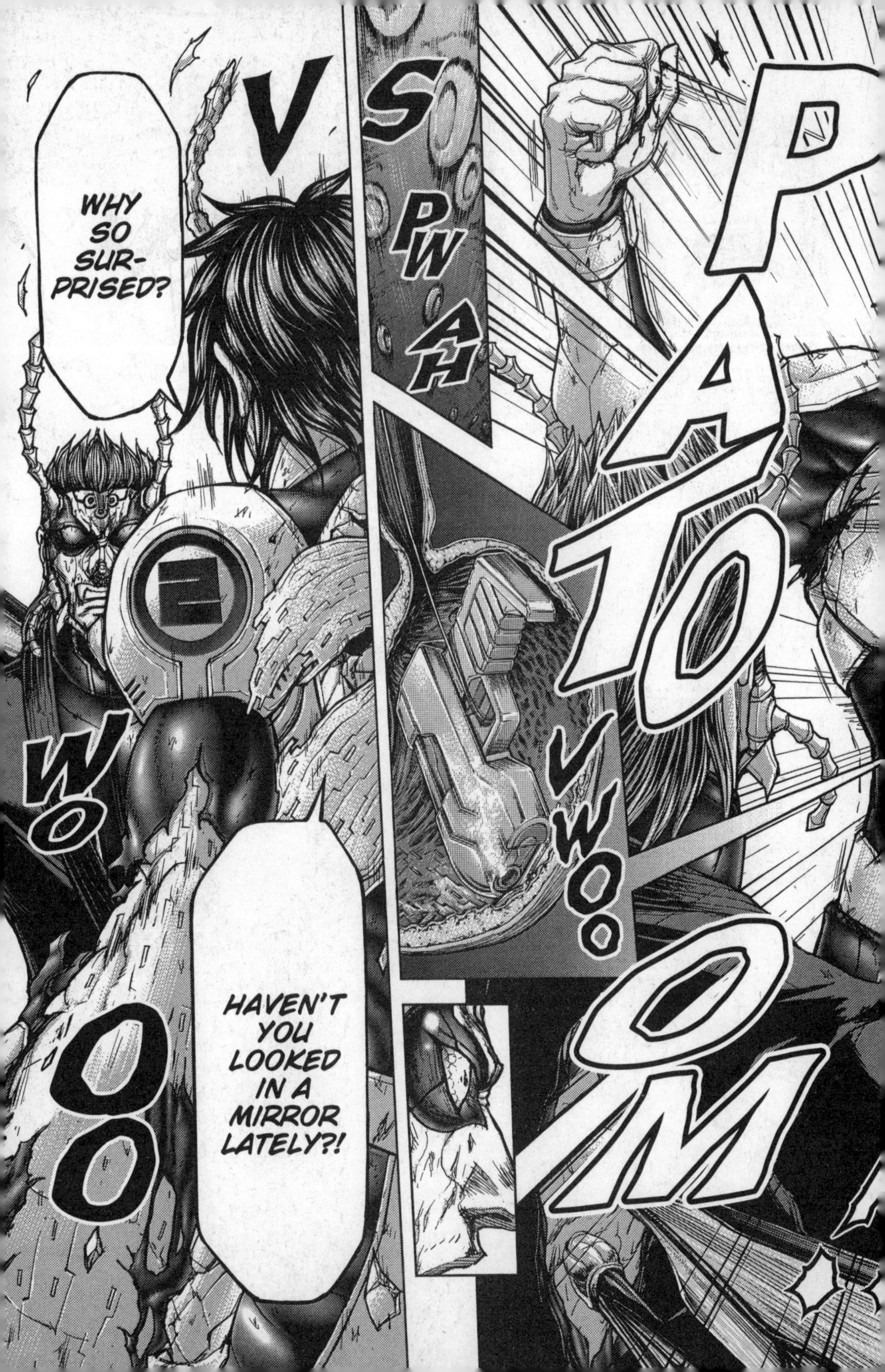
PATOOM
SPWAH
VWOOO
WHY SO SUR-PRISED?
V
WOOO
HAVEN'T YOU LOOKED IN A MIRROR LATELY?!

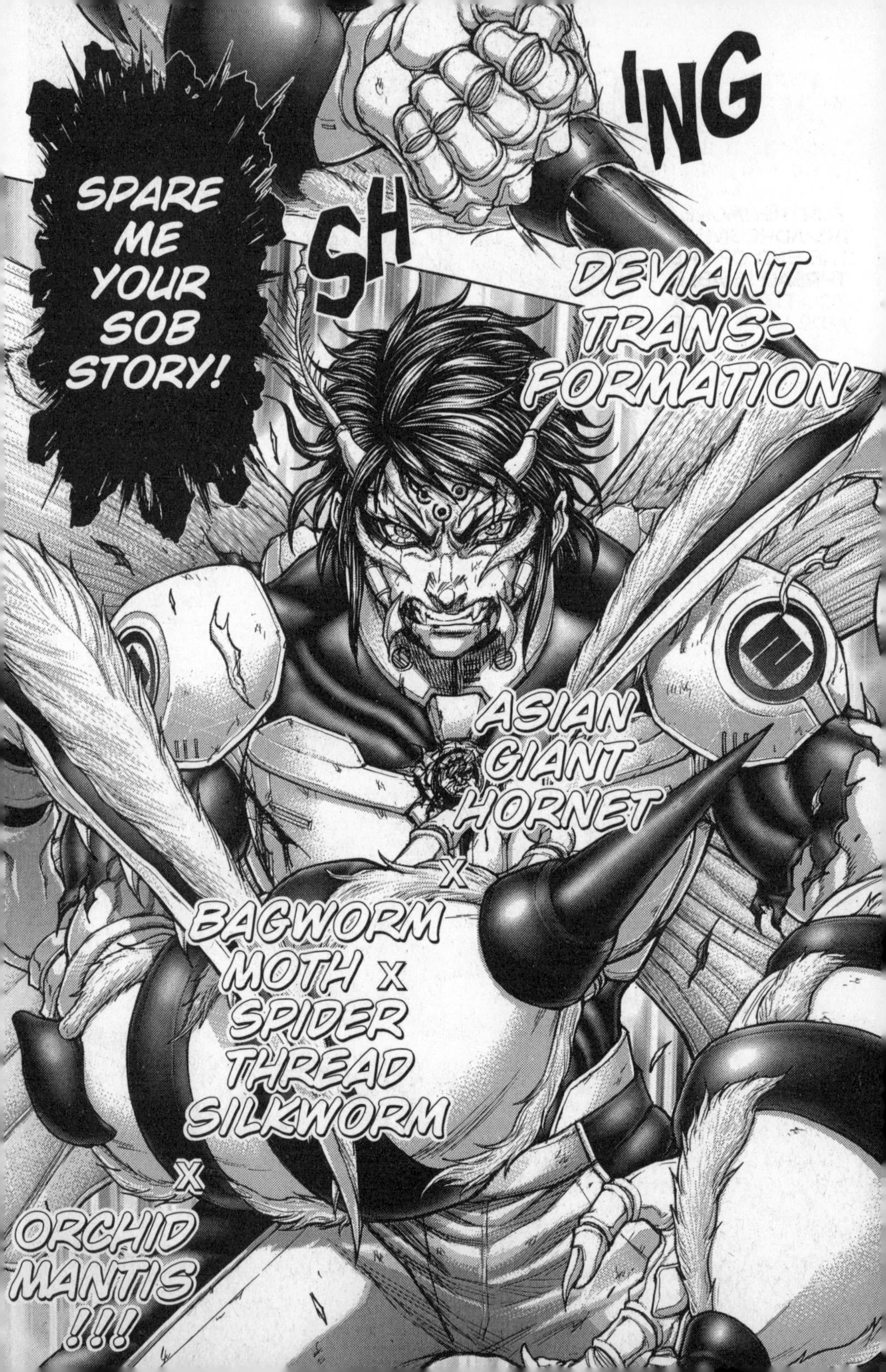
SH ING
SPARE ME YOUR SOB STORY!
DEVIANT TRANS-FORMATION
ASIAN GIANT HORNET
x
BAGWORM MOTH x SPIDER THREAD SILKWORM
x
ORCHID MANTIS!!!

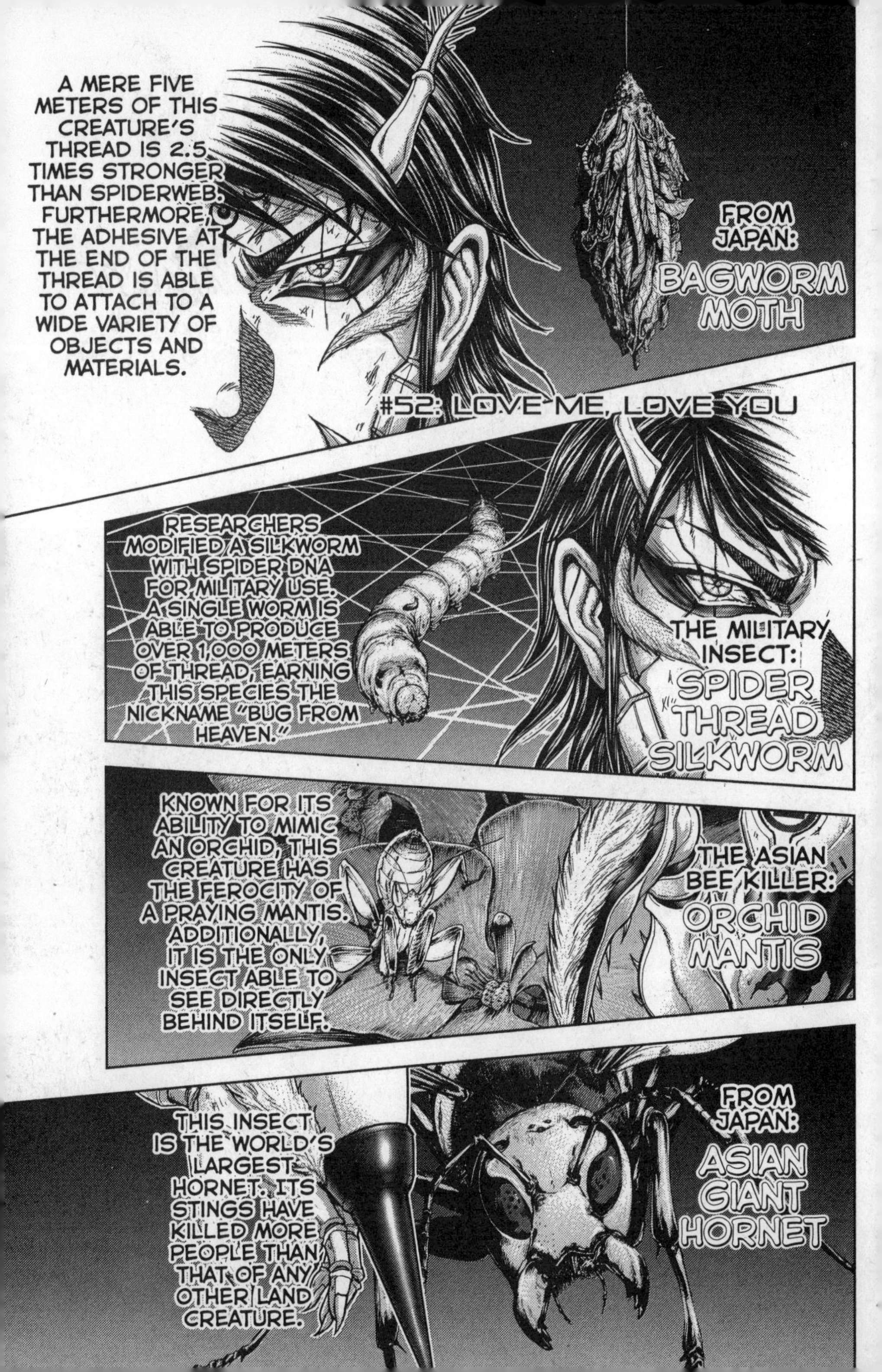
FROM JAPAN:
BAGWORM MOTH
A MERE FIVE METERS OF THIS CREATURE'S THREAD IS 2.5 TIMES STRONGER THAN SPIDERWEB. FURTHERMORE, THE ADHESIVE AT THE END OF THE THREAD IS ABLE TO ATTACH TO A WIDE VARIETY OF OBJECTS AND MATERIALS.
#52: LOVE ME, LOVE YOU
THE MILITARY INSECT:
SPIDER THREAD SILKWORM
RESEARCHERS MODIFIED A SILKWORM WITH SPIDER DNA FOR MILITARY USE. A SINGLE WORM IS ABLE TO PRODUCE OVER 1,000 METERS OF THREAD, EARNING THIS SPECIES THE NICKNAME "BUG FROM HEAVEN."
THE ASIAN BEE KILLER:
ORCHID MANTIS
KNOWN FOR ITS ABILITY TO MIMIC AN ORCHID, THIS CREATURE HAS THE FEROCITY OF A PRAYING MANTIS. ADDITIONALLY, IT IS THE ONLY INSECT ABLE TO SEE DIRECTLY BEHIND ITSELF.
FROM JAPAN:
ASIAN GIANT HORNET
THIS INSECT IS THE WORLD'S LARGEST HORNET. ITS STINGS HAVE KILLED MORE PEOPLE THAN THAT OF ANY OTHER LAND CREATURE.

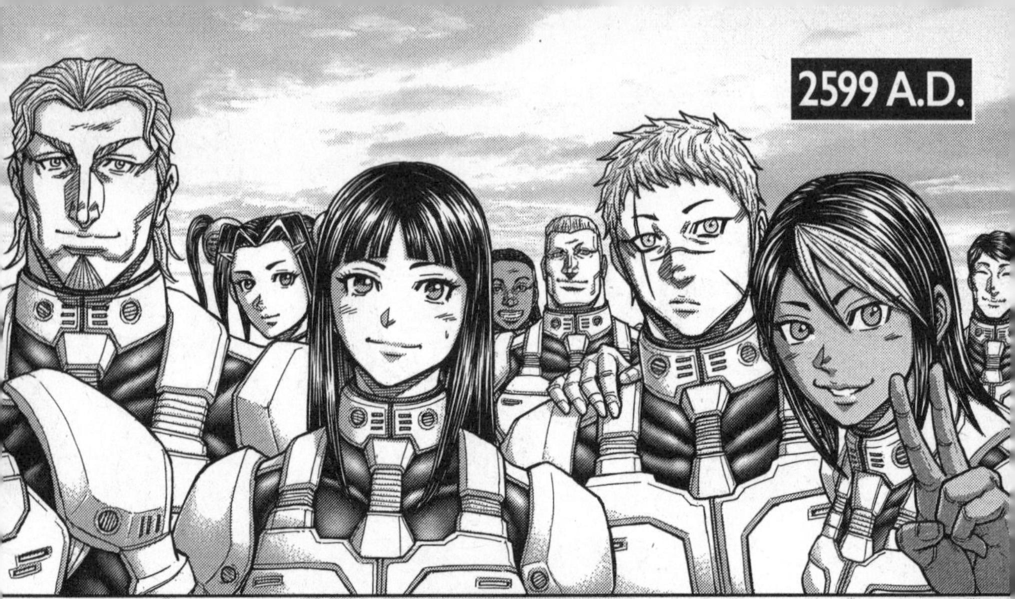
2599 A.D.
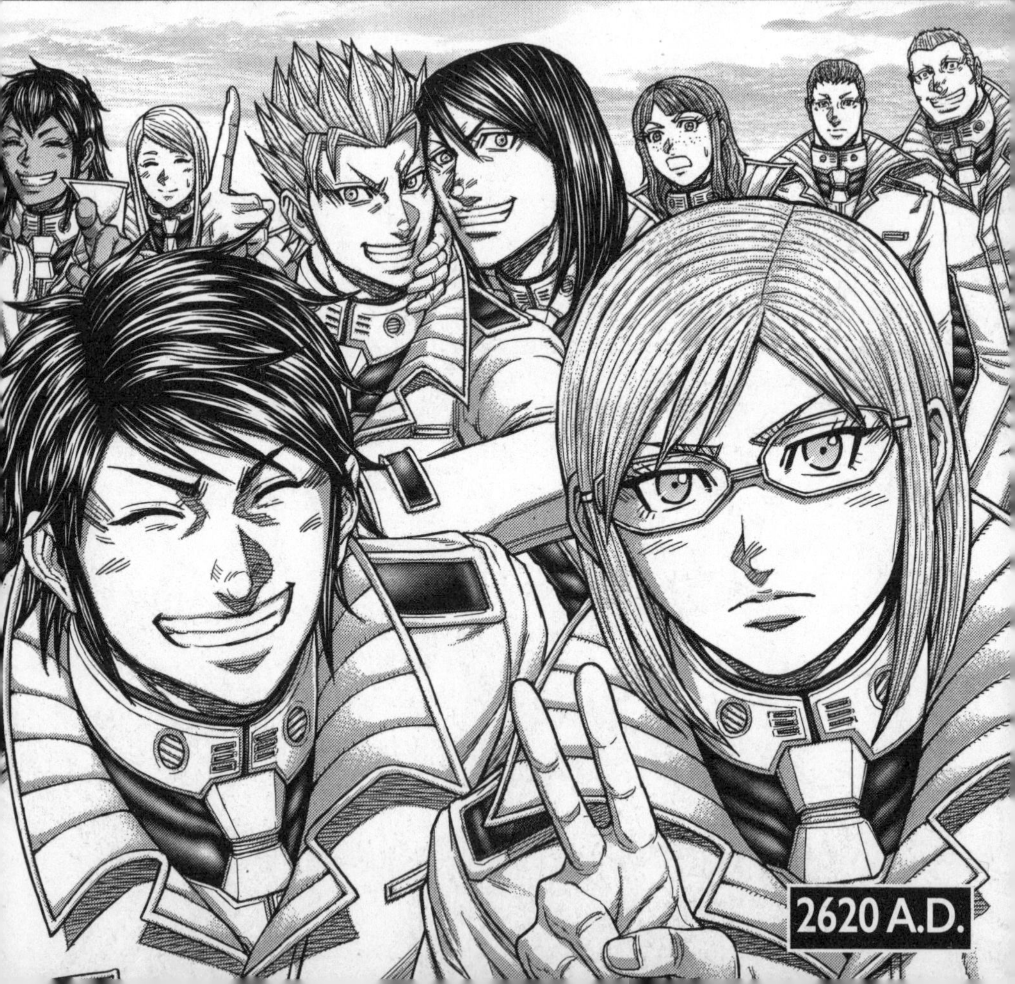
2620 A.D.

# #52: LOVE ME, LOVE YOU

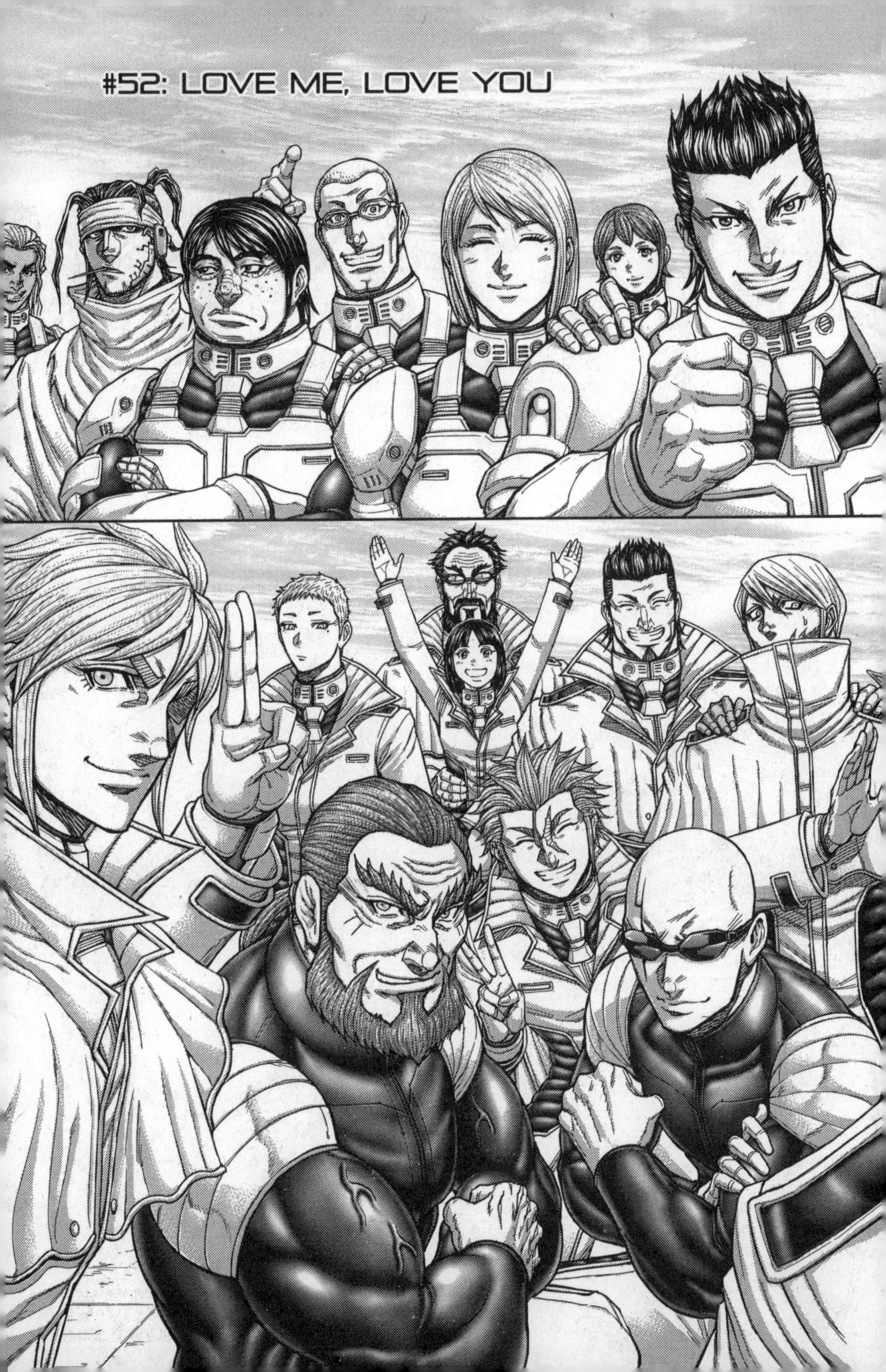

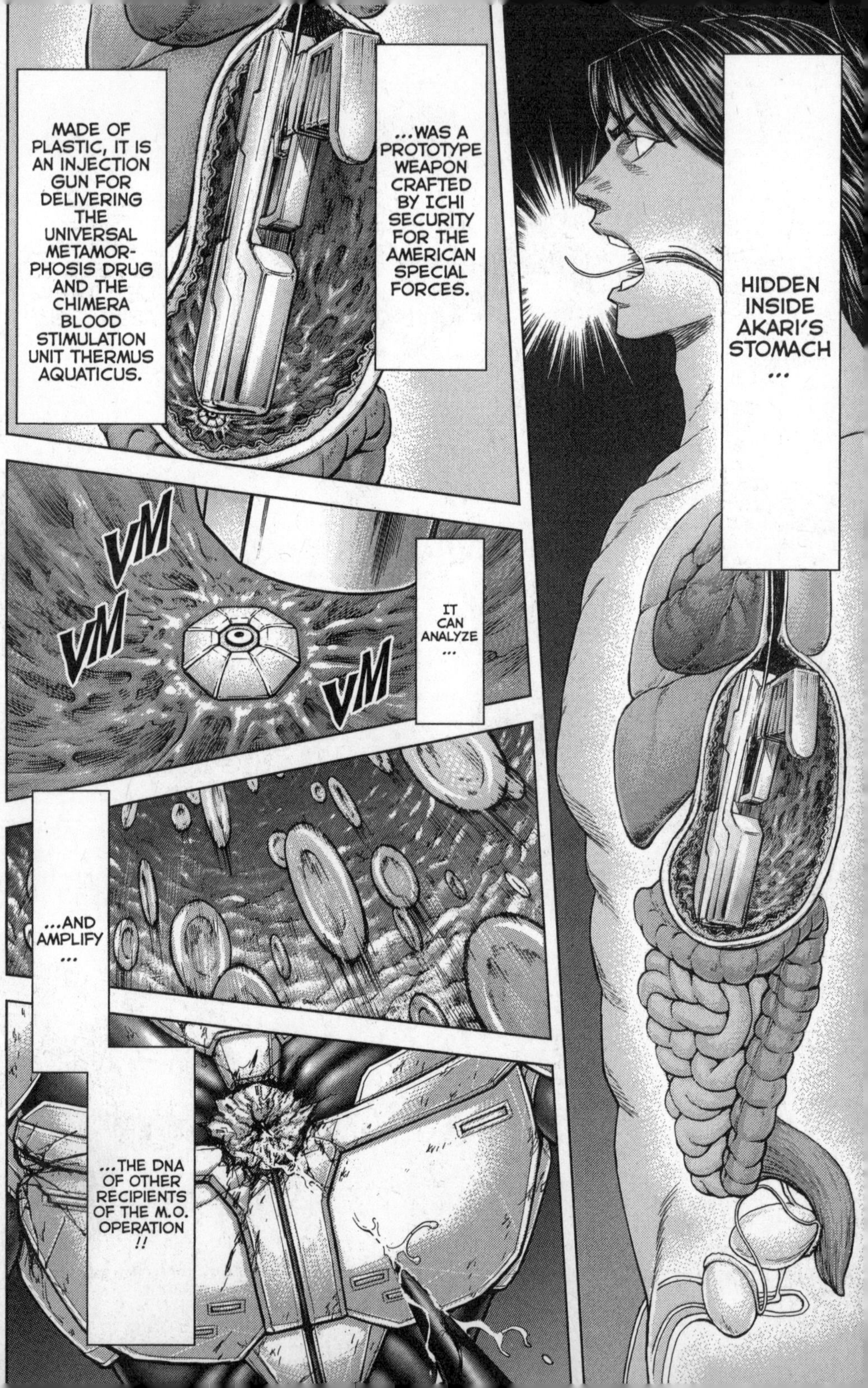
HIDDEN INSIDE AKARI'S STOMACH ...
...WAS A PROTOTYPE WEAPON CRAFTED BY ICHI SECURITY FOR THE AMERICAN SPECIAL FORCES.
MADE OF PLASTIC, IT IS AN INJECTION GUN FOR DELIVERING THE UNIVERSAL METAMOR-PHOSIS DRUG AND THE CHIMERA BLOOD STIMULATION UNIT THERMUS AQUATICUS.
IT CAN ANALYZE ...
VM
VM
VM
...AND AMPLIFY ...
...THE DNA OF OTHER RECIPIENTS OF THE M.O. OPERATION !!

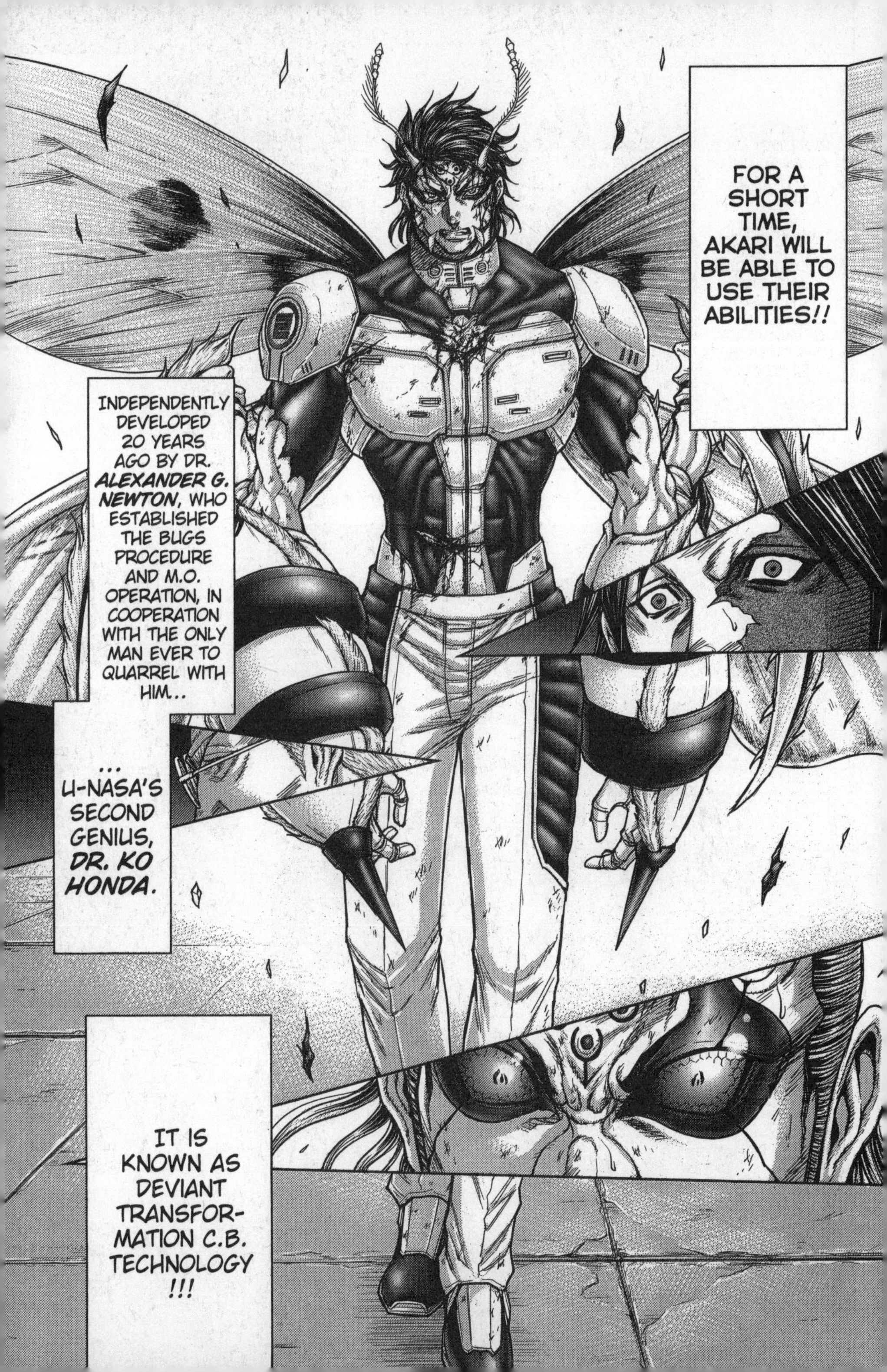
FOR A SHORT TIME, AKARI WILL BE ABLE TO USE THEIR ABILITIES!!
INDEPENDENTLY DEVELOPED 20 YEARS AGO BY DR. ALEXANDER G. NEWTON, WHO ESTABLISHED THE BUGS PROCEDURE AND M.O. OPERATION, IN COOPERATION WITH THE ONLY MAN EVER TO QUARREL WITH HIM...
... U-NASA'S SECOND GENIUS, DR. KO HONDA.
IT IS KNOWN AS DEVIANT TRANSFORMATION C.B. TECHNOLOGY !!!

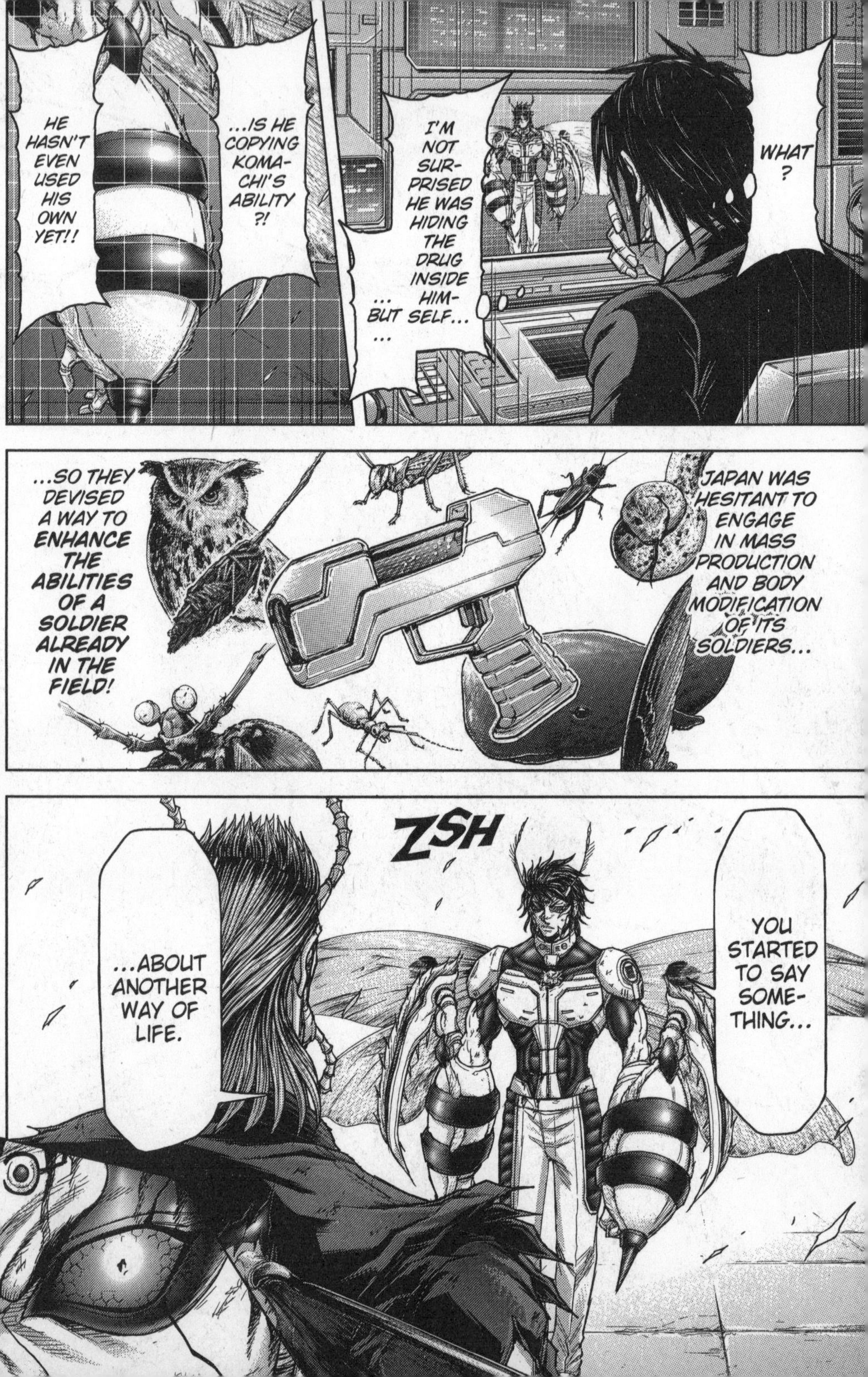
WHAT ?
I'M NOT SURPRISED HE WAS HIDING THE DRUG INSIDE HIMSELF... ...BUT ......
...IS HE COPYING KOMACHI'S ABILITY ?!
HE HASN'T EVEN USED HIS OWN YET!!
JAPAN WAS HESITANT TO ENGAGE IN MASS PRODUCTION AND BODY MODIFICATION OF ITS SOLDIERS...
...SO THEY DEVISED A WAY TO ENHANCE THE ABILITIES OF A SOLDIER ALREADY IN THE FIELD!
ZSH
YOU STARTED TO SAY SOME-THING...
...ABOUT ANOTHER WAY OF LIFE.

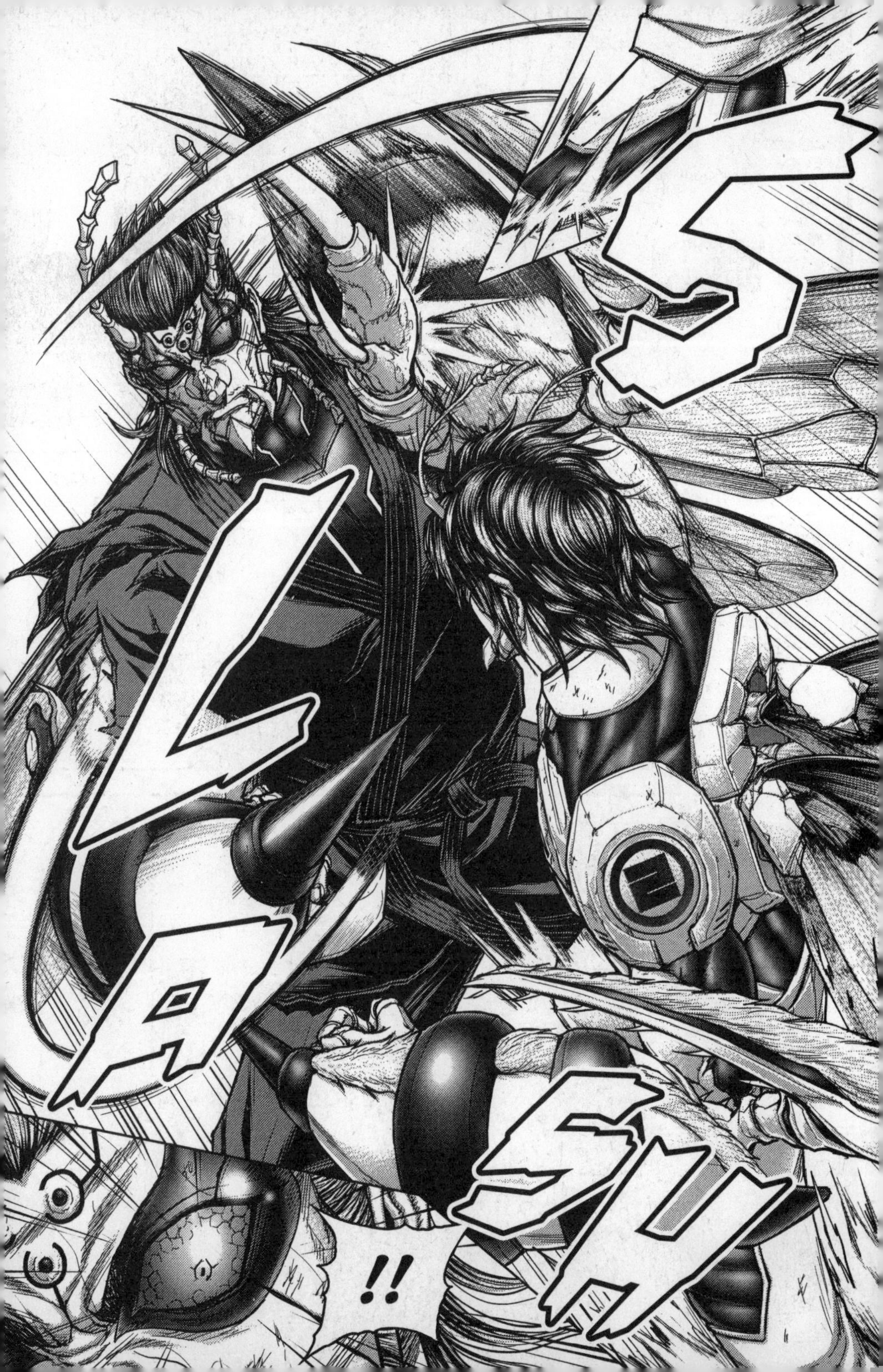
SLASH
!!

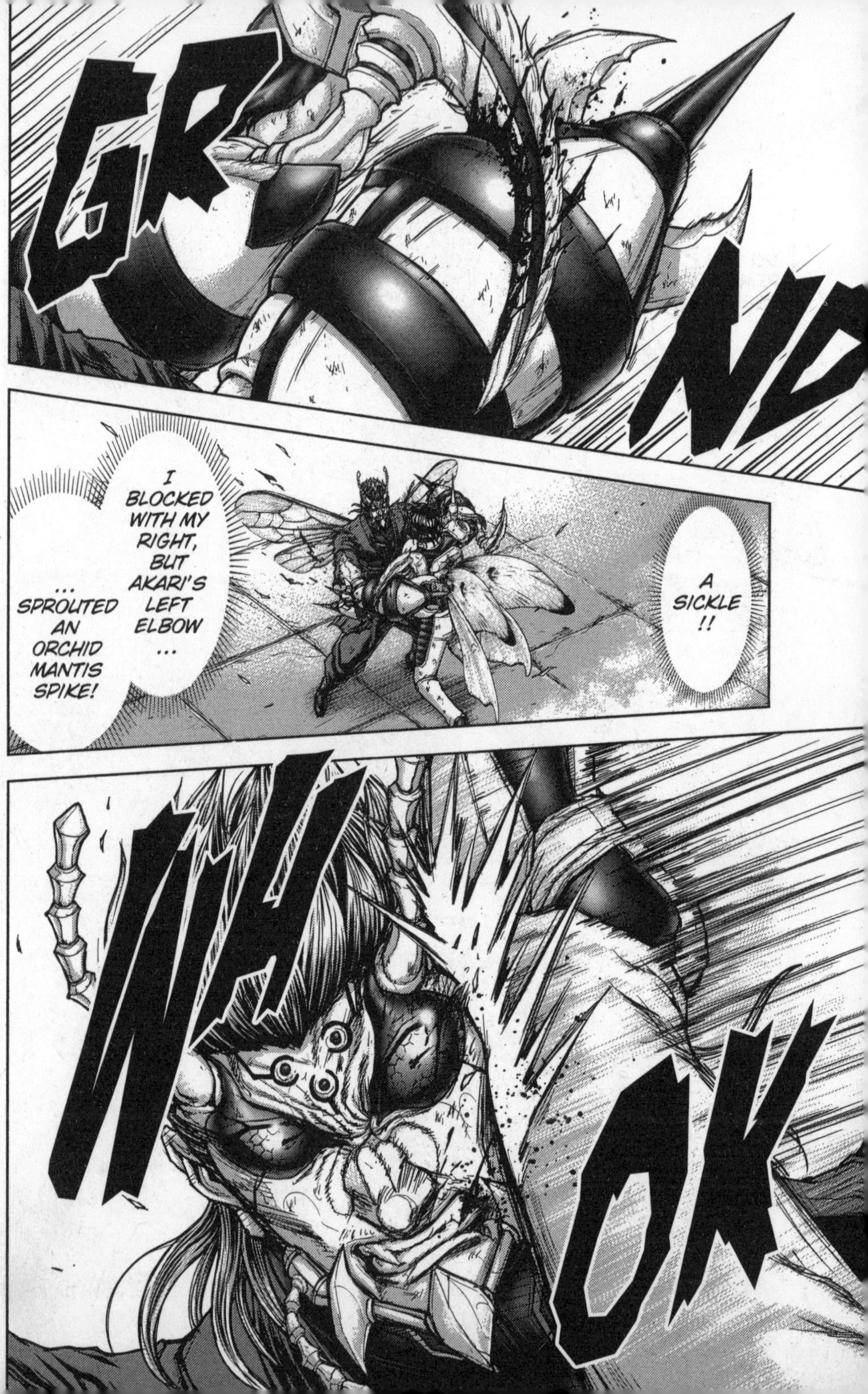
GR
ND
A SICKLE !!
I BLOCKED WITH MY RIGHT, BUT AKARI'S LEFT ELBOW ...
... SPROUTED AN ORCHID MANTIS SPIKE!
WH
OK

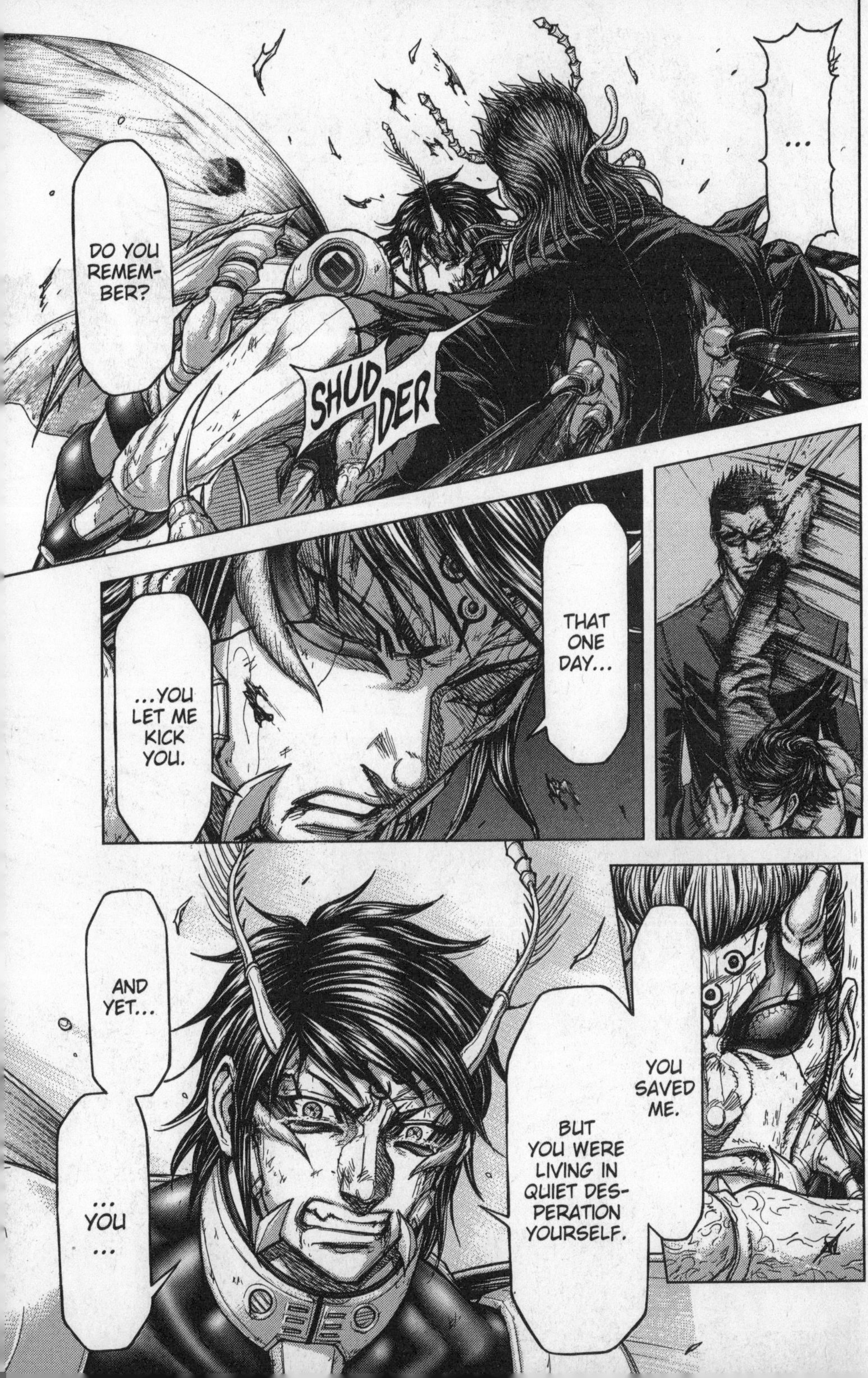
...
DO YOU REMEMBER?
SHUDDER
THAT ONE DAY...
...YOU LET ME KICK YOU.
YOU SAVED ME.
BUT YOU WERE LIVING IN QUIET DESPERATION YOURSELF.
AND YET...
... YOU ...

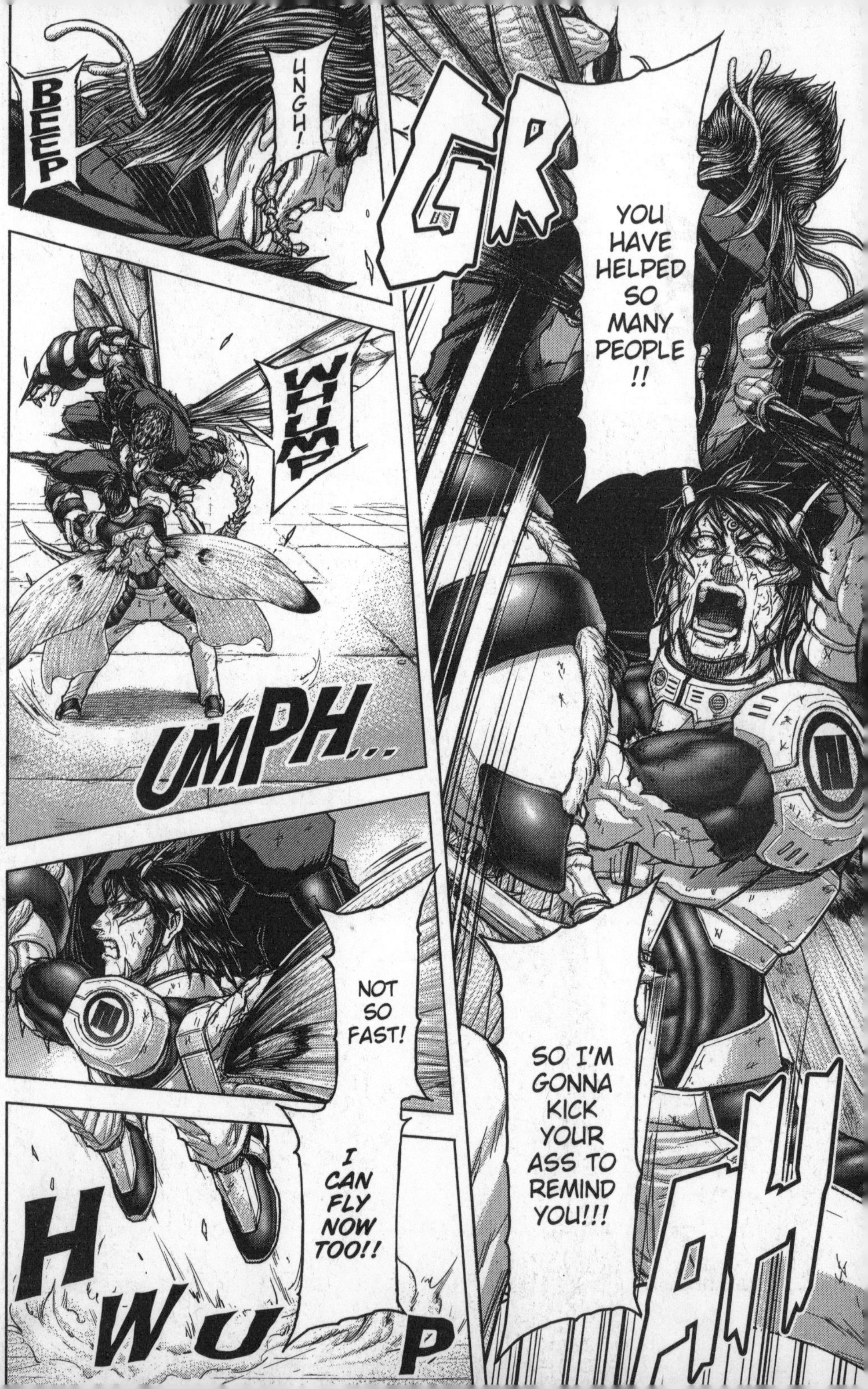
GR
YOU HAVE HELPED SO MANY PEOPLE!!
SO I'M GONNA KICK YOUR ASS TO REMIND YOU!!!
AH
BEEP
UNGH!
WHUMP
UMPH...
NOT SO FAST!
I CAN FLY NOW TOO!!
HWUP

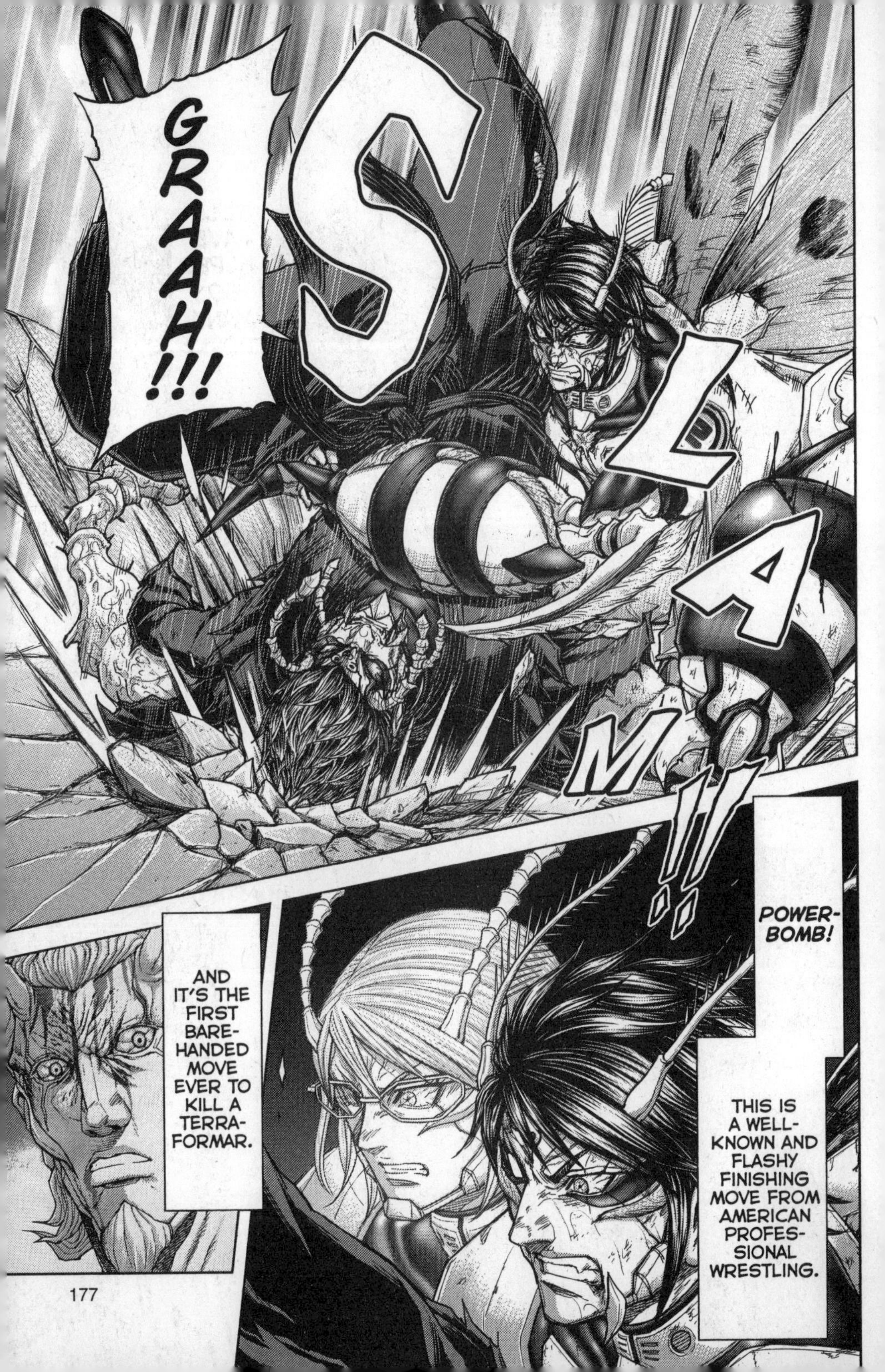
SLAM!!
GRAAH!!!
POWER-BOMB!
THIS IS A WELL-KNOWN AND FLASHY FINISHING MOVE FROM AMERICAN PROFESSIONAL WRESTLING.
AND IT'S THE FIRST BARE-HANDED MOVE EVER TO KILL A TERRAFORMAR.

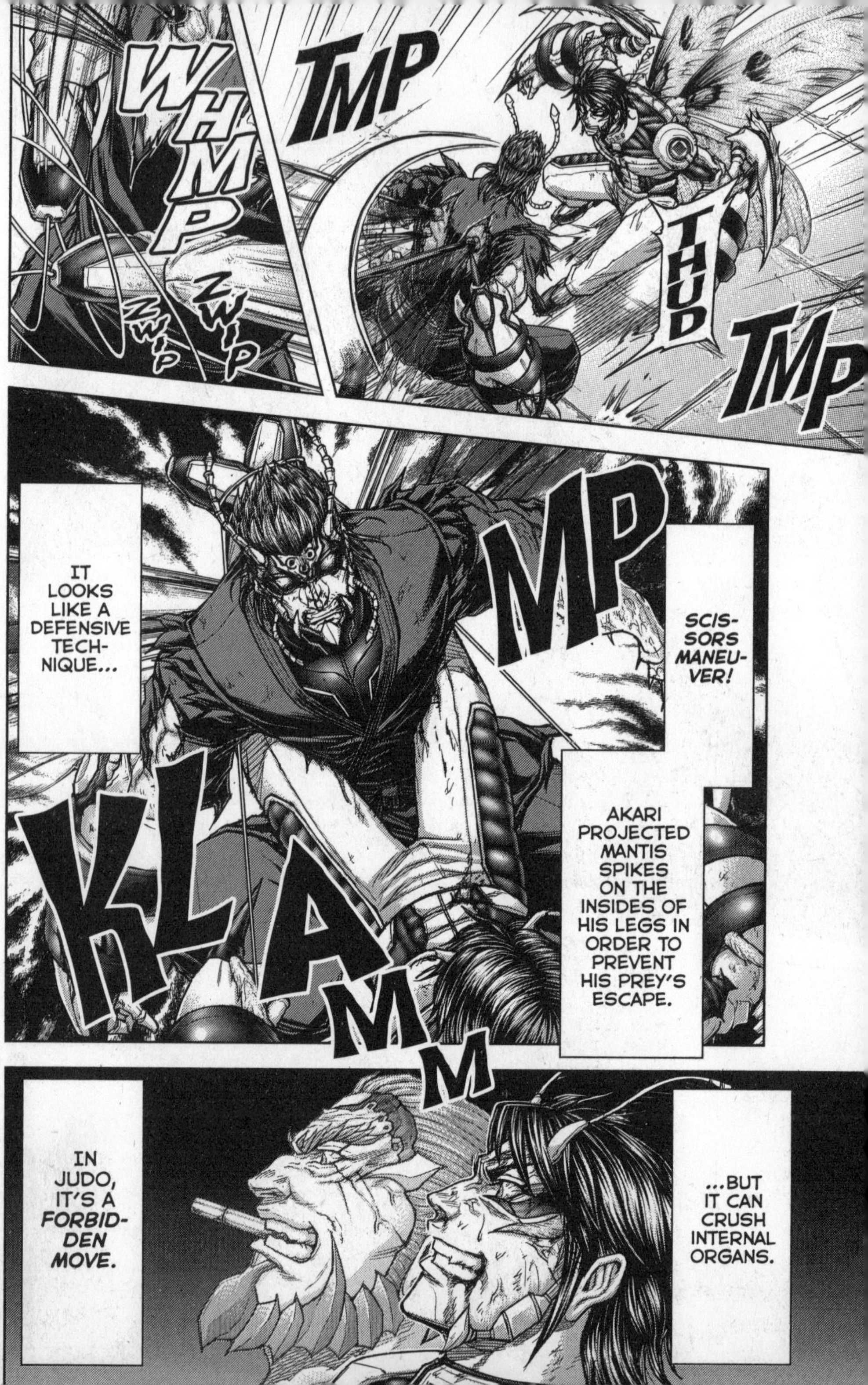
TMP
THUD
TMP
WHMP
ZWIP
ZWIP
SCISSORS MANEUVER!
MP
IT LOOKS LIKE A DEFENSIVE TECHNIQUE...
AKARI PROJECTED MANTIS SPIKES ON THE INSIDES OF HIS LEGS IN ORDER TO PREVENT HIS PREY'S ESCAPE.
KLAMMM
...BUT IT CAN CRUSH INTERNAL ORGANS.
IN JUDO, IT'S A *FORBIDDEN MOVE*.

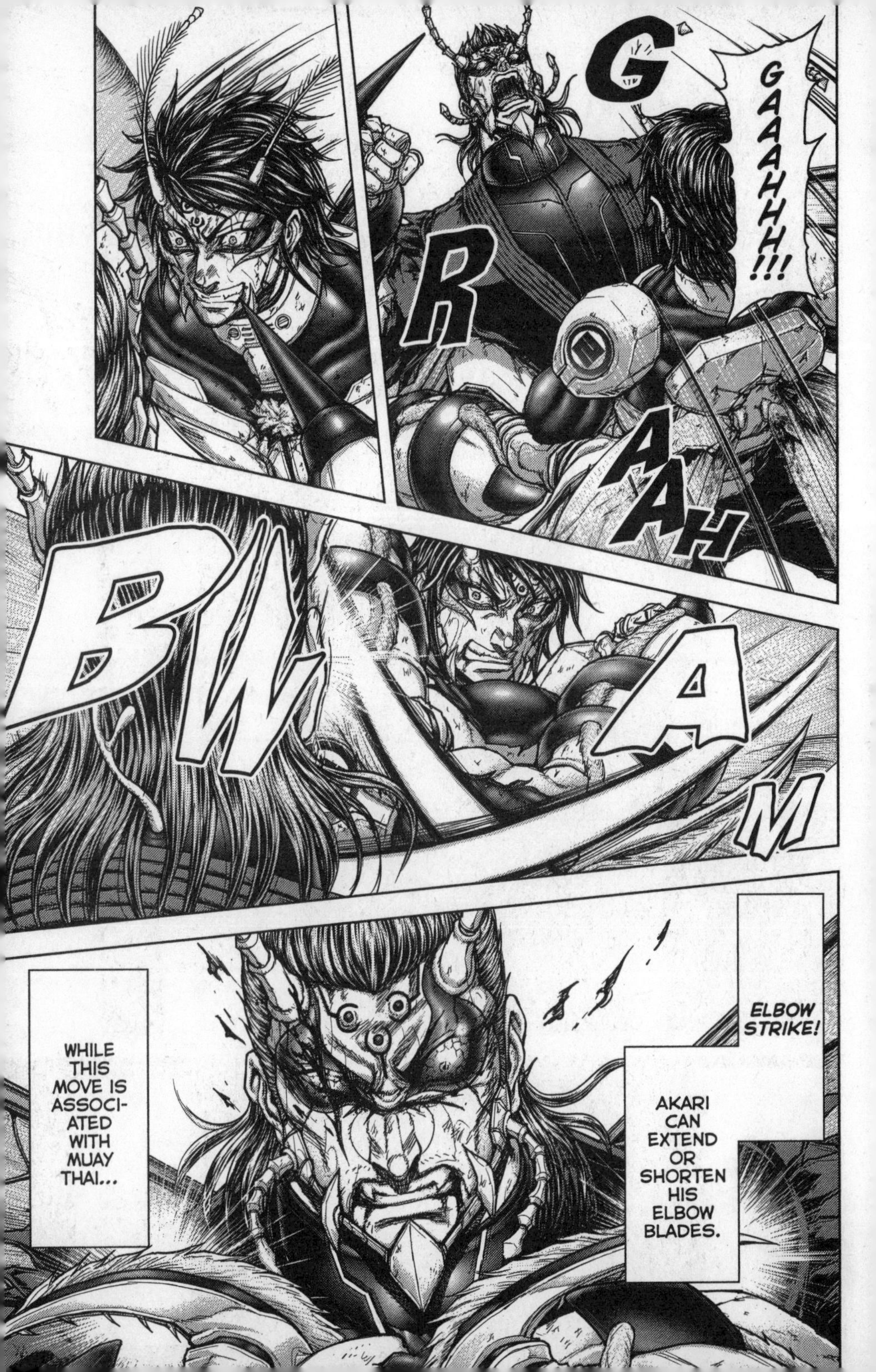
GAAAHHH!!!
GRAAH
BWAM
ELBOW STRIKE!
AKARI CAN EXTEND OR SHORTEN HIS ELBOW BLADES.
WHILE THIS MOVE IS ASSOCI-ATED WITH MUAY THAI...

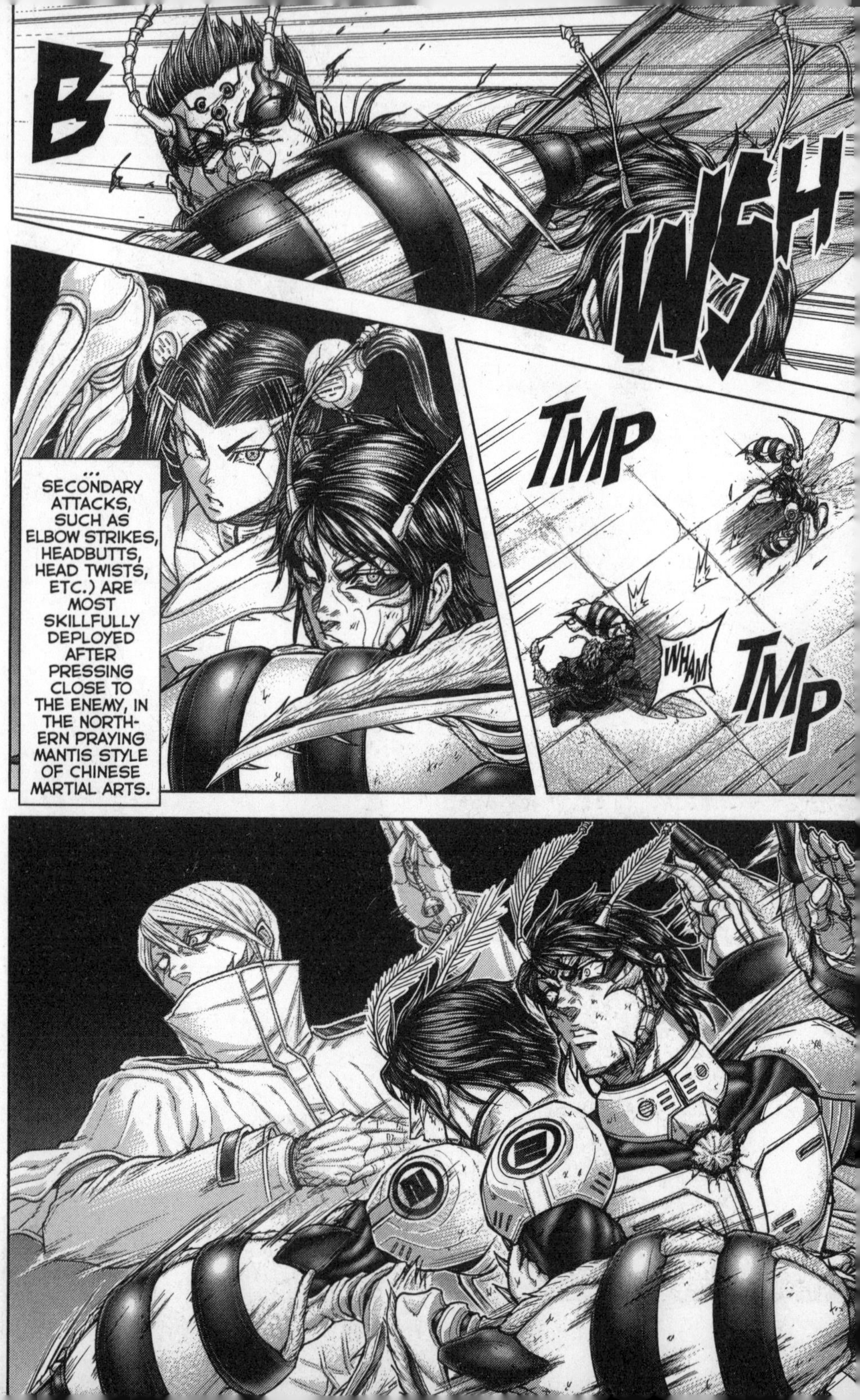
B
WSH
TMP
TMP
WHAM
... SECONDARY ATTACKS, SUCH AS ELBOW STRIKES, HEADBUTTS, HEAD TWISTS, ETC.) ARE MOST SKILLFULLY DEPLOYED AFTER PRESSING CLOSE TO THE ENEMY, IN THE NORTHERN PRAYING MANTIS STYLE OF CHINESE MARTIAL ARTS.

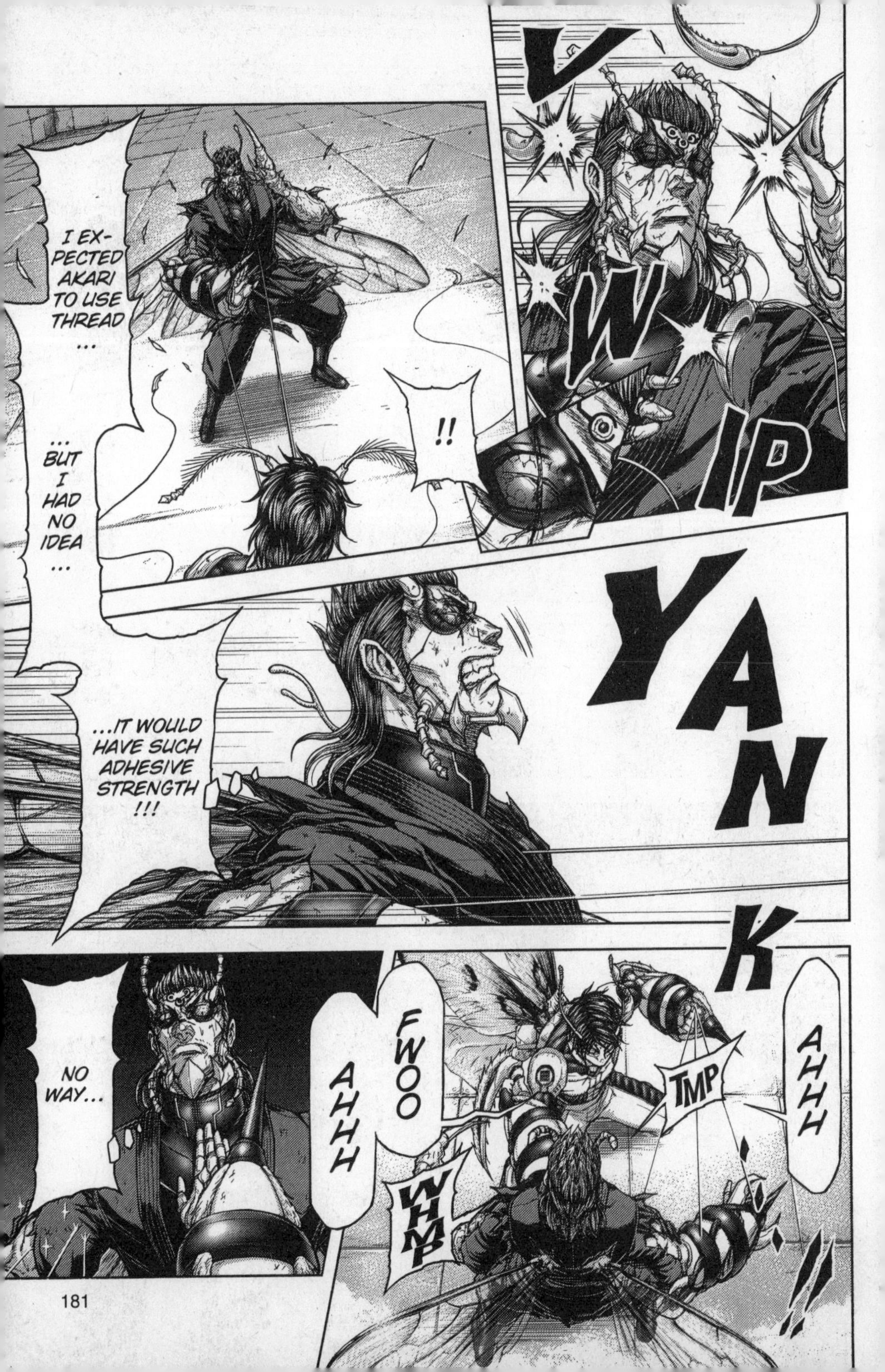
WIP
!!
I EX-PECTED AKARI TO USE THREAD ...
... BUT I HAD NO IDEA ...
...IT WOULD HAVE SUCH ADHESIVE STRENGTH !!!
YANK
AHHH
TMP
FWOO AHHH
WHMP
!!
NO WAY...

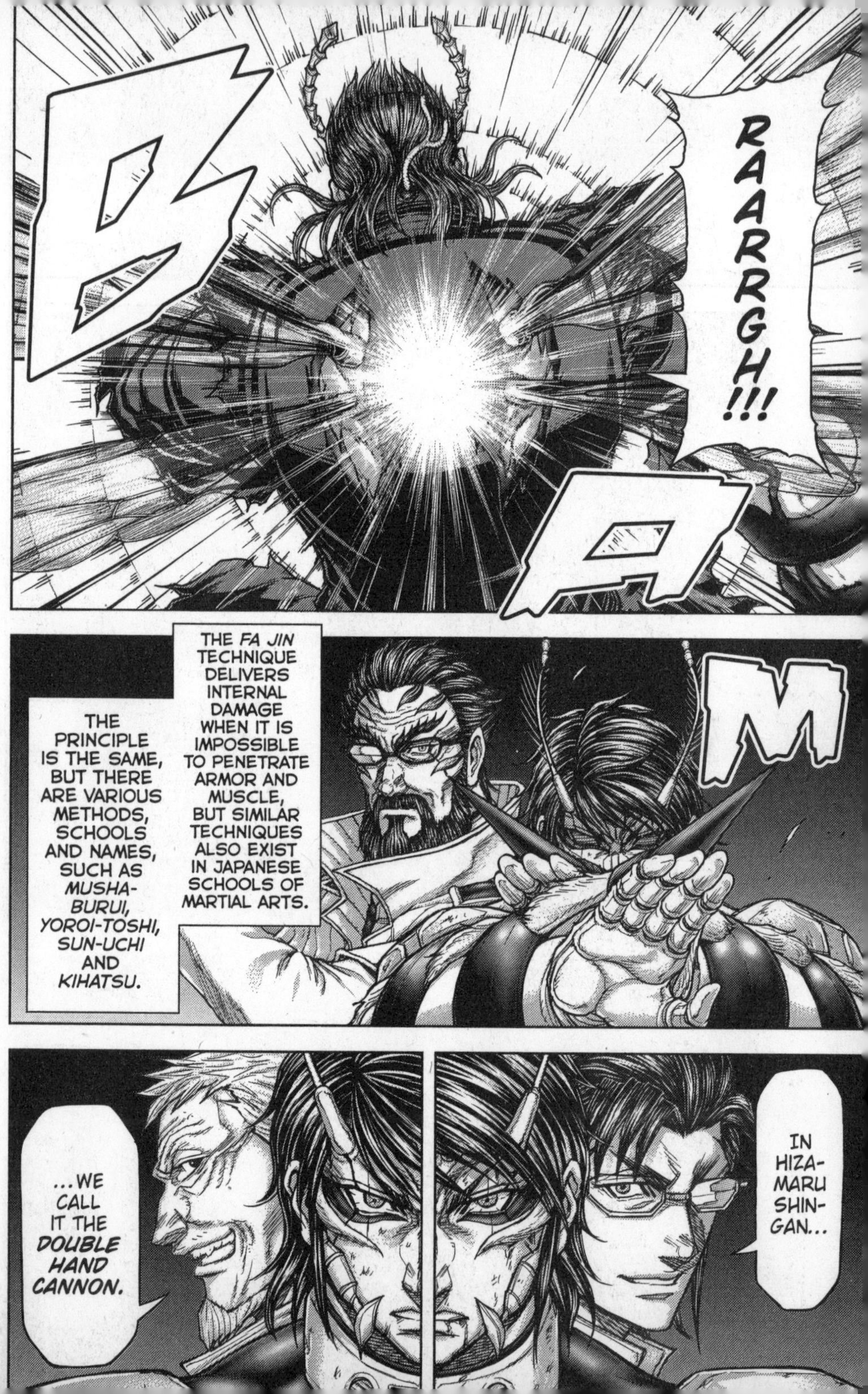
RAAARRGH!!!
B
A
M
THE FA JIN TECHNIQUE DELIVERS INTERNAL DAMAGE WHEN IT IS IMPOSSIBLE TO PENETRATE ARMOR AND MUSCLE, BUT SIMILAR TECHNIQUES ALSO EXIST IN JAPANESE SCHOOLS OF MARTIAL ARTS.
THE PRINCIPLE IS THE SAME, BUT THERE ARE VARIOUS METHODS, SCHOOLS AND NAMES, SUCH AS MUSHA-BURUI, YOROI-TOSHI, SUN-UCHI AND KIHATSU.
IN HIZA-MARU SHIN-GAN...
...WE CALL IT THE DOUBLE HAND CANNON.

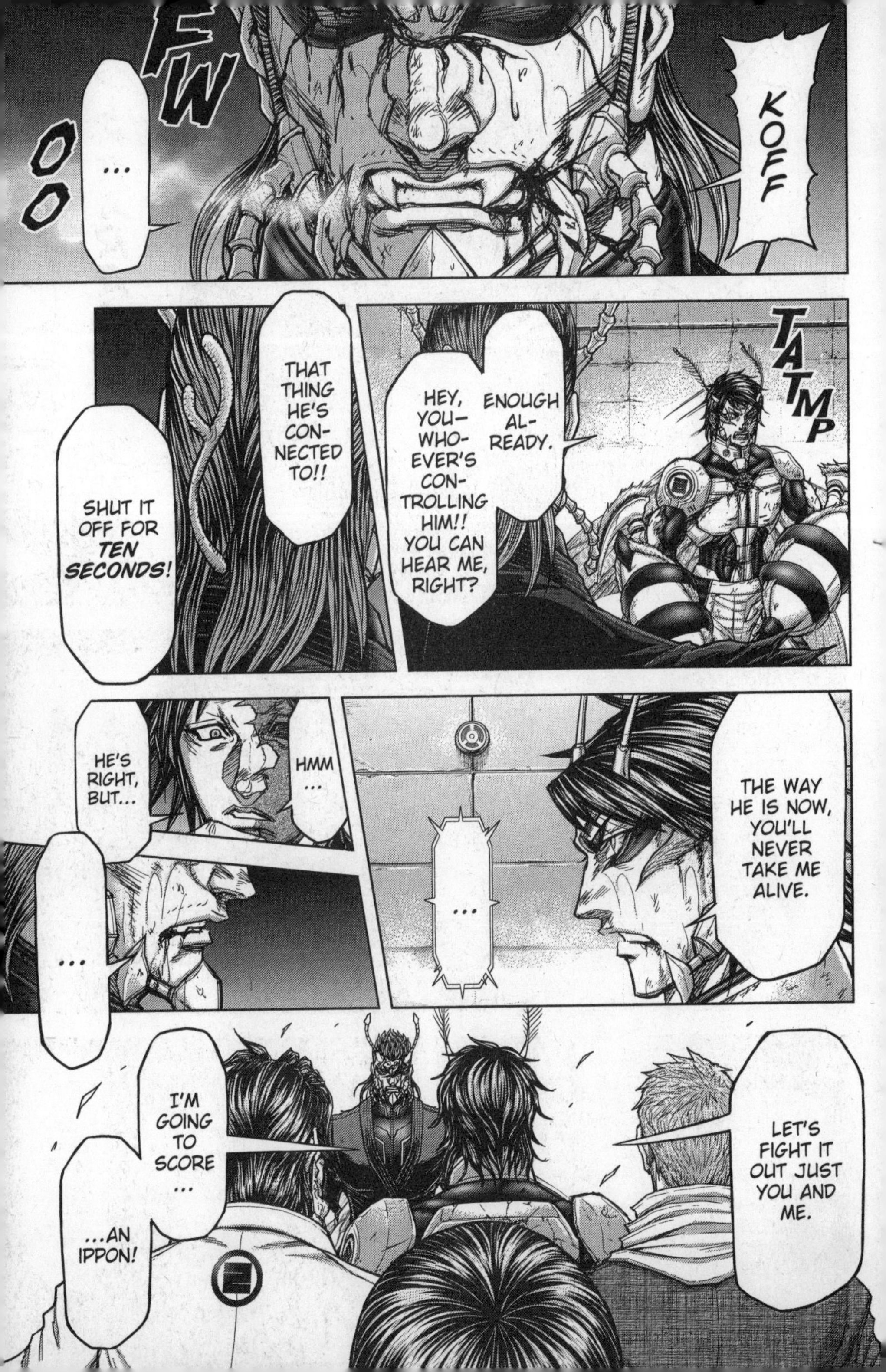
KOFF
...
FWOO
TATMP
ENOUGH ALREADY.
HEY, YOU— WHOEVER'S CONTROLLING HIM!! YOU CAN HEAR ME, RIGHT?
THAT THING HE'S CONNECTED TO!!
SHUT IT OFF FOR TEN SECONDS!
THE WAY HE IS NOW, YOU'LL NEVER TAKE ME ALIVE.
...
HMM...
HE'S RIGHT, BUT...
...
LET'S FIGHT IT OUT JUST YOU AND ME.
I'M GOING TO SCORE...
...AN IPPON!

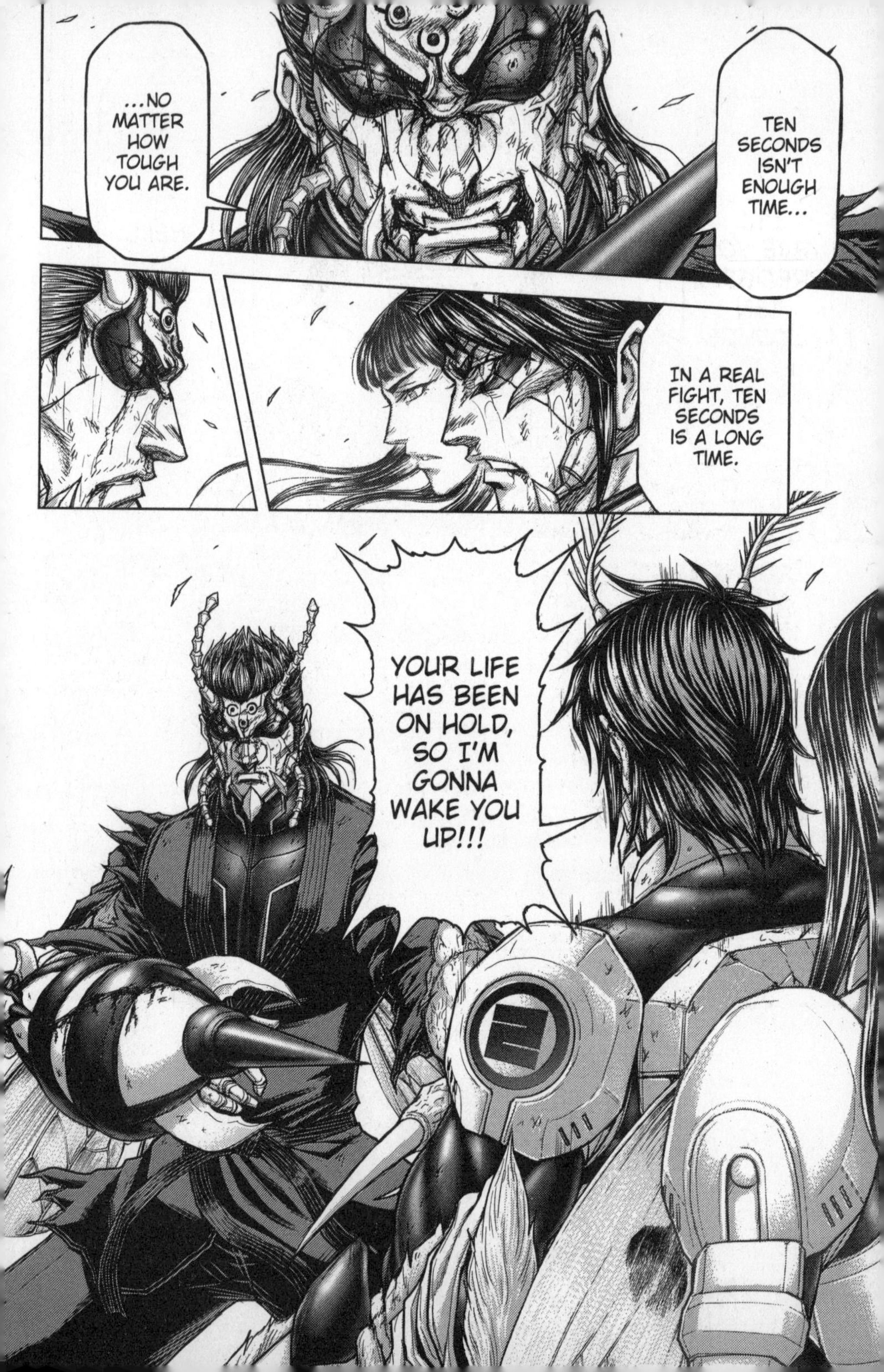
TEN SECONDS ISN'T ENOUGH TIME...
...NO MATTER HOW TOUGH YOU ARE.
IN A REAL FIGHT, TEN SECONDS IS A LONG TIME.
YOUR LIFE HAS BEEN ON HOLD, SO I'M GONNA WAKE YOU UP!!!

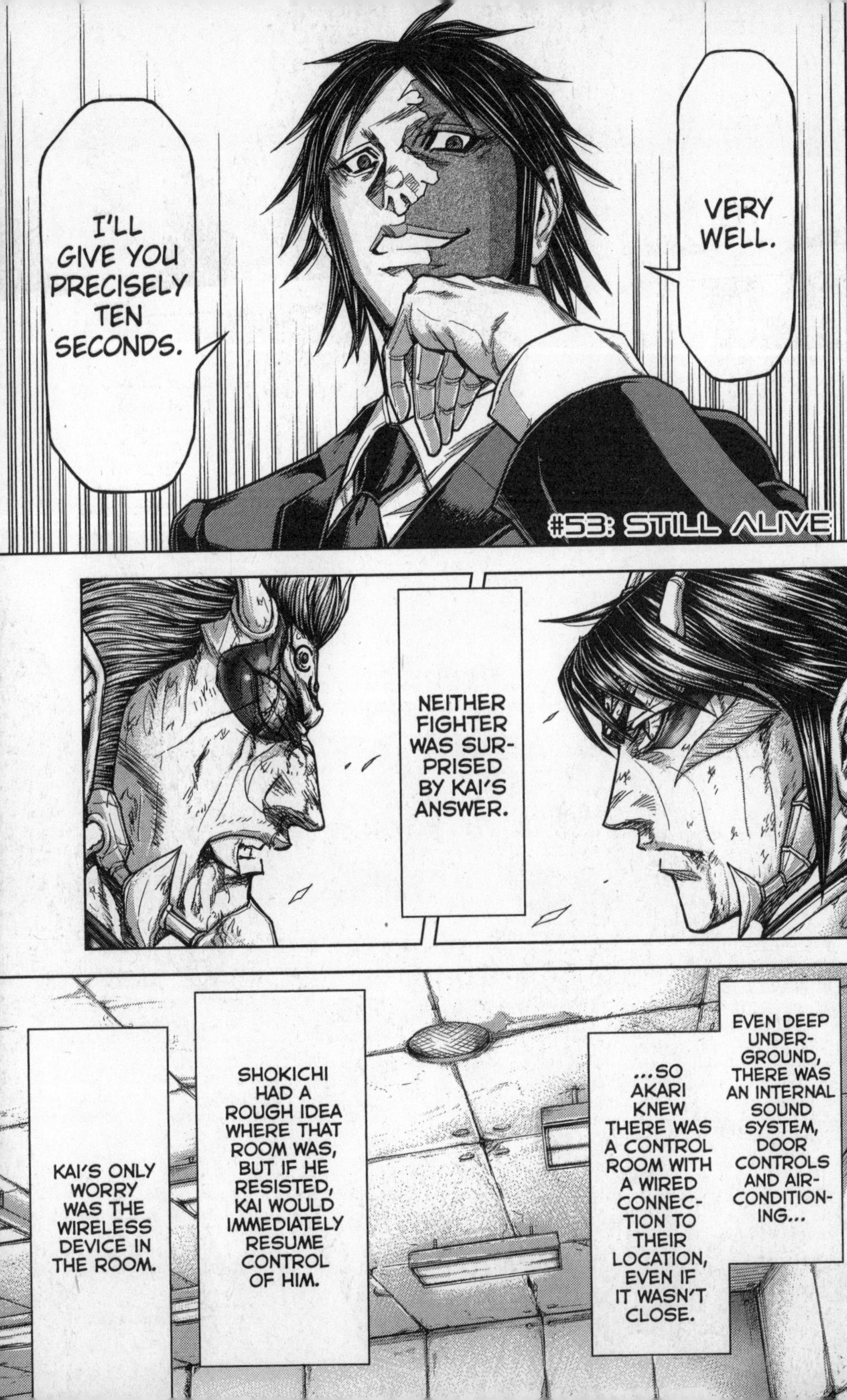
VERY WELL.
I'LL GIVE YOU PRECISELY TEN SECONDS.
#53: STILL ALIVE
NEITHER FIGHTER WAS SURPRISED BY KAI'S ANSWER.
EVEN DEEP UNDERGROUND, THERE WAS AN INTERNAL SOUND SYSTEM, DOOR CONTROLS AND AIR-CONDITIONING...
...SO AKARI KNEW THERE WAS A CONTROL ROOM WITH A WIRED CONNECTION TO THEIR LOCATION, EVEN IF IT WASN'T CLOSE.
SHOKICHI HAD A ROUGH IDEA WHERE THAT ROOM WAS, BUT IF HE RESISTED, KAI WOULD IMMEDIATELY RESUME CONTROL OF HIM.
KAI'S ONLY WORRY WAS THE WIRELESS DEVICE IN THE ROOM.

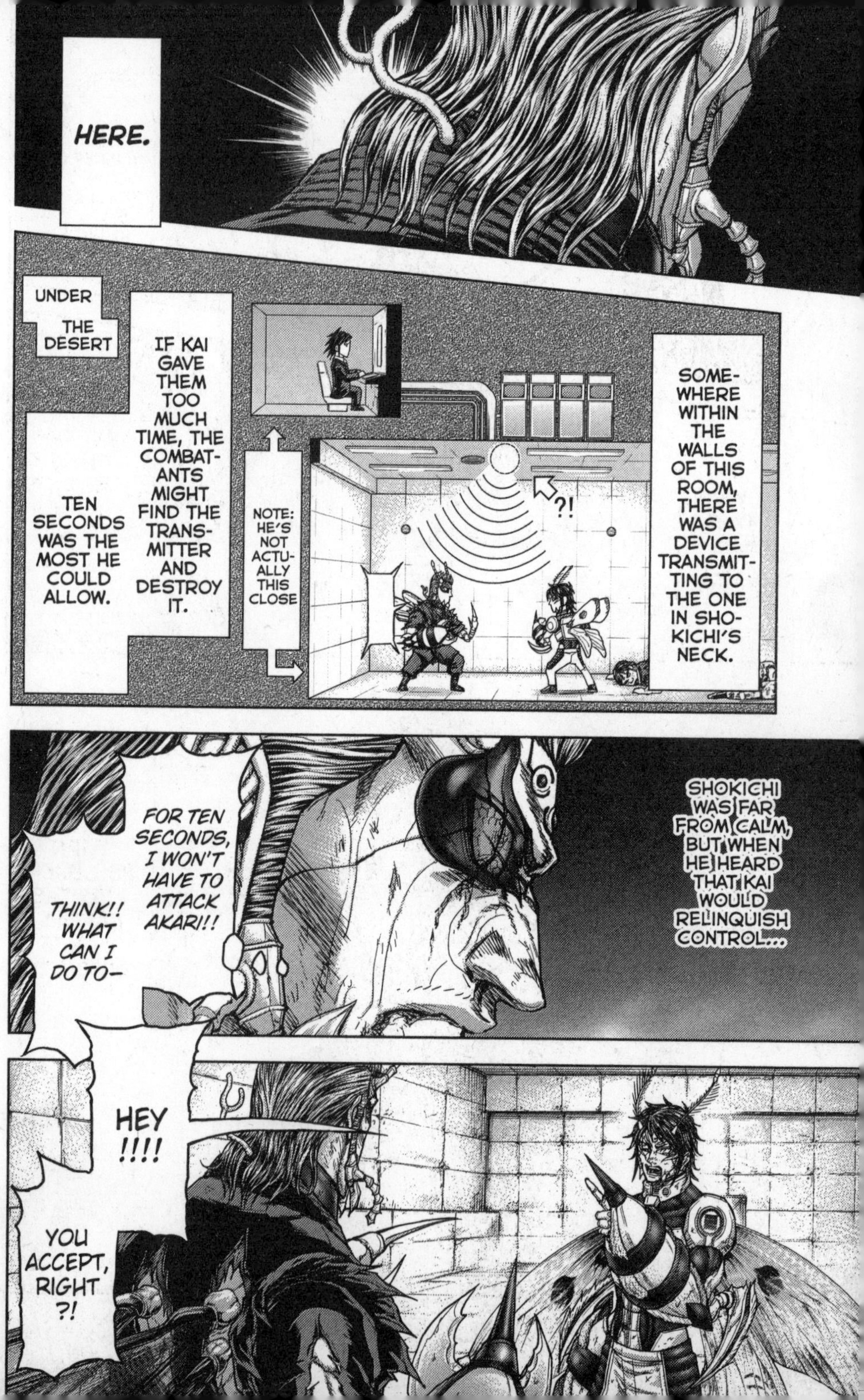
HERE.
SOMEWHERE WITHIN THE WALLS OF THIS ROOM, THERE WAS A DEVICE TRANSMITTING TO THE ONE IN SHOKICHI'S NECK.
?!
NOTE: HE'S NOT ACTUALLY THIS CLOSE
IF KAI GAVE THEM TOO MUCH TIME, THE COMBATANTS MIGHT FIND THE TRANSMITTER AND DESTROY IT.
UNDER THE DESERT
TEN SECONDS WAS THE MOST HE COULD ALLOW.
SHOKICHI WAS FAR FROM CALM, BUT WHEN HE HEARD THAT KAI WOULD RELINQUISH CONTROL...
FOR TEN SECONDS, I WON'T HAVE TO ATTACK AKARI!!
THINK!! WHAT CAN I DO TO-
HEY !!!!
YOU ACCEPT, RIGHT ?!

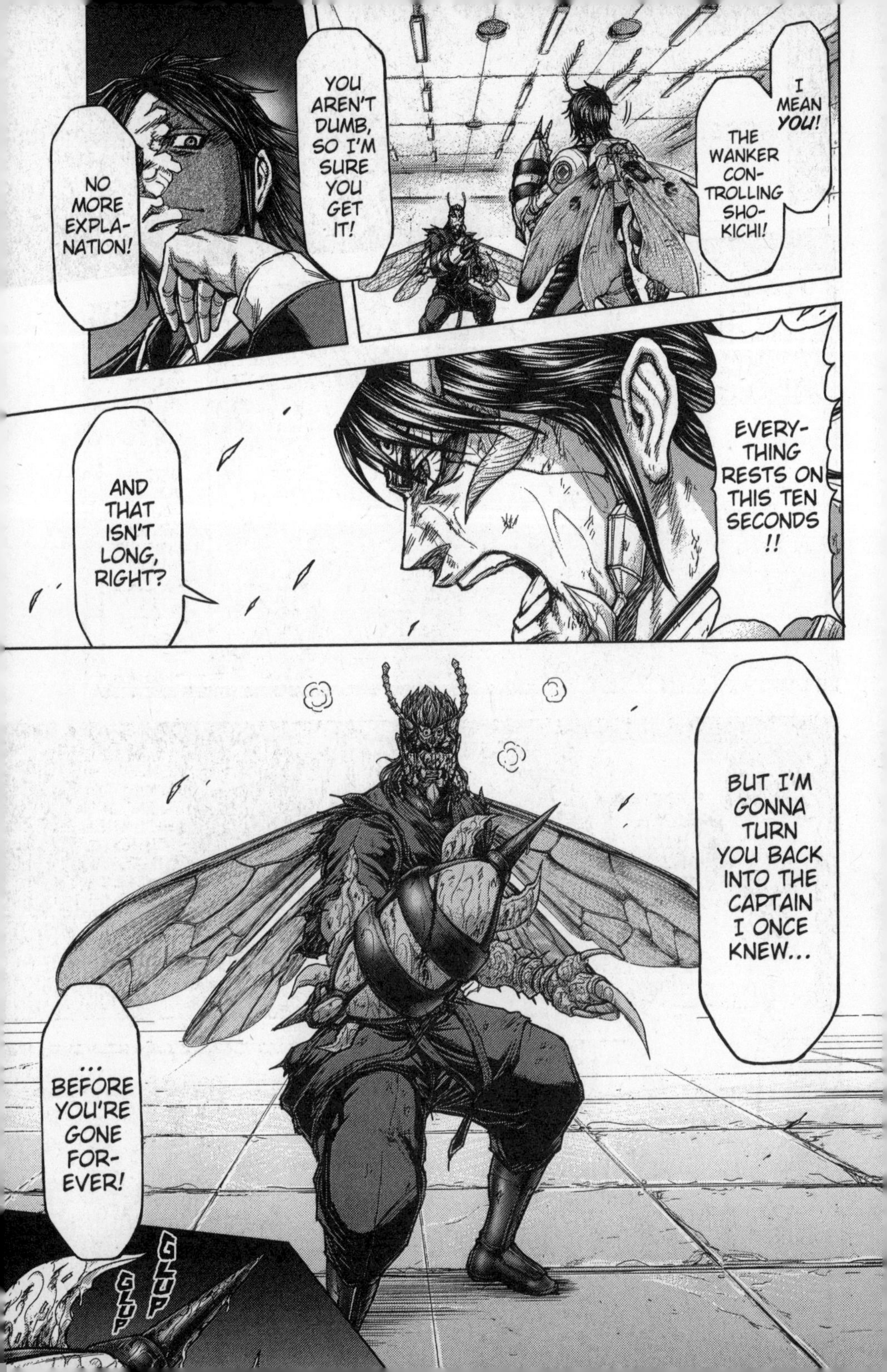
I MEAN YOU! THE WANKER CONTROLLING SHOKICHI!
YOU AREN'T DUMB, SO I'M SURE YOU GET IT!
NO MORE EXPLANATION!
EVERYTHING RESTS ON THIS TEN SECONDS!!
AND THAT ISN'T LONG, RIGHT?
BUT I'M GONNA TURN YOU BACK INTO THE CAPTAIN I ONCE KNEW...
... BEFORE YOU'RE GONE FOREVER!
GLUP
GLUP

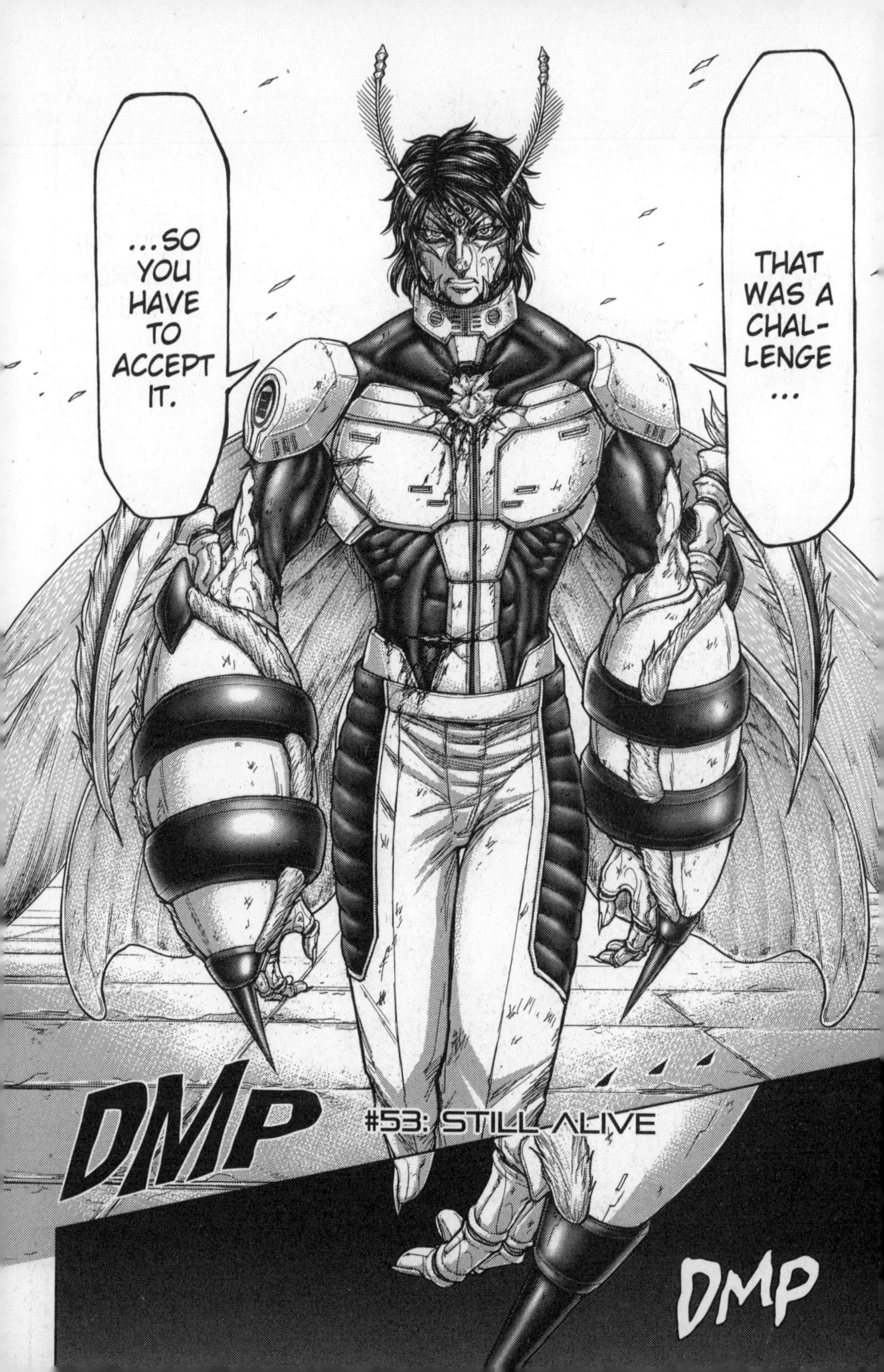
THAT WAS A CHALLENGE...
...SO YOU HAVE TO ACCEPT IT.
DMP
#53: STILL ALIVE
DMP

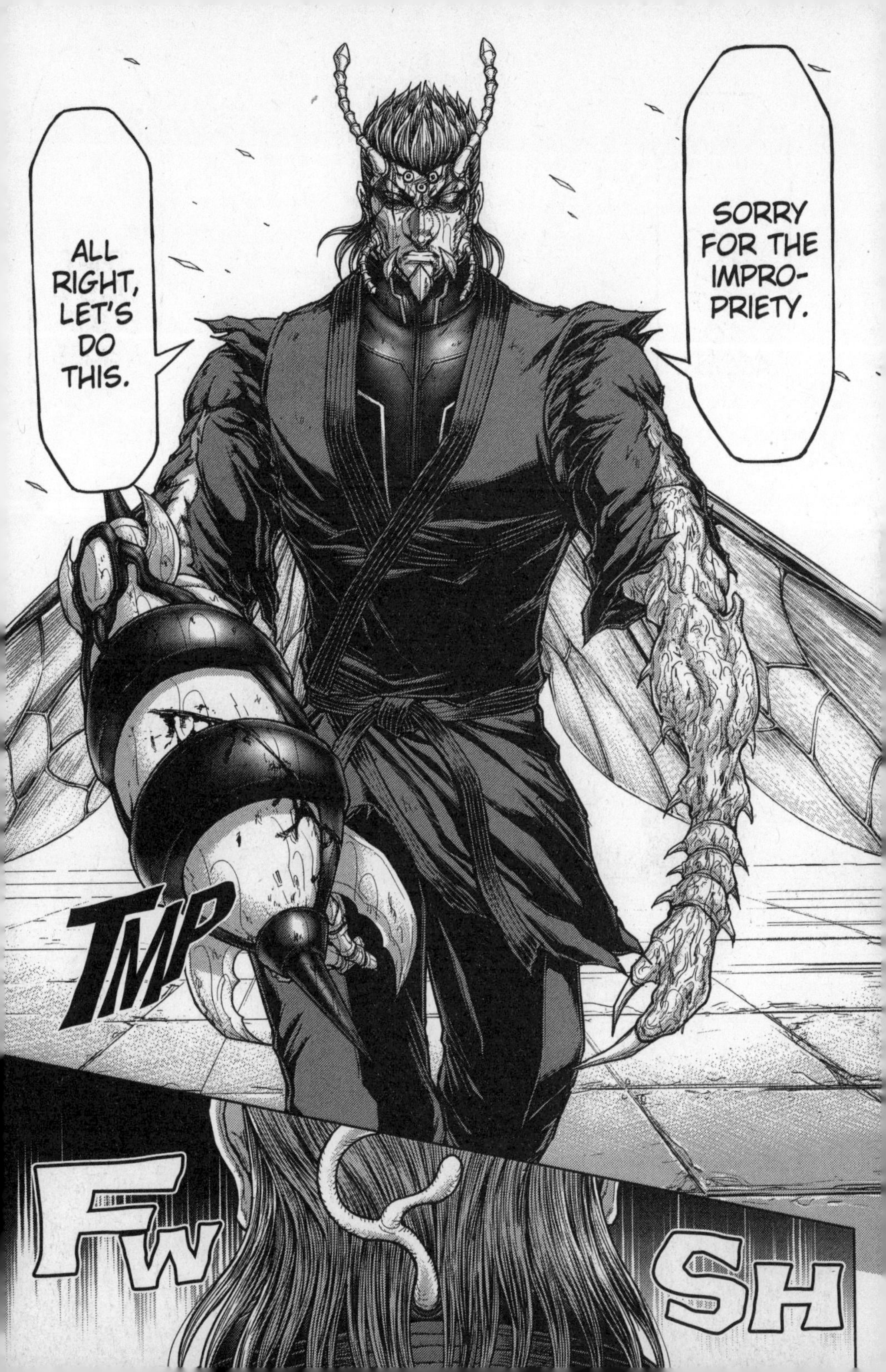
SORRY FOR THE IMPRO-PRIETY.
ALL RIGHT, LET'S DO THIS.
TMP
FWSH

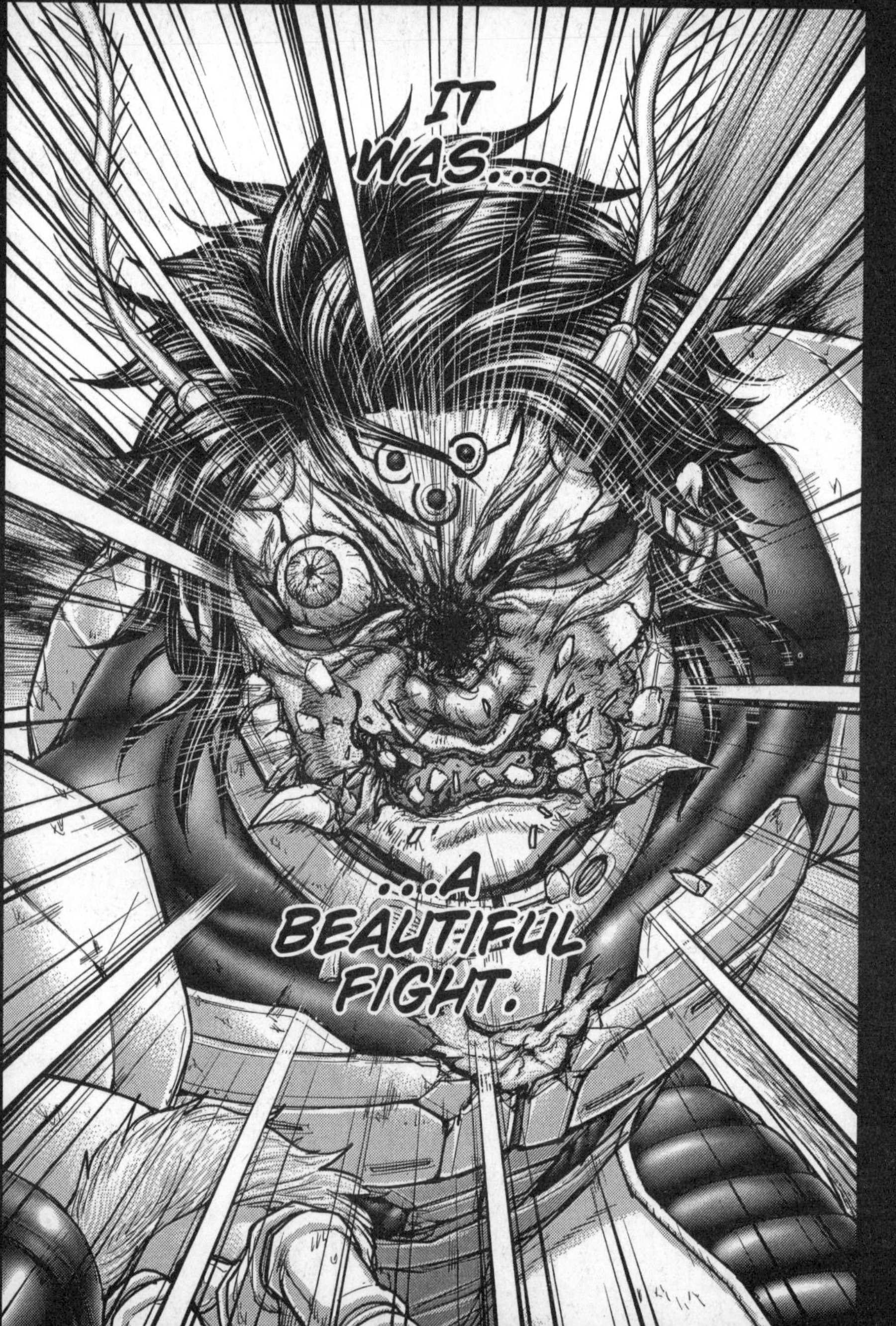
IT WAS...
...A BEAUTIFUL FIGHT.

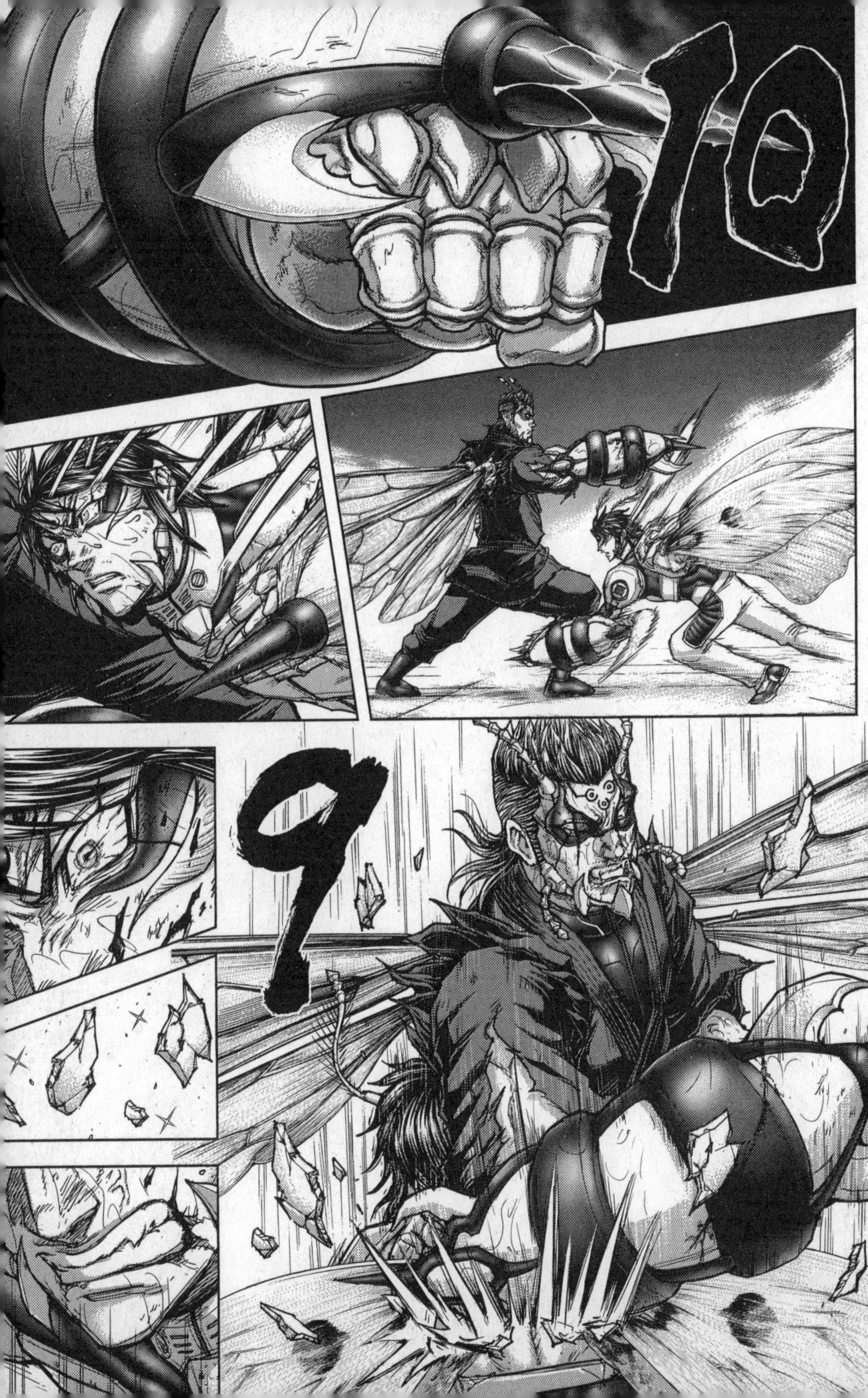
10
9

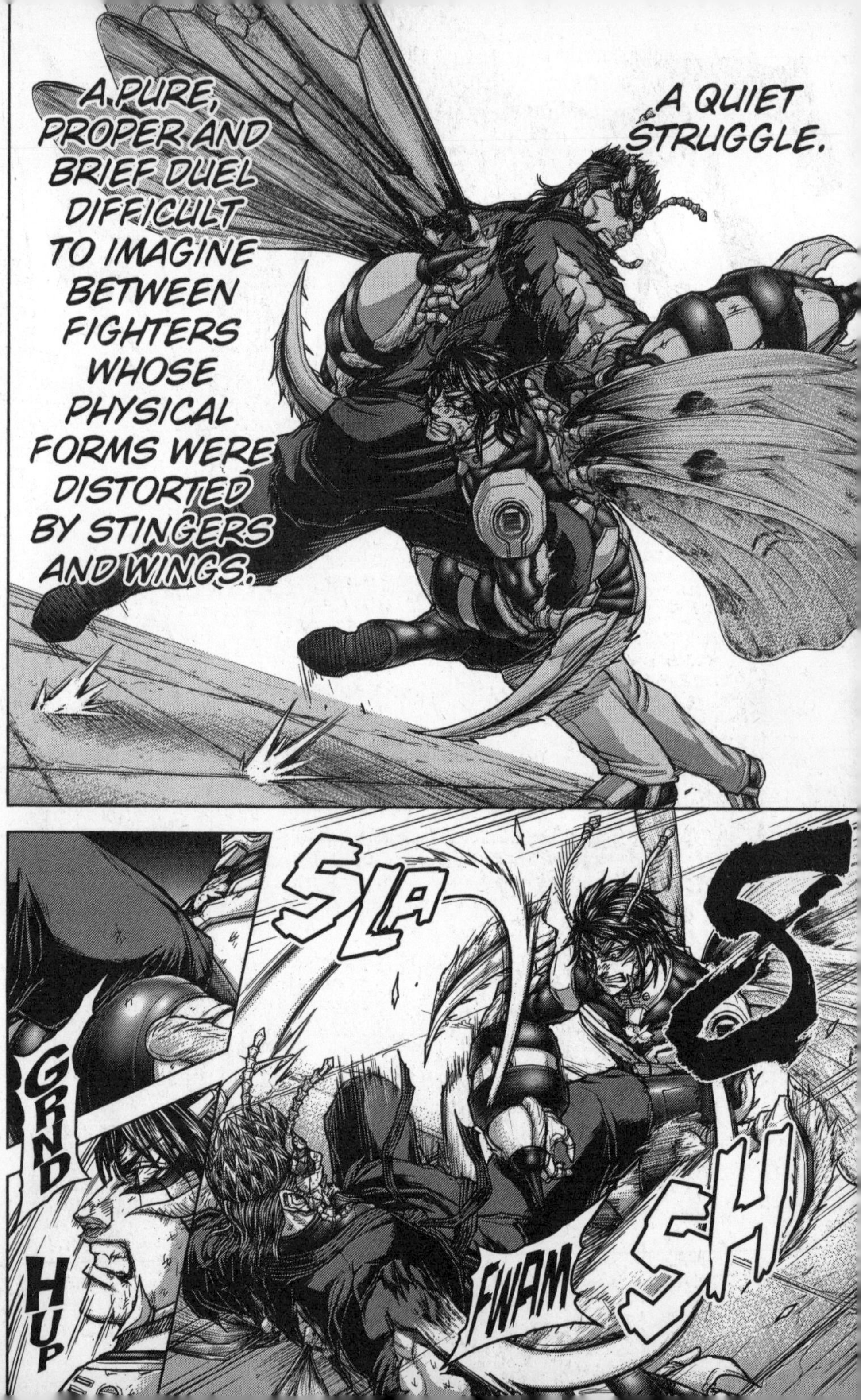
A QUIET STRUGGLE.
A PURE, PROPER AND BRIEF DUEL DIFFICULT TO IMAGINE BETWEEN FIGHTERS WHOSE PHYSICAL FORMS WERE DISTORTED BY STINGERS AND WINGS.
SLA
SH
S
FWAM
GRND
HUP

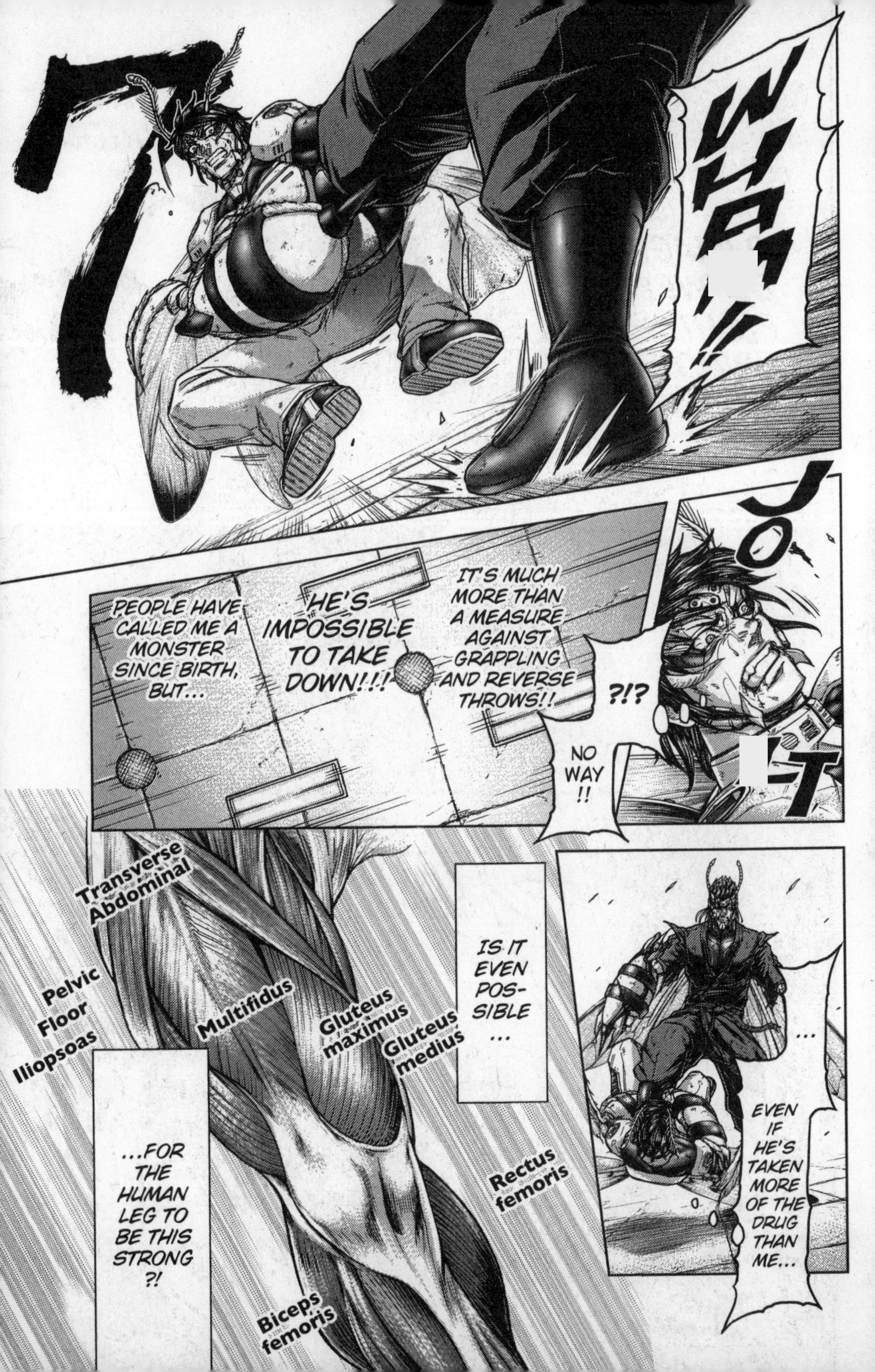
WHA
!!
JO
LT
?!?
NO WAY!!
IT'S MUCH MORE THAN A MEASURE AGAINST GRAPPLING AND REVERSE THROWS!!
HE'S IMPOSSIBLE TO TAKE DOWN!!!
PEOPLE HAVE CALLED ME A MONSTER SINCE BIRTH, BUT...
...
EVEN IF HE'S TAKEN MORE OF THE DRUG THAN ME...
IS IT EVEN POS-SIBLE...
...FOR THE HUMAN LEG TO BE THIS STRONG?!
Transverse Abdominal
Pelvic Floor
Iliopsoas
Multifidus
Gluteus maximus
Gluteus medius
Rectus femoris
Biceps femoris

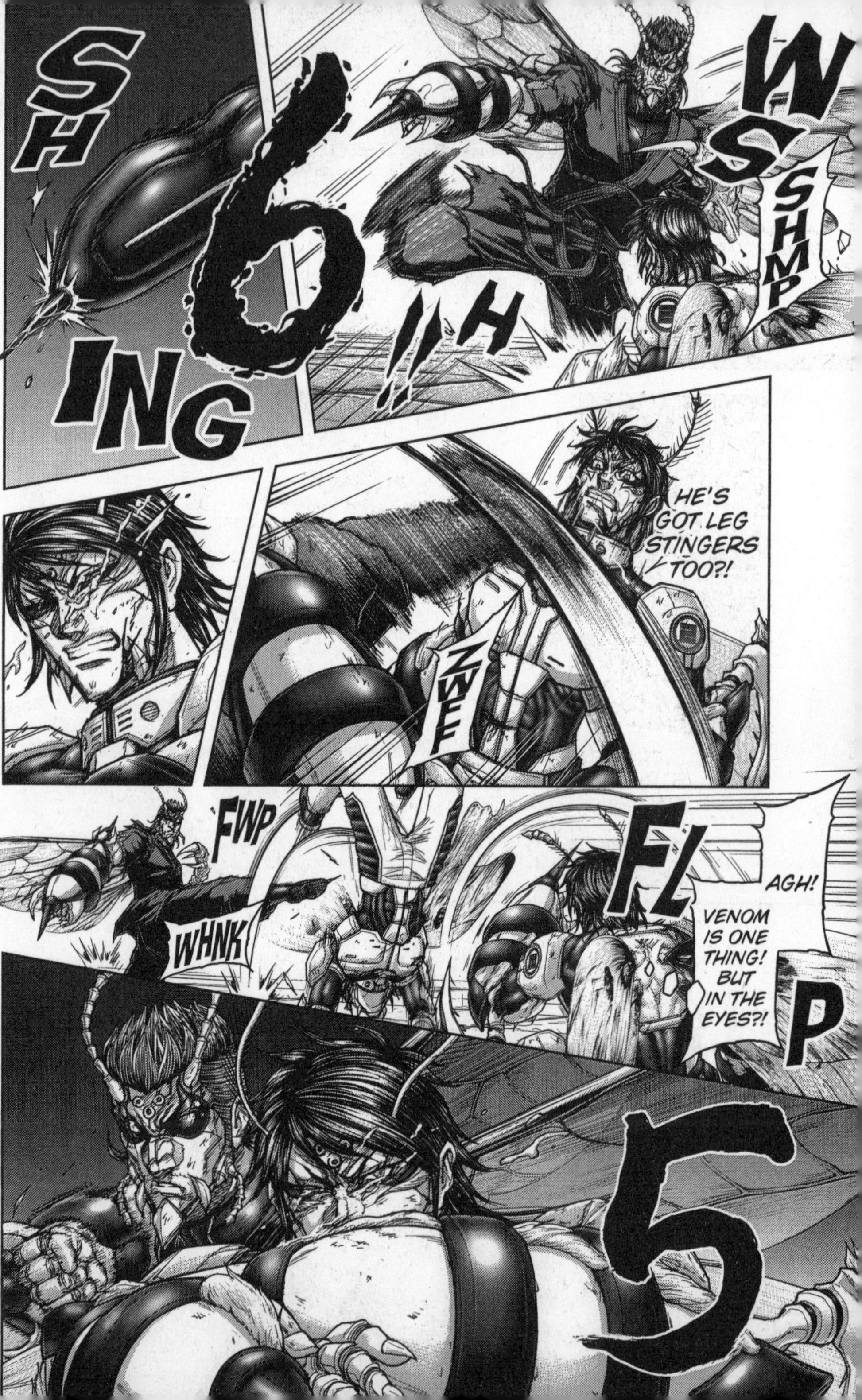
WS
SHMP
H!!
6
SH
ING
HE'S GOT LEG STINGERS TOO?!
ZWEF
FL
P
AGH!
VENOM IS ONE THING! BUT IN THE EYES?!
FWP
WHNK
5

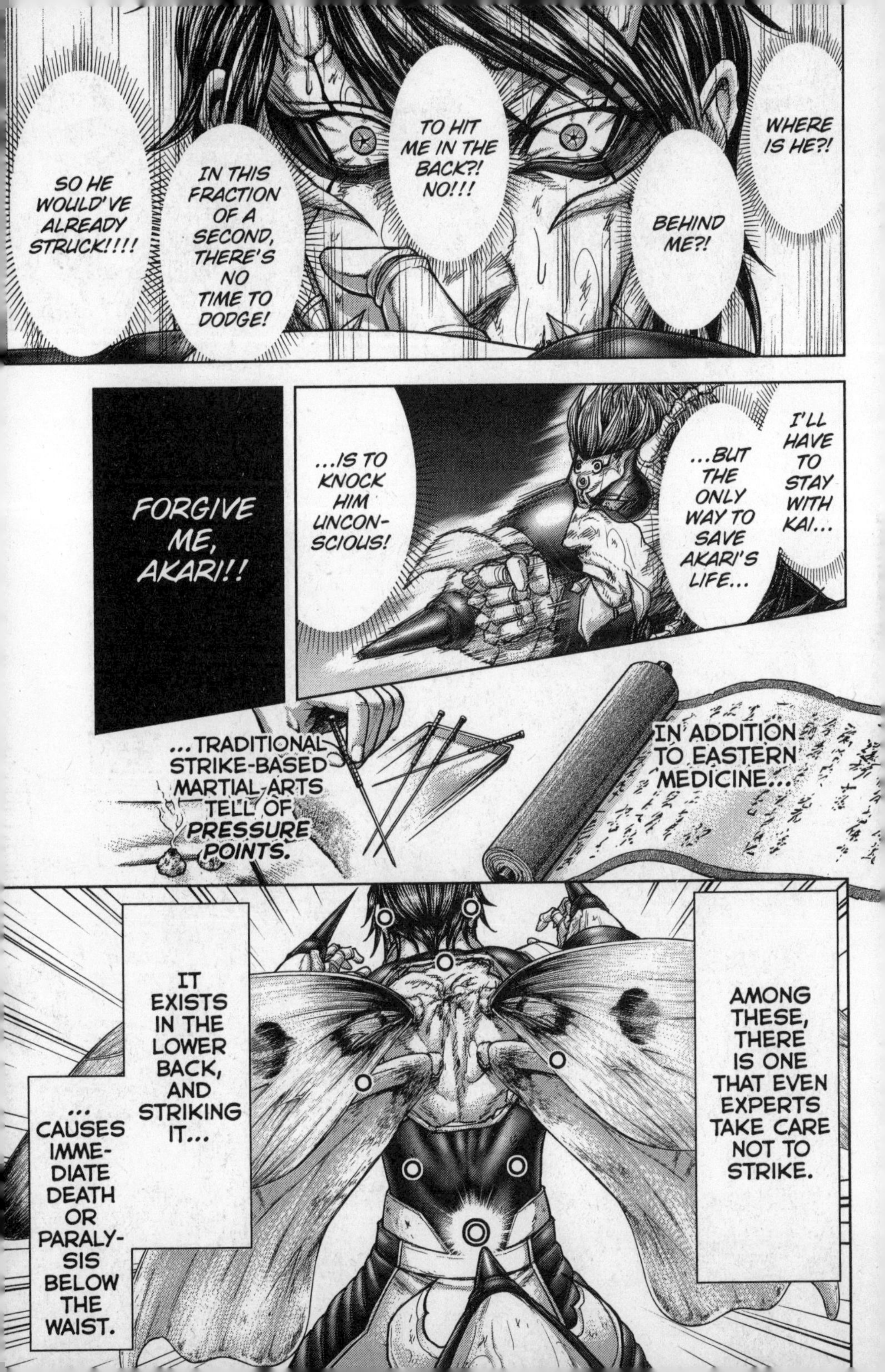
WHERE IS HE?!
BEHIND ME?!
TO HIT ME IN THE BACK?! NO!!!
IN THIS FRACTION OF A SECOND, THERE'S NO TIME TO DODGE!
SO HE WOULD'VE ALREADY STRUCK!!!!
I'LL HAVE TO STAY WITH KAI...
...BUT THE ONLY WAY TO SAVE AKARI'S LIFE...
...IS TO KNOCK HIM UNCONSCIOUS!
FORGIVE ME, AKARI!!
IN ADDITION TO EASTERN MEDICINE...
...TRADITIONAL STRIKE-BASED MARTIAL ARTS TELL OF PRESSURE POINTS.
AMONG THESE, THERE IS ONE THAT EVEN EXPERTS TAKE CARE NOT TO STRIKE.
IT EXISTS IN THE LOWER BACK, AND STRIKING IT...
...CAUSES IMMEDIATE DEATH OR PARALYSIS BELOW THE WAIST.

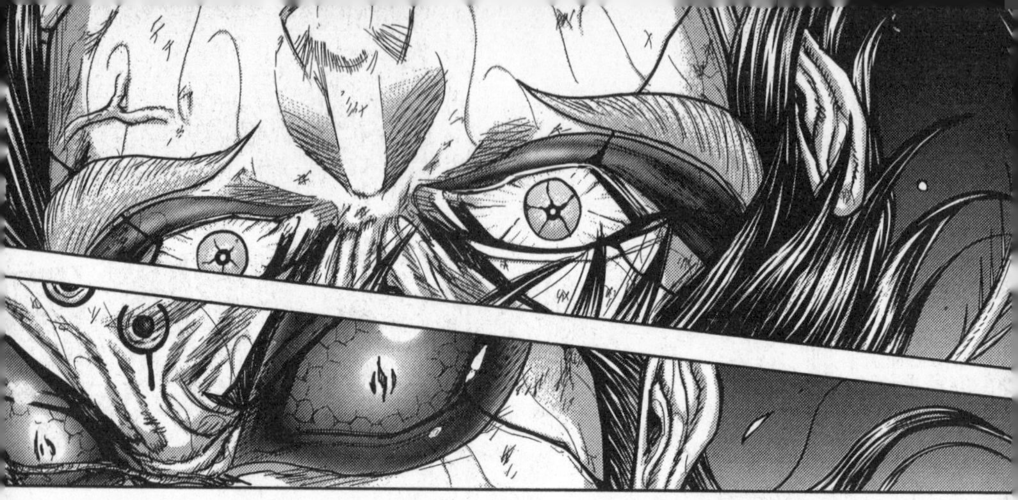

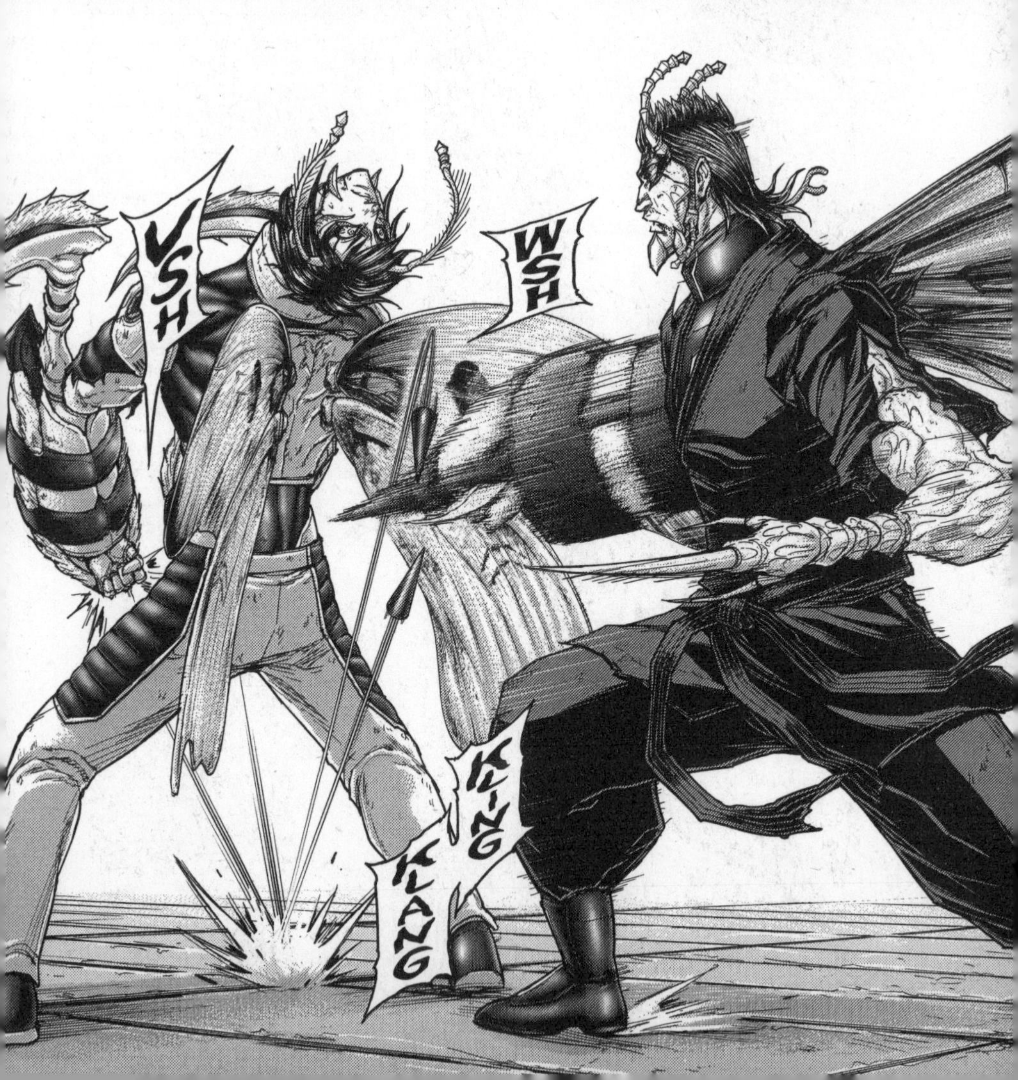
WSH
VSH
KLING
KLANG

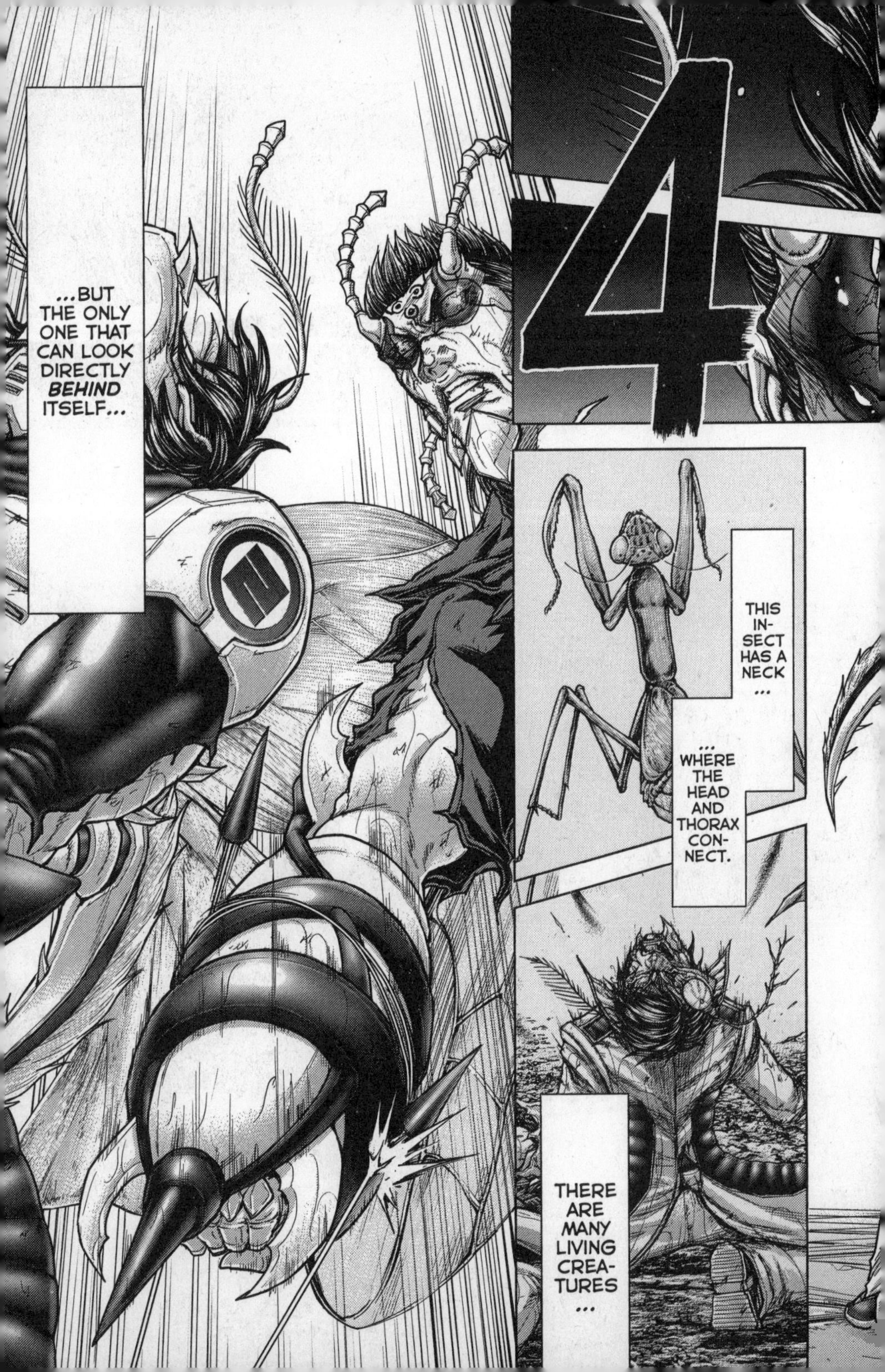
4
THIS IN-SECT HAS A NECK...
...WHERE THE HEAD AND THORAX CON-NECT.
THERE ARE MANY LIVING CREA-TURES...
...BUT THE ONLY ONE THAT CAN LOOK DIRECTLY *BEHIND* ITSELF...

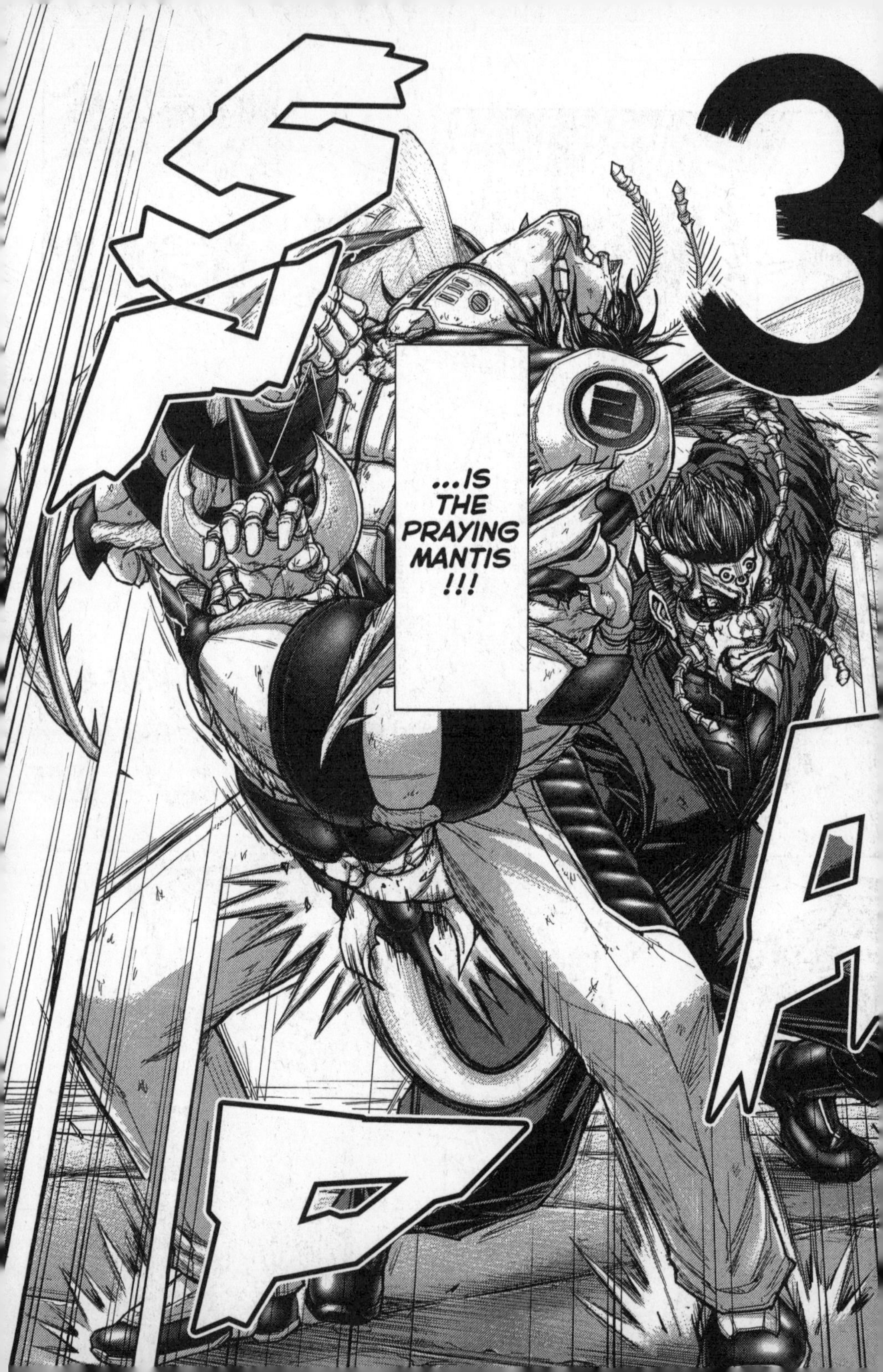
...IS THE PRAYING MANTIS !!!

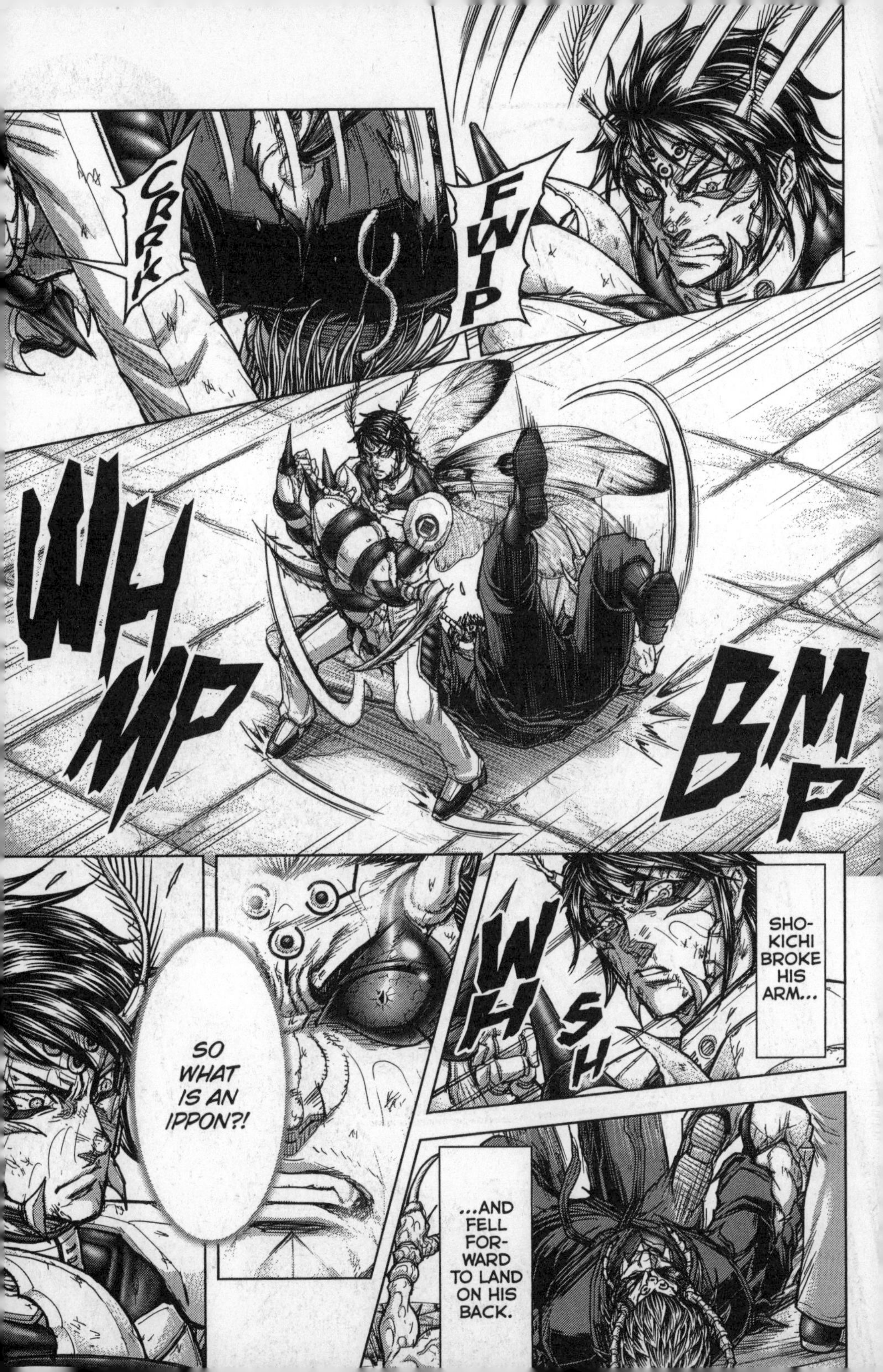
FWIP
CRAK
BMP
WHMP
SHOKICHI BROKE HIS ARM...
WHSH
...AND FELL FORWARD TO LAND ON HIS BACK.
SO WHAT IS AN IPPON?!

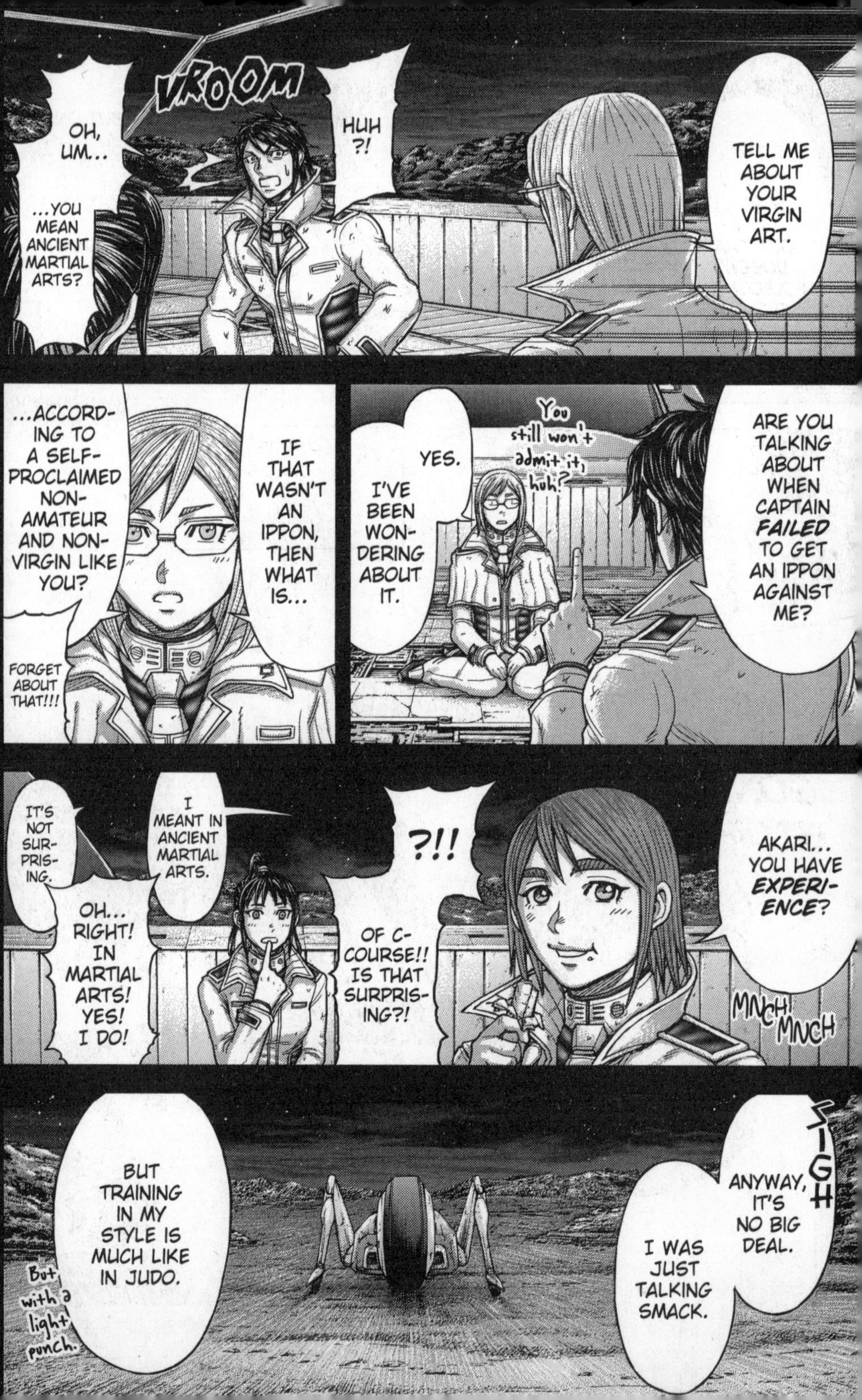
TELL ME ABOUT YOUR VIRGIN ART.
HUH ?!
VROOM
OH, UM...
...YOU MEAN ANCIENT MARTIAL ARTS?
ARE YOU TALKING ABOUT WHEN CAPTAIN **FAILED** TO GET AN IPPON AGAINST ME?
You still won't admit it, huh?
YES.
I'VE BEEN WONDERING ABOUT IT.
IF THAT WASN'T AN IPPON, THEN WHAT IS...
...ACCORDING TO A SELF-PROCLAIMED NON-AMATEUR AND NON-VIRGIN LIKE YOU?
FORGET ABOUT THAT!!!
AKARI... YOU HAVE ***EXPERIENCE?***
MNCH MNCH
?!!
OF C-COURSE!! IS THAT SURPRISING?!
I MEANT IN ANCIENT MARTIAL ARTS.
IT'S NOT SURPRISING.
OH... RIGHT! IN MARTIAL ARTS! YES! I DO!
SIGH
ANYWAY, IT'S NO BIG DEAL.
I WAS JUST TALKING SMACK.
BUT TRAINING IN MY STYLE IS MUCH LIKE IN JUDO.
But with a light punch.

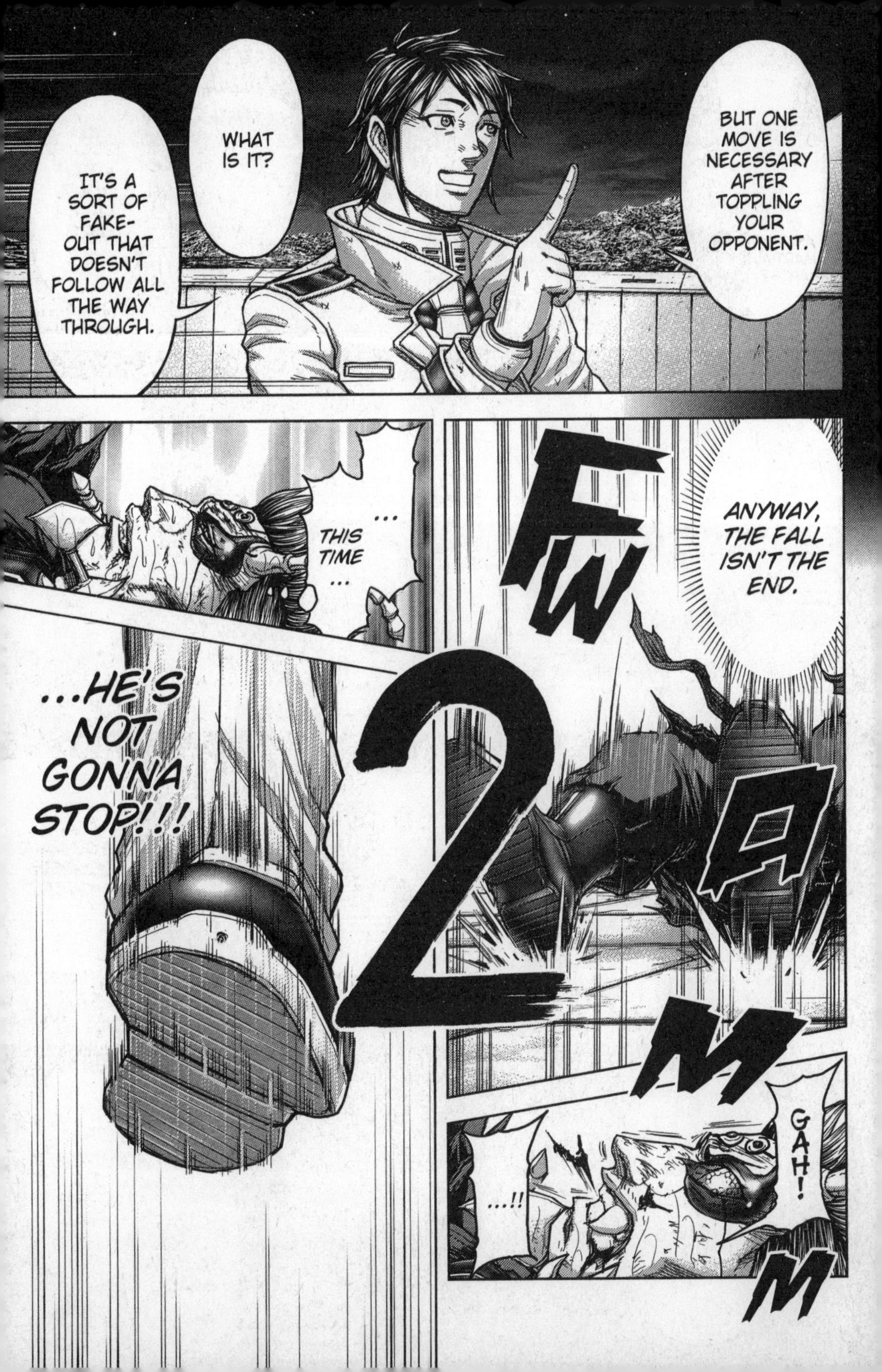
BUT ONE MOVE IS NECESSARY AFTER TOPPLING YOUR OPPONENT.
WHAT IS IT?
IT'S A SORT OF FAKE-OUT THAT DOESN'T FOLLOW ALL THE WAY THROUGH.
ANYWAY, THE FALL ISN'T THE END.
FWAM
2
... THIS TIME ...
...HE'S NOT GONNA STOP!!!
GAH!
...!!
M

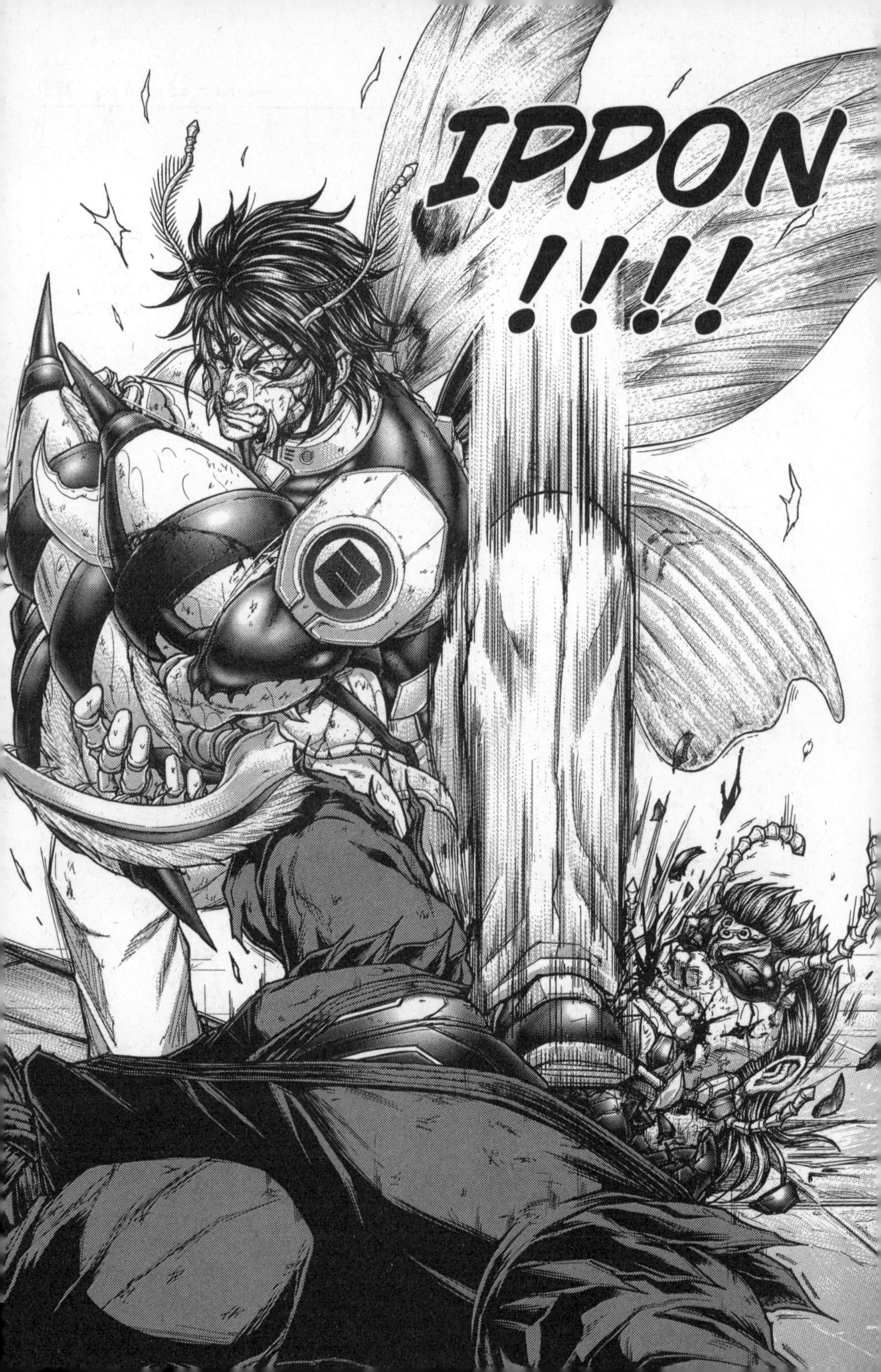
IPPON !!!!

⇐Continued from page 39!!

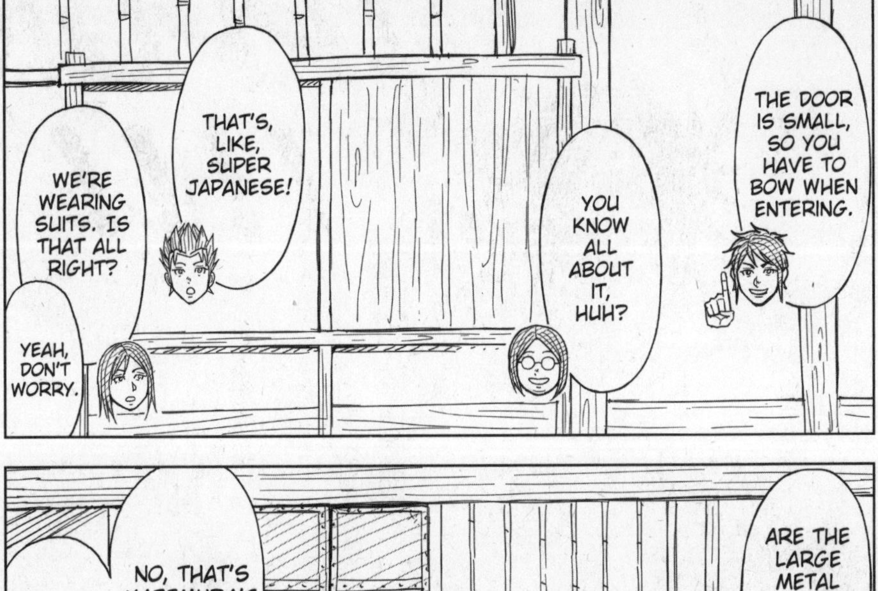
THE DOOR IS SMALL, SO YOU HAVE TO BOW WHEN ENTERING.
YOU KNOW ALL ABOUT IT, HUH?
THAT'S, LIKE, SUPER JAPANESE!
WE'RE WEARING SUITS. IS THAT ALL RIGHT?
YEAH, DON'T WORRY.

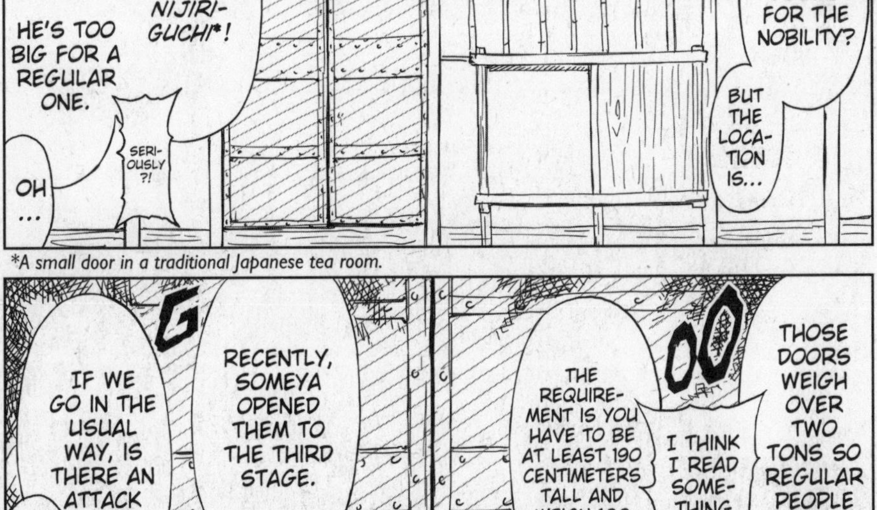
ARE THE LARGE METAL DOORS FOR THE NOBILITY?
BUT THE LOCATION IS...
NO, THAT'S KAZEMURA'S *NIJIRI-GUCHI**!
SERIOUSLY?!
HE'S TOO BIG FOR A REGULAR ONE.
OH...

*A small door in a traditional Japanese tea room.*

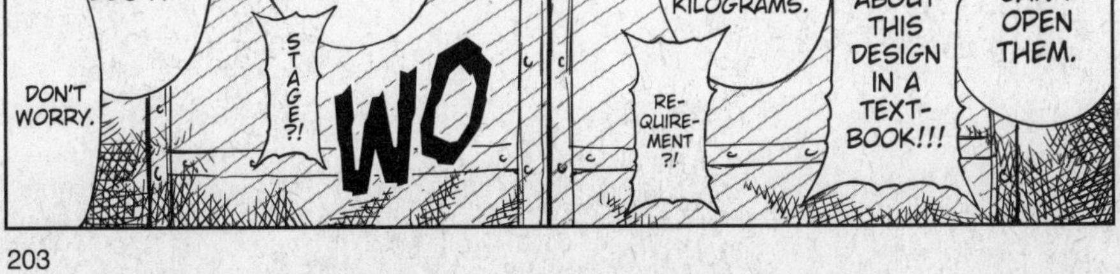
THOSE DOORS WEIGH OVER TWO TONS SO REGULAR PEOPLE CAN'T OPEN THEM.
OO
I THINK I READ SOMETHING ABOUT THIS DESIGN IN A TEXTBOOK!!!
THE REQUIREMENT IS YOU HAVE TO BE AT LEAST 190 CENTIMETERS TALL AND WEIGH 100 KILOGRAMS.
REQUIREMENT?!
WO
RECENTLY, SOMEYA OPENED THEM TO THE THIRD STAGE.
STAGE?!
G
IF WE GO IN THE USUAL WAY, IS THERE AN ATTACK DOG?!
DON'T WORRY.

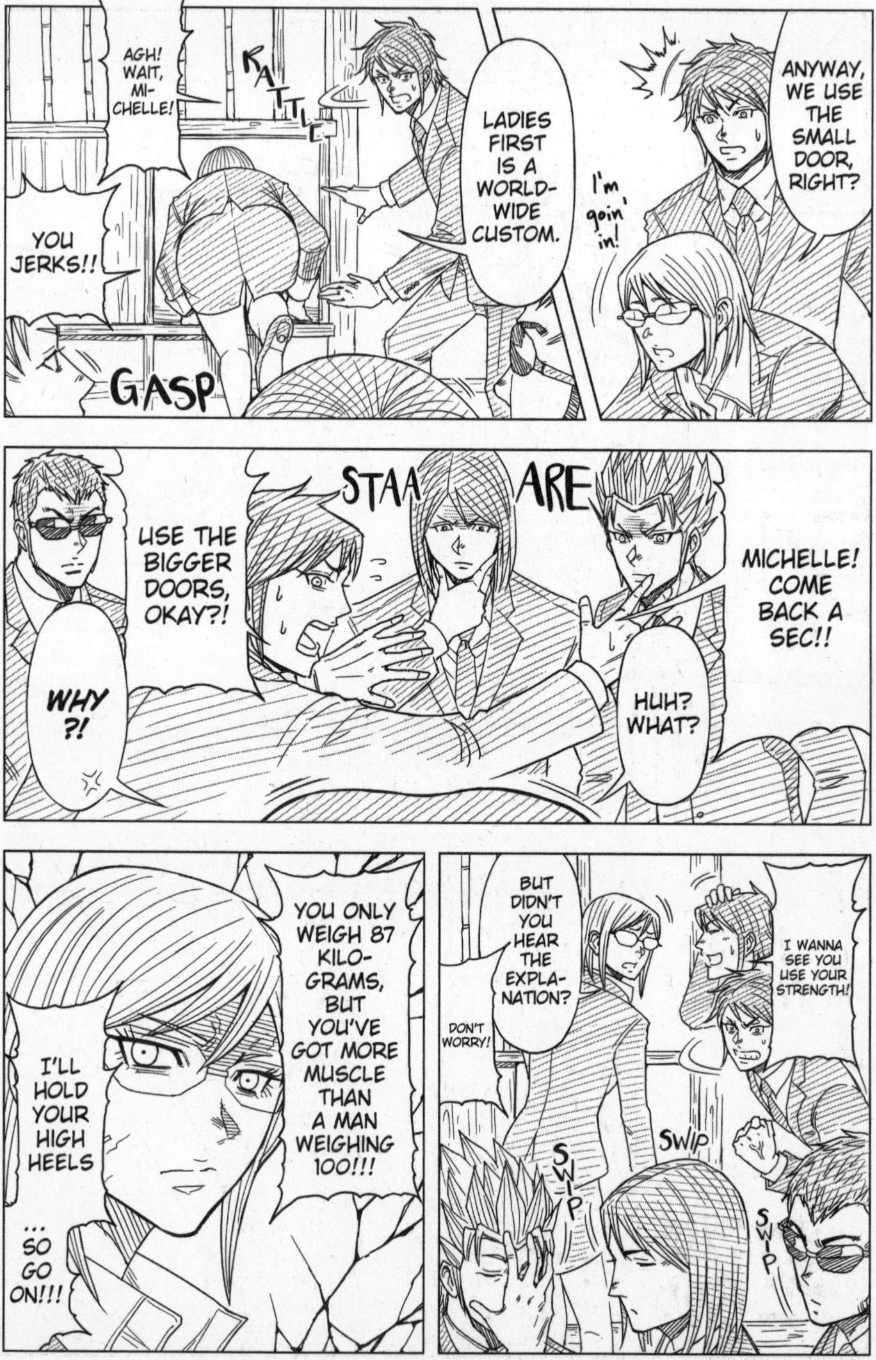
ANYWAY, WE USE THE SMALL DOOR, RIGHT?
I'm goin' in!
LADIES FIRST IS A WORLD-WIDE CUSTOM.
RATTLE
AGH! WAIT, MI-CHELLE!
YOU JERKS!!
GASP
MICHELLE! COME BACK A SEC!!
HUH? WHAT?
STAA ARE
USE THE BIGGER DOORS, OKAY?!
WHY?!
I WANNA SEE YOU USE YOUR STRENGTH!
BUT DIDN'T YOU HEAR THE EXPLANATION?
DON'T WORRY!
SWIP
SWIP
SWIP
YOU ONLY WEIGH 87 KILO-GRAMS, BUT YOU'VE GOT MORE MUSCLE THAN A MAN WEIGHING 100!!!
I'LL HOLD YOUR HIGH HEELS
... SO GO ON!!!

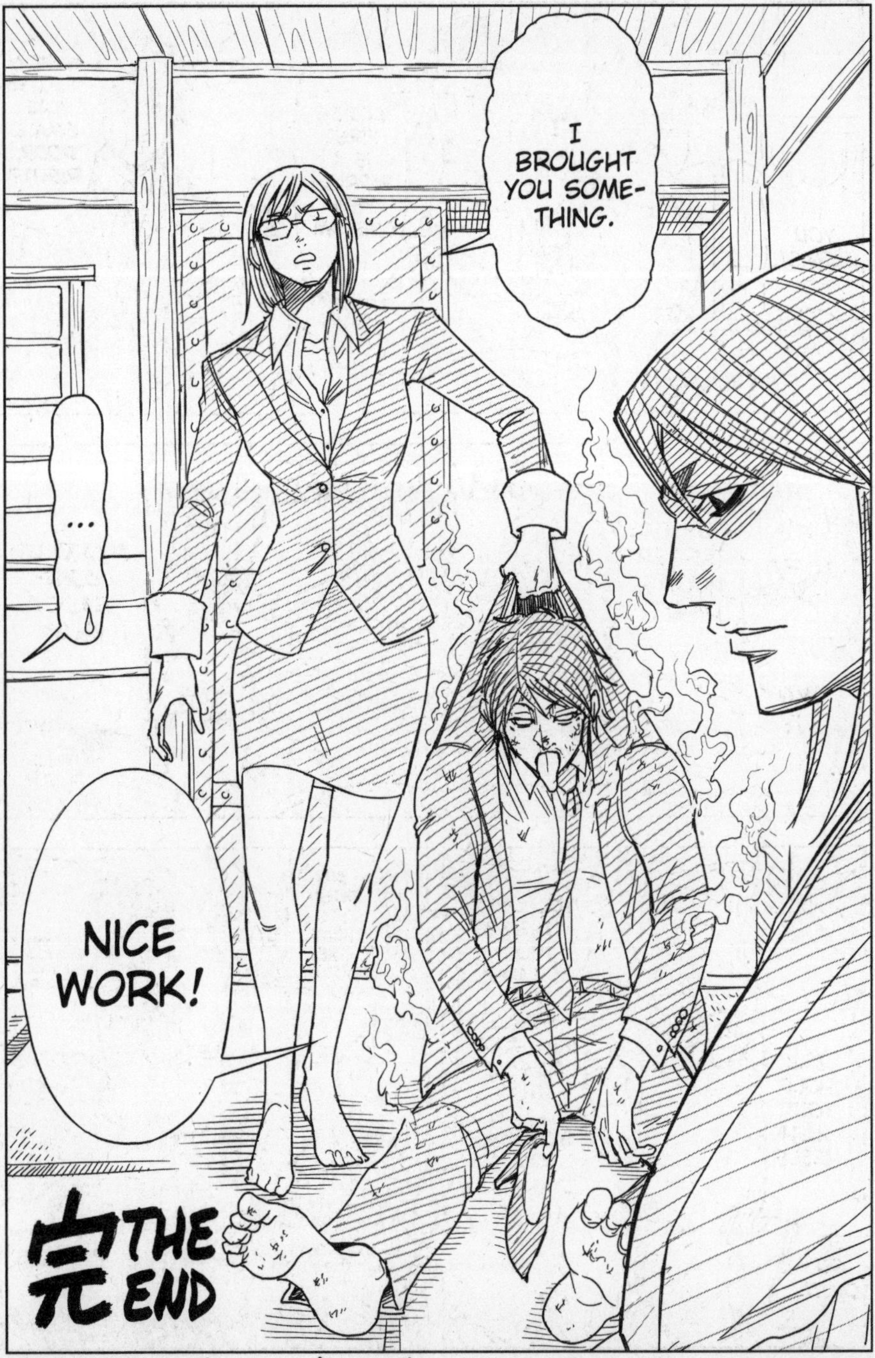
I BROUGHT YOU SOME-THING.
...
NICE WORK!
完 THE END
Parts 2 and 3 of "Instructor's Habits" may appear in later volumes. Or maybe not.

# TERRA FORMARS

Volume 22
VIZ Signature Edition

Story by YU SASUGA
Art by KENICHI TACHIBANA

TERRA FORMARS © 2011 by Ken-ichi Tachibana,Yu Sasuga/SHUEISHA Inc.
All rights reserved.
First published in Japan in 2011 by SHUEISHA Inc., Tokyo.
English translation rights arranged by SHUEISHA Inc.

Translation & English Adaptation/John Werry
Touch-up Art & Lettering/Annaliese Christman
Design/Alice Lewis
Editor/Mike Montesa

Printed in Canada

Published by VIZ Media, LLC
P.O. Box 77010
San Francisco, CA 94107

10 9 8 7 6 5 4 3 2 1
First printing, December 2019

# TOKYO GHOUL

## C O M P L E T E   B O X   S E T

STORY AND ART BY **SUI ISHIDA**

**KEN KANEKI** is an ordinary college student until a violent encounter turns him into the first half-human, half-Ghoul hybrid. Trapped between two worlds, he must survive Ghoul turf wars, learn more about Ghoul society and master his new powers.

Box set collects all fourteen volumes
of the original *Tokyo Ghoul* series.
Includes an exclusive double-sided poster.

# COLLECT THE COMPLETE SERIES

# Hey! You're Reading in the Wrong Direction!

## This is the **end** of this graphic novel!

To properly enjoy this VIZ graphic novel, please turn it around and begin reading from **right to left.** Unlike English, Japanese is read right to left, so Japanese comics are read in reverse order from the way English comics are typically read.

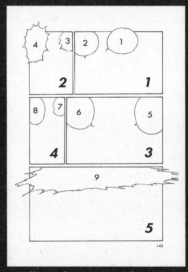

Follow the action this way

This book has been printed in the original Japanese format in order to preserve the orientation of the original artwork. Have fun with it!